Europe Undivided

Democracy, Leverage, and Integration
After Communism

MILADA ANNA VACHUDOVA

OXFORD

UNIVERSITY PRESS

OXFORD

UNIVERSITY PRESS

Great Clarendon Street, Oxford OX2 6DP

Oxford University Press is a department of the University of Oxford.
It furthers the University's objective of excellence in research, scholarship,
and education by publishing worldwide in

Oxford New York

Auckland Cape Town Dar es Salaam Hong Kong Karachi
Kuala Lumpur Madrid Melbourne Mexico City Nairobi
New Delhi Shanghai Taipei Toronto

With offices in

Argentina Austria Brazil Chile Czech Republic France Greece
Guatemala Hungary Italy Japan South Korea Poland Portugal
Singapore Switzerland Thailand Turkey Ukraine Vietnam

Published in the United States
by Oxford University Press Inc., New York

© Milada Anna Vachudova 2005

The moral rights of the authors have been asserted

Database right Oxford University Press (maker)

First published 2005

British Library Cataloguing in Publication Data

Data available

Library of Congress Cataloging in Publication Data

Vachudová, Milada Anna.
Europe undivided : democracy, leverage, and integration after communism / Milada Anna
Vachudová.
p. cm.
Includes bibliographical references.
Summary: "Europe Undivided analyses the development of East European States post-1989 and
their dynamic relationship with the EU. The author examines how the influence of an enlarging EU
has created a convergence towards liberal democracy throughout the region, and provides insights
into how the EU will function after enlargement."—Provided by publisher.
ISBN 0-19-924118-X (alk. paper)—ISBN 0-19-924119-8 (pbk. : alk. paper) 1. Europe—Politics
and government—1989– 2. European Union—Europe, Eastern. I. Title.
D2009.V33 2005

909'.097170829—dc22   2004023997

ISBN 978-0-19-924118-7 (hbk.)
ISBN 978-0-19-924119-4 (pbk.)

Typeset by Newgen Imaging Systems (P) Ltd., Chennai, India
Printed in Great Britain
on acid-free paper by
Biddles Ltd., King's Lynn, Norfolk

In memory of my parents,
Milada Vachudová (née Junová) and Jaroslav Vachuda

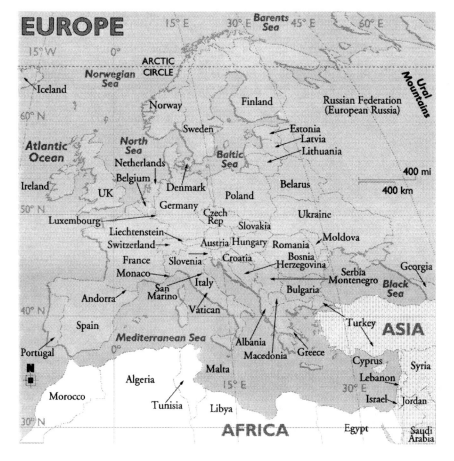

Map provided by www.worldatlas.com

PREFACE

The division of Europe shaped profoundly the lives of my parents, who were born in interwar Czechoslovakia and came of age just before and during the Second World War. The communist coup in 1948 ended their hopes of living in a (social) democratic Czechoslovakia and hobbled their careers as academics and artists. The Soviet invasion of Czechoslovakia in 1968 caught them unawares during a camping trip to the United States from which they would never return home. I have been much more fortunate as I have witnessed over the last fifteen years the end of the division of Europe. As communism unraveled in 1989 I became interested in how East European countries would transform themselves, how West European countries and institutions would respond, and whether the long-standing division of Europe could be overcome. I am deeply grateful to my parents for giving me the intellectual tools to carry out this work. I am also indebted to the Overlake Rotary Club in Washington state for my schooling at a lycee in France, and to Stanford University for its commitment to study abroad and undergraduate research. As an undergraduate at Stanford, I spent that glorious year of 1989 first in the Washington DC program, then in the Paris program, and finally conducting research in Prague. I owe a very special thanks to my senior honors thesis advisor David Holloway who supervised my undergraduate thesis on Czechoslovakia's new foreign policy, and who has generously supported my academic work ever since.

This book began as a D. Phil. dissertation at St. Antony's College at the University of Oxford. The British Marshall Commission funded my studies in the United Kingdom at a time when this suited beautifully my agenda of understanding different perspectives on a dynamic, rapidly changing Europe. The Belfer Center for Science and International Affairs at Harvard University provided a pre-doctoral fellowship that helped me complete the dissertation. At Oxford I was advised by Alex Pravda and aided in my research by Timothy Garton Ash as well as Anne Deighton and William Wallace. For comments on the book at different stages I am indebted to my Oxford examiners Andrew Hurrell and George Kolankiewicz as well as Michael Doyle, Grzegorz Ekiert, Thomas Ertman, Matthew Evangelista, Judith Kelley, Karen Ferree, Peter Hall, Stephen Holmes, Tony Judt, Andrew Moravcsik, Martin Rhodes, Thomas Risse, Richard Rose, Glenda Rosenthal, Philippe Schmitter, Thomas W. Simons Jr., Timothy Snyder, Stephen Van Evera, and Jan Zielonka. I have thanked many others in the footnotes. I could never have written the book without the input of the many individuals that I interviewed and asked for assistance in East Central and Western Europe. Dagmar Ašerová, Renata Dwan, Pavel Fischer, Sharon Fisher, Leszek Jesień, Libuše Koubská, Elena Jileva, Michael Leigh, Jiří Pehe, Pavel Seifter, Ivo Šilhavý, Jonathan Stein, Miroslav Wlachovský and Josef Zieleniec were especially generous with their time and insights. The late Pavol Lukáč was always there for me in Bratislava with his friendship and expertise; his spirit and his scholarship will be greatly missed in Slovakia and beyond. David Cameron, John Glenn, John Gould, Wade Jacoby, Judith Kelley, Charles King, Jeffrey Kopstein, Andrew Moravcsik, Mitchell Orenstein, Jacques Rupnik, Beate Sissenich, John Stephens, and Michael Ting helped me hammer out key arguments in different chapters.

During the final revisions of the manuscript I benefited greatly from the comments of Francesca Bignami, András Bozóki, Chad Bryant, Valerie Bunce, James Caporaso, Pamela Conover, Rachel Epstein, Sharon Fisher, Anna Grzymała-Busse, Evelyne Huber, Gary Marks, Alina Mungiu-Pippidi, Sinziana Popa, Thomas Oatley, Thomas W. Simons Jr., Aneta Spendzharova, and Kieran Williams. I could refine my arguments thanks as well to the comments of participants at seminars at Claremont-McKenna College, Cornell University, Harvard University, Ohio State University, the University of Washington, and Yale University, as well as at the Enlargement and European Governance Workshop of the Joint Sessions of the ECPR organized by Frank Schimmelfennig and Ulrich Sedelmeier. I also benefited greatly from the research assistance of Aneta Spendzharova. My colleagues at the University of North Carolina at Chapel Hill offered much support and extensive comments at two faculty seminars on my work. Meanwhile my students at UNC Chapel Hill were a great inspiration, and those that took my course "Undivided Europe" contributed directly to the manuscript in many ways; a special thanks goes to Chandler Abernathy, Laure Almairac, Christina Bell, Brian Harrelson, Britton Mason, Kara Petteway, Rachel Schaffer, and Maren Veatch. For their abiding interest in the project I am grateful to Laura Belin, Amy Benjamin, Robert Benjamin, Graeme Brooks, John Buretta, Tamar Herzog, Mary Anne Jorgensen, Olivia Judson, Charles Maier, Viva Moffat, Timothy Snyder, Jitka Štefková, Alec Stone Sweet, Tomáš Vachuda, and Sharon Volkhausen.

The National Science Foundation, the Center for International Studies at Princeton University, the East West Institute, the European Union Center at Columbia University, the Center for European Studies at Harvard University, and the European University Institute in Florence all supported this book in different ways. Since coming to UNC Chapel Hill, my research has been supported by the Center for Slavic, East European and Eurasian Studies, the Spray-Randleigh Foundation, the Center for European Studies, and the EU Centers initiative of the European Commission. A final thanks to Dominic Byatt, Claire Croft, and Stuart Fowkes at Oxford University Press for all of their expert work and invaluable support.

CONTENTS

LIST OF TABLES

LIST OF FIGURES

Introduction

Twice in recent history, dramatic changes have echoed across the European continent. In 1989 Soviet-style communist regimes collapsed, one by one, in East Central Europe—in Poland, Hungary, East Germany, Czechoslovakia, Bulgaria, and then Romania. Revolution and the start of democratization brought exhilaration and hope. Two years later the Soviet Union collapsed as well; the Cold War was over. In 2004, some fifteen years after the Polish round-table negotiations paved the way for Eastern Europe's first non-communist prime minister to take office, eight formerly communist states joined the European Union (EU). European Union enlargement was met with greater equanimity than the revolutions of 1989, but as an ending to the division of Europe and the start of a new era for the EU's new and old members alike, it was no less historic. These dates, 1989 and 2004, will serve as markers of contemporary European history. And candidates such as Bulgaria and Romania, still working to join the EU, will be adding their own markers in coming years. How did Europe, especially East Central Europe (ECE), make its way from revolution to integration, from 1989 to 2004?

When West Europeans contemplated the character of the newly undivided Europe in the early 1990s, two questions about East European states and societies framed the debate: where had they come from and, more important, where were they going? The answers to both questions at first glance were the same for all of them. They had come from the Soviet bloc, where "really existing" communism imposed one-party rule in politics, planning in the economy, atomization in society, and the abrogation of human rights; the system was held together with police terror, the threat of invasion, ideology, job security, and social benefits. They had all shed this system between 1989 and 1991 in order to build liberal democracies and market economies, where human rights, political pluralism, economic prosperity, and a cleaner environment would blossom in conditions of national independence.

The collapse of communism between 1989 and 1991 throughout the region, accompanied by the end of the Soviet Union itself, was indeed a critical juncture for the political development of all East European states. For many, it was also a period that set in motion forces seeking national independence: the "communist" region went from nine states in 1989[1] to twenty-seven in 1995. Yet these twenty-seven new and newly sovereign polities had not come from the same place. The first to tell you this would be the citizens: whether in samizdat writing before 1989 or in the mosaic of expressions available after 1989, what people revealed was their strong sense of national and regional diversity throughout the communist period and across the communist space. And, contrary to the appearance of uniformity from the outside, scholars had illuminated the incredible variety of polities and societies that communism had enveloped and transformed. It follows of course that differences before communism and during communism would lead to differences after its demise.

Post-communist states had not come from the same place, and they were certainly not all headed in the same direction. By 1995 the spectrum of political outcomes among the twenty-seven states was striking: from consolidated democracies to consolidated authoritarian regimes, and everything in between. This raised the question of "legacies": which inheritances from the communist and pre-communist past could explain the diverging trajectories of post-communist states after 1989? Could we make sense of the post-communist space by grouping states following similar trajectories, and by identifying the legacies that caused states to end up in one group or another?

It was not surprising, as a first observation, that states emerging newly independent from the Soviet Union after over seven decades of Soviet communism would follow trajectories very different from states of ECE. But would the states of ECE follow the same or similar paths? After all, Poland, Hungary, Czechoslovakia, Bulgaria, and Romania emerged from communism with many common legacies and attributes. They had all experienced only four decades of locally led communism in conditions of nominal state sovereignty, had existed as independent states before the Second World War and had enjoyed relative proximity to the West. They ended communism and began democratization, one after another, during that miraculous year, 1989. And for them, democratization did not coincide with national independence movements or violent conflicts, though the Czechs and the Slovaks would have their velvet divorce in 1992. All five, then six, also shared a similar geopolitical environment, and were recognized in 1993 as credible candidates for membership in the European Union.

For all of these similarities, however, Poland, Hungary, the Czech Republic, Romania, Bulgaria, and Slovakia experienced remarkable differences in the initial policies enacted by their governments in the name of building democracy, crafting a market economy, and returning to Europe. What explains the variation in political trajectories among these six states in the early 1990s? A decade later, do we see a convergence in their trajectories and, if so, how much of this convergence was caused by the leverage of the EU? These are the two questions that animate this book. For the rest of this brief introduction, I will provide a roadmap of the argument in the eight subsequent chapters, a survey of the literatures that it will engage, and an explanation of how I selected my six cases.

Map of the Argument

While each state followed its own, unique trajectory away from communism, I have identified two groups. While (more or less) all elections in the six states after 1989 were free and fair, I ask: were ruling elites pushing the polity toward liberal or illiberal democracy? By liberal democracy, I mean a political system where state institutions and democratically elected rulers respect juridical limits on their powers and the political liberties of all citizens. They uphold the rule of law, a separation of powers, and boundaries between the state and the economy. They also uphold basic liberties, such as speech, assembly, religion, and property. Important for our cases, they do not violate the limits on their powers or the political liberties of citizens in order to suppress rival political parties or groups.[2]

I start by arguing that the quality of political competition at the moment of regime change determined whether states embarked on what I call a liberal or an illiberal pattern of political change after 1989. The quality of political competition in the new democracies was initially determined by the presence or absence of an opposition to communism strong enough to take power in 1989, and secondarily by the presence or absence of a reforming communist party. Chapter 1 makes the theoretical case for why political competition is central to understanding variation in political and economic change in post-communist states. It also presents a model of the causal mechanisms that translate different levels of political competition into liberal and illiberal political and economic outcomes. Chapter 2 presents the empirical variation between domestic politics in Poland, Hungary, and the Czech Republic (the liberal states) and domestic politics in Romania, Bulgaria, and Slovakia (the illiberal ones).

What about the role of the EU and other international actors in shaping the trajectories of ECE's democratizing states? Never had new democracies emerged on a continent so busy with the activities of international organizations: besides the European Union, the Organization for Security and Cooperation in Europe (OSCE), the Council of Europe (COE), the North Atlantic Treaty Organization (NATO), the West European Union (WEU), the European Free Trade Association (EFTA), the Organization for Economic Cooperation and Development (OECD), the World Bank, the International Monetary Fund (IMF), the United Nations, and no doubt others, joined by a parade of Western non-governmental organizations, took an interest in fostering democracy and capitalism in our six East Central European states.

It was the EU that took center stage. Even before the street demonstrators had gone home in Prague in November 1989, incoming democratic leaders of Czechoslovakia, Poland, and Hungary had singled out joining the EU as their most important foreign policy goal. Joining the EU was heralded as the symbolic endpoint of the "return to Europe"; soon this symbolism was eclipsed by the economic imperative of membership. Chapter 3 presents a theoretical framework for what I call passive leverage—the traction that the EU has on the domestic politics of credible candidate states merely by virtue of its existence and its usual conduct. This includes the (tremendous) political and economic benefits of membership, the (dastardly) costs of exclusion, and the (not-so-nice) way that the EU treats nonmember states.

Yet, from 1989 to 1994 I demonstrate that the EU and other international actors had a negligible impact on the course of political change in ECE states. The EU's passive leverage merely reinforced liberal strategies of reform in Poland, Hungary, and the Czech Republic, while failing to avert, end or significantly diminish rent-seeking strategies for winning and exercising power in Romania, Bulgaria, and Slovakia. Chapter 4 traces empirically the relationship between the EU and the two groups of states from 1989 to 1994. It also reveals how the liberal states came to understand the full force of the benefits of EU membership by dealing with the EU from the outside, while the EU itself slowly came to terms with the prospect of a future eastern enlargement.

What happened once the EU started moving toward enlargement? Chapter 5 presents a theoretical framework for what I call the EU's active leverage—the deliberate policies of the EU toward candidate states. Active leverage is animated by the fact that the tremendous benefits of EU membership create incentives for states to satisfy the enormous entry requirements, setting the stage for the effectiveness of conditionality within the EU's pre-accession process. Three characteristics of this process, moreover, make it particularly powerful: asymmetric interdependence (candidates are weak), enforcement (tough but fair), and meritocracy (most of the time). The process mediates the costs and benefits of satisfying EU membership criteria in such a way as to make compliance attractive—and noncompliance visible and costly.

The benefits of EU membership (and the costs of exclusion) create one of the central puzzles of this book: why did ruling elites in illiberal pattern states respond differently than those in liberal pattern states to the incentives of EU membership?

For illiberal ruling elites in Romania, Bulgaria, and Slovakia, complying with EU membership requirements was too costly, undermining their hold on power. But I show in Chapter 6 that active leverage helped create a more competitive political system in illiberal states, changing the information environment and the institutional environment to the advantage of more liberal opposition political forces. Next, I show in Chapter 7 that active leverage helped compel all six governments to reform the state and the economy in ways that are consistent with strengthening liberal democracy and the market economy. This happened because of straightforward conditionality (to get x you must do y), but also because the pre-accession process served economic actors as a credible commitment to ongoing reform and strengthened pro-EU groups in society. I also explore in Chapter 7 the considerable variation that continues to exist among the candidate states even as they are all moving toward satisfying the domestic requirements for EU membership.

By comparing domestic politics in six countries over the course of fifteen years, I attempt to reveal chains of causation over time. I use the term "pattern of political change" deliberately to show how the absence of political competition creates similar opportunities for ruling elites to concentrate political power and extract rents over time and across countries. But as time goes by, I show that these very policies trigger similar responses by opposition elites and civic groups, similar consequences for the economy, and similar pressures from society for change. The fact that these states are credible future members of the EU, exposed to the full force of the EU's active leverage, strengthens the hand of liberal forces against illiberal ones: not in a duel where good vanquishes evil, but in an iterated electoral game where sooner or later most political actors see the benefits of moving their own political agenda toward compatibility with the state's bid for EU membership. As post-communist politics have demonstrated over and over again, with a little fine tuning most political actors—however dispirited, discredited, or despised—can find their way back into the political game and indeed back into power. Only in the run up to joining the EU, there is a twist: the EU's active leverage helps set the parameters and write the rules of the political game.

This book combines a historical institutionalist approach, demonstrating how the groups and institutions inherited from communism structure politics after 1989, with an elite-driven, instrumentalist approach, analyzing the actions that politicians take in their quest to win and hold power. Historical institutionalism explores how the existing institutions in a society shape any future changes in policy-making practices. Agency also matters: political systems become more (or less) competitive because domestic elites emerge and change in response to changing incentives in the political environment. What kinds of incentives are most compelling is in turn debated between rationalists and constructivists—between scholars that emphasize material rewards, including myself, and those that emphasize reputational and ideational rewards as motivating elite behavior.

Survey of the Literatures

This book engages many literatures in political science, most of them at the intersection of comparative politics and international relations and therefore defying easy categorization. Yet, it is helpful here to sketch the different contributions that this book may make to ongoing debates in different parts of the field. To this end, I have organized the following brief overview into three parts: (*a*) three literatures in comparative politics (post-communism, hybrid democracies, and the impact of external actors); (*b*) three literatures in international relations (international institutions, international political economy, and international security); and (*c*) that stand-alone behemoth, the study of the EU. Roughly, these three parts correspond to the three theoretical chapters— Chapters 1 (post-communism), 3 (international relations), and 5 (EU)—so many references are omitted here.

The trajectories of post-communist states diverged immediately in 1989, despite the common start to democratization occasioned by the collapse of communism: by the first democratic elections, the conditions were in place for liberal democracy in one set of states and illiberal democracy in another set. Explaining this variation, the book presents and tests a model of domestic political change based on the quality of political competition at the moment of regime change, and on how it changes over time. In so doing, the book engages the rich literature on communism and post-communism in comparative politics. It also contributes to the broader literature on democratization by considering the relationship between democratic success, economic crisis, and economic reform.

The democratization of communist states seemed in many ways incomparable to democratization in other parts of the world owing to the uniqueness of communism's impact on the polity, the economy, and society.[3] However, the behavior of ruling elites when seizing and holding power in that gray zone between liberal democracy and outright authoritarianism—be it called illiberal democracy, electoral democracy, hybrid democracy, or competitive authoritarianism—is in many respects strikingly similar across countries and regions. This book presents and tests a theory of the domestic and international conditions that turn democratic revolutions into illiberal democracies— and also that turn illiberal democracies into more liberal ones. This book thus contributes to the recent comparative politics literature on the origin, the dynamics, and the demise of democratic hybrids.[4] Most striking, it demonstrates that international actors can play an important role in either tightening or loosening the grip on the polity of elites that seek to perpetuate illiberal democracy.[5]

The impact of external actors on democratization, and on domestic political change more generally, is now one of the most exciting areas of study in comparative politics.[6] In the long-established literature on democratization in Latin America, the Caribbean, Asia, or Africa, however, the impact of external actors on democratic consolidation has usually been considered harmful or at best indifferent. The exception is democratization on the European continent, where the prospect of joining the EU is credited with supporting transition and consolidation in Portugal, Spain, and Greece as well as in the ECE states.[7] Can this kind of influence be replicated beyond the European continent? Elsewhere, states also join international organizations, and elsewhere, international actors may help make political systems more competitive. Yet, what makes the EU's active leverage so effective—the benefits and requirements of accession—is a product of very high levels of rule-based integration and shared sovereignty that are, for now, unique to the EU.

Indeed, the process of entering the EU entails a greater transformation of domestic policy-making and a greater pooling of sovereignty than entering any other international organization in the world. This raises three puzzles in international relations theory: under what domestic and systemic conditions do sovereign states create (or join) international organizations to further state interests; how does membership (or courtship) of an international organization transform state strategies and preferences; and what determines the compliance of existing (or aspiring) members with the organization's rules? These puzzles have been neglected for credible future members, as opposed to actual members, of the EU. This book shows that the tremendous benefits combined with the enormous requirements for joining the EU create incentives for compliance that are different in kind and trigger different mechanisms of domestic change in candidates than in existing members of the EU.

By exploring compliance, this book asks similar questions to the literature on the usefulness of conditionality by the international financial institutions (IFIs), chiefly as practiced by the World Bank and the IMF. Can conditionality induce elites to implement specific economic reforms? Scholars in this area have generally argued that external actors rarely, if ever, "tip the political scales in favor of reform" by using conditionality.[8] Again, the nature of the EU's active leverage is unique: EU membership is a reward of a different order, and it comes at the end of a much longer and more structured conditionality process than aid from the IFIs.

This book also contributes to the study of ethnic relations and conflict within the literature on international security. Moving states from illiberal to liberal democracy while requiring governments to satisfy membership requirements has led to the de-escalation of tensions between ethnic majorities and ethnic minorities in many prospective EU members. This is a remarkable result in the present that seems likely to endure in the future, making the mechanisms that cause this de-escalation worthy of study. In the early 1990s ethnic cleansing and war in the disintegrating Yugoslavia raised fears among policy-makers and scholars that ethnic violence could also occur in many parts of Eastern Europe, where ethnic majorities and minorities were beginning an uneasy coexistence in weak, democratizing states.[9] While violence in our six ECE states was never likely, the explanation for why it is now considered well nigh impossible can be found in this book.

Finally, this book helps answer the central question in the study of the EU: what drives European integration? And, more immediately, how did the EU arrive at such a spectacular enlargement, admitting ten new members in 2004 with several more candidates waiting in the wings? Thus far, research on the EU's eastern enlargement has focused on four issues. First, it has tracked and theorized the decisions among existing EU member states about whether and how to enlarge. Second, it has explored and speculated about the implications of enlargement for the EU's own institutions and policies. Third, it has turned to whether EU enlargement has plugged new members into a broader process of Europeanization that is bringing about political, economic, social, and even cultural harmonization among all existing EU members or even all European states. I consider these three questions, especially in Chapters 5 and 8.

I am, however, chiefly interested in a fourth question: when and how has the EU had an impact on the course of political change in aspiring member states?[10] My study is unique, as I have integrated a theory of what explains the different domestic political trajectories of ECE states after 1989 with a theory of how EU leverage has influenced these trajectories at different stages during the fifteen or more years between the start of democratization and EU accession.

Case Selection

This book focuses on Poland, Hungary, the Czech Republic, Romania, Bulgaria, and Slovakia. This selection of cases limits my ability to test theories on the entire universe of twenty-seven post-communist states. However, conducting in-depth comparisons among this limited number of cases does allow me to investigate the causal mechanisms that translate differences in well-specified initial conditions into different political outcomes.[11] It then allows me to compare the cause, the timing, and the sequence of subsequent changes. I am thus able to identify the mechanisms that translate the EU's active leverage into changes in domestic politics, comparing the impact of the EU, in broad strokes, across the six cases and across time.[12]

The cases maximize the variation on the dependent variable (political trajectories), capturing the full range of outcomes among ECE states immediately after 1989 from strong initial political competition (Poland and Hungary), to intermediate (Czech Republic), limited (Slovakia and Bulgaria), and very weak competition (Romania). They also maximize the variation on the political trajectories among ECE states vis-à-vis the EU's pre-accession process a decade later, ranging from frontrunners that hold their position (Hungary), to those that falter (the Czech Republic), to laggards that surge forward (Slovakia), and laggards that continue to lag (Romania).

Meanwhile, the most obvious structural or environmental factors that could account for the different trajectories of political change (and different levels of success in the EU's pre-accession process) vary across the outcomes. Thus, simply the strength of the economy, the country's geographic distance from Brussels or its geostrategic importance to the West cannot account for the variation in the dependent variable, as I discuss in Chapter 3. Moreover, the six cases vary across different types of communist regimes, from the least repressive in Poland and Hungary to the most Stalinist in Romania and Czechoslovakia (after 1968). The exception is the presence or absence of a large ethnic minority, which covaries in my six cases with the initial level of competition in the political system. Thus my selection of cases does not allow me to assess the relative importance of ethnic geography and political competition in determining whether states follow a liberal or illiberal trajectory after 1989.

At the same time, these six cases share crucial similarities, thus eliminating several potential explanations for their divergent political trajectories. First, all six undertook a democratic revolution in 1989 in conditions of established state sovereignty. Even in Slovakia, which would separate from the Czech Republic in 1992, Bratislava was the center of Slovak politics in 1989 allowing us, with some obstacles, to follow the dynamics of political contestation in Slovakia from the moment of regime change. Second, all have held free and fair elections, at least most of the time. Third, all six states had signed association agreements with the EU and were officially recognized as potential candidates for full membership in 1993. From 1989, they were treated as a group by the EU and received similar kinds of attention from the West. In addition to the difficulties for the researcher of taking on any more cases, I excluded Estonia, Lithuania, Latvia, and Slovenia because their "democratic revolutions" took place much later, in 1991, and were defined by emancipation from the Soviet Union or from Yugoslavia. Finally, my cases do not include a country that was not a credible future member of the EU, for example, Ukraine or Moldova, because in the second half of the book my purpose is to explain variation in political outcomes in states subject to the EU's active leverage—a goal which could not be served by a case on which the EU's active leverage had (by the EU's own choice) virtually no purchase.

Our six countries ended up in similar places, at roughly the same time, but their paths varied considerably—and diverged sharply from many of the other twenty-one post-communist states. To understand these similarities and differences we now return to the moment of regime change in 1989 to consider the importance of political competition in a democratizing polity.

Political Competition and the Reform Trajectories of Post-Communist States

East European states embarked on democratization and marketization at roughly the same time in 1989–91. They were exiting the communist system with, at least nominally, the same goal: liberal democracy and market capitalism. More than ten years on, what is striking is the multiplicity of outcomes.[1] While some post-communist states are now liberal democracies with functioning market economies, others are ruled by authoritarian regimes that have introduced only very limited economic reforms. Still others fall somewhere in between, with formal democratic institutions but illiberal politics, and with some economic reform but highly distorted markets. How do we account for this remarkable diversity?

If we compare the performance of governments across Eastern Europe since 1989, one ingredient for democratic success stands out: a competitive political system. Did the first decade of democratic government witness the alternation in power of liberal democratic parties, or the monopoly on power of illiberal parties that suppressed political competition and polarized the political system? I argue in this chapter that the divergence in democratic outcomes, and in the character of economic reform immediately after 1989 was determined by the level and quality of competition in the political system. I propose that where the collapse of communism was quickly followed by the creation and strengthening of a competitive democratic political system, we should expect relatively rapid progress in building liberal democratic political institutions and a market-based economy. In countries where the collapse of communism was followed by the creation of a noncompetitive (albeit democratic) political system, we should expect the suppression of liberal democratic institutions, and relatively slow progress toward a market economy.

Evidence drawn from the post-socialist societies over the last twelve years generally supports this basic hypothesis. Two observations stand out when we compare the empirical evidence on political freedom and economic reform across all of these post-communist states. First, as illustrated by Figure 1.1, there is a correlation between a country's political freedom rating and its

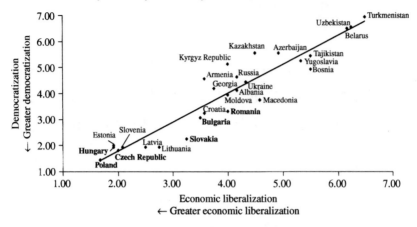

FIGURE 1.1   Democracy and economic liberalization in all post-communist states, 2001.

Note: The scales run from the highest level of democratization and economic liberalization (=1) to the lowest (=7).

Source: Freedom House (2001).

implementation of economic reform. That is, the higher a country is rated for the quality of its democracy, the more progress it has made on market reform. Figure 1.1 plots the "Democratization" scores against the "Economic liberalization" scores assigned to all twenty-seven post-communist states in Europe and Eurasia by Freedom House in 2001.[2] It reveals a very strong relationship between democracy and market reform. Moreover, strikingly similar patterns emerge using different indexes for economic reform, such as those of the World Bank and EBRD, against the Freedom House democratization index.[3]

Second, there is a correlation between the completeness of economic reforms and the level of aggregate social welfare ten years after the transition began. That is, those countries that put in place the most rapid and complete economic reforms recovered most quickly, registered the highest levels of economic growth, and generated the lowest increase in income disparities.[4] My aim here is to identify a set of causal mechanisms based on the quality of political competition that account for these correlations—that, in other words, explain the divergent political and economic outcomes in post-communist Europe.

This chapter is organized in three parts. The first part makes the case for why political competition is central to understanding variation in the course of political and economic change in East European states after 1989. I examine why the transitions create ample opportunities for rent seeking by ruling elites, and why political turnover is essential for efficient rule making in the new polities. I then explore how information asymmetries between the rulers and the voters, unchecked by rival groups and independent media, can play into the hands of rent-seeking elites in winning elections, and how political competition can abate these asymmetries over time.

The second part models the causal mechanisms that translate different levels of political competition into different political and economic outcomes. I argue that the presence or absence of an opposition to communism is the first critical ingredient for vigorous political competition. But I also argue that there is a second, less important but more surprising ingredient: a reformed communist party. The most successful recipe for a liberal pattern of political change is the alternation in power of political parties that originated from a strong opposition to communism, and from a reforming communist party. This creates the most favorable conditions for the checks and balances of a liberal democracy, but also for the consensus and compromise of a political system that avoids excessive polarization.

The third part sketches the variation that I am trying to explain in my six post-communist cases, and situates my argument about political competition within broader debates in comparative politics about the nature of post-communism. Chapter 2 presents variation among my six cases in detail. It examines states with an opposition to communism sufficiently strong to take power in 1989: Poland, Hungary, and Czechoslovakia. It then examines states where a weak opposition allowed communist rent-seeking elites to stay in power after 1989: Romania and Bulgaria, along with the hybrid case of Slovakia where the political stresses of nation building allowed rent-seeking elites to take control for many years.

1.1   Rent Seeking and Reform

The transition to a market-based democracy creates the opportunity for elites to rewrite the rules of the polity and the economy all at once. In such an environment, politicians confront strong incentives to forsake political pluralism and economic liberalism in favor of rent-seeking strategies that channel benefits to narrowly defined interest groups at the expense of society as a whole. If political competition is absent, ruling elites are free to cultivate an illiberal democracy and pursue these rent-seeking strategies—strategies that sacrifice economic welfare and ethnic tolerance.

To illuminate the economic rent-seeking opportunities created by the transition from communism, Joel Hellman presented the partial reform equilibrium model.[5] The common dilemma of the politics of economic reform was thought to be how to prevent the reversal of comprehensive reforms by the short-term *losers* in society that would suffer a decline in their standard of living. In the post-communist cases, Hellman showed that this was not true. Although comprehensive reforms did impose hardships on the majority of voters, these voters did not demand their reversal and moreover they suffered much less than their counterparts in countries that had opted for gradual reforms.

The challenge of the post-communist transition is instead to protect the momentum of reform from the short-term *winners* of partial reform. Partial reform generates rents arising from price differentials between the liberalized sectors of the economy and those still coordinated by non-market mechanisms. Arbitrage opportunities for those in a position to mediate between the reformed and unreformed sectors of the economy include the liberalization of foreign trade with incomplete price liberalization, the liberalization of prices without market competition, and the privatization of companies without new controls on state credits and subsidies for production. As Hellman pointed out, the transition from a command economy necessarily creates some arbitrage opportunities because not all aspects of a fully functioning market economy can be put in place all at once.[6] The winners of partial reform, however, seek to stall the implementation of comprehensive reform for as long as possible in order to maximize their own rents. "Instead of forming a constituency in support of advancing reforms," Hellman argued, "the short-term winners have often sought to stall the economy in a partial reform equilibrium that generates concentrated rents for themselves, while imposing high costs on the rest of society."[7]

The central challenge of reform, therefore, is to minimize rent seeking. Adam Przeworski finds that whether markets operate efficiently and generate a humane distribution of welfare depends on regulation by a democratic state that does not function as a political monopoly.[8] As Douglass North has argued, "where there are no close substitutes, the existing ruler characteristically is a despot, a dictator, or an absolute monarch. The closer the substitutes, the fewer degrees of freedom the ruler possesses, and the greater the percentage of incremental income that will be retained by the constituents."[9] Politicians who take power in a democratizing state where the quality of political competition is low may fix the rules of the transition so as to prevent turnover while profiting from the rents generated by partial reform.

Political Competition Helps Suppress Rent Seeking

Political competition limits rent seeking. It does so by exposing politicians to the scrutiny of diverse political rivals, interest groups, and voters. Politicians who face regular, competitive elections may be constrained from pursuing policies that concentrate gains to a narrow segment of the electorate while generating high social costs. There are many factors contributing to the quality of political competition, but the alternation of political parties in power stands out as the most important one. At a minimum, political turnover means that the advantages that accrue to the political parties in power are delimited by time, and scrutinized by an opposition with experience in government. Turnover creates incentives for elites to play by the democratic rules, and to write the rules more fairly, limiting the rent-seeking opportunities of those who succeed them in power.

In a noncompetitive political system, the ability of a government to maintain political power hinges on the support of a small fraction of society—a small as opposed to a large "selectorate." In such circumstances, the government has good reason to redistribute societal income from those who lack political influence—voters at large—to those who do have influence—the groups supporting the government. The government taxes society as a whole—for example, through corrupt privatization programs, partial liberalization, and ethnic scapegoating. It then transfers economic and also political resources to the narrow but influential interest groups keeping it in power.[10]

In competitive political systems, by contrast, a government must gain support from a much wider subset of society that is generally better informed. Because the need for majority support is critical, ruling parties cannot afford politically to adopt policies that tax the many to benefit the few. Instead, they are more inclined to adopt policies that are designed to disperse economic power and raise aggregate social welfare which necessarily means that economic rents are reduced.[11] The fact that resources are allocated more efficiently may foster higher levels of absolute economic growth as well as greater social cohesion. Ruling parties may also be less inclined to foster ethnic intolerance in a competitive political system where joining a coalition with an ethnic minority party may be their only ticket to power.

Competition among political parties is essential for efficient democratic politics—and its importance is greatly amplified when the rules of the democratic game are at stake. In established democracies, it may well be that competition in politics usually takes place among contending organizations, and therefore "below" the level of institutions.[12] But during transition, when the institutions of the new polity and economy are being created, it is the political parties in power that have a great deal of discretion over how new rules are written on issues as fundamental as citizenship, elections, and property rights. These political parties will only write these new rules in an efficient way if their freedom to maneuver is limited by competing groups. By efficient rules, I mean rules that are designed to curb the ability of groups associated with present and future rulers to extract political or economic rents from the transition. Institutions, following Douglass North, are not "necessarily or even usually created to be socially efficient; rather they, or at least the formal rules, are created to serve the interests of those with the bargaining power to devise new rules."[13] Where political parties are competing for the votes of a majority of well-informed citizens, politicians should write the rules more fairly and distribute the gains of economic reform more broadly in society.[14]

The character of both the communists and the opposition is critical because many of the benefits of political competition are dependent on the institutionalization of a certain kind of political party system—one that establishes competition among moderate and strong programmatic parties. Examining the post-communist cases, Timothy Frye has argued persuasively for "the perils of polarization," particularly for the success of economic reform.[15] To avoid them, all or most parliamentary parties ideally accept the overall thrust of domestic reform and foreign policy, all the while keeping up a lively culture of scrutiny and criticism to avoid in turn the pitfalls of illiberal democracy or, in other words, "democratic monopoly."[16] In Chapter 2 we will explore how each of our six post-communist cases navigate between the perils of both— of polarization and of democratic monopoly.

Political Competition Helps Overcome Information Asymmetries

An important reason why political competition is needed in the post-communist transitions is because there exists a substantial information asymmetry between the government and the citizens. Citizens are not well informed. Politicians and their associates, generally a small circle of elites, design and implement strategies for reforming the economy and the state. They have detailed knowledge about whether these reforms are complete, and what groups in society are benefiting from them. Citizens, however, have little knowledge at the outset of the transition about the alternative strategies for reform and, once reforms are underway, what groups are benefiting from them. They cannot evaluate the costs and benefits of different reform strategies for their economic welfare. But they do fear losing their jobs, and this plays into the hands of politicians who want partial reform. It is striking that in many cases the post-communist transitions enable rent-seeking elites to win successive elections and block political turnover by promising slow, halting reforms—the kinds of reforms that bring them the greatest rents while imposing the greatest costs on society.[17]

Three conditions that are common to post-communist transitions amplify the power that accrues to a government because of the information asymmetry between rulers and voters. First and most important, rivals may be weak—and the rulers may use the levers of power to keep them weak. While clientelistic groups are advantaged, competing groups may be institutionally and financially disadvantaged. Methods include blocking the registration of rival political parties, diverting state funds from inconvenient interest groups, changing the electoral laws to the advantage of the ruling parties, and neglecting to pass legislation to create a legal framework for non-governmental organizations. Rival politicians may also be co-opted, divided, harassed, and even physically assaulted by the new "democratic" leaders. This helps prevent rival politicians from assembling the strength to triumph in nominally free elections.

Second, the independent media may be weak—and rulers may still control the state-run television and large segments of the print media. State-run television can be a very powerful instrument because many citizens do not seek out other sources of information, even where they are available. In state-controlled media outlets, the rulers can portray themselves as committed democrats, implementing fair economic reforms and benefiting from close relations with powerful international actors. After decades of severe restrictions on the press, print and television journalists are typically inexperienced and unprofessional. Rulers can therefore co-opt and bribe many journalists to produce propaganda for the government. Even where journalists are not co-opted, their inexperience with investigative reporting and with the rent-seeking opportunities created by the transition plays into the hands of the rulers.

Third, voters may be susceptible to appeals to ethnic nationalism. Ethnic nationalism warps the individual and group preferences that would develop in a liberal democracy by creating a stark division along ethnic lines on all politically salient issues. This undermines social cohesion and makes politics seem like a zero-sum competition for influence between the two ethnically defined groups.[18] Politicians may rally the nation to defend the new democratic polity from ethnic minorities or from neighboring states.[19] At the moment of regime change, when individuals are struggling to understand the parameters of the new order and constructing new "mental maps," the discourse of ethnic recrimination and intolerance can be very damaging.[20]

Exploiting ethnic divisions can loosely be defined as political rent seeking: politicians collect the rents of ethnic nationalism (political power) while passing on the costs to society (ethnic recrimination). Most important, ethnic nationalism obfuscates economic rent seeking. It diverts the attention of citizens to the defense of the nation, creating common cause among all members of the ethnic majority. This disguises the benefits of partial economic reform enjoyed by the rulers at the expense of society. It often substitutes for other coverage on state-run television. It also deflects the blame for economic hardships from the government to the alleged rapaciousness of ethnic minorities at home, or of national enemies abroad.

If information asymmetries are a vital component of a rent-seeking political strategy, how does political competition help reduce them? Most important are the incentives for opposition political parties to find out what the government is doing, to make it public, and to make the case for alternative policies. Citizens seeking to limit costly policies can use this information in order to hold political parties that engage in rent seeking accountable, especially at the ballot box. The coherence and strength of the opposition parties bears heavily on the quality of the information that is gathered, and on how widely it is distributed. It also bears on how seriously this information is considered by the electorate. Over time opposition parties may find various ways to communicate with the voters despite restricted access to the electronic media. But if opposition parties are weak, fragmented, and consumed by intra-opposition battles, voters may be less likely to pay attention to them.[21] As we will see in Chapter 6, excessive fragmentation (too many small parties) and/or excessive polarization (clustering of opposition parties at the extreme left and right) can play into the hands of ruling elites seeking to suppress real political competition in the political system.[22]

1.2   Modeling a Competitive and a Noncompetitive Political System

What determined whether Central and East European states would develop a competitive or a noncompetitive democratic political system in the years immediately following the collapse of communism in 1989? Here, the key independent variable is the presence or absence of an organized opposition to the political order that preceded democracy. The presence of an opposition guarantees a certain level of political competition: at the moment of regime change there are at least two rival, organized political groups. The absence of an organized opposition creates a political vacuum that allows the old rulers to conduct the transition as they see fit. I will now sketch this process as a brief, abstract model.

In states where there is a strong organized opposition to the former political order, opposition leaders write the rules of the transition to democracy and win the first elections. Their voters may have divergent or unknown preferences on the pace of economic reform, but they clearly support democracy and prefer the exit of the old rulers. Since the first elections elevate the leadership of the opposition to the leadership of the state, their initial strategies aim rapidly to dismantle the old order. This includes creating democratic institutions that open up the political arena to competing political and interest groups—groups that were oppressed by the previous regime. Once elected to office, the opposition leaders build liberal democratic institutions and implement relatively comprehensive economic reforms. Overall, the opposition leaders are representing the interests of the opposition movement that brought them to power.

For competitiveness to become institutionalized, the most straightforward path is for the old rulers to remake themselves as credible political rivals to the new rulers in the next elections. If the reform strategies of the new rulers have met with overall domestic and international success, the old rulers will have every incentive to promise to pursue them—only better. But if the old rulers fail to reconstitute themselves as credible democratic opponents, the reform strategies of the new rulers will suffer from too much freedom. Until other rival groups gather strength, the new rulers will govern in a relatively noncompetitive political system with high information asymmetries that create opportunities for them to extract rents.

In states where no or weak opposition exists, the old rulers control the process of the transition and win the first elections. The voters may or may not prefer comprehensive political and economic reform, but they cannot express their preferences clearly because the old rulers control the terms of the first elections. Most important, they provide the information available to voters about what allegedly constitutes the best strategy for reform: the information asymmetries are therefore very high. No rival groups are strong enough to voice a coherent political alternative. Once elected to office, the old rulers are able to implement policies that benefit the few at the expense of the many. They implement only partial political and economic reform that allows a small group to extract significant political and economic rents. While the old rulers dismantle the old order to put in place democratic institutions, they attempt to block the entry of competing political and interest groups into the political arena.

The two independent variables that explain the intensity and quality of political competition in the early years of transition are exogenous to the model. They are, however, internal to the countries: the EU or other external actors play no role (yet). Political competition depends on the presence before 1989 of a strong opposition to communism. Where it exists, it evolves to form the basis of a moderate, viable political right after it is swept to power in 1989. Political competition also depends on the presence before 1989 of a reforming communist party that fosters internal debate and technocratic skills. Such a communist party has the tools to transform itself into the core of a moderate, viable political left after the unexpected switch to democracy in 1989. A surprising intervening variable lurks in the background: when countries succumb or come close to a condition of political monopoly, economic crisis can work remarkably well to invigorate democratic competition.

1.3   Explaining Variation in the Political Trajectories of East European States

With this model in mind, we turn in the next chapter to how political change played itself out in six states of East Central Europe after 1989, looking first at Poland, Hungary, and the Czech Republic where post-opposition elites took power after the collapse of communism. The puzzle in this and in the next chapter is why we see such a divergence in democratic and economic outcomes in these six states after the collapse of communism. Let me pause here to sketch the variation in my cases and situate my answer to this puzzle in the context of the ongoing academic debates in comparative politics about political change in Eastern Europe after communism.

In the six East Central European (ECE) states that I examine—Poland, Hungary, the Czech Republic, Romania, Bulgaria, and Slovakia—we see a synchronized burial of the socialist state and the leading role of the communist party in 1989, together with the emergence of democratic institutions including regular elections which are, for the most part, free and fair.[23] But we also see a remarkable divergence in the initial policies enacted in the name of building democracy and a market economy. Figure 1.2 illustrates the divergence between the two groups as measured by the "Democratization" and "Economic Liberalization" scores assigned by Freedom House to the six states in 1998. In Poland, Hungary, and the Czech Republic the first government throws open the political arena, lays the foundations of liberal democratic institutions, promotes ethnic tolerance, and begins comprehensive market reforms; this pattern breaks down in the Czech Republic after a few years. In Romania and Bulgaria, the first government suppresses political competition, subverts the new democratic institutions, uses ethnic nationalism to build legitimacy, and begins episodic market reforms; this pattern plays out in Slovakia with some delay.

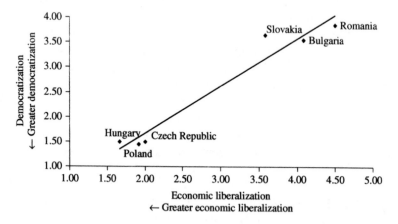

FIGURE 1.2   Democracy and economic liberalization in six ECE states, 1998.
Note: The scales run from the highest level (=1) to the lowest (=7).
Source: Freedom House (1998).

I explain this variation in the dependent variable in great detail in Chapter 2. Here, let me restate my argument that the quality of political competition determined whether states embarked on what I call a liberal or an illiberal pattern of change after 1989. The quality of political competition was initially determined primarily by the presence or absence of an opposition to communism strong enough to take power in 1989. It was determined secondarily by the presence or absence of a communist party that was already undergoing internal reform in 1989. In Chapter 2, I illustrate how the presence or absence of these two factors shaped the "competitiveness" of the political system, including the alternation of political parties in power, the effectiveness of the opposition in checking the activities of the government, the independence of the media, and the accountability of the ruling parties to citizens and groups in society.[24] The development of liberal democracy is not simply a function of having liberal democrats on hand in 1989—it is a function of an open, competitive political arena.[25]

My study is part of a broader literature in comparative politics that argues that the most important factors shaping the political and economic trajectories of East European states after communism are found among the legacies of the past. The quality of political competition at the moment of regime change is, after all, an outcome of the many different and interwoven legacies of the communist and also the pre-communist past. These different legacies are the subject of many studies that attempt to weigh their relative importance in explaining the variation in political and economic reforms after 1989.[26] The legacies include political traditions and economic development before communism, as well as protest, repression, economic reform, political organization, state institutions, and socio-economic changes during communism.[27] I will take up several of these legacies in greater detail in Chapter 3 (the next theoretical chapter) when I unpack the alternative explanations for why East European states react differently to the prospect of earning membership in the EU.

My study is different from much of this literature because instead of weighing the relative importance of different legacies I argue that at the critical juncture of regime change in 1989 the quality of political competition determines the initial political trajectory of the new democracy. However it is that some East European states developed a strong opposition to communism able to take power in 1989 and others did not, this one variable at this one rupture of history had a tremendous impact on the initial transformation of the state and the economy. The presence or absence of this opposition is the causal mechanism "created" under communism that shapes post-communism most profoundly. Put more broadly, communism's most important legacy is the character of the groups of elites that exist in 1989—both in the opposition and in the communist party.

My study is unique because it explains change over time. What determines the quality of competition—and what consequences it has for democratic politics and market reforms—changes over the years. Political competition is a dynamic factor. As we will see, a state with a very weak opposition and an unreconstructed communist party in 1989 can develop a more competitive political system over time. The quality of political competition becomes an indicator for a number of changes taking place in the polity as the transformation moves forward. In later chapters of this book, I will show how new factors, including the leverage of the EU, help improve the quality of political competition in states for which the "initial conditions" regarding the character of the elites bequeathed by communism were inauspicious indeed.

What I am attempting to do is reveal chains of causality over time, as discussed in the Introduction. I use the term "pattern of political change" to show how the absence of political competition creates similar opportunities to concentrate political power and extract rents over time and across countries; but in later chapters to show how these very policies in turn trigger similar reactions from society, consequences for the economy—and pressures for change. As Grzegorz Ekiert has argued, it is possible to show that certain specific sets of factors are of particular importance at certain stages of transformation, and that they bring about similar outcomes across post-communist states.[28]

My argument engages and draws on many studies that have helped me think about the role of political competition in the initial period of democratization. On the importance of the opposition, I wrote first with Timothy Snyder that the presence or absence of a strong opposition to communism (and of a reforming communist party) determined how ethnic nationalism and economic reform were handled by the first non-communist governments.[29] As Valerie Bunce put it, some states had "regimes-in-waiting" when communist party hegemony ended and a rough consensus on a fully liberal economic and democratic order among the elites, putting them "at the head of the parade leaving socialism."[30] M. Steven Fish demonstrated statistically that whether the first democratic elections brought to power new elites was the single best predictor of future economic reform over twenty-six post-communist cases.[31] Herbert Kitschelt conducted a systematic analysis of many factors that could account for the different outcomes in post-communist Europe, and concurred with Fish that "the temporally closest causal link to market reform runs through the victory of anti-communist forces in the first post-communist election and the establishment of civil and political rights and freedoms in that process."[32] Michael McFaul took this one step further and, emphasizing as I do the importance of the configuration of political actors at the moment of transition, argued that the ideological orientation of the more powerful actor largely determined the type of the new regime, with "democracy" emerging "therefore in countries where democrats enjoyed a decisive power advantage."[33]

On the dynamic of political competition, Joel Hellman's path-breaking article crystallized the link between state capture and economic rent seeking in the post-communist context: I attempt to explain the political genesis and, later in the book, the political demise of the perpetrators of Hellman's partial reform. Mitchell Orenstein and Anna Grzymała-Busse have done the most theoretically interesting and empirically rich work thus far on political competition in post-communist Europe. As I discuss in Chapter 2, Mitchell Orenstein has illustrated the surprising benefits of vigorous political competition for privatization in Poland as compared to the Czech Republic.[34] As I discuss in Chapter 7, Anna Grzymała-Busse has demonstrated that in Poland and Hungary strong political competition yielded a much less politicized state than in the Czech Republic or in Slovakia.[35]

Who do I disagree with? Unlike some scholars, I focus on the positive repercussions of the turnover of political parties in office, and also of the rise of new political parties when old parties are discredited by rent seeking and failed reform. I highlight the benefits of lively political competition over the possible drawbacks of instability in the political party spectrum and volatility on the part of the voters. I therefore reject the bias toward party system stability and the perseverance of political parties in power in some of the literature evaluating democratic consolidation in Eastern Europe.[36] The project led by Gábor Tóka at the Central European University in Budapest titled "The Development of Party Systems and Electoral Alignments in East Central Europe" used survey and electoral data to show that most party systems in East Central Europe did indeed remain unstable in the first half of the 1990s.[37] As Tóka argues, however, party system fragmentation and electoral volatility do *not* serve as accurate measures of democratic consolidation.[38] A small number of political parties with a loyal electorate does not necessarily signify a high quality democracy. Conversely, a large number of only weakly institutionalized political parties may exist in a "consolidated" democracy.

By focusing on which elites took power in 1989 and what kind of competition they faced in the new polity, I am privileging the role of political elites over institutional explanations of post-communist performance. I am thus arguing against scholars who attribute the political trajectories of new democracies chiefly to the design of their new institutions—to how they write their constitution, or whether they adopt a presidential or a parliamentary system.[39] While presidentialism is correlated to an illiberal pattern of political change in my cases (and across the post-communist world) after 1989, this is a consequence and not a cause of the kinds of elites dominating the institution-building process, as I have argued in the first part of this chapter.[40] Where opposition is stronger at the moment of regime change and manages to block the adoption of a presidential system, it may of course be better able subsequently to use countervailing institutions to prevent the illiberal ruling parties from gaining absolute power.

By detailing the positive role of oppositionists and of reformed communists in the post-1989 transformations, I am also arguing against the idea that the communist period was politically unproductive for the future building of liberal democracy.[41] Oppositionists in Poland and Hungary embraced Western liberal democracy and developed civic conceptions of national identity in opposition to the communist system, subduing earlier traditions of imperial expansion and ethnic nationalism. Reformed communists came to post-communism with a wealth of experience in running the state and attempting economic reform in an impossible situation.

Fundamental structural changes conducive to economic modernization also occurred or were accelerated during communism. Except in Poland, economies were brutally but effectively restructured by the collectivization of agriculture that transformed peasants into workers. More important, many societies emerged from communism with remarkable attributes that would help them manage both democracy and market reform: they had lower levels of income disparity, much higher levels of skills and education and a much lower gender literacy gap than other countries attempting the transition to democracy.[42] These structural changes have mediated the impact of the transition to capitalism, making labor forces relatively well prepared to adjust to and profit from market liberalization; for this and other reasons, the relationship between democratization and market liberalization in Figure 1.1 would look very different, for example, for Latin American states. As Philip Roeder has written, we must deepen our understanding of "the ways in which communism also transformed these societies for the better."[43]

2

Liberal and Illiberal Democracy After Communism

We turn in this chapter to how political change played itself out in my six cases after 1989. We look first at Poland, Hungary, and the Czech Republic where post-opposition elites took power after the collapse of communism; and second at Romania, Bulgaria, and Slovakia where non-opposition elites were able to dominate the transition from communism. Later in the book, we will explore in detail the variation in how oppositions developed and challenged the illiberal rulers in Romania, Bulgaria, and Slovakia after 1989. The purpose of this chapter, however, is to show how the presence or absence of an opposition to communism that is strong enough to take and hold power in 1989 puts one group of states on the road to liberal democracy, and the other group on the road to illiberal democracy.

This chapter is divided into two parts: the first part is about the liberal and the second is about the illiberal pattern of political change. Each part is divided into three sections: the first section explores the nature of the opposition and of the regime change in 1989; the second details the political, economic, and national policies of the new governments; and the third analyzes the quality of the left alternative available to voters in each state.

2.1 After Opposition: Liberal Pattern of Political Change

The presence of an organized opposition to communism jump-started the creation of a competitive political system. Revolution had to precede democracy, and the character of the elites on hand for revolution determined, in large measure, who would be elected to the first government and whether that government would attempt comprehensive political and economic reform. The presence of an organized opposition to communism at the moment of regime change strong enough to take power in Poland, Hungary and Czechoslovakia had an immediate and profound institutional effect: the rules of the political transition were negotiated between the leaders of the opposition and the leaders of the communist party. In Poland the communists had the strongest bargaining position and in Czechoslovakia the weakest: but in no case did the communists write the rules of the first elections with a free hand.[1] Indeed, the bargaining power of the communist elites had all but disappeared by the end of 1989 and the leaders of the civic movements were in a position to frame the emerging political debate.[2] While both the opposition and the communist party stood in these first elections, the voters clearly preferred the exit of the old rulers and the opposition won a sweeping victory. It is important to mark this simple political watershed: the replacement in power of the communist elites with the leaders of the opposition movements.[3]

Once in office, the post-opposition governments in Poland, Hungary, and Czechoslovakia put in place relatively comprehensive political and economic reform. By post-opposition governments, I mean governments that were formed by leaders of the pre-1989 opposition movements. They handled the two most compelling platforms of post-communist politics—the defense of the nation from its "enemies" and the protection of the average voter from economic reform—in ways that were usually consistent with liberal democracy and with marketizing reforms. (As we will see in the next section, ethnic nationalism and economic populism were easy ploys for illiberal elites seeking to win elections.) In these "founding moments," as Jakub Zielinski argues, political actors could determine which cleavages to depoliticize and which to establish as the permanent axes of political competition.[4]

Each with a different measure of success, the post-opposition governments can be credited with three outcomes: open democratic institutions, ethnic tolerance, and rapid economic reform. These are the domestic ingredients for what I call a liberal pattern of political change. First, the former dissidents built democratic institutions in such a way as to open the political arena to groups oppressed by the communist regime—including rivals to their political power. That is, they put in place a more or less level playing field for groups seeking to compete in the political arena, including the communist party and its successors, thereby creating incentives for democracy's former opponents to play by the new rules.

Second, the former dissidents set the parameters of mainstream political debate, marginalizing extreme nationalists and calling for ethnic tolerance. To win or maintain power, they did not scapegoat ethnic minorities at home, nor did they vilify the traditional enemies of the nation abroad. The appeals of nationalists, meanwhile, were relatively muted by the absence of a large, cohesive ethnic minority, though in Hungary they were amplified by large numbers of coethnics in neighboring states. If Poland, Hungary, or the Czech lands had had a large ethnic minority in 1989, ethnic tolerance in domestic politics may not have had the same character. This is an important point: we do not know how a post-opposition government would have handled this challenge, though we have good reasons to suppose that they would not have resorted to ethnic scapegoating like non-opposition politicians in other states that lacked a better source of legitimacy in the new democratic arena.

Third, the former dissidents helped electorates to understand and accept difficult economic reform as part of the democratic revolution. They persuaded their societies that the national future was in a liberal democratic and prosperous Europe for which a functioning capitalist economy was an imperative. Building democracy and building capitalism became intertwined. The consensus on the course of economic reform survived even where the post-opposition governments were voted out of power at the next elections. The electorate agreed to comprehensive marketizing reforms, though it could later reject the government for how it managed them. The most striking example is the Solidarity government in Poland that implemented a "shock therapy" reform program that led to a sharp drop in living standards but eventually propelled Poland into the economic vanguard of Eastern Europe.[5] Polish society did not resist the radical reform measures because they were closely associated with the democratic revolution.

2.1.1 Oppositions and Revolutions

Why did an opposition exist in Poland, Hungary, and Czechoslovakia that was strong enough to take control of the transition? The presence of such an opposition speaks to the structure of politics, of the economy and of society both before and during communism. It subsumes many historical and institutional developments that are beyond the scope of this book, such as the character of industrialization and political competition before the Second World War; how the communist regime co-opted, suppressed, or responded to dissent; how the communist party developed internally over the previous decades; and how state institutions were transformed under communism.[6] But the condition of the opposition could already be detected in the 1950s: H. Gordon Skilling notes the rise of the intellectuals in the years of de-Stalinization in what he calls the "more liberal states" of Hungary, Poland, and Czechoslovakia—states where there was "much greater toleration and even encouragement of specific dissent and sometimes acceptance, to some degree, of fundamental opposition"—in contrast to Bulgaria or Romania. Tolerance of intellectual interest groups was coupled with the inclusion of more actors in policy-making, though usually in a very limited way, and conversely also with more protest against communist rule.[7]

In Czechoslovakia this tolerance ended categorically during the normalization period following the Soviet invasion of August 1968 that militarily suppressed the reform movement known as the Prague Spring. Normalization re-established the quasi-totalitarian system of the fifties though in a gentler form; Ernest Gellner dubbed it "Stalinism with a human face."[8] Three forces had taken part in the

Prague Spring: society, reform-minded elites, and the communist party. During normalization, the communist party renounced all reform; it ended the dialogue between the party, dissidents and society; and it forced or coerced many elites to emigrate. Still, isolated groups of dissidents emerged and attracted new members, regrouping from 1977 around the anti-communist manifesto Charter 77 which reminded the Czechoslovak communist government that it was violating the human rights provisions of the 1976 Helsinki Final Act.[9] The legacy of the Prague Spring—of the opening to democracy and of the direct challenge to communist rule—shaped a small but forceful opposition with echoes of support in society and abroad.[10] It is the other half of our equation, the communist party, which suffered irreversible decay after the Soviet invasion.[11] As we will see, the Czech Republic would pay a heavy price for the normalization-era purges of reformers from the communist party and the subsequent twenty years of rigid party rule, because these would leave the communist party without the intellectual resources to reform itself after 1989.

Hungary and Poland also experienced a crackdown on opposition to communism and on reformers within the communist party. The normalization following the Hungarian Revolution of 1956 was brutal and sweeping. The imposition of martial law on Poland in 1981 to suppress the Solidarity movement was also very forceful.[12] Yet, in both Hungary and Poland, for a variety of reasons including the timing of the crackdowns, the choices of communist rulers, and the nature of protest, opposition groups as well as the reformers in the communist party arrived at the collapse of communism in 1989 in better form than their Czechoslovak counterparts.[13]

Yet, in Czechoslovakia as well as Poland and Hungary, oppositionists did regroup during the 1980s around the goal of reversing the destruction of civil society and establishing rival groups to the communist party that could fight for democracy and human rights.[14] The "refolutions" and revolutions of 1989 would thrust them suddenly, dramatically and quite romantically into high politics.[15]

In Poland, the communist party invited the opposition movement Solidarity to the Roundtable negotiations on power sharing in the early months of 1989. This move was all the more fantastic for the fact that the communist leaders who concluded that Poles would only accept desperately needed economic reforms at the hands of a Solidarity-endorsed government were the same leaders that had imposed a harsh martial law in 1981 to save Poland from Solidarity.[16] In partially free elections held on June 4 1989, Solidarity won every seat that it was allowed to contest.[17] Solidarity hesitated, but ultimately decided to form a government: Prime Minister Tadeusz Mazowiecki took office on August 24 1989 and his finance minister Leszek Balcerowicz launched Poland's "shock therapy" program on January 1 1990.[18] The former shipyard worker and Solidarity leader, Lech Wałęsa, was elected president in 1990. Solidarity splintered and dissolved; in the first completely free parliamentary elections, held in October 1991, no single party received more than 13 percent of the vote and eighteen "clubs" were formed within parliament. The leading vote-getters were post-Solidarity Freedom Union (UW) at 12.31 percent, and the post-communist Alliance of the Democratic Left (SLD) at 12 percent. This was liberal democracy in its more vibrant (and chaotic) form: Poland had three governments in the next two years and waves of strikes (mostly by public sector employees), but political and economic reforms proceeded apace.[19] Then it was the turn of the former communists to govern again as Polish voters adjudged that the post-Solidarity governments had become inefficient and immodest. In the 1993 elections the former communist party, now named the Alliance of the Democratic Left (SLD), won 37 percent of the seats, and formed a coalition with the ex-communist satellite Polish Peasant Party (PSL) that won 29 percent of the seats; together they controlled 66 percent of the seats for four years until the 1997 elections.

In Hungary, the communist party entered into talks in 1989 with the Opposition Roundtable, which brought together nine opposition groups and parties.[20] The Roundtable was first set up by the opposition itself to harmonize the activities of different opposition organizations.[21] Unlike Poland's Solidarity movement and Czechoslovakia's Civic Forum movement, the Hungarian opposition was already organized into political parties by 1989, including the Alliance of Free Democrats (SZDSZ), the Federation of Young Democrats (FIDESZ), the Hungarian Democratic Forum (MDF), the Christian Democratic People's Party (KDNP), and the Independent Smallholders' Party (FKGP). The Roundtable with the communists agreed the rules of the transition, but it was competition among the anti-communist parties that took center stage in the run-up to the first free elections in 1990. The elections were won by the Hungarian Democratic Forum (MDF), the right-wing post-opposition party—defeating the center-right and center-left post-opposition parties as well as the reforming communists. The MDF formed a coalition with the Smallholders and the Christian Democrats, con-trolling 59 percent of the seats. The agenda of the first democratic government of Prime Minister Jószef Antall reflected very closely that part of the opposi-tion that it represented. Indeed, the first post-opposition government in Hungary overplayed its hand in defending ethnic Hungarian minorities abroad. In 1994 the former communist party, renamed the Hungarian Socialist Party (MSZP), won an absolute majority of the vote, but elected to form a coalition with the centrist liberal post-opposition Alliance of Free Democrats (SZDSZ); together they controlled 72 percent of the seats in parliament until the 1998 elections. The second free elections returned the former communists to power in Hungary just as they had in Poland.

In Czechoslovakia, the communist party was different: it did not reform and it did not negotiate in 1989 until the pressure of street demonstrations brought it down in a matter of days. Czech oppositionists and students organized into the Civic Forum (OF), backed by hundreds of thousands of people in the streets, forced the communist leadership to resign. A transitional non-communist government took power in December 1989, dissident leader Václav Havel became president, and the Civic Forum (along with its Slovak counterpart Public Against Violence, VPN) won the first free elections in June 1990 by a landslide. Before the June 1992 elections, the Civic Forum split into three political parties. Civic Forum Finance Minister Václav Klaus, a quiet economist under the communists, founded the Civic Democratic Party (ODS) and rapidly took center stage in Czech politics. Klaus campaigned on a radical free market platform, and rallied the Czechs to the neoliberal teachings of Friedrich Hayek and Margaret Thatcher; his policies in office would prove far less straightforward. The ODS won the 1992 elections decisively and formed a coalition with another post-Civic Forum party, the Civic Democratic Alliance (ODA) as well as the Christian Democratic bloc (KDU-ČSL), controlling 53 percent of the seats until the 1996 elections. Prime Minister Klaus negotiated the end of Czechoslovakia; an independent Czech Republic came into existence on January 1 1993.

We now turn to a closer study of why we find little political or economic rent seeking in Poland and Hungary, and rather more in the Czech Republic. First we examine how political parties that originated in the opposition to communism play a pivotal role in building liberal democracy during the first transition years. Second we consider the importance of a reformed communist party that gets back, quickly, into the political game.

2.1.2   Liberal Policies

We have explored in Chapter 1 the opportunities for rent seeking that exist for political parties that hold power during transition. So why did politicians in Poland, Hungary, and Czechoslovakia behave like liberal democrats immediately after 1989? Why did they put in place liberal institutions and economic reforms that limited their own rents? The key is to pay attention to the existence of the opposition movements before 1989 as groups that selected their leaders and thus—unexpectedly—also selected the leaders of the new democratic polity. The Western model of liberal democracy, rule of law, and market capitalism was deeply internalized by individuals long before the regime began to change in 1989.[22] Opposition groups selected their leaders not only for their proto-political skills, but also for their devotion to the core political and economic beliefs held by the opposition.

Without discounting the courage and the foresight of the opposition leaders, we can therefore understand the policies of the post-opposition governments as reflecting the interests, beliefs, and codes of conduct of the opposition groups that brought them to power.[23] Adam Michnik wrote most eloquently before 1989 about his conviction that how Solidarity activists behaved and the values they espoused under totalitarian rule would be profoundly reflected in the character of the political order that would follow communism. The values he and other dissidents promoted in Solidarity included liberalism, toleration, forgiveness, and nonviolence.[24] We need not, therefore, imagine the oppositionists deciphering the preferences of a majority of citizens after taking office in 1989, or even heroically forecasting the long-term interests of society as a whole. We can simplify their interests to a profound rejection of certain aspects of the communist system, and a sincere affirmation of liberal democracy.[25] These opposition groups were fighting for the inclusion of diverse parties, groups and opinions into politics. They were also fighting for national reconciliation with ethnic minorities at home and with historical enemies abroad. They held strong normative views that led them to include democratic pluralism and to exclude ethnic chauvinism and economic populism from debates in the nascent democratic polity. They held divergent views, however, on the virtues of economic liberalism with some dissidents calling for a road between socialism and capitalism enticingly called "the third way."[26]

By definition, these new governments initially had a relatively free hand. The communist party was discredited, most of the opposition was represented in government (except in Hungary), and other groups in society were only beginning to (re)form. Society had given them a broad mandate to dismantle communism, create democracy, transform the economy, and take the country into the West: but the details were left to the new government. The civic movements Solidarity and the Civic Forum would soon dissolve, leaving former oppositionists to try their hand at running normal political parties. Still, the first post-opposition governments were relatively successful in laying the foundations of liberal democracy and market capitalism because they had formed preferences conducive to this project long before communism had ended. Here, to paraphrase Douglass North, the private objectives of those with the bargaining strength to alter institutions did produce institutional solutions that turned out to be relatively efficient over the long term.[27]

On issues of national reconciliation, some post-opposition governments exploited the revolutionary moment to begin certain policies more "European" than their societies had expected.[28] Czechoslovakia's Civic Forum leader and first democratic president Václav Havel took a dramatic step toward reconciliation with Germany in 1990 by apologizing for the expulsions of ethnic Germans from Czechoslovakia after the Second World War—even though Czech citizens stood nearly united in their support for the expulsions.[29] Poland's Solidarity movement was guided by a group of intellectuals that had rethought Poland's nationality policy during the 1970s and 1980s, embracing a liberal approach to ethnic minorities in Poland, and to Poles living abroad in formerly Polish lands. Ingeniously promoting "European standards," even some that did not exist, Foreign Minister Krzysztof Skubiszewski overcame myriad obstacles to establish good relations with almost all of Poland's neighbors, including those with sizeable Polish minorities, even as every single state that had bordered Poland before 1989 disappeared.[30]

In contrast, Hungary's first post-opposition government led by the Hungarian Democratic Forum (MDF) had foreign policy priorities that were less evidently liberal. Its leaders came from that branch of the opposition movement that had worked tirelessly under communism to support Hungarian minorities in neighboring states. The brutal persecution of Transylvania's ethnic Hungarians by the communist dictator Nicolae Ceauşescu in Romania in the 1980s defined their experience of opposition.[31] The Antall government exasperated Western leaders and Hungarian citizens alike for the whole of its term with its obsession with the treatment of ethnic Hungarian minorities in neighboring states, at the expense of other projects. The priorities of the MDF illustrate clearly how the policies of the first democratic governments reflected the interests of those opposition groups from which they hailed.[32]

On issues of economic reform, post-opposition governments also had significant freedom that they used to implement a range of market-oriented reforms. Polish, Czech, and Hungarian post-opposition governments all supported a comprehensive transition to a market economy. Why did liberal elites implement rapid economic reform, particularly "shock therapy" in Poland, given the risk that the resulting economic downturn would lose them the next elections?[33] Two answers stand out:

First, post-opposition governments had to move (relatively) rapidly with reform to please their core interest groups as well as the electorate at large. For most voters, democracy was inextricably linked to building capitalism. The new governments could expect to be punished for the short-term economic hardships caused by reform—but they could also expect to be punished if the economy was reformed too little. We need not therefore solve the mystery of how a government, even of former dissidents, could be so heroic and self-sacrificing as to implement reforms knowing it would lose power. Alan Jacobs argues that governments seeking re-election may adopt policies with short-term costs but long-term benefits because these policies are understood to improve their chances of re-election: Interest groups may value the long-term benefits; voters may value them as well; the government may enjoy electoral slack (or believe it does); and some concentrated group of voters may actually gain from these reforms even in the short term.[34]

All four of these possibilities were at play in the Polish case. But the existence of Solidarity and the way that it legitimized economic reform by way of the democratic revolution were still critical. People declared themselves ready to suffer in the short term for long-term gain, and they supported the Mazowiecki government even as their living standards deteriorated dramatically.[35] For many Poles, the very decisiveness of the Balcerowicz reforms was welcomed after years of impasse, and Polish reformers expected this support. But it is likely that these new politicians also misunderstood how easy it would be for voters to throw out the heroes of the revolution for whatever party could present itself as a better manager of the new capitalist economy. The Poles did subsequently vote Solidarity out of power after a wave of protests swept through Poland in 1993. But as Grzegorz Ekiert and Jan Kubik argue, the Poles voted out the post-opposition government because they disapproved with some of the ways that it was handling the economy, not in retaliation for the economic hardships caused by marketizing reforms.[36]

Second, the catalyst for costly short-term economic reforms demanded by the transition was more reliably economic crisis than deeply held convictions about the benefits of economic liberalism.[37] Thus Poland's Solidarity reformers, brought to power by workers and presiding over a communist majority in the Sejm, pushed through radical "shock therapy" in 1989 because the Polish economy was imploding. The Czech Republic's self-proclaimed free market zealots in the ODS, by contrast, put off many fundamental reforms to win re-election in 1996 because the Czech economy was not in (visible) crisis. Hungary's communitarian right-wing MDF also put off many reforms with an eye on the 1994 elections, leaving Hungary's reformed communists to impose a sharp austerity program as the economy slid toward collapse in 1995.

Economic crisis had unexpected democratic benefits in many post-communist states by acting as a catalyst for political turnover.[38] Voters will punish a government for the decline in living standards brought about by the short-term economic repercussions of reform. However, if the thrust of the reforms has the support of the majority of the electorate, the new government will not promise to reverse them—only to manage them better. No mainstream political party is likely to upset the overall thrust of economic reform—so it matters relatively little who wins the elections. Rapid reform thus strengthens the polity by promoting the alternation of different political parties in power and implicating all of them in the project of reform.

Economic crisis also created an immediate demand for the left, which had unexpectedly good results in Poland and Hungary, giving reformed communists a way back into the democratic political game. In Romania and Bulgaria, playing to fears of economic reform allowed unreconstructed communists to stay in power, but eventually economic crisis created a demand for new parties of whatever origin. As we will see in Chapters 6 and 7, economic crisis helped break the democratic monopoly of the ruling party in Romania in 1996, in Bulgaria in 1997, and also in the Czech Republic in 1997.

The value of economic crisis sketched here is in opposition to much of the democratization literature that worries that crisis will destabilize and even destroy democracy, especially at low levels of economic development.[39] It is also in opposition to the "postcommunist breakdown-of-democracy" literature that predicted that economic crisis would destabilize and delegitimize democracy.[40] Bela Greskovits argues that, on the contrary, democratization became the political vehicle of economic stabilization and transformation.[41] Once economic crisis and other factors have enhanced the quality of political competition in post-communist states, I argue in Chapter 7 that locking ruling parties into a two-step of liberal democracy and economic reform, whatever their political stripes, is part of the leverage of the EU on domestic politics.

2.1.3   Time Horizons and the Quality of the Left Alternative

Does the presence of an organized opposition to communism at the moment of regime change guarantee liberal democracy and economic reform? If there is an organized opposition to communism, then there are automatically at least two powerful, rival groups: the opposition right and the communist left. The quality of political competition is higher, and at least one political turnover immediately takes place. But for the communists to leave the stage is not enough. If the communist party becomes a credible challenger to the opposition as a modern social democratic party, then a competitive political system becomes institutionalized rapidly after 1989 (Table 2.1).

The Polish and Hungarian communists set the example: after losing the first democratic elections, they transformed themselves into social democratic parties and won the second free elections—in Poland in 1993 and in Hungary in 1994.[42] The economic insecurity and hardship of the transition created a strong demand by voters for a political left. The communist successor parties in Poland and Hungary reinforced the liberal democratic equation by providing a moderate, non-nationalist left-wing as an alternative for voters weary of economic reform. Most important, these parties operated with the same long time horizons as the post-opposition parties when evaluating their chances under democratic institutions.[43] Having lost power and regained it, they never

TABLE 2.1   State of the opposition and the communist party, 1989

Nature of the opposition to communism	Nature of the communist party	
	Reforming	Unreconstructed
Strong	Poland Hungary	Czech Republic
Weak	Slovakia	Bulgaria Romania

behaved as if losing power again would threaten their future in national politics. Unlike the communist successor parties in Romania and Bulgaria discussed in the second part of this chapter, they had successfully reinvented themselves and had few incentives to resort to illiberal methods in order to prevent future political turnovers.

What is more striking is that the Polish and Hungarian socialist parties did not promise to reverse economic reform; they only promised to restructure the welfare state, shoring up social safety nets for those disaffected by reform.[44] They deftly portrayed themselves as better "managers" of the economy—"as reformers who knew how to minimize reform's social costs."[45] Once in office, they paid strict attention to continuing market reforms and impressing international institutions and investors with their constancy as economic liberals. After all, they had to establish their credibility as political parties suitable for running the government in a market democracy. Indeed, in Hungary it was the former communist party, its hand forced by economic crisis, that implemented sweeping economic liberalization and fiscal austerity after its election in 1994.

What is also striking is that the Polish and Hungarian socialist parties made no use of ethnic nationalism directed against minorities or historic enemies to win or maintain power. As I wrote with Timothy Snyder, they differed from their counterparts in Bulgaria and Romania in that they did not need to resort to ethnic nationalism to establish their identity. In fact, they were the alternatives to more patriotic parties that hailed from the former opposition. In Poland the post-opposition parties were reprimanded by some voters for the immodest role of the church in politics, while in Hungary the post-opposition parties were reprimanded for privileging the protection of ethnic Hungarians in neighboring states over political and economic reform at home.[46]

Why did the Polish and Hungarian communists reform so skillfully? Confronted by a strong opposition to the communist regime, these parties had opened themselves to dialog with society and to internal reform already in the 1980s. As I wrote with Timothy Snyder, "the Polish and Hungarian communist parties had made some attempts at internal reform during the 1980s and had allowed internal debate on a limited range of issues. A few modernizers had even sought to move their comrades toward something like West European social democracy. Meanwhile, factional differences within these parties were a response to the strong opposition movements discussed earlier. None of this is to say that Polish and Hungarian communists were crypto-democrats before 1989, only that some of them were sufficiently prepared to take advantage of the changes that followed."[47] This background helps to explain the relative ease with which these post-communist parties have become social democratic parties akin to those of Western Europe.[48]

Anna Grzymała-Busse shows that the legacies of communism determined the resources and strategies available for party regeneration. How the communist parties transformed themselves after 1989 depended on the "portable skills" they had acquired based on their organizational practices under communism. The practices that set the stage for successful reform by Poland and Hungary's communists were elite advancement based on technical expertise, experience with policy reform, and negotiation with the opposition.[49]

The case of the Czech Republic demonstrates the importance of competition in the political system—beyond the opposition credentials of the first government.[50] That is, even if these credentials are outstanding, as they were in the Czech lands, post-opposition governments need checks on their power. The Czech communist party exited government in the autumn of 1989 and subsequently remained true to its communist ideology; it was the second or third largest party, but an impossible coalition partner for any other party in parliament.[51] The historic Social Democratic Party (ČSSD) was recreated in 1990, but many years passed before it gathered political strength. Consequently the left as a whole was divided and weak for the first six or more years. This handed the post-opposition parties a comfortable majority in parliament after the first—and also after the second and the third—free elections. These successive right-wing governments were hailed as evidence of the Czechs' devotion to neoliberal reform and to the free market. These post-opposition governments, however, had far too much freedom because there were far too few checks on their political power.[52]

As time and politics wore away at their commitment to liberal democracy, and as the non-oppositionist Václav Klaus maneuvered his way to the helm, the post-opposition governments led by the Civic Democratic Party (ODS) started blocking the entry of other groups into the political arena in a clear bid to limit competition.[53] Abby Innes argues that the split of Czechoslovakia was partly orchestrated by Klaus and the ODS, operating virtually free of public or institutional constraints—just like their counterparts in Slovakia.[54] Meanwhile, to stay in power, they delayed many key marketizing reforms that would cause unemployment and price rises, while the free hand they enjoyed led to corrupt privatization, theft of state assets, and bank fraud linked to the ruling political parties.[55] Comparing Poland and the Czech Republic, Mitchell Orenstein vividly depicts how the absence of strong political competition enabled major reform mistakes to continue unabated: "Democratic policy alternation in the Polish case slowed the progress of privatization programs. However, it also slowed the adoption of mistaken policies, and allowed for more substantial interim policy corrections. The result is that Poland is now widely believed to have slower, but higher-quality, privatization, with a substantial positive effect on economic growth and productivity."[56]

Ironically, the absence of a reformed communist party left the Czech Republic without the right amount of competition in domestic politics—and also without the right amount of consensus in foreign policy. The reformed communist parties in Poland and Hungary gradually persuaded a substantial portion of their core voters on the 'conservative' left to take a pro-Western stand: to support membership in NATO, membership in the European Union (EU), reconciliation with Germany and liberal market reform. On NATO, for example, a strong political consensus developed in 1990–1 in Poland and Hungary and held fast until membership was attained in 1998. All mainstream political parties of the left and the right supported NATO membership as a matter of basic state interest. In the Czech Republic, by contrast, the unreformed communist party remained vehemently anti-NATO, anti-EU, anti-German and anti-reform—while attracting as much as 20 percent of the vote. Meanwhile the newly established ČSSD did not exert itself to create a consensus within its own ranks or among its electorate. Instead, social democratic politicians remained lukewarm on NATO and on reform (though not on the EU) as part of their ongoing struggle to woo voters away from the communists. All together, this makes the Czech Republic a hybrid case, as we will explore in greater detail in Chapter 7.

One of the insights of this chapter is therefore that strong political competition among cohesive and moderate opposing political parties develops most easily when you have a post-communist left as well as a post-opposition right. If it reforms itself, the communist party becomes a credible, vocal, and non-nationalist "opposition" to the rulers almost immediately after the first democratic elections in 1989, drawing on its established organizational base. For many, it was amazing and even shocking that a party allegedly so hated by the population for forty-five years, however well reformed, could win over the majority of the voters just a few short years after the end of communism. For many reasons, however, in the words of Valerie Bunce, the return of the left in Poland and Hungary proved to be "an investment in democratic governance."[57] We can sum up this investment as creating the conditions for the right balance of competition and consensus among the political parties in the national parliament.

We now turn to the states that faired far worse than the Czech Republic. They did not have a reforming communist party in 1989, but they also did not have a strong opposition to staff the first democratic government. Instead, unreconstructed communists and opportunists took control—or indeed remained in control—in conditions of weak political competition and growing polarization.

2.2 No Opposition: Illiberal Pattern of Political Change

The absence of a strong, organized opposition to communist rule in Romania, Bulgaria and Slovakia created a political vacuum at the moment of regime change that enabled non-opposition governments to hold power.[58] By non-opposition governments, I mean governments that were not formed by leaders of groups that had opposed communism. Unreconstructed communists[59] (in Romania and Bulgaria) and opportunists (in Slovakia) won power by using the fear of economic reform and the defense of the nation to forge a new political identity and maintain their political viability. They exploited the lack of competition in the political system to control information and to control the new institutions of the democratic state. Illiberal democracy took hold: the elections were mostly free and fair, but the ruling elites had little interest in fostering the institutions of a liberal democracy.[60] Despite their democratic rhetoric, the non-opposition governments presided over what I call an illiberal pattern of political change: they warped democratic institutions, sabotaged economic reform and fostered intolerance in their efforts to concentrate and prolong their power.[61]

The absence of a strong opposition in Romania and Bulgaria in 1989 meant that there was no need for the communist party to formulate a liberal democratic reform program. Indeed, the comparative advantage of the Romanian and Bulgarian communist parties lay with patronage disbursement, not with designing policies that would pluralize the polity and liberalize the economy. Such policies were understood as a threat to their domestic power base. Romania's and Bulgaria's communist elites put a brake on domestic change to prevent political pluralism and comprehensive marketizing reforms from undermining their power, while Slovak elites pressed for a fundamental change—a sovereign Slovak state—to help consolidate theirs. The absence of a strong opposition in Slovakia in 1989 allowed nationalists and opportunists to develop a powerful political party based on Slovak nationalism that used Slovak state-building to create a partly new, highly clientalistic patronage network. Pauline Jones Luong describes the behavior of all three aptly in her finding that elites support innovation where they perceive their relative power to be increasing, and resist changing the status quo and its distribution of power where they perceive their power to be declining.[62]

To win elections, Romanian, Bulgarian, and Slovak communists and nationalists promised to protect the average voter from economic reform, and to protect the nation from its "enemies." For elites competing for popular support during the transition to democracy, Jack Snyder makes a similar argument that "nationalism is a convenient doctrine that justifies a partial form of democracy, in which an elite rules in the name of the nation yet may not be fully accountable to its people." Nationalist elites are more able to "hijack" political discourse when "representative institutions, political parties, and journalistic professionalism are weakly established," and "when its citizens lack the skills needed for successful democratic political participation."[63] In our illiberal pattern states, we see that the concentration of power in the hands of rent-seeking elites, unchecked by other political forces, allows them to mislead electorates about the long-term costs of halting economic reform and of ethnic nationalism. In power, they harness domestic institutions to suppress political competition and corrupt marketizing reforms, further concentrating power in their own hands. Later in the book, we will explore how opposition parties and civic groups gradually gather strength and challenge the rent-seeking elites in all three states. Already below, we see that at least in Bulgaria and Slovakia opposition forces are developing as an important counterweight to the illiberal rulers.

2.2.1 Oppositions and Revolutions

Why were the oppositions to communism so weak in Romania and Bulgaria that they could not manage to wrest power from the communist party in 1989—in what was after all supposed to be the moment of democratic revolution? Why was the opposition in Slovakia so weak that illiberal forces gained so much ground after 1989? These are intriguing questions that, as I mentioned above, are outside of the scope of this book. What must be stressed here, however, is that there are very significant differences in the oppositions that did exist after 1989 in these three states. They were not strong enough to take and hold power in 1989, but the similarities just about end there. In this section I examine in turn each of the oppositions to communism, and then each of the "revolutions" that ended communism in Romania, Bulgaria, and Slovakia.

Romania had virtually no moderate, organized opposition to communism. Its ruthless, extremely oppressive form of communism evolved into the dictatorship of communist leader Nicolae Ceauşescu. Under the Ceauşescu regime, Romanian intellectual dissidents were few, and the creation of clandestine opposition organizations was impossible: "The only alternatives were desperate isolated gestures—immediately followed by imprisonment and forced exile."[64] Oppression does not lead to moderation, and opposition to Ceauşescu that did exist was often pushed to extremes: one of the most active groups espoused a totalitarian, fascist ideology associated with the inter-war Iron Guard. Since there is little trace of liberal democratic thought in the history of Romania's ruling elite, it is possible that the Romanian opposition would have been illiberal irrespective of the brutality of the communist regime. However, liberal democratic ideas did not prevail among Hungary or Poland's ruling elites in the interwar period, but gained currency as part of the opposition to communism.[65] Absent the brutality of the Ceauşescu regime a liberal intelligentsia in Romania may well have taken shape in opposition to communism. Instead, many Romanian intellectuals and other proto-dissidents emigrated to the West, and most never looked back. The success of Romania's communist party in stunting pluralism in Romania after 1989 was as much a consequence of the incoherence and weakness of the opposition which protested its takeover of the Romanian revolution as of the lengths that Iliescu and other leaders were willing to go to subdue it. The incoherence and weakness of this opposition is a direct legacy of the draconian nature of Ceauşescu's totalitarian rule.[66]

Bulgaria in contrast had a rainbow of disparate civic groups that could exist in the more relaxed though extremely pro-Soviet atmosphere of Bulgarian communism. The end of communist leader Todor Zhivkov's rule in November 1989 unified much of Bulgaria's diverse opposition. Grouping historic social democratic and Christian democratic parties, ecological movements, a trade union, religious and human-rights groups, and various other kinds of political formations, the Union of Democratic Forces (UDF) announced its existence on November 23 1989. Zhelyu Zhelev, an academic philosopher and Bulgaria's leading dissident, was elected chairman of its coordinating council. While this recalls in many ways the birth of the Civic Forum in the Czech lands, the UDF lacked the coherence to outwit the communists, or the authority to force them to resign at the behest of demonstrators, who were absent from the streets of Bulgarian cities in the autumn of 1989.

Slovakia demonstrates most clearly how important it is for opposition groups to exist before the end of communism, and to transfer their agendas and their leaders to post-opposition governments at communism's end. As a part of Czechoslovakia, Slovakia did create the "superstructure" of a regime change driven by opposition groups. To mirror the Czech Civic Forum (OF) and negotiate with the outgoing communist government, an umbrella pro-democracy organization called Public Against Violence (VPN) was created in November 1989. But this spontaneous organization could claim only a hand-ful of "authentic" dissidents, and did not vet the elites that stepped forward to take the helm (except for links with extreme right-wing forces).[67] Opposition to communism in Slovakia had been weaker than in the Czech lands after 1968, as had liberalism in political thought before communism.[68] Slovak intellectuals had generally adapted themselves to the communist regime, while Slovak society generally perceived the communist period as one of progress. As a result, in comparison to the Czech lands, "the polarization of Slovak society was not so deep; the dividing line between the official and alternative structures was not so sharp." By 1988, for example, there were only 19 signatories of Charter 77 in Slovakia, as compared to 1,900 in the Czech lands (though Slovaks did turn to other forms of dissent such as envir-onmental movements and the Catholic Church).[69] Of those PAV members who were unbending supporters of liberal democracy and of a civic conception of statehood, none emerged to dominate politics in Bratislava in 1989–90 as Václav Havel did in Prague. Opportunistic politicians began to fill the political vacuum in Bratislava with Slovak nationalism, gaining by 1992 a remarkable purchase on Slovak politics despite low levels of public support for Slovak independence.

Communism ended in the autumn of 1989 in all three states: the leading role of the communist party was terminated, basic human rights such as the freedom of speech and the freedom of assembly were adopted, and multiparty elections were scheduled. These were tremendous, revolutionary, changes. But the way that communism ended, and the way that the early years of democratization played themselves out were very different than in the liberal pattern states.

In Romania the communists, led by the former Ceauşescu lieutenant Ion Iliescu, were able to use economic populism and nationalism to repackage themselves as the defenders of Romanian interests on the road away from communism. Romania's aborted revolution was violent. Demonstrations against the regime began on December 16 in Timişoara where at least ninety-seven people had died by December 21. On this day Ceauşescu called a pro-communist rally in Bucharest that turned against him and forced him to flee. Fighting allegedly erupted between members of the Securitate and members of the armed forces that had turned against the regime, with protestors caught in the crossfire, leaving at least 1,104 dead overall.[70] The Council of the National Salvation Front (FSN) formed on or before December 21 1989 by Iliescu executed Ceauşescu and his wife and broadcast some version of their death on national television, but kept the bulk of Ceauşescu's apparatus and protected members of the much feared Securitate, even those responsible for the December violence.[71] Several dissidents joined the FSN, but they had little more than an ephemeral role, legitimizing Iliescu's seizure of power.[72] The FSN was able to "kidnap" the Romanian democratic revolution in late 1989 because the Ceauşescu regime had created vast communist networks (whose members recognized the FSN as the protector of their interests), and because the Ceauşescu regime had severely repressed the opposition.[73] In the electoral campaigns of 1990 and 1992, the weak and fractious opposition was unable to advance a convincing alternative program to that put forth by the FSN and its propaganda machine. It was also undercut by Romania's presidential system that favored Iliescu and his ruling party.

After winning the presidency (with 85 percent of the vote for Iliescu) and a majority in both chambers of the parliament (with 66 percent of the vote) in May 1990, the FSN became "a party devoted to the protection of Romanians in their own nation-state."[74] Its offshoot,[75] the Democratic FSN (DFSN), won the parliamentary elections in September 1992 with 27 percent of the vote, and formed a minority government with the tacit support of three extremist parties (which together received 15 percent).[76] In July 1993, the DFSN merged with several small parties and renamed itself the Party of Social Democracy in Romania (PDSR). The PDSR entered in 1995 into a formal coalition with the extremist parties that had propped up its minority government since the 1992 elections. Though its name changed twice, Iliescu's party of former communists was in 1996 the only one in East Central Europe to have held power continuously since the revolutions of 1989.

In Bulgaria the communists managed to hold on to power in 1990 by presenting themselves as the defenders of the Bulgarian nation, and as the protectors of the Bulgarian voter from the harsh consequences of market reform. In so doing, they emulated the success of Romania's communist elites. Bulgarian communist elites, however, did not use the tools of ethnic nationalism nearly as harshly as their Romanian counterparts, nor did they resort to violence. They had to contend with an opposition that managed to remain (more or less) united in the UDF, that held power in 1991–2, and that helped elect a strongly pro-Western president. From 1989 to 1994 a series of virtual electoral stalemates between the unreconstructed communists and the inexperienced opposition produced weak, often incompetent, Bulgarian governments: these brought neither systematic economic reform nor the entrenchment of a liberal democratic state. Still, when compared to its Balkan neighbors in the 1990s, Bulgaria was stable, peaceful and relatively tolerant; when compared to Romania, it was politically vibrant.[77]

Political change in Bulgaria began on November 10 1989, when Todor Zhivkov was ousted in a palace coup. The coup was preceded not by mounting popular pressure but by a carefully orchestrated plot among several of Zhivkov's lieutenants, including Andrei Lukanov and Petur Mladenov; Mladenov took the top post in both the party and the state apparatus. The communists soon took the plunge: in January 1990 they changed their ideological profile from Marxist–Leninist to "modern Marxist," and in April they renamed themselves the Bulgarian Socialist Party (BSP).[78] The UDF pressed for negotiations that took place from January to May 1990, yielding an agreement to hold elections almost immediately in June 1990. The UDF believed that these elections would serve as a simple referendum on communist rule, and were confident of victory. The BSP promised the Bulgarian people gradual reform that would shield them from the economic penury of the "shock therapy" that the UDF had prepared for the Bulgarian economy. Helped by intimidation in the countryside, the BSP gained an absolute majority of 211 of 400 seats in the June 1990 elections.[79]

Ineffectual government, internal BSP divisions, and social unrest brought new elections in Bulgaria in October 1991: the UDF won a narrow plurality and formed a minority government which depended upon the tacit support of the ethnic Turkish party, the Movement for Rights and Freedoms (MRF). The UDF government, led by Filip Dimitrov, greatly improved Bulgaria's relations with the West and introduced essential market reforms. Unlike oppositionists in Poland and Hungary, the UDF focused on what Rumyana Kolarova calls "backward-looking justice": instead of implementing radical economic reform and shoring up democratic institutions, the UDF government prioritized retribution and restitution. Given the nature of Bulgaria's communists, this may be understandable, but according to Kolarova the Bulgarian public preferred "forward-looking impartiality."[80] After just one year in power the UDF government fell in October 1992, ushering in a BSP-dominated government of "experts" led by Lyuben Berov.[81] In the elections of December 1994, a BSP-led coalition won a resounding victory with 43.5 percent of the vote, and an absolute majority of 125 out of 240 seats in parliament. In a foreboding prop-aganda document published in March 1995, the new BSP government led by premier Zhan Videnov blamed the UDF opposition for the bulk of Bulgaria's problems, while making virtually no mention of the consequences of forty-five years of rule by the BSP's communist antecedent.

In Slovakia, the communist government resigned in December 1989: the Czechoslovak communist party gave up control of the federal Czechoslovak government as well as the government of the Czech and Slovak federal republics at the same time. The Public Against Violence (VPN), regrouping those opposed to communist rule, took power in Bratislava, but was gradually eclipsed by nationalists who pushed for greater Slovak autonomy as the core strategy for increasing their political power.[82] From the perspective of those seeking to maximize power, Slovak nationalism made good sense: the leaders of a unit of a confederation or of an independent state must automatically wield more political and economic power, with fewer constraints on that power, than the leaders of a unit of a federation. For Slovakia's new nationalists, the power of independence was amplified by the opportunity to redesign political and economic institutions as part of the ongoing transition.[83]

After the June 1990 Czechoslovak elections, Vladimír Mečiar was appointed prime minister of the Slovak federal republic, having risen quickly through the ranks of the VPN.[84] The first Mečiar government (June 1990 to April 1991) ended when Mečiar was charged with abuse of power and removed from office in a no-confidence vote. He quit the VPN to form his own party, the Movement for a Democratic Slovakia (HZDS). Many prominent VPN members who would later become Mečiar's bitterest ene-mies resigned their posts and joined the HZDS, including Michal Kováč, the future president. The HZDS won the next elections in June 1992. Apart from rhetoric, the most objectionable action of the second Mečiar govern-ment (June 1992 to March 1994) was stopping privatization and then transforming it into an opaque, corrupt system of rewarding loyal Mečiar supporters. By autumn 1993, the misuse of power by the ruling parties had resulted in open conflict between Mečiar and President Michal Kováč. A second group of HZDS deputies left the party in protest, bringing down the government in a no-confidence vote in March 1994 (a first group had left in protest in 1992).

The next government, led by Prime Minister Jozef Moravčík (March to October 1994), made considerable progress in shoring up democratic institutions, promoting ethnic tolerance, mending relations with Western institutions, fixing privatization and moving forward with economic reform. Five rightist, centrist, and leftist parties formed the Moravčík government, which relied on the tacit support of the ethnic Hungarian parties, thus regrouping every moderate political party in the Slovak parliament including the reformed communist party, the Party of the Democratic Left (SDL).

This enlightened Slovak government was short-lived: the elections of October 1994 returned Mečiar to power, installing the most "nationalist" government since 1989 in Slovakia. Sharon Fisher argues that although nationalism was pivotal to the discourse of the HZDS, it was of little importance to the party as an ideology: nationalism was instead a very effective tool enabling the HZDS to carry out an authoritarian concentration of power.[85] Mečiar's HZDS received a plurality of 35 percent of the vote; it formed a coalition with the extremist right-wing Slovak National Party (SNP) and the neo-communist, Trotskyite Association of Workers of Slovakia (ZRS), which received 5 and 7 percent of the vote respectively.[86] To signal that ambitious reforms were afoot, the HZDS gave the education ministry to the extreme nationalists, and the privatization ministry to the Trotskyites (whose "ideology" turned out to be personal enrichment). If the 1992 elections halted the development of liberal democracy in Slovakia, then the 1994 elections heralded its reversal as the full force of "Mečiarism" hit Slovakia for the next four years.[87] Many of its perpetrators operated on the basis of communist-era networks and habits, and thus represented a certain continuity with the old regime that had been masked by the drama of the independence movement.[88]

It bears emphasizing that the 1994 elections were extremely close. The "opposition" to Mečiar lost voters because it included a cacophony of competing parties. More shocking, it wasted many of its own votes that were cast for small center-right parties that failed to cross the 5 percent threshold to enter parliament.[89] Despite some efforts, these small parties did not manage to merge with one another or with larger parties. There was ample evidence from opinion polls that they were unlikely to get enough votes (allegedly, the results of at least one opinion poll were fixed to attract voters by convincing them otherwise). Meanwhile, the 1994 elections need not have taken place at all: the Party of the Democratic Left (SDL) insisted on elections in the autumn of 1994 instead of supporting the Moravčík government until the next scheduled elections in June 1996. Though it had made progress since 1989, the Slovak opposition was still too fragmented and inchoate, lacking the consensus and the skills to cooperate effectively against the illiberal parties and to avert Slovakia's additional four years of suffering under Mečiarism.

2.2.2   Illiberal Policies

Now we turn to the policies implemented by the PDSR in Romania, the BSP in Bulgaria, and the HZDS in Slovakia that help create illiberal democracy in the three states. The non-opposition leaders of the PDSR, the BSP, and the HZDS had no normative project before them except to win and to maintain power.[90] They had typically not spent years contemplating their state's transformation into a liberal democracy, nor did they represent groups that had resisted communist rule. Instead, they had typically spent years doing rather well under communism. What they did after 1989 was to preserve and rebuild a domestic power base of political and economic elites beholden to them for patronage. In what follows I will briefly examine policies connected to (*a*) the concentration of political power; (*b*) the corruption of economic reform; and (*c*) the use of ethnic nationalism in domestic politics.

The Concentration of Political Power

The most prolonged and effective campaign to concentrate political power in the hands of the former communist nomenklatura occurred in Romania. The deliberate strategy adopted in 1990 by Iliescu and the FSN was to monopolize power by "retaining the substance of authoritarian centralism" and by quelling emerging political pluralism.[91] The role of Ceauşescu's Securitate in harassing opposition political parties at the behest of Iliescu is murky but incontestable. Iliescu also used more subtle means to undermine the pro-Western intelligentsia, such as appointing nationalists and communists to all cultural positions, excluding non-communists from the Romanian Academy, and protecting the Ceauşescu-era academic establishment.[92] Iliescu brought under his control the state-run television and several influential newspapers; the newspapers *Romania libera* and *Ziua* were independent and critical, but their readership barely extended beyond Bucharest.

Described as "Romania's original contribution to Eastern Europe's post-communist history," the use of armed miners to suppress the opposition vividly depicts the authoritarian ambitions of the Iliescu regime.[93] Some 300,000 Romanian students, teachers, and professionals who supported democracy and decommunization began a rally in April 1990 in Bucharest's University Square against Iliescu's usurpation of power. But the protesters did not construct a political party, nor did they address the nation as a whole. Iliescu, meanwhile, campaigned throughout the country and the FSN engaged in a vigorous anti-intellectual campaign. After Iliescu's triumph in the May 1990 elections, what was left of the (then) dispirited rally was driven away by some 10,000 miners that were transported to Bucharest from the Jiu valley in special trains on the dawn of June 14. The miners, armed with wooden staves and iron bars, beat the protestors with the help of officers of the Securitate.[94] Encouraged to embark on an anti-intellectual rampage, the miners moved on to destroy the headquarters of opposition newspapers and political parties, and to attack anyone they suspected of opposition to the government.

The BSP in Bulgaria had from the outset much more limited possibilities for dampening political competition. In the peculiar conditions of 1989 and 1990, the UDF was strong enough to force the communists to accept certain institutions of a liberal democracy. UDF leader Zhelyu Zhelev was elected president by parliament in August 1990 after it was discovered that his predecessor Mladenov had supported the use of tanks against demonstrators in 1989. In 1992, Zhelev became the first president of Bulgaria elected directly by the population. The UDF also helped install a powerful and independent Constitutional Court that ruled frequently against legislation proposed by the UDF as well as by the BSP. The Constitutional Court blocked attempts by the BSP to control the judiciary and usurp power from the president and the parliament. Meanwhile, no strong, charismatic leader like Iliescu in Romania or Mečiar in Slovakia emerged from the ranks of the BSP to seduce the electorate and to forge cohesion inside the BSP.

What is striking is how the BSP managed to portray itself as the defender of democracy and of the economic well-being of Bulgarians, and to portray the UDF as anti-democratic and extremist on account of its support for retribution and for comprehensive economic reform. The BSP frightened especially the rural electorate with warnings that the UDF would implement "a Polish-style" reform. The BSP, like the PDSR, had a monopoly on the information received by most voters in the countryside where the BSP maintained extensive control of local government. After the BSP won a parliamentary majority in the 1994 elections, it moved to consolidate its national control of the public television and radio. Interviews conducted with journalists by the Bulgarian Helsinki Committee found widespread reports of censorship among journalists including direct political interference in the content of newscasts. Many considered that their freedom had deteriorated considerably as a consequence of the BSP victory in the 1994 elections.[95]

The steps taken after the 1994 elections in Slovakia by Mečiar and the HZDS to evade accountability to rival democratic institutions and to concentrate political and economic power were dramatic and ruthless.[96] The HZDS made unabashed moves to contravene normal parliamentary procedures and the rulings of Slovakia's Constitutional Court. It took complete control of all parliamentary committees (except environment), and excluded opposition parties from oversight bodies.[97] In an act of political revenge on the former HZDS members who toppled Mečiar's cabinet in March 1994, the HZDS attempted to get one opposition party, the Democratic Union (DU), evicted from the national parliament, and to oust President Kováč on charges of treason. It illegally stripped a HZDS defector of his parliamentary mandate, and passed dozens of laws that were found to violate provisions of the constitution such as the separation of powers and the rights of the citizen. The HZDS also took control of the public media, the intelligence services, and the privatization process, giving it even better tools for rewarding loyalists and undermining opponents than simply its majority in parliament.

The 1994 onslaught on political competition in Slovakia was spearheaded by new legislation that gave Mečiar's HZDS partisan control over the public media.[98] The ruling coalition replaced seventeen of the eighteen members of the boards overseeing Slovak Radio and Television. Meanwhile, Slovak economic elites that benefited from massively corrupt privatization bought and attempted to control private media outlets. Independent newspapers, television and radio, however, became vociferous critics of the HZDS government and grew in popularity despite being harassed by government agencies and blasted as the tools of the "enemies" of the Slovak nation.[99]

The illiberalism of the HZDS coalition also led, as Kieran Williams has shown, to the gross misuse of the means of coercion and surveillance, in particular by the security intelligence service, SIS.[100] The SIS monitored and harassed opposition politicians, trade unionists, clerics, and journalists. Its higher command was dominated by some eighty reactivated officers of the communist secret police, the StB. The SIS and its HZDS director, Ivan Lexa, allegedly organized the kidnapping of the son of President Kováč in August 1995, and the murder of Róbert Remiáš, a friend of a witness to that kidnapping in April 1996. Peter Tóth of the independent daily *SME* investigating Lexa and the SIS was physically assaulted by a SIS officer, his car was firebombed, and his newspaper was heavily sued.[101] These are perhaps among the most egregious known actions of the SIS under Mečiar, but it also engaged in other politically motivated criminal activities.

The Corruption of Economic Reform

Partial economic reform in all three states benefited economic elites from the old regime. This was a small group of highly placed officials and enterprise managers, and not the large group of workers employed by state-owned enterprises that the PDSR, the BSP, and the HZDS were claiming to protect. Ironically it was the very rich and the very poor in society that relied on the state—one for maintaining clientalistic networks centered on state-owned enterprises, state-owned banks, and state-directed privatization, and the other for meager pensions and low-paying jobs in the public sector. In general, citizens in Romania, Bulgaria, and Slovakia were more suspicious of the market: the absence of an opposition to communism, or of a reforming communist party at the end of communism left these societies with a weaker consensus on the desirability of market capitalism. This made it easy for rent-seeking elites to win elections by promising slow, cautious reform.

Rather than easing the transition for workers or improving aggregate economic welfare, slow reform protected and enriched communist-era managers whose inefficient state enterprises should have been restructured or forced into bankruptcy. Often, money poured from the state budget through these enterprises straight into the managers' pockets, while mounting debts were dumped back on the state. Privatization also became remarkably corrupt, with governing elites handing out state property to economic cronies for a fraction of its actual worth. For these intertwined circles of political and economic elites, comprehensive and transparent economic reforms proved much too costly: why forego the ongoing benefits from partial reform?[102] Capturing the state yielded vivid and immediate pay-offs because of the opportunities to exploit the transition to a market-based economy.

John Gould shows that illiberal democracies tend to choose privatization programs that primarily reward insiders. Insiders "sought to use privatization as a vehicle to transfer the positional assets they inherited from Communism into material assets." Gould presents data showing that illiberal governments in Slovakia, Croatia, and Serbia presided over "insider capture" of the privatization process with important negative effects for economic growth and economic equality.[103] As Stephen Holmes observes, "successful office holders throughout the post-communist world have no immediate interest in the creation of political transparency or a rule governed polity and economy."[104]

Stalled economic reforms, corrupt state institutions, and insider privatizations also suppressed the interest groups with foreign contacts that would normally develop in a functioning market economy with strong links to the global economy.[105] Foreign investors were reluctant; they were scared away by uncertain reform and uncertain access to EU markets—and deliberately kept away by rent-seeking elites enjoying the spoils of insider privatization. As Figure 2.1 demonstrates, the lower levels of economic liberalization in Romania and Bulgaria correlate with lower levels of foreign direct investment in these countries from 1990 to 1995. Figures 2.1 and 2.2 also illustrate the peculiar position of Slovakia: substantial market reforms were put in place between 1990 and 1992 as part of Czechoslovakia's economic reform program, but illiberal politics and insider privatization kept foreign investors away.

Using United Nations and World Bank data, Heather Grabbe and Kirsty Hughes show similar discrepancies. They estimate the cumulative foreign direct investment (FDI) inflows for 1990–6, per capita, as follows for our six cases: Hungary $1,256, Czech Republic $674, Poland, $351, Slovakia $190, Romania $70, and Bulgaria $60.[106] (This is echoed in Figure 7.1 in Chapter 7.) The low levels of FDI in the illiberal states are significant, since elsewhere foreign investors played a key role in integrating firms into global networks

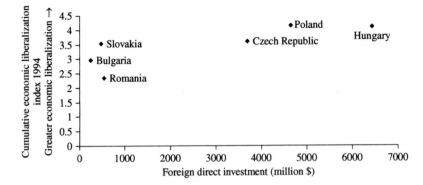

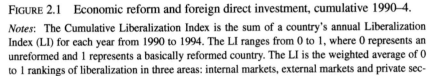

FIGURE 2.1   Economic reform and foreign direct investment, cumulative 1990–4.

Notes: The Cumulative Liberalization Index is the sum of a country's annual Liberalization Index (LI) for each year from 1990 to 1994. The LI ranges from 0 to 1, where 0 represents an unreformed and 1 represents a basically reformed country. The LI is the weighted average of 0 to 1 rankings of liberalization in three areas: internal markets, external markets and private sector entry.

Source: Economic liberalization index from De Melo, Denizer and Gelb (1996); foreign direct investment from World Bank (2002*b*).

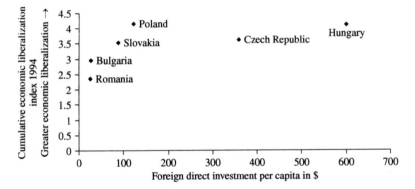

FIGURE 2.2   Economic reform and foreign direct investment per capita, cumulative 1990–4.

Source: Economic liberalization index from De Melo, Denizer and Gelb (1996); foreign direct investment from World Bank (2002*b*).

of production and marketing, and in shifting exports towards more advanced stages of production.[107] For Romania and Bulgaria, which in 1989 had (along with Poland) the most impoverished economies of the region, halting reform brought great hardship without accomplishing the transition to the market. For Slovakia, corrupt reform robbed the state and drove foreign investors away from an economy that had otherwise shown considerable promise.[108]

The seven years of Iliescu's regime in Romania provide a textbook case of the capture of a partially reformed economy by former communist cadres linked closely to the ruling political parties. The PDSR attracted the votes of Romania's desperately poor rural workers and farmers, but it acted vigorously to protect the interests of Romania's increasingly rich economic nomenklatura. Economic backwardness played into the hands of the FSN in 1990: an uneducated rural population accounting for over 50 percent of the electorate and a generally desperate economic situation throughout Romania meant that many Romanians quickly fell for the FSN's promises.[109] With measures such as augmenting supplies of food and fuel, Iliescu and his friends did, in the words of Ivo Banac, manage "to restore a semblance of normality to Romania."[110] The draconian austerity program imposed by Ceauşescu in the 1980s to pay off foreign debt by squeezing domestic consumption, combined with widespread fear of untrammeled and savage capitalist forces from abroad, stoked by the FSN, meant that the Romanian electorate was uniquely unprepared to understand the benefits of comprehensive economic reform for the Romanian economy.[111]

The circles of economic elites close to Iliescu that benefited from partial reform overlapped quite dramatically with members of the communist security services. Dennis Deletant argues that "Securitate officers, with their specialist knowledge and their foreign contacts, triggered the creation of a veritable economic mafia. Using their privileged commercial expertise these officers set up private import-export businesses and by exploiting their positions within the Foreign Trade Ministry and other government agencies . . . cornered a significant part of Romania's export activity."[112] Romania's opportunistic communist elites, dubbed "entrepratchiks" by Katherine Verdery, were indeed hard at work.[113]

The links of Bulgaria's BSP governments with the former communist cadres that stole with impunity from the Bulgarian economy after 1989 defy easy description. Bulgarian economic reforms, especially in the fields of privatization and banking reform, were woefully slow and foreign investment was negligible. After 1994, the Videnov government reversed certain economic reforms, such as the privatization of agriculture. BSP politicians were involved in the theft of the assets of state enterprises, the appropriation of loans from state banks, and the very lucrative arbitrage opportunities that existed in the foreign export business. The BSP's privatization plan excluded foreign investors and gave favorable state credits to Bulgarian businesses, thus catering to the former communists that controlled much of the private economy. The financial mismanagement of the banking sector by BSP-led governments allowed savings to be directed toward "shadowy financial-industrial groups" which had the effect of bankrupting several banks and contributing to the eventual collapse of the banking system in 1996.[114] BSP governments also allowed companies to reap profits from massive illegal exports that exploited the differential between subsidized domestic prices and world prices. In 1995, firms owned by close friends of BSP premier Zhan Videnov had exported enough wheat to cause a severe grain shortage for several weeks. In the winter of 1996–7, a poor harvest and illegal exports caused bread shortages and a twenty-fold increase in bread prices, helping to bring down the Videnov government in January 1997.[115]

Divisions inside the BSP between Marxist ideologues, reformers, and "entrepreneurs" combined with incompetence among BSP officials to create a more anarchic situation than in the Romanian or Slovak economy. Communist enterprise managers and other economic elites could increasingly manipulate or bypass the BSP government even as they stole from the Bulgarian state.[116] Zhelyu Vladimirov argues that these circles of "apparatchik-experts" developed a specific corporate and conspiracy spirit, forming a spontaneously emerging institution that gradually took hold of the very state.[117] Venelin Ganev shows with careful detail how the powerful economic conglomerate Multigroup systematically undermined the capacity of state institutions and the organizational coherence of administrative agencies.[118] However, there is no question that Bulgaria's economic nomenklatura knew who their political protectors were: reportedly all of Bulgaria's 1,000 millionaires and five billionaires in 1994 were BSP members. Thus Videnov presided over an unprecedented redistribution of national wealth.[119] It is also tempting to conclude that the penury of a Polish-style shock therapy would have been a blessing for the great majority of the BSP's voters as compared to the economic immiseration that they endured.

In Slovakia, Czech-led reforms before 1992 had already liberalized much of the economy, making many rent-seeking opportunities of Hellman's lucrative "partial reform" equilibrium inaccessible to Slovakia's ruling parties. But their ability to capture the privatization process after 1992 and distribute its spoils among a small circle of elites was striking. Mečiar allied himself with Slovakia's communist-era enterprise managers who considered Czech-led reforms a threat to their economic power.[120] These industrialists were grouped in the Union of Industry (ZP) that became a cornerstone of Mečiar's domestic power base, accounting for 64 percent of Slovak gross domestic product in 1994. Initially wary of privatization, the industrialists embraced it once they were "in a position to dictate conditions, so that foreigners and ordinary citizens would be excluded and management would be able to acquire firms for a fraction of their book value."[121]

Mečiar consolidated personal control over privatization toward the end of his second government in 1994, rewarding HZDS insiders with control over key state enterprises and with lucrative privatization deals. The Moravčík government attempted to reverse some of the more problematic privatizations, but its time in power was too short. After the 1994 elections, the HZDS-controlled parliament transferred decision-making power for privatization sales from the government to the National Property Fund (FNM). John Gould details how the FNM, as a quasi-private entity, could make decisions entirely free of public scrutiny: henceforth Mečiar-appointed loyalists engaged in "a non-transparent and quasilegal insider privatization program" including "the sales of Slovakia's largest industrial enterprises to often-unidentified Mečiar allies at a fraction of their real value."[122] Meanwhile, FNM officials openly used xenophobia to justify their exclusion of foreign bidders—who were anyhow not beating down the doors to invest in Mečiar's Slovakia. During Mečiar's third government, the HZDS joined the extreme right-wing party the SNS in openly seeking to block foreign investment in favor of building what was called a "domestic entrepreneur class."[123]

The Slovak underworld blossomed under Mečiar: a privatization triangle evolved between the HZDS, the security services, and the crime syndicates, made possible by the FNM's concealment of the identity of new enterprise owners. The SIS contracted politically-connected work out to criminal gangs, which in turn competed with one another to muscle in on the privatization handouts of the HZDS.[124] As gangland killings began taking place on Bratislava's streets and HZDS politicians were spotted in the company of underworld thugs, it is not known to what extent the HZDS was losing even its own control of the FNM.[125]

The blatant political abuse of privatization was perfectly evident to the opposition and the independent media, but calls for oversight of the FNM were to no avail.[126] The toll on the economy was substantial: the privatization of enterprises at only 28 percent of their book value in 1996 and 18 percent in 1997, usually into the hands of friends and relatives of the leaders of the ruling parties, robbed the state of desperately needed revenue.[127] Meanwhile, in the absence of foreign investment, uncompetitive enterprises were kept afloat through heavy borrowing, which led to a doubling of the country's external debts, from $5.4 billion in 1994 to $10.5 billion in 1998.[128]

Ethnic Nationalism and Political Rent Seeking

The contrast between how oppositionists and non-oppositionists handled ethnic questions was sometimes stark. The post-opposition governments in Poland and in the Czech lands in 1990 and 1991 celebrated the multiethnic nature of their states (easier to do with no large ethnic minorities) and worked to regulate relations with neighboring states that had been historical enemies. The non-opposition governments in Romania and Slovakia warned that the nation's sovereignty and territorial integrity were under threat from ethnic minorities and neighboring states. They encouraged individuals to blame their economic hardships on the rapaciousness of ethnic minorities, even though minorities tended to suffer from much higher levels of unemployment. They cycled through all of the available ethnic enemies: for example, Slovakia's HZDS started with the Czechs, continued with the Hungarians and the Roma (Gypsies)—and finished with opposition politicians, independent journalists and even Western academics. For some groups of elites, nationalist appeals aimed against ethnic minorities and foreign powers were an attractive way to compete for popular support.[129]

Ethnic geography—a matter of historically conditioned perceptions rather than "pure" demography—helped determine the salience of ethnic nationalism as a political strategy. As pictured in Table 2.2, Poland, Hungary, and the Czech Republic are relatively homogenous, while in Romania, Bulgaria, and Slovakia one ethnic minority comprises about 10 percent of the population. There are some 1.7 million ethnic Hungarians in Romania (7 percent of the total population), 800,000 ethnic Turks in Bulgaria (10 percent), and 600,000 ethnic Hungarians in Slovakia (11 percent).[130]

TABLE 2.2   Ethnic Geography of East Central Europe, 1991/1992

Country	Total population	Largest minorities as percentage of the population in 1991/1992	Minorities approximate numbers
Poland	38,419,603	Ukrainian 0.78	300,000
		Belarusian 0.52	200,000
		German 0.52	200,000
Hungary	10,375,323	Roma 3.9	404,461
		German 1.69	175,000
		Slovak 1.06	110,000
Czech Rep	10,298,731	Moravian 13.2	1,359,432
		Slovak 3	308,962
		Roma 0.49	50,000
Romania	22,760,449	Hungarian 7.12	1,620,199
		Roma 1.8	409,723
Bulgaria	8,472,724	Turkish 9.7	822,253
		Roma 3.4	287,732
Slovakia	5,268,935	Hungarian 10.76	566,741
		Roma 1.53	80,627
		Czech 1.01	53,422

Source: Bugajski (1994). For similar data, see European Commission country profiles at: http://europa.eu.int/comm/enlargement/enlargement.htm. Estimates of the probable number of Roma are 35,000 in Poland; 482,000 in Hungary; 200,000 in the Czech Republic; 700,000 in Bulgaria; 1.5 million in Romania; and 500,000 in Slovakia. See Zoltan Barany (2002: 160–61).

The success of Romanian, Bulgarian, and Slovak illiberal elites in exploiting feelings that ethnic minorities posed a threat to the national majority can be attributed to three main factors: minorities form a significant portion of the population; history lends credibility to assertions that the minority harbors a separatist agenda; and minorities have formed cohesive political organizations.[131] Moreover, the political activism of ethnic Hungarian minority groups combined with the forceful advocacy of the Hungarian government after 1989 provided "external validity" to the accusations of the Romanian and Slovak governments that Hungarian minorities posed a threat to the nation.[132] Finally, the susceptibility of the electorate to strategies of ethnic scapegoating also depended on the use of nationalism by the communist regime to shore up their legitimacy—practiced in its most extreme and coercive form by Bulgaria's Zhizhkov against ethnic Turks, and by Romania's Ceauşescu against ethnic Hungarians.[133]

In Romania, Iliescu's unreconstructed communists exploited ethnic nationalism to win national elections and establish domestic legitimacy as the defenders of the Romanian nation.[134] The ethnic Hungarians of Romania viewed democratization as an opportunity to rebuild their organizations, restore Hungarian-language schools, and work toward local self-administration. But the political cohesion of Hungarians in Transylvania was portrayed by the FSN (and later the DFSN and the PDSR) and by the extreme nationalist parties as threatening to the Romanian majority. In March 1990, the extremist group Vatra Românească (Romanian Cradle) incited anti-Hungarian riots in Târgu-Mureş; an unknown number of Hungarians and Romanians were killed in what has so far been the only instance of large-scale, organized ethnic violence within the six states considered in this book since 1989. The governing FSN did not condemn Vatra for the violence; instead, it blamed Hungarian extremists and their patrons in Budapest. Weeks later the FSN affirmed the "unitary" character of the "Romanian national state" and deplored Hungarian "chauvinism, irredentism and extremism." Prime Minister Petre Roman claimed to have discovered a Hungarian–Transylvanian government-in-exile.[135] In its first months in office, the FSN government passed up, quite spectacularly, the opportunity to repudiate its nationalist inheritance from the Ceauşescu regime.

The increasing influence of Romanian extremist parties and organizations, combined with the refusal of the government to meet minimal Hungarian demands in the spheres of education and local administration (often delivered with accusations of "treason" in parliament), led the Hungarian Democratic Alliance of Romania (UDMR) to radicalize its program. After years of consciously moderating its agenda, the UDMR decided at the Cluj Congress in late 1994 to work for territorial autonomy. In January 1995 the UDMR set up a council on local administration, grouping Hungarian mayors and ethnic councilors. This council was declared illegal by the government and denounced by virtually all of Romania's other political parties.[136] Nationalist politicians and extremist groups capitalized on the moves toward territorial autonomy to press their case that the Hungarians seek secession and that the Budapest government may intervene militarily on their behalf.

Between 1989 and 1996, the cycle of national animosity and political isolation of minorities proceeded the furthest in Romania. Whenever Iliescu appeared to be in danger of being overtaken by his reformist opponents, the nationalist card was played "in all of its crudity."[137] The climate created by Iliescu's unreconstructed post-communist party during its seven unbroken years of power moved many opposition parties to adopt nationalist rhetoric as a *sine qua non* of Romanian domestic politics. Meanwhile, the PDSR depended on the support of extreme nationalist parties, which ceaselessly pushed it to radicalize its discourse and its policies. All the while, the reaction of the Hungarian minority—its moves towards self-administration and calls for territorial autonomy—made it an easy target for nationalists and an impossible ally for moderates. By 1995, domestic political discourse in Romania was steeped in ethnic nationalism aimed against the ethnic Hungarian minority.

Illiberal elites used nationalism to win early elections in different measures. Bulgaria's BSP chiefly engaged the population's fear of economic reform; its use of ethnic scapegoating was muted compared to that of Romania's PDSR or Slovakia's HZDS, but nevertheless present. The BSP moved decisively in 1990 to reverse the brutal and violent forced assimilation campaign of ousted communist leader Zhizkov against Bulgaria's Turkish minority, and resisted the organized protests of nationalist groups opposed to reinstating the basic rights of the ethnic Turks. However, the BSP capitalized on the echoes of Zhizkov's anti-Turk nationalism, presenting itself as the defender of the majority ethnic Bulgarian population and the Bulgarian nation state.[138] The BSP used ethnic nationalism when campaigning for votes, and enjoyed the support of Bulgaria's small extreme-nationalist parties.[139] Some Bulgarian scholars and observers claim, however, that ethnic nationalism aimed against the ethnic Turks did not gain much "purchase" on Bulgarian society, which prides itself on a history and a culture of tolerance.[140]

In the first election campaign in 1990, the BSP exploited fear of the Turks by telling Bulgarians that a politically empowered MRF would seek cultural autonomy, which would inevitably lead to territorial autonomy, and then the return of Turkish domination. In the run-up to the October 1991 elections, the BSP continued to appeal to ethnic nationalism, and formed an electoral coalition with several small extreme-nationalist parties.[141] Socialist candidates claimed that the MRF did not allow democracy in regions where it had influence, and that the MRF and the UDF were in some kind of an unholy alliance directed against ethnic Bulgarians.[142] Bulgaria's 1991 constitution and electoral law passed by the BSP prohibited the creation of political parties based on religious or ethnic identity. The socialist-controlled Central Electoral Commission then banned the MRF from participating in the October 1991 elections, but this decision was reversed by the Constitutional Court. For its part, the MRF has generally curbed its radical elements and has never called for territorial autonomy, helping to keep the intensity of majority–minority antagonism at a much lower level than in Romania.[143]

The BSP's 1994 electoral campaign also promoted Bulgarian ethnic nationalism by linking economic problems to the Turks. As education minister, the 1994 BSP government appointed Ilcho Dimitrov, an extremist politician who had taken part in the assimilation campaign of the 1980s, and who vowed to restrict Turkish language education. By 1994, however, Antonina Zheyazkova argued that Bulgarians had at least come to accept the existence of a Turkish party as normal.[144]

In Slovakia, Mečiar created his political base by rallying Slovak nationalism behind the cause of an autonomous Slovakia. He found that the call to rally around the Slovak nation was especially effective if the nation was in danger, and hinted (at politically propitious times) that the Czechs, the Roma, and the Hungarians posed a threat. From the outset, the HZDS government elected in June 1992 refused Hungarian initiatives to strengthen minority rights, and rejected changes to the draft Slovak constitution designed to move Slovakia toward a civic definition of the state.

In response to the deepening intolerance of the second Mečiar government and, in particular, to plans for redistricting regional administration, Hungarian groups proposed in December 1993 the creation of a territorially autonomous district uniting Hungarian areas situated along the Slovak–Hungarian border. The principle of territorial autonomy was immediately condemned by all Slovak political parties, and subsequently abandoned by Hungarian representatives. By January 1994, Hungarian groups had reduced their demands to cultural and educational autonomy, expanded language rights, and a greater role in local administration.[145] The short-lived call for territorial autonomy exacerbated political tensions, as nationalists charged that the Hungarians threatened the integrity of the Slovak state. The third Mečiar government renewed earlier attacks on the educational autonomy, language rights, and parliamentary representation of the Hungarian minority. The language law of November 1995 restricted the use of minority languages by decreeing, for example, that all official communication involving any aspect of state or local government must be in Slovak. We will turn to a closer study of the relationship between the Slovak and Romanian governments, the ethnic Hungarian minority groups, and the Hungarian government in Chapter 6.

2.2.3   The Quality of the Left Alternative and Time Horizons

Returning to the broader comparison of liberal and illiberal pattern countries, we can reflect again on the importance of a reforming communist party for the success of post-communist reform. In every single country of post-communist Europe, the transition to a market economy created a strong demand for the left. Voters suffering from the economic hardships of market reform—voters angry about the present or scared about the future—sought to vote for a classic left-wing party that would promise them help from the state. The transition thus raised fundamental questions of balance between economic liberalization and managing the social costs of liberalization to maintain social cohesion. The election of moderate left-wing parties in Poland, Hungary and eventually the Czech Republic has helped maintain social cohesion which has, in turn, had benefits that feed back into the capitalist economy including fewer strikes, greater investor confidence, and the diminishing fortunes of extreme left- or right-wing parties.

In Romania and Bulgaria voters had no moderate left-wing alternative to the unreconstructed communist party: this prolonged the grip on power of the communist parties that were not forced to exit in 1989. And the PDSR and the BSP naturally fought to keep their position as the only left-wing party available to voters disaffected with economic reform. The irony therefore is that on election day the PDSR and the BSP capitalized on the economic misery of the population that they helped create by way of economic corruption and partial reform. The Czech Republic also lacked a reformed communist party, and this has hurt its transition to a liberal democracy, but the Czechs *could* choose to elect another major leftist party, the social democrats, once they became weary of economic reform. Romanian and Bulgarian voters who sought protection from the market did not have an alternative to the PDSR and the BSP, except perhaps tiny extremist parties on the far left.

Why did the PDSR and BSP not reform themselves into moderate social democratic parties? Besides the immediate incentives to suppress political competition, corrupt economic reform, and exploit ethnic nationalism that we have discussed above, there are at least three, more structural, factors at play. First, the PDSR and the BSP were not forced to exit government in 1989 and thus to break their pre-existing patronage networks. This empowered those in the party that resisted reform. Even the Hungarian communist party which was quite reformed before it left power in May 1990 still had a great deal of "divesting" of these networks to do in the early 1990s.[146]

Second, under communism the Bulgarian and especially the Romanian communist parties allowed little internal debate and underwent little or no internal reform: communist officials consequently lacked the creativity, the vision, and the knowledge about Western social democracy to transform their party in 1989.[147] This was a two-way street in Poland and Hungary before 1989: more reform-minded communist parties created "space" for oppositions to exist, and oppositions challenged communist cadres to policy innovation and, perhaps, ideological introspection. In Bulgaria and Romania, the old communist leaders had resisted calls for perestroika-style reforms from Moscow; after communism collapsed, the new communist leaders looked to these limited reforms as a model instead of looking to the West.

Finally, these parties had no experience with economic reform. Whereas Hungary had pursued economic reforms since 1968, and Polish communists had behind them the experience of reforms in the 1970s and the accord with Solidarity in 1980, very little colored the gray pattern of communist life in Romania and Bulgaria—and in Czechoslovakia after 1968. These communist parties were unresponsive even to Soviet leader Mikhail Gorbachev's urgings for economic reform in the waning days of communism in 1989. In Hungary and also Poland, a significant portion of the elites that worked as technocrats for the communist state subsequently worked for the democratic state. Their experience in government and their technical skills turned out to be an asset. Romanian, Bulgarian, and Czechoslovak elites that had worked for the communist state were, on balance, more ideological and a greater burden by way of their persistence in the bureaucratic structures of the democratic state.

In contrast to Romania and Bulgaria, voters in Slovakia did have a moderate left-wing alternative because after 1989 the core of the Slovak communist party moved toward genuine social democracy.[148] But by the time this new party had consolidated itself, Vladimír Mečiar had succeeded in drawing elements of the left and the right into his populist and nationalist Movement for a Democratic Slovakia (HZDS). Much like the PDSR and the BSP, he promised to protect the average voter from economic reform while robbing the Slovak state of millions of dollars through insider privatization. However, the existence of a reformed communist party in Slovakia would pay dividends in the future by giving voters a moderate left alternative to the HZDS in the 1998 elections.

Illiberal political parties operate with different time horizons as compared to liberal parties. They behave as if losing power represents an extraordinary event and possibly the end of their role in national politics. This is important because it is those rulers who equate losing an election with the end of their political career who are most likely to use illiberal methods to prevent political turnover. These rulers are probably wrong to think that any political party is ever so discredited that it cannot reinvent itself and win in future elections. They are probably right, however, in our cases to think that if they ever do regain power, the opportunities for rent seeking will be much more limited.

The PDSR, the BSP, and especially the HZDS behaved as if their time horizons did not extend beyond losing office. They pushed through as much insider-friendly legislation and as many corrupt privatization projects as possible. In Bulgaria, as we will see in Chapter 6, the BSP stole so much from the public purse that its government was driven out by street riots—despite its comfortable majority in parliament. More impressive are the PDSR in Romania and the HZDS in Slovakia that managed to fine tune their extraction of resources to keep the economy from crashing. But in Slovakia, the ruling HZDS pushed through literally hundreds of privatization deals, trade agreements with Moscow, and loans in the eleventh hour of its term, leaving the country poorer, with unwanted ties to Russia, and with crippling debt.

Regular political turnover teaches political parties to work with longer time horizons that are more conducive to liberal democracy. As Valerie Bunce has argued, party turnover means "losers learn that they can win, and winners learn that they can lose."[149] Where it exists, political parties in power are usually looking past the possibility of losing the next elections to the probability of winning the ones after that.

2.3   Conclusion

In this chapter I have attempted to show how the quality of political competition at the moment of regime change helped determine the character of the new polity. The presence or absence of an opposition to communism was the key factor: in East European states where the opposition was strong, the communists were forced to quit power and dissidents-turned-politicians wrote rules and built institutions that helped install political pluralism and comprehensive economic reform. In states where the opposition was weak and divided, unreconstructed communists and other opportunists used the defense of the nation and the defense of the voter from economic reform to win and maintain power. These rent-seeking elites made their voters pay a heavy price by promoting intolerance in society and by stealing from the state. Concentrating political and economic power allowed these elites to slow down and partly to control the transition from communism.

I have also argued for two other factors that have aided the quality of political competition in the democratizing states: I have argued for the reform of the communist party and its swift return to government, providing voters a non-nationalist left-wing party that symbolizes greater protection from the hardships of the transition economy. The reform of the communist party moreover helps establish a moderate post-opposition and a moderate post-communist pole in politics that encourage lively competition against the backdrop of a parliamentary consensus on basic goals such as economic reform and joining Europe. I have also pointed out the salutary effect of economic crisis which, in conditions of weak political competition or outright democratic monopoly, has helped create a demand for new parties in government. As we will see in Chapter 6, this eventually happens even where unreconstructed communists or nationalists have managed to monopolize power and also monopolize the left. More broadly, this chapter points to the positive effects of the alternation of different political parties in power. Table 2.3 summarizes the turnover of political parties in our six states from 1989 to 2002.

TABLE 2.3   The alternation of political parties in power, 1989–2004

Poland

1989	Opposition movement Solidarity rules with communists.
1991	*Complete alternation*: post-opposition right Solidarity coalitions led by UW
1993	*Complete alternation*: post-communist left coalition SLD + PSL
1997	*Complete alternation*: broad coalition of right parties led by AWS
2001	*Complete alternation*: post-communist left coalition SLD + PSL

Hungary

1990	*Complete alternation*: post-opposition right defeats communists, forms coalition MDF + FKGP + KDNP
1994	*Complete alternation*: post-communist left and post-opposition center form coalition MSZP + SZDSZ
1998	*Complete alternation*: post-opposition right forms coalition FIDESZ + FKGP + MDF
2002	*Complete alternation*: post-communist left and post-opposition center form coalition MSZP + SZDSZ

Czech Republic

1990	*Complete alternation*: opposition movement Civic Forum defeats communists
1992	Partial alternation: post-opposition right forms coalition ODS + ODA + KDU-ČSL
1996	No alternation: post-opposition right forms same coalition ODS + ODA + KDU-ČSL
1997	(Government falls: brief centrist government)
1998	Partial alternation: "opposition agreement" soc dems ČSSD + ODS
2002	Partial alternation: soc dems ČSSD + center-right parties

Slovakia

1990	*Complete alternation*: Public Against Violence defeats communists
1992	Partial alternation: HZDS forms coalition with SNS
1994	(Government falls: brief centrist government of moderate parties)
1994	No alternation: HZDS forms coalition with SNS + ZRS
1998	*Complete alternation*: left and center-right parties in broad coalition SDK + SDL + SOP + Hungarian SMK (with cabinet posts)
2002	Partial alternation: center-right parties form coalition SDKU + KDH + ANO + Hungarian SMK (with cabinet posts)

Bulgaria

1990	No alternation: post-communist BSP wins first free elections
1991	(Government falls, caretaker government)
1991	*Complete alternation*: opposition forms coalition UDF + Turkish MRF (no cabinet posts)
1992	Partial alternation: UDF government falls after only one year; lengthy "technocratic" government supported by BSP + Turkish MRF

1994	Partial alternation: BSP wins majority, rules alone
1996	(Government falls due to economic crisis; caretaker UDF government)
1997	*Complete alternation*: coalition of center-right UDF + small center parties
2001	*Complete alternation*: coalition of center-right NMSS + Turkish MRF (with cabinet posts)

Romania

1990	No alternation: post-communist FSN landslide in first free elections
1992	No alternation: post-communist FSN/PDSR minority govt.; later PDSR forms coalition with extremist parties PRNU + PRM + PSM
1996	*Complete alternation*: opposition CDR forms broad coalition including Hungarian UDMR (with cabinet posts)
2000	*Complete alternation*: post-communist PDSR wins majority, rules alone
2004	Elections in November.

In January 1995, it was clear that in many ways Poland, Hungary, and the Czech Republic were "ahead" of Romania, Bulgaria, and Slovakia in creating political pluralism, and prosperous capitalism. But in my details of domestic politics in Bulgaria and Slovakia, I have signaled the presence of opposition parties and civic groups that were becoming more and more organized, cohesive, and moderate over time. While they were still immature and weak in 1995, where we leave this narrative, they were giving the ruling parties, the HZDS and the BSP, a run for their money. They were challenging them in the Constitutional Court, they controlled the presidency; and more and more they were incorporating international actors and international goals, especially EU membership, into their political strategies. We will rejoin the efforts and the development of these opposition groups in Chapter 6.

Now, having identified the initial domestic ingredients that determined the trajectories of East European states after communism, we turn to a new question: when and how did the EU and other international actors start having an impact on the course of political change in our six states?

The Passive Leverage of the European Union

We have identified the following problem: while some democratizing states of post-communist Europe developed a competitive political system after 1989 and laid the foundations of liberal democracy, other states moved toward illiberal democracy. These states failed to implement comprehensive political and economic reforms because a non-competitive political system allowed rent-seeking elites to win and maintain power. We now turn to how the prospect of European Union (EU) membership was treated by the governing elites of Poland, Hungary, the Czech Republic, Slovakia, Bulgaria, and Romania during the first five years of transition.

It is striking how rapidly and universally membership in the EU (then the European Community) became the destination of the revolutions of 1989. By the end of 1990 the five governments had all embraced joining the EU as their most important foreign policy goal. Despite fears of diminished national sovereignty and increased economic vulnerability, EU membership emerged as a matter of national interest because it offered tremendous geopolitical, sociocultural, and economic benefits. In turn, the magnitude of these benefits created a profoundly asymmetrical power relationship between aspiring candidates and the EU because they depended so much on the EU whereas the EU depended on them but little. This "asymmetric interdependence" would shape all of their dealings with the EU—until they became full members and perhaps even thereafter.

I use the concepts of "passive" and "active" leverage to separate theoretically the kinds of influence that the EU can have on credible future members. By passive leverage I mean the attraction of EU membership, and by active leverage I mean the deliberate conditionality exercised in the EU's pre-accession process. For the first five years after 1989, the EU exercised only passive leverage over its six credible future member states in this study. The reaction of the liberal pattern and the illiberal pattern states to this passive leverage, however, diverged substantially. Joining the EU became the common foreign policy goal of all six states, but meeting the domestic requirements of EU membership did not necessarily emerge as a matter of immediate government industry. In other words, the foreign policy goal was not necessary followed up with the requisite domestic policies. Only the liberal pattern governments of Poland, Hungary, and Czechoslovakia satisfied or anticipated EU requirements in key areas of domestic policy-making; the illiberal pattern governments of Romania, Bulgaria, and, eventually, Slovakia did not. While all five (then six) governments declared EU membership as their foremost foreign policy goal, illiberal pattern governments distinguished themselves from liberal pattern ones by jeopardizing their state's progress toward EU membership.

Why were the benefits of EU membership treated differently in different East European capitals?[1] The explanation returns us to domestic politics: the cost to governing elites of fulfilling the EU's domestic requirements varied after 1989 according to their dependence on ethnic nationalism and economic corruption to win and keep political power. For illiberal governments, the costs of adapting domestic policies to EU requirements were too high. Their political power depended on domestic strategies that were incompatible with the EU's requirements of liberal democracy and comprehensive economic reform. Complying with the implicit and later explicit norms of EU member-ship would require these ruling elites to implement policies that would weaken their domestic power base.

Applying for EU membership would put the domestic politics of all of the candidates under close scrutiny by EU officials and institutions once the EU began exercising its active leverage. Joining the EU is in this sense an unusual foreign policy goal because it can only be attained by profound changes of domestic policy. But for a few years, while there was only passive leverage, illiberal pattern governments could have it both ways. They could solicit EU membership as a matter of foreign policy, but practice economic and political rent seeking as the daily bread of domestic politics. Governments in Romania, Bulgaria, and Slovakia exploited low levels of political competition at home and of scrutiny from abroad to conduct a sort of foreign policy "arbitrage." They pretended to be seeking EU membership under the cover of their near monopoly on the transmission of information between their polities and the West. And they exploited the embryonic nature of the EU's conditionality policies to win a level of inclusion and approbation from the West that made these claims more credible.

This is the first of two chapters that explores the relationship between East European states and the EU during the period of passive leverage. In Chapter 4, I show how (differently) passive leverage played itself out in the EU's rela-tionship with liberal and illiberal pattern states from 1989 to 1994. In this chapter, I first examine theoretically the EU's passive leverage, explaining the benefits of membership and the costs of exclusion that make membership so attractive. Second, I look at alternative explanations for why East European states reacted differently to the incentives of EU membership.

3.1 Theorizing Passive Leverage

By the force of the attraction of its markets and institutions, the EU exercised "passive leverage" on the democratizing states of Eastern Europe after 1989. Passive leverage is the traction that the EU has on the domestic politics of credible candidate states merely by virtue of its existence and its usual conduct. This includes the political and economic benefits of membership, the costs of exclusion, and the way the EU treats nonmember states, as summarized in Table 3.1. But it does not include any deliberate policies to influence the states in question or to pave the way for their eventual membership—this is active leverage.

For the EU to have leverage or "traction" on domestic politics, a state must be a credible future member of the EU. The EU's 1957 founding Treaty of Rome stipulates only that the EU is open to all European countries. After 1989, Poland, Hungary, and Czechoslovakia were widely perceived as the most likely candidates for EU membership (if the EU did enlarge) because of politics and geography: they were considered the frontrunners in the transition to liberal democracy, and they were situated along the border of the EU. Bulgaria and Romania joined them as the only other two states that renounced communism in 1989 in conditions of uncontested state sovereignty. Since 1995, the list of states that are considered credible future EU members has increased dramatically. We return to the question of which states are credible future EU members and why in Chapter 8. For our six cases here, however, their geographic eligibility to take part in the EU's pre-accession process (once it existed) was never in doubt.

TABLE 3.1   Passive leverage

Political benefits
Protection of EU rules
Voice in EU decision-making

Economic benefits
Access to EU market
Transfers from EU budget
Increased investment + growth
Increased entrepreneurship + skills

Benefits are shaped by:
Costs of exclusion when neighboring states are joining
EU treatment of nonmembers

Additional benefit:
EU membership conditionality as a catalyst for domestic reform

Why do states seek to join the EU? Let us turn now to a theoretical discussion of the benefits of EU membership for states in general. This discussion applies not just to the six states in this study, but to all official candidates and proto-candidates for EU membership (especially the post-communist ones). At its height before ten new states joined the EU in May 2004, this totaled some eighteen states: Poland, Hungary, the Czech Republic, Slovakia, Romania, Bulgaria, Slovenia, Estonia, Lithuania, Latvia, Malta, Cyprus, and Turkey were official candidates; and Croatia, Serbia-Montenegro, Macedonia, Albania, and Bosnia-Hercegovina were, officially, potential candidates.

3.1.1 The Protection of Rules and the Benefits of Voice

If we look at the relationship between the EU and states outside of it through the lens of international relations theory, we can add to the strictly economic benefits of membership discussed below two other benefits: the protection of EU rules, and a voice in EU policy-making.[2] For international relations scholars, the political reasons for *joining* the EU—centered on the reduction of uncertainty in order to increase prosperity through cooperation—are much the same as the reasons for *creating* institutions.[3] Most important, joining the EU would regulate relations with powerful neighbors by way of a desirable set of clear and well-established rules. Stanley Hoffmann and Robert Keohane describe a new institutional form that enables "rich and strong states to act more effectively on a collective basis, and [permits] poor and weak countries to gain acceptance into a club of prosperous states, governed by rules that apply to all members."[4]

The debate within international relations about whether and how multilateral institutions influence state strategies unites institutionalists and realists on the importance of rules for weak states. The rules of institutions, in Robert Keohane's words, "may create a presumption in favor of the norm that principles of conduct must be generalized to all members of the institution, imparting greater consistency of behavior and favoring weaker states."[5] Similarly, Joseph Grieco finds that weaker states may favor institutionalized relations with their stronger partners if the rules "provide sufficient opportunities for them to voice their concerns and interests and thereby prevent or at least ameliorate their domination by stronger partners."[6] The protection of EU rules through membership satisfies both approaches—and the chief motivation for seeking the protection of EU rules was early vulnerability to EU protectionism.

For all of its geopolitical rhetoric, the EU was still primarily a successful project of economic integration in the early 1990s, and its greatest source of power remained its enormous market.[7] At this time, as we see in Figure 3.1, all of the non-EU economies in Europe taken together were inconsequential

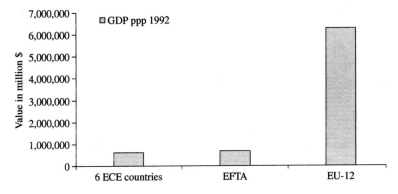

FIGURE 3.1   EU, EFTA and ECE GDP compared, 1992.

Gross Domestic Product (GDP) purchasing power parity (ppp).

Notes: The six ECE countries are Bulgaria, Czech Republic, Hungary, Poland, Romania and Slovakia. The EFTA countries are Austria, Finland, Iceland, Liechtenstein, Norway, Sweden, and Switzerland.

Source: Calculations based on World Bank (2002*b*).

compared to that of the EU and highly dependent on its markets. The EU's trade partners—rich West European and poor East European states alike—had to abide by rules governing access to its markets, but had no hand in writing these rules, nor could they control how the rules might be changed. This created a substantial power discrepancy, which most plausible EU members chose to end by way of membership: witness the accession of all but two of the wealthy European Free Trade Area (EFTA) states, whose advanced economies allowed for substantially greater autonomy than those of East European states.[8]

The Europe Agreements on association with the EU signed in 1991 did not satisfy East European states for the same reasons that the European Economic Area did not stave off the membership applications of the EFTA states, culminating in the accession of Sweden, Finland and Austria to the EU in 1995. The EFTA states like East European states found themselves obliged to adopt a great proportion of the *acquis communautaire* without any participation in the decision-making process of the Commmunity. Unilateral adjustment to the EU's trade rules did minimize the costs of being on the outside of the EU economy.[9] But much of the sovereignty that would formally be lost through accession was thus already gone in practice—without the benefits of full membership.[10] The costs of exclusion from aspects of "the EU economy" motivated concessions not just from the rich EFTA states on the terms of their admission, but also from isolated members on the project of European Monetary Union (EMU).[11]

How much a particular state values the protection of EU rules that membership would afford it depends on how the EU chooses to treat it as a nonmember. This explains why protection by EU rules mattered so much to Poland, Hungary, and Czechoslovakia in the early 1990s. As we will examine closely in Chapter 4, exports from Eastern Europe threatened EU producers in the "sensitive sectors," triggering an array of protectionist safeguard clauses that the EU insisted on including in the Europe Agreements. Meanwhile, export-led growth turned out to be of paramount importance to the transition from planned to market economies taking place in Eastern Europe. In this way Poland, Hungary, and Czechoslovakia were more "provoked" to apply to the EU than the EFTA states, which enjoyed virtually unrestricted access to EU markets for all but agricultural goods. And it is possible that latecomers to the accession process such as Serbia or Albania will be more complacent about full membership, because the EU has recently backed up its geopolitical goal of stabilizing the Balkans with economic instruments such as market access that were previously blocked by domestic economic interests in various members.

As we will see in the next chapter, East European elites became aware in 1990 and 1991 of the nature of the EU as an economic actor and the weakness of their own bargaining position in a relationship of asymmetric interdependence.[12] Institutionalists have shown that "power in an interdependent relationship flows from asymmetry: the one who gains more from the relationship is the more dependent."[13] By playing by the EU's rules, attempting a wholesale reorientation of their trade to EU markets, embarking on the EU's pre-accession process and seeking EU membership, East Central European (ECE) elites adopted what amounted to a strategy of maximizing their dependence on the EU: Figure 4.2 in the next chapter illustrates the tremendous rise in their dependence on trade with the EU from 1991 to 2002. For ECE states, the only way to eventually decrease their vulnerability to the EU was to become a part of it.[14] The behavior of the candidate states supports Andrew Hurrell's argument that "the more prepared the dominant power is to accept a rule-constrained hegemonic order, the more acceptable is a strategy of bandwagoning for the weak states."[15] In this case, it is the EU's institutional form that makes "incorporation" an acceptable strategy for candidates. The fact that the EU is an open and effective international organization as opposed to a powerful neighboring state matters profoundly.[16]

Joining the EU offers a much brighter economic and geopolitical prospect to East European states than their existence as the weak neighbors of powerful West European states. Lloyd Gruber in *Ruling the World* argues that states faced with the possibility of joining a powerful regional organization like the EU will do so to avoid the costs of exclusion. However, Gruber argues that this organization caters to the interests of the states that designed it—and *not* to the interests of the latecomers, who would prefer that the organization did not exist at all. Referring to the preparations that East European states have had to make to enter the EU, Gruber asks, "were governing parties in these formerly Communist countries happy about all this?"[17] As we will see in the next chapter, that rather depends on the domestic agenda of the governing parties in question. But overall the answer is a resounding "yes." The relationship between the EU and its aspiring eastern members is indeed all about power, but it is a more comfortable, diffuse power moderating the special interests of individual EU member states in the political sphere and, over time, the economic one as well.

Indeed, in some ways the existence of the EU would have been a boon for Eastern Europe's new democracies even if they never got to join it. The aggregate terms of trade have very likely been considerably better than any that East European states could have negotiated bilaterally with each of the EU's twelve, then fifteen, member states. Moreover, while the EU projected the aggregate special economic interests of its members in its external trade policy, the commitment to rules dampened the ability of EU governments to use foreign economic policies to bully small neighbors for nationalistic ends. Given the firm hand of the European Commission in foreign economic relations, extortion was difficult. Thus Greece was eventually forced to desist in its trade blockade against Macedonia, and Italy was similarly pressured into moderating its intimidation of Slovenia. Thus Germany in the 1990s was unable to use its economic weight including access to the critical German market to coerce special compensation for Germans expelled from Czechoslovakia and Poland after the Second World War. As Figure 3.2 shows, the Gross National Income (GNI) of the six states in this study was only about one third of the GNI of united Germany in 1992.

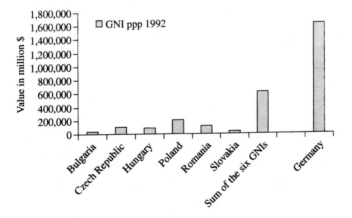

FIGURE 3.2   German and ECE GNI compared, 1992.

Gross National Income (GNI) purchasing power parity (ppp).

Source: Calculations based on World Bank (2002*b*).

Since East European states can in fact become members of the EU, the argument that the existence of the EU is beneficial to them is much clearer. We turn now to the economic benefits of EU membership for poor entrants, which are compounded for post-communist states by the benefits of using EU membership as a catalyst for reform.

3.1.2   The Economic Benefits of Membership and the Costs of Exclusion

For East Europeans emerging from forty years of communism, the original attraction of the EU was as a choice of civilization, as a democratic political community, as a guarantor of security—and as a promise of Western economic prosperity. Soon the overriding and enduring appeal became economic performance. For poor states whose GDP per capita is below the EU average—and this includes all of Europe's post-communist states—EU membership is considered "enormously beneficial."[18] The prosperity of Portugal, Spain, Ireland, and Greece bears witness to the overall economic benefits of EU accession for relatively poor countries. EU membership brought them economic modernization, access to new export markets, and improvements in the regulatory environment as well as transfer payments that were macroeconomically significant. It also brought substantial inflows of foreign direct investment.

More interesting perhaps is that qualifying for EU membership has influenced the unique transitions of East European states from planned to market economies. Chapter 7 will focus on how the process of joining the EU at the same time as consolidating democracy and building market economies has shaped domestic policy choices in the applicant states. Indeed, as we will see, the discipline imposed by the EU's accession process has had much to recommend it—not least because it has served as a commitment device reassuring foreign investors and domestic economic actors that elected officials will stay the course of reform.

Here my point is more straightforward, simply that being an EU member has many economic benefits for East European states. One study forecast long-term total gains to the new member states ranging from 23 to 50 billion Euro.[19] Entering the EU is expected to raise output and growth rates by stimulating entrepreneurship, foreign direct investment (FDI) and technology transfers. Studies indicate that because of raised investor confidence FDI inflows have already been concentrated in those post-communist states that were at the front of the queue to join the EU.[20] Locking the applicants into the EU legal and regulatory frameworks also promises to improve administrative capacity and, all together, facilitate fuller insertion into the EU and global economy—thereby bringing substantial opportunities for higher returns to the national budget over the long run. Transfers from the EU to the national budget are also considerable even though East European entrants receive lower subsidies from the Common Agricultural Policy (CAP) and from the Structural and Cohesion Funds than did the previous economic laggards to join the EU. We will analyze in Chapter 8 the argument that the EU's more limited financial transfers to the East European entrants make it unlikely that they will be able to emulate the economic success of Spain, Portugal, and Ireland following their entry into the EU.

The costs of exclusion are in any case even more striking than the benefits of membership. For those that fail to enter an enlarging EU along with their neighbors, the economic consequences are grave. A steady flow of aid, expertise, and foreign direct investment is diverted away from states that do not join the EU towards those that do.[21] The opportunities for trade also bear the costs of exclusion as exports to the EU run the ongoing risk of incurring various forms of contingent protection, while market access for agricultural goods remains restricted. This takes on unusual importance given the sheer size of the EU market and the striking poverty of the proximate alternatives, particularly of the post-Soviet market. All the while the EU market from which a nonmember is excluded will continue to expand—causing what Richard Baldwin has termed the "domino effect" of enlargement.[22]

The costs of exclusion weigh heavily on relatively rich states as well as poor ones. Walter Mattli in *The Logic of Regional Integration* has shown that economic integration can cause three kinds of negative externalities for states left outside: trade diversion, investment diversion, and aid diversion.[23] When states consequently suffer a significant performance gap, measured in terms of forgone growth, they will seek membership. Studying West European states outside the EU from 1960 to 1992, Mattli shows that "out of twenty applications for membership by eleven countries, eighteen were submitted after one or—more typically—several years of growth rates mostly substantially below the average growth rates of EC countries."[24] Joining the EU has costs: a considerable loss of sovereignty and, for wealthy members, usually net contributions to the EU budget. But only states that have an independent source of economic wealth—and here the chief example is Norway with its discovery of vast oil reserves in the North Sea—can afford to shrug off the costs of exclusion; our East European states cannot.

Indeed, there are few persuasive economic arguments against EU membership for East European states (although we will see in Chapter 8 that some scholars suggest that the net economic benefits are in fact modest). A possible advantage of staying outside is the ability to protect national industries and small-scale farming from outside competition. But the imperative of exporting to the EU prompted most East European states to sign trade agreements which, as described below, already supplied domestic markets with Western industrial and agricultural goods in response to high consumer demand before EU membership was even on the table. These agreements could have been designed to give local producers more time to improve quality and marketing to compete with Western products. Still, pulling out of these agreements—or having never signed them—would cause economic disruption that would far outweigh the benefits of protectionism as it would further restrict access to the critical EU market while delaying structural reform and frustrating consumer demand for Western products.[25] More broadly, as James Caporaso suggests, the demands of the global economy may argue against successful protectionism by individual economies— and for joining the European Union as a way to mitigate the negative externalities of globalization through regional cooperation.[26] We will return to this in Chapter 7 when we ask how much of the domestic policy change we see in the applicant states can be attributed to the EU's active leverage— and how much to the less deliberate processes of Europeanization or globalization.

3.2   Explaining Variation in the Response to EU Membership Incentives: The Domestic Costs of Compliance with EU Requirements

All together, the considerable benefits of EU membership create one of the central puzzles of this book: why did ruling elites respond differently to the incentives of EU membership? After all, there were so many reasons for our six ECE states to turn away from Moscow and seek EU membership that through the lens of international relations theory this outcome seems highly overdetermined. The answer is that for some ruling elites the domestic costs of complying with EU rules were much higher than for others. The cost to governing elites of fulfilling the EU's domestic requirements varied after 1989 according to their use of restricted political competition, economic corruption, and ethnic nationalism to win and keep power. In liberal democracies, ruling elites depended little on these strategies to win power. In illiberal democracies, however, ruling elites used all three strategies (in different measures).

As we will see in the next chapter, the political and economic agendas of governments in the liberal states overlapped (more or less) with the implicit (and later explicit) requirements for joining the EU. Explaining this, Walter Mattli and Thomas Plümper argue that leaders in "more democratic countries had a strong incentive to implement politically costly and protracted 'institution-building' reforms that constituted a natural stepping stone towards EU application." However, leaders in "less" democratic countries, facing lower electoral accountability, were much less concerned with the general well-being of the population, and therefore felt less pressure to embark on such difficult reforms.[27]

Illuminating further the contrast between these groups, I argue that the domestic requirements of EU membership proscribed the very mechanisms by which governing elites in illiberal states consolidated political power and cultivated their domestic power base: limited political competition, partial economic reform and ethnic nationalism. Meeting EU requirements threatened to undermine the domestic power of ruling elites in Romania, Bulgaria, and Slovakia by strengthening opposition forces, limiting rent-seeking opportunities for economic cronies, and precluding ethnic scapegoating as an easy ploy for rallying support. Although citizens overwhelmingly wanted to join the democratic, prosperous West, few had any knowledge about how different state strategies might bear on this goal. In a non-competitive political system, the ruling parties were able to control information about the state's relationship with the EU much like they controlled information on what were allegedly the best strategies for political and economic reform. Meanwhile, political parties in opposition were too weak and divided to get their message through an electronic media that was only partially free.

It is not surprising that the illiberal pattern governments would forsake the generalized benefits of EU membership to protect their political and economic rents. But why did they not distance themselves from the EU altogether? It turned out that they could not abandon the project of building closer ties with the EU because this project was so popular with the electorate,[28] as shown in Table 3.2, and because it offered immediate economic rewards including greater market access and international development aid. So Bulgaria, Romania and Slovakia signed Europe Agreements and put in their applications for EU membership in step with Poland, Hungary, and the Czech Republic.

Since the future requirements of membership were not specified and surveillance of domestic politics was only sporadic, from 1989 to 1994 governing elites in Sofia, Bucharest and Bratislava could thus demand EU membership while pursuing rent-seeking domestic strategies with impunity. They were in a position to practice a sort of foreign policy arbitrage because they were the dominant intermediary between Western actors, domestic political actors, and the domestic media. They kept up a rhetoric of working in earnest to join the EU, because Western acceptance strengthened their domestic credentials as reformers, while Western loans and trade agreements provided much-needed economic resources. There is evidence that it is indeed counterproductive for international actors to provide these kinds of resources to governments disposed against reform as they help them "postpone, rather than pursue, adjustment."[29]

Ethnic nationalism was a tempting tool for winning elections in Slovakia, Bulgaria, and Romania (and elsewhere in post-communist Europe) because of

TABLE 3.2   Support for EU membership, 1992 and 1996

Country	Support for full EU membership (percentages of those surveyed)				
	1992		1996		
	For full membership	Against	For EU accession	Undecided	Against
Poland	80	7	70	12	7
Hungary	83	4	47	16	15
Czech Republic	84	7	43	23	11
Romania	88	2	80	8	2
Bulgaria	73	2	49	17	4
Slovakia	86	7	46	25	9

Notes: The question in 1992 asks: *"If [country] were to join the European Community as a full member in the future, would you feel strongly in favor, somewhat in favor, somewhat opposed or strongly opposed?"* The table combines the answers into two groups.

The question in 1996 asks: *"If there were to be a referendum tomorrow on the question of [country's] membership in the EU, would you personally vote for or against membership?"*

Sources: Eurobarometer (1993: 28, 47) and Eurobarometer (1997: 36).

the substantial information asymmetries that existed between political leaders and citizens. Many voters did not understand that ethnic nationalism at home delays or prevents substantial gains in wealth and security by the special means of EU membership. Governing elites in nationalist pattern states pushed the electorate towards shortsighted identity politics and an identification of the state with the ethnos, while also hailing a return to the prosperous and democratic West. Likewise, voters did not understand that partial reforms that kept state enterprises afloat and price regulations in place had the opposite effect of shielding them from the hardships of economic reform. Partial reforms exacerbated economic suffering and allowed small groups of elites to get rich, all the while putting the country behind for EU membership. Meanwhile, opposition parties were too weak to provide credible alternative strategies for dealing with the protection of the nation and the reform of the economy.

Ruling parties in Slovakia, Bulgaria, and Romania did articulate *foreign* policies that called for rapprochement to the EU and NATO. The interests of society and the state were sacrificed, however, in the economically corrupt and nationalist *domestic* strategies they adopted in order to hold power in the period of democratization. These eventually compromised the state's application for EU membership and curtailed relations with foreign economic actors.

The prospect of EU membership multiplied the international effects of domestic policy choices, making the opportunity costs of "illiberal" politics at home unusually high. Absent this prospect, a government propped up by ethnic nationalism would at most compel the suspension of some international aid and the withdrawal of some foreign investment—as long as it resisted foreign military adventures. In post-communist Europe, a government legitimized by clientelism and ethnic nationalism could make society pay the high price of delaying or forsaking EU membership.

3.2.1   Alternative Explanations

Why did the political elites in power in East Central European capitals respond differently to the prospect of obtaining the benefits of EU membership? Institutionalist theory has helped us understand under what conditions states seek the benefits of cooperating with other states through international institutions; but it cannot explain the variation we observe among ECE states. I argue above that the answer to the puzzle of why we see so much variation in the responses of governments to the incentives of EU membership is found in the costs that compliance imposes on the domestic power base of ruling elites. But can we instead explain this variation without considering the tenor of domestic political change in each country after 1989? Let us consider briefly four alternatives to domestic politics: a state's position in the international system, geography, economic prosperity, and prospects for membership.

The first competing explanation is coercion: realists treat regional integration as a way for hegemonic states to impose cooperation on weaker states.[30] Realists may therefore consider that the EU is asserting its economic and political might, taking advantage of the feeble position of post-communist states in order to impose rules and regulations and dominate domestic politics against the will of local elites too weak to protect their sovereignty. If this were the case, we would expect to see the weakest states succumbing to this coercion more readily than the strongest. Instead, some of the politically and economically stronger states made progress most quickly in satisfying accession requirements and unilaterally adopting 80,000 pages of EU norms and standards. In fact, the EU did not impose cooperation on the candidates; many EU member states were indifferent to enlargement in the early 1990s, as we will see in the next two chapters. Realists also treat regional integration as an alliance created to counter the rising power of a threatening state. But on this logic we would expect to see all East European states doing their utmost to join the EU and NATO in order to counter the threat of a resurgent Russia.[31]

The second competing explanation is geography: The success of reform aimed at entering the EU has been explained as a function of a post-communist country's geographical distance from the border of the EU. This can be discounted because of Slovakia's as well as Croatia's poor performance in the 1990s despite their proximity to the EU. Nevertheless, there is clearly a strong correlation between geography and liberal democracy. Jeffrey Kopstein and David Reilly develop a more subtle analysis where the strict geographic proximity of a post-communist state to the West is combined with openness to create a new measure called "accessibility." They find that "states that are near the West but have established barriers to interaction are less likely to be influenced by Western ideals and practices than a state that is near and receptive."[32] But this raises the very question that this book seeks to answer: what domestic factors determine the level of "openness" to outside influences?

The third competing explanation is economic prosperity: many observers of the EU accession process consider that the relative progress of post-communist candidates toward EU membership is a function of their economic starting point at the moment of democratization in 1989. Since all six states confront similar strategic environments and economic incentives, systemic theories of international relations, be they realist or institutionalist, might also predict that all six states endeavor with equal commitment—but varying ability—to join the EU. On this logic, variation in how states respond to the incentives of EU membership can be explained by relative levels of per capita income, because these determine a state's ability to meet the EU's accession requirements. The evidence, however, does not bear this out: per capita income in 1989 does not correlate with progress toward EU membership in the subsequent five years. The most prosperous states did not make the greatest progress toward meeting EU requirements.[33] Moreover, economic ability did not bear on the strictly political requirements for EU membership that were the cornerstone of EU conditionality in the mid-1990s. Meeting at least these political requirements could have brought substantial economic rewards that the less prosperous countries ought to have been most keen to earn.

It is however more compelling to define modernization broadly, and to argue that the progress of industrialization and urbanization in the nineteenth and early twentieth centuries determines a country's likelihood of democratic and capitalist success after the collapse of communism. A composite rating would include such measures as the skill level of the population, the development of infrastructure, and the capability of the public administration, but need not be reflected in per capita income in 1989. This would help account for Poland's success despite its impoverished economy in 1989. More interesting, it could help build a theory of why strong oppositions to communism developed in some states but not in others. Rich Czechoslovakia as well as rich Yugoslavia would still be the outliers: while they spawned liberal democracies (the Czech Republic and Slovenia), they also spawned illiberal ones

(Slovakia and Croatia) where little or no opposition to communism existed before 1989. In both cases, as discussed below, politics trumped economics as a political vacuum allowed questions of nation—the struggle for sovereignty and the presence of a large ethnic minority—to shape domestic political change.

More recently, GDP per capita or even modernization broadly defined cannot explain why some candidates move more quickly through the pre-accession process than others. Bulgaria, for example, has implemented political and economic reform more successfully than Romania since 1998. As we will see in Chapter 7, the explanation again returns us to domestic politics and the choices that are made by the political parties that hold power.

The fourth competing explanation is the prospect of membership: for the EU's own internal reasons, different East European states may enjoy different membership prospects, and consequently different levels of attention and aid from Western actors. Following the logic of this explanation, governments in Poland and Hungary paid attention to the requirements of EU membership because they were convinced that their membership prospects were good by the steady attention and encouragement of a wide range of Western actors. This was a virtuous circle, but to the south it was the opposite, a vicious one. Governments in Romania and Bulgaria could be less sure for several reasons that they enjoyed the same likelihood of joining the EU: they were poorer and geographically more distant, offering fewer opportunities for Western investors while threatening to send greater quantities of cheap labor and cheap goods westward that would compete with EU workers and producers. Romania and Bulgaria consequently benefited from less attention and less funding from Western institutions, government officials and private investors. Altogether this made it much less obvious to ruling parties that they should conduct domestic policy-making with reference to EU requirements, while also lowering their ability to do.

There is of course some truth to this argument. Romania and Bulgaria are geographically more distant from the EU, and therefore they were of less immediate geopolitical concern and economic interest to EU governments in 1989. They were also thought of as less "European" for historical reasons. While uprisings in Hungary in 1956, Czechoslovakia in 1968, and Poland in 1981 are stamped in the minds of West Europeans as attempts by these societies to join the liberal democratic West, no equivalent events took place in Romania or Bulgaria before 1989 attesting to the liberal democratic aspirations of Romanian and Bulgarian citizens. And as 1989 was drawing to a close, Romania and Bulgaria seemed also to end communism in the least "democratic" way.

For all of this, however, the evenhandedness and equality that Romania and Bulgaria enjoyed from EU governments after 1989 is stunning. We will ask ourselves in later chapters if the EU's obsession with treating Romania and Bulgaria just like Poland, Hungary, and Czechoslovakia (the Visegrad states) in the early 1990s was a mistake because it conferred domestic legitimacy on illiberal elites. However, here I can say with confidence that rulers and citizens of Romania and Bulgaria had many reasons to believe that they enjoyed the same membership prospects as the Visegrad states.[34] I will show in Chapter 4 that the EU refrained from differentiating among the five countries in the early 1990s. I will show in Chapter 5 that it was the meritocracy of the EU's pre-accession process that helped make the EU's active leverage so powerful in the late 1990s. And I will show in Chapter 6 that reform-oriented domestic elites could, and did, rehabilitate illiberal pattern states very quickly in the eyes of the EU even if they could not quickly overcome economic backwardness and weak state capacity.

3.3 Conclusion

In this chapter I have explained the EU's passive leverage as the attraction or magnetism of EU membership, absent any deliberate policies toward prospective members. The EU's passive leverage is based on the political benefits of membership (that also have important economic implications): a voice in EU affairs, and the protection of EU rules. The benefits of international institutions for states seeking to join them are much the same as the benefits theorized by institutionalist scholars for why states choose to create them—and they appear in both situations to be particularly beneficial for weak states. The EU's passive leverage is also based on the straightforward economic benefits of membership: inclusion in the internal market and receiving financial transfers from the EU budget. Finally, it is shaped by the overall cost of being excluded from the EU, which is largely determind by how the EU treats nonmembers.

EU membership was embraced as the foremost goal of foreign policy after 1989 by all five (then six) states in this study (and by many of their neighbors). Yet as we will see in Chapter 4 and then again in Chapter 6, the cost to ruling elites of fulfilling the EU's implicit and explicit domestic requirements varied after 1989 according to the nature of their domestic power base. For ruling elites in Poland, Hungary, and the Czech Republic, the costs were minimal because the thrust of the anticipated requirements overlapped with their political and economic agendas. For Romania's PDSR, Bulgaria's BSP and Slovakia's HZDS along with their extremist coalition partners, however, this cost was prohibitive because of their dependence on ethnic nationalism and economic corruption to win and keep political power. Yet, the conditions of passive leverage until 1994, during which time the EU used hardly any conditionality to structure its relations with its new democratic neighbors, allowed ruling elites in the illiberal democracies to sign agreements with the EU and demand EU membership while pursuing rent-seeking domestic strategies with near impunity.

Now we turn to the details of the relationship between the EU and both the liberal and the illiberal pattern states from 1989 to 1994. While all of the benefits of joining the EU described in this chapter may not be immediately evident to elites on the ground in Eastern Europe in 1989, we see in Chapter 4 how they come to have a greater and greater appreciation of the advantages of full membership through dealing with the EU from the outside.

The Impact of Passive Leverage: The EU and Eastern Europe, 1989–94

East European elites learned hard lessons about power and vested interests by dealing with the European Union (EU) in the early 1990s. To understand why the EU's passive (and later active) leverage became so powerful, I trace in the first part of this chapter how elites in liberal states came to treat EU membership as such an all-consuming goal of foreign and domestic policy. While deeply held convictions about joining the Western democratic community shaped the opposition groups whose leaders took power in 1989, we will see how their resolve hardened in response to the material incentives of membership—especially in response to the economic costs of trading with the EU from the outside. In the first part of this chapter I also sketch the milestones in the development of relations between the EU and Eastern Europe more generally, because EU policies tended to crystallize in response to the persistent demands of the three frontrunners, known as the Visegrad states. The liberal states put forward demands that the EU open markets and design a pre-accession process—as opposed to reacting to demands by the EU or other international actors to change their own policies.

From 1989 to 1994, the Polish, Hungarian and Czechoslovak (later Czech) governments took cues from Western policy and Western advice, but the liberal democratic project was their own. I argue therefore that during this period the EU merely *reinforced* the domestic strategies of reform in the liberal pattern states that we have explored in Chapter 2. By this I mean that the EU did not play a decisive role in motivating liberal reform—and absent the existence of the EU, we could expect all three states to follow broadly similar trajectories of political and economic reform in the early 1990s.

I turn to the impact of the EU's passive leverage on the course of domestic political change in the illiberal states in the second part of this chapter. Again, I show that in this period from 1989 to 1994, the EU's passive leverage did not have a decisive influence on domestic politics. In illiberal pattern states, the EU's passive leverage failed to avert or modify the rent-seeking behavior of governing elites. Pressure from the EU and other international actors was sporadic and had little success in changing their domestic policies in key policy areas. Still, the EU did set the stage for its more active leverage during this period by committing to an eventual enlargement and by beginning work on the requirements for (and therefore the grounds for exclusion from) an eastern enlargement.

4.1   The EU and the Liberal States

The interaction between Eastern Europe's frontrunners and the EU during 1990, 1991, 1992, and 1993 revealed to East European elites and publics the benefits of EU membership—and these benefits were amplified by the difficulties of dealing with the EU from the outside. The EU stood to gain from its political and economic relationship with Eastern Europe. But Eastern Europe stood to gain much, much more. This gave the EU significant bargaining power when dealing with East European states, especially those serious about economic reform—and it showed no compunction in using it. As Andrew Moravcsik has argued, such patterns of "asymmetrical interdependence" have determined relations between the EU and candidate states in the past—and also among EU member states during major treaty negotiations.[1] The underlying logic is that more "interdependent" countries tend to benefit more from liberalizing markets, and are thus willing to make concessions to reach agreements. For political elites in emerging market economies in Eastern Europe, trade and integration with the EU was soon treated as a matter of economic survival, and their relative weakness vis-à-vis the EU became well understood.

The episode that defined the relationship between the EU and Poland, Hungary, and Czechoslovakia was the negotiation of the Europe Agreements (concluded about one year before the division of Czechoslovakia on January 1, 1993). Whatever its support for freedom and democracy, the EU acted decisively to protect producer interests in the EU as opposed to easing the economic hardships of transition in the East. By December of 1989, EU leaders were also worrying about the repercussions of an eastern enlargement for the momentum and the institutions of European integration, launching the ongoing "widening" versus "deepening" debate. Could a suddenly undivided Europe hinder, halt or even reverse (West) European integration?

The irony is that France, the state most interested in stalling EU enlargement to prevent "widening" from undermining "deepening," was also the state that hardened the resolve of East European governments to attain full EU membership by insisting on the highest levels of protection from East European imports. The effects of competition from East European producers, even in the "sensitive sectors," would by all accounts have been modest had the EU thrown wide open its markets after 1989. EU miserliness prompted Polish, Hungarian, and Czechoslovak leaders to work in concert and with determination to scuttle any alternatives to full EU (and NATO) membership, prefacing all moves toward regional cooperation with declarations that they were not establishing any kind of rival economic or defense organizations.[2]

In the end, the position within the EU against enlargement of the "deepeners" and of certain groups of producers did not prevail since enlargement would turn out to be a matter of net economic and geopolitical interest for the EU as a whole.[3] But producer groups have managed to capture EU policy-making in other cases to great effect; witness the endless delays in reforming the EU's Common Agricultural Policy (known as the CAP). It is therefore interesting to note here just how much the EU's early policies toward Eastern Europe were shaped by their concerns, and how later attempts by the EU to construct a more effective foreign policy, discussed in Chapter 8, have hinged on loosening their grip on the EU's external economic policies.

In this part I will look first at the goal of the 1989 revolutions to "return to Europe"; second at the negotiation and implementation of the 1991 Europe Agreements; and third at the earliest steps by the EU toward an eastern enlargement. I use the term "Visegrad states" to refer to Poland, Hungary, and Czechoslovakia: these three states embarked on a regional cooperation effort in 1990 known as the Visegrad triangle. Like policy-makers and journalists at the time, I find it useful shorthand for Eastern Europe's three self-appointed frontrunners in the early years of the transition. I use the name European Union or EU (except in direct quotes) even though before 1992 it was called the European Community or EC.

4.1.1 The Return to Europe

For states emerging from communism in 1989, the EU was closely associated with the democratic stability and prosperity of Western Europe. Opposition elites who had spent years battling communism and plotting an exit from the Soviet bloc hailed EU membership as the final marker of their country's escape from Moscow and its "return to Europe." The Civic Forum called for the inclusion of Czechoslovakia in the process of European integration in the first "samizdat" version of its foreign policy agenda, crafted in the Magic Lantern in the early days of the revolution in November 1989.[4] By then, Poland's first Solidarity-led government had already taken office in August 1989, and called for closer relations with the EU as had Hungary's still-communist government.

The slogan "return to Europe" captured the aspirations of East Central European publics and elites alike to "rejoin" the community of West European democracies from which East Central European states had been "kidnapped" by Joseph Stalin after the Second World War (though only Czechoslovakia had been a democracy during the interwar period). For many, Western or Central Europe (with Paris or London or Berlin as the hub) was the natural political and cultural home of the Czech, Polish, and Hungarian nations.[5] Moscow had forced them into the Soviet sphere at gunpoint.[6] What is fascinating is that by the end of 1989 membership in an international economic organization, the EU, had become the destination of this cultural and social–political journey "back" to Europe. To a great extent elites and publics now equated Europe with the EU. And for them, the appeal of EU membership was initially as much a question of beliefs about their identity and culture as it was a matter of geopolitical and economic interest.

The goal of the revolutions of 1989 was to reproduce West European freedom and prosperity—and the prospect of EU membership gave hope that building democracy and capitalism to catch up with Western Europe could be a success. After all, formerly authoritarian and backward states such as Spain and Portugal had made great strides in the wealthy European club.[7] The nature of the EU was also attractive to the dissidents who had suddenly become politicians. The EU symbolized, for them, the triumph of cooperation and integration over nationalism and war. Many dissidents considered the revolutions of 1989 as the beginning of a new order in Europe in which the EU and the Conference on Security and Cooperation in Europe (CSCE) could play a founding role—in contrast to the Atlantic Alliance, which they considered as much an anachronism of the Cold War as its Soviet-led counterpart the Warsaw Pact.[8]

For its part, the EU embraced in 1989 and 1990 its role as the instantiation of the ideal of European freedom and prosperity. Jacques Delors, President of the Commission, explained early in the autumn of 1989: "As many European leaders have already stressed, it is our Community, a Community based on the rule of law, a democratic entity and a buoyant economy, that has served as the model and the catalyst for these developments. The West is not drifting eastward, it is the East that is being drawn toward the West."[9] West European politicians delighted in welcoming triumphant Polish, Hungarian, and Czechoslovak dissidents turned politicians to their capitals. These visits were moving for both sides, symbolizing the hard won freedom of Eastern Europe's new democracies.

The year 1990 became the year of boundless discussions about the "new architecture of Europe." The EU, self-confident and dynamic due to the success of the Single Market project, took center stage in the debate. Indeed, the EU's member states as well as outsiders expected it to take the lead in the region as the cornerstone of the new European architecture. The member states took important steps in 1990 to create a unified EU policy by giving the Commission authority to construct political as well as economic relations with

East European states. The Commission soon assumed the role of coordinating aid to Eastern Europe on behalf of the G-24 as well as the EU. With the completion of the Single Market project in view, the Commission embraced building relations with the EU's eastern neighbors as the new project that would guard its own prominence in EU affairs while preserving the momentum of integration.

For their part, the new democratic politicians of Poland, Czechoslovakia, and Hungary embraced membership in the EU as a culmination of their democratic revolutions. The EU was perceived as a union of rich countries, easily capable and morally obligated to help their eastern neighbors through this difficult period. They believed that the EU would offer them membership soon, in order to lend political and economic support to their fledgling democracies. This support would be motivated by the West's moral and historical obligations to the countries it abandoned to the Soviet Union at Yalta. It would also be motivated by the EU's interest in democratic and economic stability along its eastern borders. The simultaneous transition to democracy and market capitalism risked endangering democracy as populations suffering from economic reform turned on their weak new democratic institutions.[10] Czechoslovak President Václav Havel warned, "Instability, poverty, hopelessness and chaos in the countries which have rid themselves of totalitarian rule could threaten [the West] just as much as it was threatened by the military arsenals of former totalitarian governments."[11]

As it happened, the risk of democratic failure and economic collapse in East Central Europe in the early 1990s was one that EU member governments seemed willing to take—as opposed to the risk of opening their markets to East European goods. The EU's common foreign policy was still far too weak to command market access as a tool for bolstering stability in the East. East Central Europe's post-opposition governments soon realized that the EU had no plans to admit them rapidly—indeed, it would not even commit to an eventual enlargement or open its markets. Questions of cultural affinity and deeply held beliefs about joining the Western democratic community, symbolized by the slogan "return to Europe," soon formed only a backdrop to the questions of trade and economic adjustment that dominated relations between East European states and the EU in the early 1990s.[12]

4.1.2 Negotiating the Europe Agreements

In 1990 the EU initiated negotiations on association agreements called "Europe Agreements," governing the economic and political relations between the EU and the East Central European states. At their core, these were trade agreements. If East Central Europeans were disabused of their hopes of quick membership, they continued to expect that their trade with the

West could be regulated in such a way as to support economic reforms. But the EU took negotiating positions that East Central Europeans regarded as unfair or even unjust. Proud of their achievements in the revolutions of 1989, confident of their own European credentials, and believing themselves entitled to better treatment at the hands of their richer Western neighbors, the East Central Europeans were brought face to face with their own weakness.

The agreements, signed in December 1991, were anticipated as preparing the way for full membership, offering a first set of rules regarding both political and trade relations with the EU. Hungarian Foreign Minister Géza Jeszenszky explained, "This document is expected to pave the way for us towards full membership in a few years' time, i.e. towards Hungary's full political and economic integration into Europe, assuming, of course, that Hungary takes all the required steps."[13] As Steven Weber aptly put it, Poland, Hungary, and Czechoslovakia "delivered dramatically on their side of the ledger." Each country moved rapidly to establish the basic institutions of a market economy with regulation, tax, and legal codes designed to make them "EU-compatible."[14] In the Europe Agreements they agreed to bring their laws pertaining to the EU's internal market in line with EU practice; this included laws on intellectual and commercial property, public procurement, banking, financial services, company accounts and taxes, indirect taxation, technical rules and standards, consumer protection, health and safety, transport, and the environment. This was dubbed "harmonization without representation," but it was generally understood by political and economic elites as positive.[15]

But the experience of negotiating access to the EU market was difficult and demoralizing. The Polish negotiator (and later Foreign Minister) Andrzej Olechowski recalled "a jungle of complex quotas and haggling over the precise details of dried mushrooms."[16] In September of 1991, a French veto of an infinitesimal increase in meat quotas prompted his delegation to walk out of the negotiations.[17] Access to the EU market, however, was essential to the success of the transition from state socialism to market capitalism. Poland, Hungary, and Czechoslovakia were reorienting their exports dramatically from east to west. Foreign trade was the most dynamic sector of their economies, and by 1991 nearly half of their exports were directed to EU markets. But the EU did not hasten to promote economic restructuring and growth by granting generous market access. Instead, EU negotiators of the "Europe Agreements" with East European states acted decisively to protect the interests of powerful producer groups within the member states.[18]

While the agreements provided for a steady liberalization of trade over a ten-year period, in the "sensitive sectors" where East European exports would be most competitive—steel, textiles and agriculture—the EU demanded long transition periods, extensive antidumping safeguards, and, for agriculture,

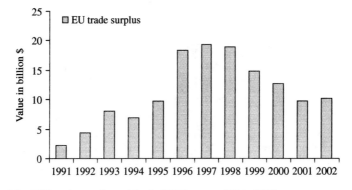

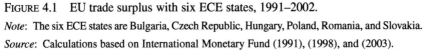

FIGURE 4.1   EU trade surplus with six ECE states, 1991–2002.

Note: The six ECE states are Bulgaria, Czech Republic, Hungary, Poland, Romania, and Slovakia.

Source: Calculations based on International Monetary Fund (1991), (1998), and (2003).

permanent restrictions. Meanwhile, in the sectors where West European goods would be most successful, the Europe Agreements locked in market access. In 1991, 1992, and 1993, as industrial production fell, the EU was able to constrain eastern exports to its markets and accumulate a large and growing trade surplus with its East Central European partners.[19] Many argued that this surplus, depicted in Figure 4.1, exceeded the export of technology and capital that was necessary to propel the economic transition—though many economists have pointed to the benefits of the inflow of Western technology and of the shock of sudden competition from Western producers in accelerating the transformation of the economy.[20]

The text of the Europe Agreements explicitly declared that they were more advantageous to the weaker party in what was recognized as the asymmetric relationship between the EU and Eastern Europe; the opposite turned out to be true. The association agreements contained three kinds of unfavorable economic provisions. First, higher tariffs were maintained on "sensitive goods" such as steel, textiles, and agricultural products: goods in which the East Central Europeans had a comparative advantage.[21] Second, a 60 percent local origin rule was included, and numerous other non-tariff barriers were allowed.[22] Third, the agreements contained seven safeguard provisions, allowing for the implementation of "contingent protection" on any good at any time. This sort of protection was doubly worrisome, for even the possibility of its use deterred domestic and foreign investment.[23] Although most observers paid more attention to the first kind of protection, the third proved to be more important. During the negotiation of the agreements, newer EU members endeavored to write in specific clauses protecting particular industries, while older members of the EU held back, well aware that they could rely upon safeguard measures to protect themselves.[24]

The result was frequent and unpredictable protectionism. A 1993 survey concluded that "protective devices" affected between 40 and 50 percent of all exports from eastern and central Europe.[25] A 1994 European Bank for Reconstruction and Development (EBRD) study found nineteen anti-dumping and twelve other restrictive measures in force, along with a number of other "voluntary export restraints" effectively imposed on East Central European states. The authors of this EBRD study called EU trade policy "the main threat to eastern European exports and investment."[26] A study of the Polish Ministry of Agriculture found that the terms of the agreement were "decidedly unfavorable" to the development of Polish agriculture; a Western analyst considered the agriculture provisions of the agreements "nothing short of criminal."[27] The editors of the *Financial Times* noted that while the EU accumulated a $13 billion trade surplus with all of Eastern Europe in 1992, its total imports from the same countries amounted to less than 60 percent of its imports from Switzerland. In their view, "The terror felt by EU member states—demonstrated by the fact that the Europe Agreements contain seven safeguard clauses—is pathological."[28] In 1992, Poland, Hungary and Czechoslovakia accounted for only 1.42 percent of the EU's total imports, and only 2.07 percent of the EU's imports in the "sensitive" sectors.[29]

It is indeed difficult to account for the protectionism of the association agreements by way of rationally considered economic interests. Economists concur that while the welfare benefits of free trade with the EU would have been substantial for East Central Europe, the effects on EU producers would have been modest, even making no allowances for the growing eastern market for West European products. Jim Rollo and Alisdair Smith conclude that "no rational economic explanation for the EU's sensitivity with respect to trade with Eastern Europe emerges."[30] Riccardo Faini and Richard Portes write that "it is virtually impossible to find significant negative effects" of "opening trade with [East Central Europe] at the national, regional, or sectoral levels."[31] A study commissioned by the European Commission found that medium-term gains far outweighed (very small) short-term reductions in output, and that the EU's poorer south would have benefited immediately from free trade with eastern Europe.[32] To many, the trade provisions of the association agreements demonstrated that the EU remained subservient to vested interests, and that its approach to trade with East Central Europe was "shaped more by direct commercial interests and policy priorities of its own than by any general considerations with regard to the international repercussions of the dissolution of the Soviet bloc."[33]

The consequences of the EU's protectionism are difficult to assess overall. There is no question that the Visegrad states were able to dramatically reorient

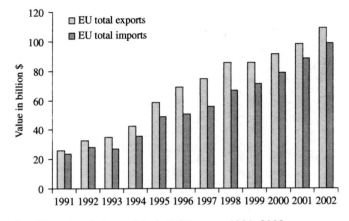

FIGURE 4.2   EU trade relations with six ECE states, 1991–2002.

Source: Calculations based on International Monetary Fund (1991), (1998), and (2003).

their trade to the West, as illustrated in Figure 4.2. Between 1988 and 1992, Czechoslovakia increased its share of the EU's total imports by 96 percent; Hungary by 40 percent; and Poland by 62 percent although, as we saw above, their overall share of EU imports was tiny.[34] After 1992, however, the dynamism of the Visegrad states' export growth slackened (see Figure 4.2) and many blamed the safeguard and other protectionist measures in the Europe Agreements. Meanwhile, as Table 4.1 shows, between 1991 and 1994 the image of the EU deteriorated in the Visegrad states—quite likely as a consequence of EU protectionism and stalling on enlargement.[35] (The question of the EU's image is distinct from the support of respondents for their country joining the EU in Table 3.2) Two trade disputes sketched below—one over meat and the other over fruit—help illustrate for us the atmosphere as well as the substance of EU relations with the liberal states in the early 1990s.

The meat and livestock ban of April 1993, our first example, sparked the first trade war between the EU and its eastern associate members.[36] EU officials had detected a case of foot-and-mouth disease in Italy, and traced the infection to Croatia. In response, the EU imposed total bans on the import of livestock, meat, and dairy products from eighteen Central and East European countries. Hungary, Poland, and the Czech Republic protested that their countries had been free of the disease for decades, and invited EU inspections. They also retaliated by banning the import or transit of EU livestock, meat, and dairy goods. Poland's Minister for Foreign Economic Cooperation Jan Krzysztof Bielecki turned the tables on the EU, officially justifying the ban by the appearance of foot-and-mouth disease in Italy. Still, the EU ban continued for some 100 days. Ironically, it was ended under the pressure of French

TABLE 4.1   The image of the EU, 1991–2003

Country	Image of the EU: positive and (neutral) percentages of those surveyed									
	1991	1992	1993	1994	1995	1996	1997	2001	2002	2003
Poland	**49**	**48**	**37**	**42**	**46**	**58**	**56**	**44**	**46**	**47**
	(32)	(31)	(32)	(23)	(19)	(24)	(27)	(32)	(31)	(27)
Hungary	**42**	**34**	**36**	**32**	**30**	**33**	**42**	**51**	**59**	**45**
	(28)	(34)	(32)	(28)	(28)	(32)	(30)	(31)	(26)	(35)
Czech Rep	**46**	**45**	**37**	**34**	**26**	**33**	**34**	**46**	**43**	**42**
	(29)	(36)	(40)	(40)	(36)	(42)	(38)	(24)	(26)	(29)
Romania	**52**	**55**	**45**	**51**	**50**	**65**	**56**	**70**	**72**	**75**
	(11)	(16)	(21)	(25)	(18)	(21)	(25)	(13)	(10)	(13)
Bulgaria	**46**	**51**	**42**	**37**	**27**	**42**	**50**	**70**	**64**	**72**
	(16)	(12)	(17)	(23)	(15)	(19)	(17)	(17)	(21)	(16)
Slovakia	**37**	**35**	**44**	**37**	**31**	**34**	**46**	**48**	**47**	**51**
	(34)	(43)	(39)	(37)	(35)	(44)	(38)	(33)	(33)	(32)

Note: The question gave respondents three choices: *positive, neutral*, and *negative*. The figures in bold are for positive and those for neutral are within brackets.

Sources: For 1991–95, Eurobarometer (1996: 44–51). For 1996–97 Eurobarometer (1998: 8–16). For 2001–03, Eurobarometer (2001), (2002a), and (2003).

farmers who were in need of supplies from Polish farmers. Hungary, Poland, and the Czech Republic estimated their losses in the tens of millions of dollars, and noted that the ban had made it impossible for them to meet several yearly quotas. All three Visegrad states agreed that the ban had been a transparent attempt to eliminate competition, but officials suggested that the greater loss was in their confidence in the EU.[37]

Fruit restrictions imposed by the EU in 1993, our second example, came on top of complaints from the East Central Europeans that EU export pricing was undercutting their own agricultural sectors, and that the EU was dumping surplus grain on markets in Russia and Ukraine.[38] In July and August 1993, the EU imposed minimum prices on several fruits imported from East Central Europe. The EU was paying its farmers the difference between production costs and market prices so that they could compete in the east, while forcing eastern farmers to price their products out of western markets. While all parties knew that such actions were envisioned by the safeguard clauses of the association agreements, the Visegrad states were additionally annoyed by the lack of any advance notice and took note once again of the inadvisability of trading with the EU from the outside.[39] The Visegrad leaders were by now quite determined to secure a promise of full membership, as well as a roadmap for the preparations and the timing of the pre-accession process.[40]

4.1.3 Commitment, Criteria, Timetable

Although governing elites in Prague, Budapest, and Warsaw desired more explicit and active guidance from Brussels, the EU needed to do little—except hold out the credible promise of membership—to encourage these states to make policy choices consistent with future membership. The EU provided not only a goal for foreign policy, but its prevailing rules and practices provided templates or at least clues for the domestic policies necessary to achieve it. The goal of joining the EU thus reinforced liberal reforms in these states chiefly by creating "a normative focal point" for domestic adjustment efforts. Well before joining the EU and even before any accession requirements were clearly spelled out, liberal pattern states engaged in "anticipatory adaptation" of the rules and norms associated with EU membership.[41] In Poland and Hungary, for example, by 1995 all new legislation had to be checked for conformity with EU legislation. These new rules and norms in turn shaped the development of political and economic interests in each state.[42]

The period before 1995 when the EU exercised only passive leverage was marked by Polish, Hungarian and Czech officials demanding more guidance from the EU (and better terms of trade)—and not by the EU making demands on them to change domestic policies. There was certainly much room for improvement in their domestic policies in many areas. But the considerable deficiencies that existed in liberal states went largely unnoticed or uncommented by the EU. One notable exception that I examine in Chapter 6 was the pressure exerted on Hungary to moderate its foreign policy toward neighboring states harboring ethnic Hungarian minorities.

Meanwhile, as we have seen, all of the liberal pattern states reoriented their trade as rapidly as possible from east to west. They became much more dependent on the West for trade and, as a result of their successful economic reform programs, they were able to attract much more foreign direct investment (FDI) than the illiberal pattern states.[43] Here, however, the Czech Republic stands as another notable exception because it tried to minimize foreign direct investment in the early years. The voucher privatization program launched by the government of Václav Klaus in 1992 was designed to keep enterprise shares in the hands of Czech citizens.[44] This was part and parcel of attempts by the Klaus government to limit political competition and concentrate economic power in the Czech Republic between 1992 and 1996, making the Czech Republic a "hybrid" case as discussed in Chapter 2 and again more fully in Chapter 7.

The countries that attracted significant FDI inflows between 1990 and 1997—Hungary, Poland, and eventually also the Czech Republic—were among the best performers in EU markets.[45] This is important because rapid economic reform weakened the interest groups tied to the communist and early transition status quo, and strengthened individuals and groups that benefited from trade with Western Europe.[46] This, in turn, reduced their willingness to upset relations with the EU and to scare off foreign investors by supporting nationalistic politicians. Economic links with Western Europe, meanwhile, amplified the preferences of domestic actors for marketizing reform, while also "pluralizing" communist-era distributions of income and power.[47] Building dense links to the EU economy and rewriting domestic laws to comply with EU standards helped empower domestic economic actors favorable to future integration into the EU, while weakening domestic actors that might oppose it.

Pressure for an Enlargement Policy

Visegrad leaders sought to change the terms of their relationship with the EU by pressing for a promise that membership was forthcoming, for the criteria by which their applications would be judged, and for a timetable of what they must do by when. The agenda of the three governments for the next ten years crystallized around these three goals: a commitment to enlargement, a list of membership requirements, and a timetable outlining the steps toward full membership. Polish, Hungarian, and Czech politicians returned over and over again to Western capitals to make eloquent pleas for the EU to open the doors to new member states from the east. Only in 1993 did the EU loosely commit itself to an eventual eastern enlargement—on a still unknown timetable, should the candidates meet (still unspecified) requirements.[48] Patience would be needed: The criteria would be spelled out in the 1997 Opinions and Accession Partnerships, and a timetable would follow in 2001.

Opposition to enlargement among EU member states generally stemmed from fear of competition with East European goods, fear of diminishing payments from the EU budget, or concern that the EU's federal project would be derailed and its institutions ensnared by admitting new members. "Widening" versus "deepening" dominated the debate about the future of the EU. French leaders especially Commission President Jacques Delors and French President François Mitterrand admonished that the end of the Cold War should in no way hinder or modify the projects underway among the (then) twelve members of the EU.[49] These "federalists" opposed enlargement, while so-called intergovernmentalists such as the United Kingdom and Denmark supported it—not least to thwart the federalists.

By 1990 the divergent approaches to enlargement of the EU's key member states were already on display.[50] The French opposed it, to protect "deepening," to protect France's pivotal role in the EU, and to protect French farmers, though they could not resist many pretty words about democracy and a united Europe. Belgium, the Netherlands, and Luxembourg tended to fall in behind France to protect the federal vision of the EU that privileged them as small member-states. The British supported enlargement, because it served their interests in diluting European integration, extending free trade and expanding the zone of liberal peace on the cheap. This left the Germans to cast, cautiously, the deciding vote in favor of enlargement for reasons of national security and economic opportunity. They were backed by other geographically proximate states—Denmark, Norway, Sweden, and (fitfully) Austria. However, the Spanish, the Portuguese, the Greeks, the Irish and sometimes the Italians opposed enlargement, in so far as it threatened to impoverish their producers and to dramatically reduce the payments they received from the EU budget. Over the next thirteen years the Germans backed by the British and the Scandinavians would have to railroad the French and pay off the poorer members, repeatedly, before a deal could be done.[51] And as time passed, even France was forced to admit that an eventual eastern enlargement was in the interest of the EU (and of France), thus French strategy shifted from preventing enlargement to slowing it down.[52]

The first attempt on the part of the French to head off enlargement came early: French President François Mitterrand proposed in January 1990 a European Confederation of concentric circles, eventually joining the entire continent in a political framework but keeping East European countries definitively out of the inner EU core.[53] He revived it from time to time as a useful method for cooperation as he predicted that it would be decades before the East European states could qualify to join the EU.[54] A second attempt came during the negotiation of the Europe Agreements in 1990 and 1991: the EU delegation refused to formally link the association agreements with the possibility of full membership; the three East Central European delegations had to struggle mightily to include a preamble stating that *they* understood the association agreements as preparation for full membership. When the finished accords were signed in December 1991, they were quickly ratified by national parliaments in the East—but not by those in the West, which were extremely slow.[55] This was of little practical importance because transition agreements with identical terms of trade went into force immediately, but such a public display of how politically inconsequential the agreements were for the EU member states was considered demeaning in Poland, Hungary, and Czechoslovakia.[56]

Many West European politicians viewed the determination and the fitness of Poland, the Czech Republic, and Hungary to join the EU in the near term as unfortunate.[57] Given the economic climate in Western Europe in the early 1990s, the revolutions of 1989 were ill-timed. The foundation of European integration, economic prosperity, had been eroded by high unemployment, low growth, and an overextended welfare state. Economic stagnation had in turn compelled West European governments to take a short-term and thus tight-fisted view of financial assistance and market access for the new democracies. Meanwhile, as the

Second World War faded into history, the political imperatives of postwar European unity seemed to fade as well.[58] European integration was feared to be adrift: the Maastricht Treaty and its aftermath only heightened confusion about the EU's purpose and form. In this nervous climate, it was argued that the "widening" of the EU to the east would preclude needed "deepening" of West European integration.

One message sent to the governments of Poland, Hungary, and Czechoslovakia in 1991 and 1992 was that they could not qualify for EU membership in the foreseeable future, so it would be most logical for them to cooperate and integrate with one another instead.[59] The Visegrad Triangle—Quadrangle after the split of Czechoslovakia—had indeed been launched by Polish, Hungarian, and Czechoslovak leaders in 1990–1 to foster cooperation and integration on the logic that these three states faced similar social, economic and geopolitical challenges.[60] But all three governments were put on their guard to prevent any appearance that Visegrad cooperation could be a substitute for EU membership. [61] In fact, a tangible success of the Visegrad effort in the early 1990s was cooperation in putting pressure on the EU to set the stage for enlargement. Visegrad showed that states may cooperate among themselves as part of their strategy to win membership in an attractive international institution.[62]

Visegrad was first and foremost a triumph of marketing: the term "the Visegrad group" became shorthand for the politically and economically most advanced, most "Western" post-communist states.[63] Visegrad cooperation helped convince the West that these countries were the stars of the transition to communism—that figuratively, as well as literally, they had the least distance to travel to return to Europe. The emergence of their new political leaders from the bosoms of spirited protest movements attested to the fact that they also had the most developed civil societies. Simply put, Visegrad cooperation helped convert revolutionary capital into diplomatic recognition and positive articles in the international press. By way of Visegrad, Poland, Hungary and Czechoslovakia also made the geographic, cultural, and political claim that they were the heart of Central Europe, and of Europe as a whole.[64]

Three years after the revolutions of 1989, Visegrad leaders had become practiced in scuttling any alternatives to their full membership in the EU. Besides the European confederation, Western politicians and observers had suggested that the East European states join EFTA, or take on an "affiliate," "partial," or "political" membership in the European Union.[65] For Visegrad leaders, all of these signified second-class status in the EU, making them second-class citizens in Europe; the political symbolism (added to the economic imperative) of full membership was too powerful for any of these schemes to succeed.[66]

On October 28, 1992, the four Visegrad prime ministers met in London for their first joint summit with EU leaders. They requested once again a timetable and criteria for membership. The EU promised instead an intensification of dialogue, but host British Prime Minister John Major indicated that a list of criteria would be presented at the December 1992 Edinburgh summit of the European Council.[67] The European Commission added to the expectations by proposing that the EU liberalize trade with its associate members at the Edinburgh summit.[68] In the event, the Edinburgh summit was an attempt to rescue the Maastricht treaty (signed in February 1992) after its referendum defeat in Denmark, and to resolve a host of organizational, financial, and security issues that had plagued the EU during 1992. Consumed by these problems, EU leaders agreed neither on the criteria for membership nor on the liberalization of trade with the East.[69]

The reaction of the Visegrad prime ministers was immediate and to the point. In January 1993, Hungarian Prime Minister Joszef Antall called full membership a question of economic life and death; Polish Prime Minister Hanna Suchocka said that Poland must secure entry into the EU by the year 2000; and Czech Prime Minister Václav Klaus fumed that his new Czech Republic was already prepared for full membership.[70] In an attempt to reduce some of this pressure before the Copenhagen summit of June 1993, the Danish government called a pre-summit conference for April 1993. There, East Central Europeans were urged to trade with one another and with their eastern neighbors. The Poles, Czechs, Slovaks, and Hungarians pointed to their freshly signed Central European Free Trade Agreement (CEFTA), and asked once again for criteria and a timetable.[71] In early June 1993, representatives of the four Visegrad states issued a joint appeal for the EU to "set the date and define conditions for full membership," adding that after the fall of communism and the hardships of reform, their publics "should at least be given hope."[72]

The Copenhagen and Essen Summits of the European Council

The Copenhagen summit of the European Council in June 1993 was a turning point, laying the foundations for the EU's pre-accession process.[73] The EU formally committed itself to admitting, eventually, its eastern associate members if they met the criteria for membership. It also provided a first set of very general but also far-reaching requirements known as the "Copenhagen criteria." These were welcome moves: during the previous two years the EU's refusal to pave the way for enlargement and the EU's protectionism had caused a great deal of bad feeling toward EU members among both elites and publics in the Visegrad states. Describing the breakthrough at Copenhagen Alan Mayhew observes, "it is an interesting comment on the European Union that while there was little discussion or dispute on the common objective of accession, the minor trade concessions proved very difficult to negotiate."[74] Indeed, as we will discuss in Chapter 5, by 1993 all EU members seemed in agreement that enlargement should eventually go forward because it was in the long-term geopolitical and economic interest of the EU, but there remained many disagreements regarding the timing of enlargement and the distribution of its expected short-term economic costs.

The Copenhagen criteria, for their part, stipulated that candidate states could become EU members as soon as they had achieved democratic stability, the rule of law, human rights, and respect for and protection of minorities. To satisfy the Copenhagen criteria, discussed in detail in Chapter 5, the candidates would also have to prove the existence of a functioning market economy, the capacity to cope with competitive pressures and market forces within the Union, and the ability to take on the obligations of membership including adherence to the aims of political, economic and monetary union.[75]

The Copenhagen criteria would eventually take on great importance as the focal point of the political and economic conditionality of the EU's pre-accession process. For the time being, however, the Copenhagen criteria were too general to have much of an impact on the liberal states. By any account, they were making progress toward them in the mid-1990s. The general expectations of the EU in many areas coincided with the political and economic agenda of the liberal pattern governments. When they did not, as in reform of the state administration or privatization, this remained largely hidden for want of a systematic, first-hand evaluation by any external actor. The Czech Republic in particular would later yield surprises as corrupt privatization and financial schemes were found to riddle the vaunted economy.

Hungary, Poland, and the Czech Republic announced in 1994 that they would submit formal applications for full membership. With their ratification by EU parliaments finally completed, the European Agreements went into force on February 1, 1994. The agreements set up cabinet-level Association Councils bringing together government officials and parliamentarians from both sides to oversee their implementation. Hungary took advantage of the first meeting of the Councils, on March 7, 1994, to announce its intention to apply for full membership. Hungary applied on April 1, 1994, and Poland followed seven days later.[76] Czech Prime Minister Václav Klaus maintained that his country was already prepared for full membership, but (to make the Czech Republic stand out) he stated that he would delay formal application until 1996. The Czechs took the opportunity to reiterate that the EU should liberalize trade with its eastern neighbors.[77] As pictured in Table 4.2, all ten East European associate members filed official applications for membership between 1994 and 1996.

The Essen summit of the European Council reaffirmed Germany's pivotal role in pushing the enlargement process forward as a reflection of its own

TABLE 4.2   Europe Agreements and applications for EU membership

	Date of Europe Agreement	Date of application for membership
Hungary	December 1991	March 1994
Poland	December 1991	April 1994
Czechoslovakia	December 1991	
Romania	February 1993	June 1995
Bulgaria	March 1993	December 1995
Slovakia	October 1993	June 1995
Czech Republic	October 1993	January 1996
Estonia	June 1995	November 1995
Latvia	June 1995	October 1995
Lithuania	June 1995	December 1995
Slovenia	June 1996	June 1996

Source: European Commission.

geopolitical and economic interests. On March 23, 1994, German Chancellor Helmuth Kohl reacted positively to the pending membership applications of Hungary and Poland, expressing his own view that it was "unthinkable" that the Oder-Neisse line would remain the eastern boundary of the Union.[78] Kohl pledged that the upcoming German presidency of the EU from July to December 1994 would be used to accelerate the expansion process. The German presidency was marked by an essentially German–French disagreement over the timing of expansion. In late July, the Commission had proposed a number of steps to prepare the East Central Europeans for membership, including a timetable for harmonizing legislation and a pledge to address imbalances in agricultural trade.[79] At a September summit of EU and associate member foreign ministers, Germany and France accepted the first proposal, and soon afterwards asked the Commission to draw up a White Paper detailing the steps that associate members should take to prepare themselves for the EU's internal market.[80] Beyond this point, German proposals began to meet French resistance. First, the French opposed German plans to regularize contacts between EU and associate member foreign ministers. Then the French began to resist German plans to invite the East Central Europeans to the final day of the Essen summit.[81] By the time of the summit (December 9–10), however, Kohl had orchestrated an impressive compromise, winning French support for moving forward on enlargement in exchange for a plan for a Mediterranean free-trade zone and for increased EU aid to France's southern neighbors.

The Essen summit reaffirmed the Union's intention to expand to the east, announced that the Union would first be reformed by the 1996 Intergovernmental

Conference, and suggested that accession might proceed at the turn of the century. A "pre-accession blueprint" was to be prepared for the six associate members (the Visegrad states plus Romania and Bulgaria) by spring 1995, and for Slovenia and the Baltic states after they signed association agreements.[82] This was important, because it opened up the accession process to any associate member and it also tasked the Commission to launch the pre-accession process by creating Agenda 2000 and writing the Opinions, described in the next chapter. Although the summit was seen as a victory for Germany and a significant breakthrough for enlargement, it did not offer the East Central Europeans a clear timetable for membership. The Poles and Hungarians set one for themselves, saying that they expected to join the EU in the year 2000; the Czechs predicted 1999.[83]

4.2   The EU and the Illiberal States

While Polish, Hungarian, and Czech leaders were making demands on the EU, Bulgaria and Romania, later joined by Slovakia, were keeping a relatively low profile. They did demand—and receive—equal treatment from Western Europe, more or less. It was never as affirming for a Western leader to host a barely redone communist or a disreputable nationalist as to host a hero of the struggle against communism such as Czechoslovak President Václav Havel or Polish President Lech Wałęsa. Romanian, Bulgarian and later Slovak leaders were invited less often to Western capitals. More important, EU leaders discussed whether these states were in fact liberal democracies eligible for closer relations with the EU. During the 1989–94 period, they considered using conditionality and even put in place instruments to do so, but they decided against differentiation among the five (later six) states. With some delays, the EU negotiated and signed (almost) the same Europe Agreements with all six—and all six also gained admittance to the Council of Europe and signed up for NATO's Partnership for Peace. No one challenged the illiberal pattern states when they proclaimed their intention of qualifying for EU membership.

I argued in Chapters 1 and 2 that the character of political change in East European states immediately after 1989 depended on domestic factors, primarily on the quality of political competition. I argue in Chapter 3 and in this chapter that during the first five years (1989–94) of democratic politics international factors played a marginal role in the composition and the policy choices of the first post-communist governments. In this period, the EU exercised only passive leverage: this failed to avert or stop rent-seeking behavior in illiberal pattern states, while (merely) reinforcing the trajectory toward democratic pluralism and market capitalism (such as it was) in liberal pattern states, as we saw above.

The EU's passive leverage, stemming from the benefits of EU membership, was so compelling that the leaders of *all* East European states declared that they were doing their utmost to qualify for membership. Societies throughout the region wanted to join the EU and expected, on the government's own account, that the state was making progress toward membership. We will see in Chapter 6 that once the EU developed its active leverage it had so much traction on the domestic politics of credible future EU members because the potential benefits of membership were so appealing. Rulers that disqualified their states from EU membership by conducting illiberal politics and partial economic reform could not turn their back on the EU. Their participation in the EU's pre-accession process opened the door to criticism of their domestic policies, strengthening the hand of their domestic opponents.

But while East European states were only subject to the EU's passive leverage, illiberal pattern governments could get away with having it both ways. Passive leverage induced all governments to sign up for future membership rhetorically, as a matter of declared state policy—but it did not inspire their compliance with EU rules in domestic policy-making. The strategies adopted by these first governments in response to international incentives—to the "passive leverage" of the EU—distinguished liberal and illiberal pattern states from one another well before the EU had even committed itself to enlargement. The litmus test of the sincerity of a government's EU strategy was whether or not it pressed for specific accession criteria: liberal pattern governments pleaded for a list, while illiberal pattern governments could already be heard complaining of unwarranted attention to internal affairs. In this section I will explore how the EU treated the illiberal pattern states from 1989 to 1994: the idea of using conditionality existed already in 1989, but it was practiced so weakly that it had little impact.

4.2.1 Inclusion versus Differentiation

Early in 1990 the EU was already confronted with political and economic policies in Romania that were quite drastically at odds with the declared project of building liberal democracy and a market economy. Political developments in Bulgaria caused more muted concern. How did the EU handle Romania at a time when it was just beginning to wrestle with its emerging role as the core of an undivided Europe? Given the divergent views about whether to pursue enlargement at all, it is not surprising that the EU lacked a coherent policy during this period toward states embarking on a trajectory that would distance them from qualifying for EU membership. The dominant approach, which was also the most expedient, was to avoid isolating new governments by adopting the same policies toward all five East European states that "revolted" against communism in 1989. It is worth remembering here that in 1990 the Soviet Union and

Yugoslavia had not yet dissolved, while East Germany was fast disappearing and Albania was completely marginalized, leaving only our five states seeking agreements with the EU. Were the years 1990 and 1991 a missed opportunity for EU leaders to avert "illiberal democratization" by differentiating among these five states in a more consequential way?

There were two sides to the debate about how to treat Romania and Bulgaria that could be roughly termed as "inclusion" versus "conditionality." And had the EU chosen to sanction Romania, a separate debate would have taken place about whether Bulgaria merited the same treatment (echoing the debates in 2004 discussed in Chapter 8). On one side, policy-makers argued that conditionality could generate isolation, economic hardship, and under- mine democracy as excluded governments and societies turned back to the protection of Moscow. They argued for inclusion as a way to change govern- ment policies over time through engagement and cooperation. On the other side, policy-makers argued that it was wrong to maintain the same relations with governments embarked on such different trajectories of reform, and that including Romania and Bulgaria in the EU's programs would undermine democracy by empowering undemocratic forces.[84] The outcome, as we see below, was that inclusion carried the day against differentiation.

The EU's first opportunity to use political conditionality was in the timing of the negotiation and conclusion of the Trade and Cooperation Agreements, precursors to the Europe Agreements. They were signed quickly in the spring of 1990 with Poland, Hungary, Czechoslovakia, and even Bulgaria, though the Bulgarian government was still composed entirely of communists. President Petur Mladenov tried to present Bulgaria as an example of reform communism that could satisfy Moscow, and of democracy that could engage the West. Bulgarian Socialist Party (BSP) leaders were far from making a credible case that they had become liberal democrats, but they did make a favorable impression by reversing the assimilation campaign against Bulgaria's Turks. The BSP was internally ambivalent about its orientation to the West despite its pro-EU rhetoric. Much of the party favored preserving a close relationship with Moscow and generally kept its distance from Western leaders and organizations.

The Trade and Cooperation Agreement with Romania was initialed on June 8, 1990, but its conclusion was postponed when later in June the Romanian gov- ernment trucked several thousand miners to Bucharest to attack the protestors. By this time, the European Commission was also overseeing PHARE aid and more generally aid on behalf of the G-24. It sent fact-finding teams to judge whether prospective PHARE recipients met five conditions: commitment to the rule of law, respect for human rights, the establishment of multiparty democracy, free elections, and economic liberalization. On July 4, 1990 the G-24 foreign ministers decided that Romania did not qualify for PHARE aid because of the violent government crackdown on pro-democracy protestors using armed miners in Bucharest. G-24 PHARE aid to Romania was delayed until January 30, 1991.

In July 1990 the representatives of EU governments debated the merits of suspending altogether the negotiation of a Trade and Cooperation Agreement with Romania. France, Italy, and other member states argued that marginalizing Romania could jeopardize the democratization process rather than encourage it; the United Kingdom, the Netherlands and others disagreed but did not prevail. France was accused already in 1990 of supporting the agreement with Romania despite the violent crackdown for two rather different reasons: to slow down or prevent enlargement by including such a miscreant in the process; and to exploit economic opportunities flowing from the long-time affection of Romanian elites for France.[85] Doina Cornea, one of the few Romanian dissidents who had openly denounced Ceauşescu, attacked Iliescu's confiscation of the revolution and called on the West to stop all aid to Romania until a real democracy was in place.[86] Little had improved in Bucharest when the European Council did sign the agreement with the Romanian government in October 1990. The European Parliament also delayed its consent, but not for long: it ratified Romania's Trade and Cooperation Agreement in February 1991.

Next came the question of whether the EU should sign a formal association agreement, a Europe Agreement, with Romania and Bulgaria. The fact that the EU dodged a commitment to a future eastern enlargement in the Europe Agreements played into the hands of illiberal ruling elites in Romania and Bulgaria: if the agreements had been more explicitly linked with future accession, EU member states might have taken a harder look at the qualifications of their new associate members. To qualify for a Europe Agreement states had to "give practical evidence of their commitment" to the five conditions listed above that had already been set out for PHARE aid. As Karen Smith writes, "Geopolitical concerns seem more important in this decision than a positive appraisal of Bulgaria's and Romania's fulfillment of the criteria for concluding Europe Agreements."[87]

The Council did delay the start of talks with Romania because of another round of violence against demonstrators in Bucharest in September 1991: undeterred by torrents of bad press in the West, Iliescu had called in the miners yet again. In April 1992, the Commission proposed that the Europe Agreements with Romania and Bulgaria contain a clause making them conditional on respect for human rights, democratic principles, the principles of the market economy, and also respect for the rights of minorities. The clause was an early attempt to give the EU a way to exercise political conditionality: it signaled that Bulgaria and Romania did not fully meet established criteria for a Europe Agreement, and that the agreement could be revoked if political and economic reforms did not proceed apace. The Council was concerned about offending

Romania and Bulgaria, but did decide to follow the Commission's recommendation and include the clause in the Europe Agreements that were signed with Romania on February 1, 1993, and with Bulgaria on March 8, 1993. Romania and Bulgaria protested because the first three Europe Agreements did not contain such a clause. After the division of Czechoslovakia, however, the Czech Republic and Slovakia signed new, separate Europe Agreements with the EU in October 1993 that also included this clause (see Table 4.1).[88]

What impact, if any, did these delays have on the Romanian government? There is evidence that the delays did moderate the use of physical violence on the part of the Romanian government. President Iliescu's aids allegedly advised him that the West would let slide many things but not government-sponsored violence making headlines in the Western media.[89] However, there is no evidence that the delays led to greater inclusion of opposition political parties and civic groups in the policy process, access for them to the media, or indeed less scapegoating of ethnic Hungarians or opposition "subversives." Moreover, there is little indication that the delays had any domestic repercussions for the Iliescu government, which was able to present the agreements as testaments of the West's approval of the Romanian government and gloss over the delays.[90] Table 4.1 shows a significant drop in positive views of the EU in Romania (and Bulgaria) from 1992 to 1993 which likely reflects negative publicity about the protectionist measures included in the Europe Agreements, making Iliescu's position even more comfortable.

4.2.2   Moving Toward Conditionality

From the earliest days, the European Commission presented the incentives of EU membership as a tool for promoting liberal democracy. Writing in 1992 to persuade EU member states to make a commitment to an eastern enlargement, the Commission observed: "By offering this perspective, the Community will provide encouragement to those pursuing reform and make the short term economic and social consequences of adjustment easier to bear. This perspective will also provide a stimulus to investment and discourage excessive nationalism."[91] The clause making the Europe Agreements conditional on respect for democratic standards, the principles of the market economy and the protection of ethnic minority rights was the first decisive move toward conditionality in the EU's relations with its eastern neighbors. It also heralded the EU's deepening concern about ethnic intolerance throughout Eastern Europe as the wars worsened in the former Yugoslavia.

When the EU did commit itself to an eastern enlargement at the Copenhagen summit in June 1993, the tables started to turn against the illiberal governments—but it would take two or three more years before their situation became uncomfortable. The EU began the process of developing the tools to interact purposefully with the eastern candidates. It finally set out the general political and economic conditions of membership in the so-called Copenhagen criteria, but it did not evaluate the candidates in terms of these requirements. For the illiberal pattern governments, the only ramification of manifestly failing to the meet the Copenhagen criteria—even in the prominent area of ethnic minority rights—was the threat of exclusion from a first wave of EU expansion. Such an exclusion seemed very distant in 1993—and in fact it would take the EU four more years to separate the "ins" from the "outs."

The EU and other international actors discouraged the use of physical violence or blatantly undemocratic acts, but they had little impact on the substance of domestic policy-making in the illiberal pattern states until active leverage was fully developed. In theory, the EU could have revoked Europe Agreements, but it preferred to wait until the Commission researched and published long Opinions on the applications of each of the candidate states in July 1997. However, even sooner than that, Western governments and EU officials started to abandon the norm in international politics of not interfering in the domestic affairs of other states. They began to point out the discrepancies between the behavior of governments claiming to aspire to EU membership, and the membership requirements laid down in the Copenhagen criteria. As we will see in Chapter 6, this practice gathered steam in 1995—and it has continued ever since.

4.3 Conclusion

The passive leverage of the EU—not just the benefits of membership but also the costs of exclusion and the treatment of nonmembers—invigorated the quest of liberal pattern states in the early 1990s for full EU membership. However, even in the liberal pattern states, passive leverage alone was not self-sustaining: as EU leaders continued to avoid committing to an eastern enlargement in 1990, 1991, and 1992, this discredited moderate parties who had all thrown their lot in with "Europe." For this reason, the EU's passive leverage declined over time, and an EU that had remained passive (or that had later changed its mind about enlarging) could have caused a backlash against moderate parties.

But there is reason to believe, as we will see in the next chapter, that the EU's reluctance to enlarge along with the economically brutal way that the EU took advantage of the asymmetric interdependence in its relationship with East European states set the stage for the effectiveness of the EU's active leverage. Although lack of access to the EU market hurt Visegrad economies, EU protectionism did drive home the imperative of full membership. The Visegrad states in particular might have felt less pressure to play by the rules of the EU's pre-accession process in the early 1990s had they not experienced the ambivalence of certain key EU members toward enlargement, key members that could use noncompliance to grind the process to a halt.

The passive leverage of the EU did not, however, change the course of democratization in the illiberal pattern states in the early 1990s. The EU and other international actors moderated the behavior of illiberal elites on the margins, but clearly failed to change their way of governing, in particular the kinds of domestic policies that they implemented to please their domestic power base. The marginal role of international actors may be surprising given the general expectation that Europe's international institutions would be intimately involved in building Europe's new democracies. There existed the perception that international actors and especially the EU were shaping the course of the transitions—and certainly both EU leaders and East European leaders invoked the role of international actors in the democratization process a great deal.

What were the consequences of the absence of more active leverage on the part of the EU? Most important, elites in Romania, Bulgaria, and Slovakia were able to "play it both ways" for a long time—seeking membership as a matter of foreign policy, but engaging in ethnic intolerance and economic corruption as a matter of domestic politics. The illiberal governments exploited the time lag, subordinating foreign policy (joining the EU) to domestic politics (rent-seeking). Ethnic nationalism came to permeate domestic political discourse in Romania and Slovakia. Economic corruption disfigured economic reform in all three states, distorting new institutions, undermining the belief of citizens in the market economy, and robbing the coffers of the state. Economic links with the West were much slower to develop, further impoverishing the population. But as we will see in the next chapters, the EU's active leverage, once developed, would play a role in breaking the hold of illiberal rulers by improving the quality of competition in domestic politics in Romania, Bulgaria, and Slovakia after 1994.

5

The Active Leverage of the European Union

We ended Chapter 2 and Chapter 4 on the same note: the substantial divergence between the political and economic trajectories of the liberal pattern and the illiberal pattern states after five years of transition. On the first of January 1995, Romania was governed by unreconstructed communists in coalition with extremists; Bulgaria by unreconstructed communists alone; and Slovakia by nationalist populists in coalition with extremists. The three ruling parties, the Party for a Democratic Romania (PDSR), the Bulgarian Socialist Party (BSP), and the Movement for a Democratic Slovakia (HZDS), respectively, were embarked in vigorous and creative attempts to concentrate political power and extract economic rents from the transformation. To the south, ethnic cleansing and war devastated Bosnia-Hercegovina and Croatia, while Croatia and Serbia became the pariahs of Europe as the sponsors of genocide.

On the first of January 2000, Eastern Europe looked quite different. Those states that were credible future members of the EU had all developed a more competitive political system. They were almost all moving forward with political and economic reform, and making progress toward EU membership within the framework of the EU's pre-accession process by adopting EU rules. David Cameron shows that while all post-communist countries have made progress in economic liberalization since the early 1990s, the gap between the accession candidates and the other countries in the extent of sectoral and regulatory reform increased dramatically over the 1990s. More striking is the divergence between the two groups in meeting liberal democratic standards: between 1991 and 2001, "while the accession candidates extended rights and liberties to such an extent that most of them were comparable in that regard to many of the member states of the EU, the other post-communist states actually experienced a *decrease* in the average score; in the latter group, rights and liberties were, on average, *less* extensive and secure in 2001 than they had been in 1991!"[1]

In the three accession states that I have labeled illiberal pattern states in this study, coalitions of political parties that vowed to open up the political arena, respect the rule of law, implement comprehensive economic reform, promote ethnic tolerance and qualify for EU membership had won elections in 1996 in

Romania, in 1997 in Bulgaria, and in 1998 in Slovakia. The imperative of a "return to Europe" was evoked once again—and it was popular to quip that the new reform governments were starting where Poland and Hungary had started in 1989. For the most part, the new ruling parties followed through on their promises, changing domestic policies and adopting specific EU rules in order to pave the way for EU membership and the "return to Europe." In Romania and Slovakia the very composition of the new coalition governments signaled a radical change since they included political parties representing the Hungarian minority and distributed government portfolios to ethnic Hungarians.

We have explained the variation in the domestic trajectories of East European states after 1989 in Chapters 1 and 2, and the variation in their responses to the external incentives of EU membership in Chapters 3 and 4. Now, how do we explain this general convergence? What are the domestic and international factors that caused shifts in the political and economic trajectories of East European states? I argue that of greatest importance are two key factors that change and interact over time: the quality of political competition, and the EU's active leverage flowing from pre-accession process.

As we considered the prospects for liberal democracy in post-communist states in Chapters 1 and 2, we looked first to the legacies of the communist and pre-communist past; legacies that cannot be changed. Political competition, however, is dynamic: polities can become more (or less) competitive over time as a consequence of political, economic and social developments. The EU's pre-accession process is also dynamic: states can move forward (or back) in the process over time. Meanwhile, the EU's active leverage reinforces domestic political change: it elicits compliance as candidates seek to qualify for membership, and the process of complying transforms the polity, the economy and groups in society over the medium term. As candidates move through the pre-accession process toward membership, it becomes less likely that the polity will slide back by becoming less competitive or rolling back reform.

This chapter takes a step back and unpacks active leverage—much as Chapter 3 explored the theoretical and empirical underpinnings of passive leverage. I argue that the EU's active leverage is so powerful because it builds on the benefits of membership, described in Chapter 3. It is also powerful because of the requirements of membership and because of the three characteristics of the pre-accession process—asymmetric interdependence, enforcement, and meritocracy, described in this chapter. I show how the EU's pre-accession process mediates the costs and benefits of satisfying EU membership criteria in such a way as to make compliance attractive—and noncompliance visible and costly.

The next two chapters, Chapter 6 and Chapter 7, demonstrate how the EU's active leverage has had a role in a two-step process of convergence toward liberal democracy and compliance with EU rules. In the first step, illiberal pattern states replace overtly rent-seeking governments in national elections with more reform-minded governments that bring them into compliance with the EU's general political criteria. In the second step, governments in both liberal and illiberal pattern states implement substantial reform of the state and of the economy as they make their way through the EU's pre-accession process aiming to complete the negotiations and enter the EU.

What are the mechanisms by which the EU's active leverage influences the evolution of domestic politics during each step? I argue in Chapter 6 that the relationship between the EU and credible future members gradually changed the domestic balance of power in illiberal states against rent-seeking elites, undermining the strength of their domestic power base by making the political system more competitive. The EU's active leverage was only marginally effective in moderating the domestic policies of illiberal pattern governments directly. But active leverage did help create a more competitive political system by working through society to change the information environment and the institutional environment to the advantage of more liberal political forces.

Once in power, these more liberal political forces pursued EU membership in earnest: I argue in Chapter 7 that the conditionality of the EU's pre-accession process compelled all governments to reform the state and the economy, embarking on politically difficult or inconvenient reforms instead of delaying them. The pre-accession process also locked governments into a predictable course of economic policy-making that served as a credible commitment to ongoing reform for internal and external economic actors. Since this argument has two distinct steps, Chapter 6 and Chapter 7 each have a separate section exploring alternative explanations to the argument presented in that chapter. By unpacking active leverage in this chapter, I lay the groundwork for Chapters 6 and 7 that investigate in detail the mechanisms of EU influence on domestic politics.

By no means is this two-step process of convergence inevitable; moreover, it has come with costs and dangers that I will explore in detail in Chapter 8. Now that eight post-communist candidates have obtained membership and more are very likely to do so, the record of the EU's active leverage in compelling states to pursue political and economic reform certainly seems impressive. However, there is also considerable scholarly disagreement about the outcome: how beneficial has the process of qualifying for EU membership been for Eastern Europe's new democracies? After I have presented my argument about how EU leverage works and what impact it has on domestic policy choices in aspiring member states, I will put it in the context of the wider debate on the merits and demerits of EU conditionality in Chapter 8.

This chapter covers the EU's active leverage and is organized in four parts. The first part explains why three characteristics of the pre-accession process—asymmetric interdependence, enforcement, and meritocracy—have made the EU's active leverage particularly effective. The second part examines carefully the substantial requirements of EU membership that have made the EU's active leverage so far-reaching. The third part explains in more detail the various "tools" of the pre-accession process that the EU has used to exercise active leverage. The fourth part compares the EU's active leverage to the influence of the Council of Europe and NATO, two international organizations that East European states also sought to join after 1989.

5.1   Active Leverage and the Characteristics of the Pre-Accession Process

The substantial benefits combined with the enormous requirements of membership have afforded the EU unprecedented leverage on the domestic politics of aspiring member states. We can generalize to any institution and hypothesize that the leverage on credible candidates created by the prospect of membership varies according to two factors: the magnitude of the benefits of membership, and the magnitude of the entry requirements. The greater the benefits of membership, the greater the *potential* political will in applicant countries to satisfy intrusive political and economic requirements.

Following this logic alone, we could conclude that the benefits of EU membership for East European states must be immense: at no time in history have sovereign states voluntarily agreed to meet such vast domestic requirements and then subjected themselves to such intrusive verification procedures to enter an international organization. The requirements of EU membership bear on virtually every aspect of the work of a national government, placing very substantial demands on the executive, the legislature, and the judiciary. Securing EU membership may begin as a foreign policy goal, but it becomes a mammoth project of domestic politics. In addition to the benefits and the requirements of membership, I argue that there are three characteristics of the pre-accession process—of the way that the EU "delivers" political and economic conditionality—that have made the EU's active leverage, summarized in Table 5.1, so effective.[2] They are (a) asymmetric interdependence; (b) enforcement; and (c) meritocracy

TABLE 5.1   Active leverage

Characteristics of the pre-accession process	*Requirements of EU membership*
Asymmetric interdependence	Copenhagen political criteria
Enforcement	Copenhagen economic criteria
Meritocracy	Acquis communautaire

across countries and across time. These characteristics amplify the incentives to comply with the EU's membership requirements because they make the EU's threat of exclusion as well as its promises of membership more credible. I will now examine each of them in turn.

5.1.1 Asymmetric Interdependence

The EU does not coerce candidates into meeting the membership require-ments. Indeed, some EU member states would be indifferent to, if not pleased by, the defection of some or all of the candidates from the accession process—a fact that makes the conditionality of the pre-accession process all the more powerful (as long as the process itself is not put in question). This bears emphasis: the initial wavering of the EU and its lukewarm approach to enlargement made conditionality more powerful. The relationship of "asym-metric interdependence" that I introduced in Chapter 3 made the conditional-ity of the EU's pre-accession process credible: while the EU depended but little on economic or political ties with any particular candidate, East European states depended on integration with the EU for their economic survival and eventual prosperity. Robert O. Keohane and Joseph S. Nye showed that relative bargaining power in international negotiations tends to track relative preference intensity.[3] As we saw in Chapter 4, the East European states showed a very intense preference for an accession agreement, and consequently their position in dealing with the EU was very weak.

This imbalance allowed the EU to make believable threats of exclusion, turning up the heat on illiberal states by threatening to keep them out of the pre-accession process entirely, but also on liberal states by threatening to keep them out of the first wave of enlargement because they were dragging their feet on certain reforms. For this reason, 1996–7 in Poland and 1998–9 in the Czech Republic were remarkably fruitful years for reform of the state and of the economy. However, geopolitical and domestic considerations did give greater bargaining power to the candidate states late in the process—for example, giving Poland too much confidence after 1997 that Germany would not allow it to be excluded from the first wave of enlargement, or allowing Poland to cast doubt on the preference of its citizens for entry in the context of its accession referendum.[4]

Is this a case of successful, noncoercive international leverage on domestic outcomes as a consequence of carefully assembled policies? Not quite: the EU's *passive leverage*—flowing from the benefits of EU membership—certainly did not come by design. What is striking, however, is that the EU's *active leverage*—flowing additionally from the requirements of EU membership and the structure of the pre-accession process—did not come by design, either.[5] There was hardly a "civilizing" project on the part of EU leaders to democratize and stabilize

Eastern Europe by using the tools of EU enlargement. Originally the requirements of EU membership and the structure of the pre-accession process were
designed to keep undesirable states out of the EU; they were not designed to coax
and cajole every eligible state into making itself desirable.[6]

My point here is that asymmetric interdependence, stamped very clearly on
the early stages of the accession process, made conditionality more powerful.
Let us imagine an EU that was eager to expand rapidly to the states of Eastern
Europe after 1989 in order to prove its growing geopolitical importance to the
United States. Such an EU would not have wielded the same active leverage
on domestic politics as an EU that took its time deciding whether or not it
would go forward with an eastern enlargement at all. To put it another way,
most West European governments and officials did not care about improving
the public administration, the banking system or even the environment in
East European states. They learned to care about these things as they became
convinced that EU enlargement was in their national interest, given the
alternative of foregoing EU enlargement in a post-Cold War Europe. (How
many West European politicians would return to the relative simplicity of
a divided Europe if they could is an interesting but quite different question.)
We will take up the question of what motivated EU governments to pursue
enlargement to Eastern Europe again in greater detail in Chapter 8.

5.1.2 Enforcement

Asymmetric interdependence is paired with the enforcement of the EU's accession requirements. If states insist on pursuing EU membership, they are voluntarily subjecting their domestic policy process to the examination and evaluation
of the EU. The power discrepancy exposed by trade relations between the EU
and neighboring states becomes even more stark when these states choose
to take part in the "pre-accession process": the requirements for accession are
massive, and they are nonnegotiable. Here the voluntary aspect bears emphasis.
The complex, laborious, intrusive, and sometimes demeaning process of seeking admittance to the EU is triggered by the candidate's application for membership. An application is submitted on the understanding that the EU's vast
requirements cannot be changed, and that compliance with the requirements
will be (more or less) enforced. Explaining the Commission's recommendation
to exclude Slovakia from negotiations in 1997, Commissioner for External
Relations Hans van den Broek put it like this: "With all respect for the sovereignty of Slovakia I have to make plain that if a state wishes to become an EU
member, it has to respect its fundamental rules and also convince [the EU] about
it."[7] Many of the tools of the EU's active leverage that I discuss below in part
four were designed to help the EU gather information about the compliance of
candidate states with the EU's requirements.[8]

Ultimately, the EU's pre-accession process is designed to make candidates demonstrate their commitment to EU policies well before they join. This helps to explain the relative effectiveness of EU conditionality vis-à-vis the eastern candidates in comparison to previous enlargements, and also in comparison to the uses of conditionality by the international financial institutions (the IFIs)—the World Bank and the IMF. Miles Kahler's "bargaining model" predicts successful implementation of IFI programs when governments are asked to make commitments and take policy actions *before* external support is offered.[9] But while IFIs generally hand over a considerable part of the reward they have to offer (loans and other financial assistance) in the early stages of their relationship with a government, the EU holds back its greatest reward (membership) until a later stage when the expectation that conditionality will induce compliance has all but run its course. While IFI conditionality can certainly compel governments to take dramatic economic steps in the short term to secure assistance, the scope and the incentives for compliance are more limited and different in kind.[10]

Leading up to the first eastern enlargement in 2004, enforcement was taken more seriously than during previous enlargements for two reasons. First, earlier applicants for EU membership had less to do: the acquis was far less substantial, especially before the completion of the internal market. Sweden, Finland, and Austria did join after the completion of the internal market, but they had already adopted much of the EU acquis as participants in the European Economic Area (EEA). Since they joined in 1995, European integration has moved forward quite dramatically in areas of more "political" integration such as border control, immigration, and foreign policy, in addition to the traditional areas of economic integration centered on the single market and the common external tariff. Earlier applicants also had less to do because they had established civil societies and market economies, whatever their prior difficulties with democracy. East European candidates have had to create a civil society and a functioning market economy, as well as a democratic polity. Reconstructing the state so that it can oversee all of this and also implement the acquis has posed a great challenge. All told, when faced with implementing the acquis, for East European candidates the starting point is further back and the acquis target is moving forward more quickly than for previous candidates.

Second, enforcement has taken center stage because of the EU's interest in making sure that candidates generally do comply with the EU's membership requirements before accession. This has been a function of the number of candidates: by 2003 there were ten official candidates and five protocandidates from Eastern Europe, a tremendous number in comparison to previous enlargements. It has also been a function of the gravity of the problems that unqualified candidates from Eastern Europe could, it was feared, import into the EU. These have included ethnic conflict, unstable political institutions, weak oversight of financial markets, and the inability to combat international crime, in addition to the cardinal sin of having public administrations that are too weak to implement the single market acquis. At the same time, the economic backwardness of the East European candidates has given the EU other powerful reasons to delay accession until the requirements are met. These reasons have included the fear of competition from low-wage workers and low-priced goods, and concern about the implications for the EU budget of so many economically backward new members joining the EU at once.[11]

For EU officials, the lessons of past enlargements underscore the importance of enforcement, especially the lesson of the Greek accession. The logic of inclusion was at play for Greece in 1981. The Commission's Opinion on the Greek application in 1976 argued that Greece was not prepared for membership. But EU governments decided to let Greece reform its state administration and implement the acquis *after* accession so that membership in the European Community could nurture and protect its new democracy. In the years that followed, Greece adopted the EU acquis at a snail's pace. Thirty years later, Commission officials argue that inclusion has worked for Greece. But they also argue that Greece would have been better off if the EU had used the leverage it had on the Greek government *before* it joined to push for more comprehensive reforms as a condition of accession. And they observe that the EU could not wait—for political, budgetary and institutional reasons—for twenty or thirty years until gentle inclusion transformed such a quantity of new East European members.[12] The accession of five or ten or fifteen countries as ill prepared as Greece when it joined in 1981 would be a full-blown disaster for the EU. More generally, the geopolitical context of a Europe divided by the Cold War militated against setting rigorous membership requirements for Greece; in contrast, the geopolitical context of an undivided Europe, with a long queue of candidates for membership, gave EU leaders all the more reason to insist that requirements be met.

5.1.3 *Meritocracy Across Countries and Over Time*

While asymmetric interdependence and enforcement both give credibility to the EU's threats of exclusion, meritocracy gives credibility to its promises of eventual membership. So far the EU has adopted a roughly merit-based approach to enlargement: an applicant's place in the membership queue has corresponded to the progress it has made toward fulfilling the EU's requirements. All of the candidates are subject to the same requirements and are evaluated in a manner that has proved to be more or less based on merit. The pre-accession process could not work without enforcement, and enforcement could not work if the process was not generally considered to employ objective and technical standards for evaluating whether candidates qualify to move forward in it. The European Commission's evaluations and the European Council's decisions about the status of candidate applications have been accepted as reflecting accurately the state of reform. Though officials from the candidate states may find factual mistakes or may disagree with the interpretation of a particular passage in the Commission's Opinions and Regular Reports, it is striking how in general they accept the logic and the overall fairness of the process.[13]

More remarkable, there have been few charges that the Commission's assessments or the Council's decisions have been driven by short-term political interests—for example, that a candidate's reforms have been portrayed as lagging behind because (for political, economic or budgetary reasons) some EU member states would prefer to exclude that country from the first wave of enlargement. Governments would cease to devote so much political capital to meeting the requirements of membership if it was obvious that the quality of preparations for any individual candidate could be trumped by domestic politics in EU member states. While strict requirements mean a great deal of work for applicant states, in principle they protect those applicants who, for structural reasons, are difficult for EU member states to absorb. For EU electorates, it would be more popular to admit a state with a low potential to export workers, and for the EU budget, it would be more convenient to admit a state with low demands on the agricultural and cohesions funds—irrespective, in both cases, of how well large swaths of the acquis had been adopted. If meritocracy did not prevail, a candidate with strong patrons in the EU could also expect special treatment. In these ways, at least in principle, a merit-based accession process creates rules which tie the hands of governments not just in aspiring member states, but also in existing ones.

Another aspect of the meritocracy principle is that it extends across time in one country as well as across countries. The EU's good opinion, once lost, is not lost forever. In other words, however dismal a country's past record of respecting democratic standards and even human rights, it can "rehabilitate" itself by implementing the necessary reforms under a future government. When I interviewed them, opposition politicians and civil society leaders in Romania, Bulgaria, and Slovakia emphasized that this message was very important in motivating political action, especially among the young, and fostering cooperation among different civic groups and political parties.[14] When the Luxembourg European Council decided to invite only five of the ten candidates from Eastern Europe to begin negotiations in 1998, EU leaders and the Commission went to great lengths to reassure the five states excluded from negotiations that they were still very much in the running for membership and that they would be invited to begin negotiations in the near future. To make the point, they were invited to begin screening immediately (see below).

The Commission meanwhile pushed very hard for the two groups to be called the "ins" and the "pre-ins," as opposed to the "ins" and the "outs."

To give the most striking example of meritocracy across time, Serbia-Montenegro is a credible future member of the EU, and as such has a clear and relatively certain track toward membership despite its history of state-sponsored ethnic cleansing. Among our cases here, Slovakia was able to affect a dramatic reversal of its EU fortunes. EU Commissioner for External Relations Hans Van den Broek explained in the spring of 1998 that, "The question is not whether Slovakia will enter the EU, but when this will take place. The answer is in the hands of the Slovak government."[15] After ousting the undemocratic HZDS in the autumn 1998 elections, and keeping it out of government in the 2002 elections, Slovakia joined the "ins." Therein lies a certain twist to the story: although Slovakia could rehabilitate itself, Vladimír Mečiar could not. The EU clearly stated that a Mečiar-led Slovak government would not be allowed to sign the accession treaty because the EU dismissed the idea that Vladimír Mečiar could politically reinvent himself. Ion Iliescu, by contrast, who was returned to the presidency of Romania by elections in 2000, has been grudgingly accepted as the best that Romania can do.

Meritocratic Tensions

Even though in hindsight we can see that the EU's decisions have reflected the merit of the applicants, there have certainly been palpable tensions along the way among EU officials and governments about the proper uses of conditionality. Some prioritized using conditionality as a tool to build prosperous, liberal democracies in Central and Eastern Europe. Others preferred to highlight the shortcomings of the candidates in the face of the requirements as a way to delay enlargement. Certain politicians and Commission officials seemed to embody both of these tendencies in a single individual.

The situation was indeed complex also as regards the timing of the first eastern enlargement and the number of countries invited to join.[16] An EU government or official could support an *inclusive* first enlargement out of concern that more backward states would fall out of the process entirely if they were excluded. Or, support for an inclusive first enlargement could be motivated by an agenda to slow down and put off the entire enlargement process by including the laggard states that would likely take much longer to complete their preparations for membership.

In the obverse, support for an *exclusive* first enlargement could be motivated by a desire to keep the enlargement process moving forward on the basis of merit and ensure the timely completion of negotiations with the most advanced states. On this view EU leverage should be maximized and not squandered by admitting candidates prematurely. Or, support for an exclusive enlargement could be a way to limit the entire enlargement project to only a few of the most desirable states, thus minimizing the repercussions for the EU's institutions and federalizing projects. Here we could cite the preference in 1997 of Commission President Jacques Santer for only starting negotiations with Poland, Hungary, and the Czech Republic in 1998. Estonia and Slovenia were doing roughly as well as the frontrunners, but including them would (and did) open the floodgates for other candidates from the Baltic and the Balkan region.[17] It also dashed the hopes of some politicians and officials that if the EU limited the eastern enlargement to only three states then the EU's institutions would not need further reform in preparation for enlargement.[18]

Why does the EU's pre-accession process function as a meritocracy? This characteristic is harder to explain than asymmetric interdependence and enforcement. The meritocratic nature of the pre-accession process was not foreordained, and indeed in the early 1990s it appeared that the odds were against it as East European states signed undifferentiated Europe Agreements with the EU. Germany supported enlargement, but its very strong preference was to admit the countries geographically proximate to its borders. Since these turned out to be amongst the best-prepared candidates, Germany supported a meritocratic approach to the pre-accession process. (What would have happened if our illiberal pattern states had bordered Germany and our liberal pattern states were located further east?) By all accounts, however, German officials had little premonition that the process they helped create would lead to eighteen candidates and protocandidates by the year 2000. If they had been told this at the German-led Essen European Council in 1994 that tasked the Commission to develop the pre-accession process, they would have been surprised.[19]

For its part France certainly lacked a vision of a far-reaching enlargement; in 1993 and 1994 it was giving in to Germany's demands to admit its eastern neighbors for fear of losing influence within the EU if it opposed it.[20] The British and the Scandinavians did, however, always support a broad, open-ended process—the British to spread the zone of liberal peace and undermine deepening; the Scandinavians to give *their* nearest neighbors, the Baltic states, a chance at membership. This is only a schematic overview, but the important point is that the balance of interests among EU member states did favor enlargement.[21]

The decision to open the door to enlargement led the European Council to task the European Commission to design and implement a merit based pre-accession process. José Torreblanca argues that EU members created a "shared normative framework" to govern enlargement to overcome their diverging interests. This concept is similar to my concept of meritocracy in that he points to the fact that once this framework was created, the member states considered themselves obligated to respect it, for example, by treating all candidates equally and by evaluating them on the basis of merit. [22] While EU members made the decision to enlarge based on interest, the decision when to enlarge to which countries was to be guided and constrained by this set of rules.

Looking at the broader picture, the meritocratic nature of the pre-accession process together with the benefits of membership have brought about what participants and observers generally agree is the unanticipated outcome of a very long list of new candidates for EU membership. That the Council and the Commission created this "meritocratic" process for enlargement has had profound consequences for the EU. In theory and so far in practice, any state that can prove itself "European" and that can meet the requirements is considered a credible future member. As a result, pressures are mounting both to keep the process and to change it, as we will see in Chapter 8. In 1994 few imagined an officially recognized membership queue of more than six or eight states. In 2000, as pictured in Table 5.2, the number was eighteen, and possibly

TABLE 5.2   The queue to join the European Union, 2000

EU-15 in order of accession	Official candidates in order of application	Protocandidates
		Promised membership in 1999 Stability Pact for SE Europe
France	Turkey 1987	Croatia
Germany	Cyprus 1990	Macedonia
Italy	Malta 1990	Serbia-Montenegro
Belgium	Hungary 1994	Albania
Netherlands	Poland 1994	Bosnia-Hercegovina
Luxembourg	Slovakia 1995	=33 members
	Romania 1995	
United Kingdom 1973	Latvia 1995	
Ireland 1973	Estonia 1995	*Past + Future Candidates?*[a]
Denmark 1973	Lithuania 1995	Norway (1992)
Greece 1981	Bulgaria 1995	Switzerland (1992)
Spain 1986	Czech Republic 1996	Ukraine
Portugal 1986	Slovenia 1996	Moldova
Sweden 1995	=28 members	Belarus
Finland 1995		Georgia
Austria 1995		Independent Kosovo
		=40 members

[a] Switzerland's membership application was frozen after Swiss voters rejected participation in the European Economic Area in a referendum in 1992. Norway completed accession negotiations, but Norwegian voters rejected EU membership in a referendum in 1994. Morocco's application was rejected in 1987 on the grounds that it is not a European country.

rising. Unintended though it may be, this outcome is not particularly surprising. European integration has from its inception evolved in response to external pressures and internal initiatives, without a long-term plan or a clearly defined goal.

The Role of the Commission

There is broad agreement that supranational officials in the EU enjoy more autonomy than the officials of any other international organization. But has the EU's executive bureaucracy, the European Commission, had an independent impact on how the EU's enlargement process has unfolded since 1989? This question engages the debate between neofunctionalists and intergovernmentalists on the nature of what drives European integration.[23] Neofunctionalists would expect to find that yes, the Commission and other supranational actors have had an important independent impact on enlargement policy.[24] Intergovernmentalists would expect that the policy was determined almost exclusively by national governments who only delegated authority to the Commission to achieve specific, well-defined goals.[25] We explore the role of the Commission briefly here not to resolve this debate, but to help illuminate more of the complexities of answering the broader question posed by this chapter: where did the EU's active leverage come from, and how does it work?

There are three different ways to make the argument that the Commission has had an important role in shaping and channeling the EU's active leverage.[26] They are: first, that it has set the agenda and de facto controlled the pre-accession process; second, that it has served as a powerful broker in that process; and third, that it has promoted a large enlargement to strengthen its own position.[27]

First, how might the Commission have shaped the agenda on enlargement? Discussing the role of the Commission in the enlargement process, many have pointed to "the community method" in action: the Council delegated the development of the pre-accession process to the Commission, leading to the Commission's Agenda 2000 proposals in 1997. It also tasked the Commission with gathering information about the candidates, writing the Opinions on the candidates, and then monitoring their ongoing compliance with the EU's membership requirements. The Council delegated all of these tasks to the Commission because they were complex, technical, and labor intensive. Indeed, EU governments asked the Commission to monitor the adoption and implementation of policies as diverse as those to reform the public administration, safeguard the independence of the central bank, modernize the judiciary, improve the environment, harmonize transport policy, reinforce borders, bolster civil society, and fight racism.

When it came time to decide on the Commission's recommendations about the status of an individual candidate, the member states accepted the Commission's recommendation every time instead of opening up a debate on the issues at hand among themselves. They accepted the Commission's recommendations because of the technical complexity, but also the political complexity of the issues: once the Pandora's box of picking apart the Commission's recommendations was open and each member state weighed in with their preferences, the bargaining and disagreement could become very time-consuming and costly. It was easier to set up a framework for evaluating the candidates, as discussed above, and then simply accept the Commission's recommendations with no modifications—especially since these recommendations were supposed to be based on a "meritocratic" assessment of the candidates' preparations for membership. On this view, the Commission kept the eye of the EU governments on the goal of enlargement and helped them side-step myriad minor but contentious issues.[28] If EU governments had debated every issue every step of the way, some believe that the 2004 enlargement would likely have taken place much later.[29] The Commission also helped member states respond to the tremendous external "shock" of the collapse of communism that left many EU governments with confused preferences about EU enlargement. As a policy entrepreneur that supported enlargement, the Commission helped induce cooperation between EU member and candidate states by generating and selling new conceptions of the future of European integration.[30]

Second, how might the Commission have acted as an important broker between the candidates and the member states? Since the Commission's recommendations carried so much weight given the technical and complex nature of the enlargement process, the Commission had considerable discretion in how it "presented" various matters to the Council. From the perspective of the candidate states, many EU officials believe that the Commission acted as "more than an honest broker"; the candidates were in a much weaker position than the member states, and the Commission would generally take their side in matters that affected the momentum of the enlargement process.[31] The Commission as the "guardian of the treaties" could logically adopt the dual position of (a) admitting only prepared candidates; and (b) admitting in a timely manner all candidates that were prepared. It could use its skills in brokering compromise agreements to keep the enlargement process moving forward.[32]

But the Commission's role as the "guardian of the treaties" need not have automatically counseled Commission officials to support an extensive and timely enlargement. The Commission could interpret the objectives of the EU treaties, especially the vague declarations of working toward an ever closer union, as being at loggerheads with admitting 10–20 new states to the EU.

Indeed, for many, this is a quite separate puzzle: how could the Commission that has traditionally been a stalwart supporter of moving towards a federal "United States of Europe" support such a vast enlargement that seems to make this goal impossible? The historical record, however, reveals that the Commission has consistently supported enlargement as a way to reform EU institutions and to deepen European integration.[33] From as early as 1990, the Commission promoted the efforts of East European states to secure a closer relationship with the EU. In their quest for trade concessions and for a timetable for enlargement, East European candidates could generally count on the support of the Commission. Less subject to direct pressure from producers than EU governments, the Commission routinely "ran interference" between the candidate states and the attempts of member states to curtail their access to the EU market.[34]

Understanding the Commission's role may require a third line of analysis: how might the enlargement process increase the power and strengthen the position of the Commission? Most simply, enlargement creates a tremendous amount of work for the Commission, fortifying its claims for greater resources and more staff. Once the pre-accession process is in place, the addition of each candidate represents more work for the Commission—and this may be particularly important as the most advanced candidates start exiting the Commission's purview by becoming full members. More important, as we already discussed above, the Commission is tasked with much of the work generated by enlargement, and this strengthens its position. Desmond Dinan argues that "as much as any other factor, the imminence and importance of future enlargements strengthen the Commission's claim to remaining at the center of the EU's institutional system, in full possession of its existing powers and prerogatives."[35]

The counterargument to all three of these arguments is that the Commission is restrained from acting in any way that runs counter to the interests and wishes of the member states: the Commission is held in check by the preferences of the member governments at every turn.[36] This, of course, leaves open the possibility that member governments deliberately seek to avoid disputes (as well as extensive technical work) by delegating some tasks and decisions to the Commission. But the Commission only makes proposals and recommendations that the member states signal ahead of time will be acceptable to them. It only acts as a broker in the ways that the member states want it to. Finally, it only amasses resources and responsibilities as suits the interests of the member states.[37]

Whether the role of the European Commission in the eastern enlargement is one of a disciplined agent of the EU governments, as intergovernmentalists would expect, or of an independent policy entrepreneur, as neofunctionalists would predict, will not be resolved here.[38] The preliminary evidence from my interviews points to a two-step argument. The European Commission did move on enlargement and design the pre-accession process (particularly Agenda 2000) in line with the wishes of the majority of the member states, as described in the previous section. It also took a careful sounding of member states preferences at each step.[39] But since dealing with Eastern Europe was such an unexpected, unfamiliar, and confusing issue for many EU member states, the Commission was able to benefit from (and perhaps amplify) some of the unintended consequences of the pre-accession process. In particular, the number of candidates that have emerged has made enlargement a very substantial and ongoing project for the EU, and the Commission remains at the heart of the process. It is possible that EU governments did not understand the consequences of a merit-based pre-accession process for the scope of the EU's enlargement to Eastern Europe—quite simply, for the potential number of applicants and the difficulties of turning candidates away once they enter the process.[40] This invites investigation of whether the Commission's role in the accession process really did tip the scales in favor of a large enlargement, and whether this has created a "gap" in member state control over the course of European integration.[41] The answer lies in the future: it depends (in part) on whether the enlargement framework, including the meritocracy-driven pre-accession process, forces EU member states to grant full membership eventually to all states that can jump through the hoops of the pre-accession process, even though they would rather keep some of them out. We will look in particular at the dilemmas posed by the EU's long courtship with Turkey in Chapter 8.

5.2   The Requirements: The Copenhagen Criteria and the Acquis

We turn now to a close investigation of the EU's formal accession require-ments that are at the heart of the EU's active leverage. They can be divided into roughly three groups: the Copenhagen political criteria, the Copenhagen economic criteria, and the acquis communautaire (referred to below as the acquis). The Copenhagen political and economic criteria, issued in 1993, are very general. The EU's priorities and intentions, however, have been clarified by the detailed assessment of each candidate in light of these criteria, first in the Opinions of 1997 and then subsequently in the Regular Reports published on the progress of each of the candidates every year. The acquis is very specific: in some 80,000 pages it organizes into a single body all of the laws, norms, and regulations that are in force among EU member states. A fourth, less formal requirement of EU accession has been dubbed the "good neigh-borliness" requirement by Karen Smith.[42] To prevent importing "foreign policy problems" into the EU, it requires East European states to resolve disputes and establish good relations with their neighbors. As I will explore in detail in the next chapter, this was the requirement that was enforced first and most vigorously by EU governments alongside the provision of ethnic minority rights in the early 1990s.

5.2.1 The Copenhagen Criteria

The Copenhagen requirements animating the EU's pre-accession process reflect a broad consensus in favor of liberal democracy, market capitalism and the peaceful resolution of disputes.[43] Adopted at the Copenhagen summit in June 1993, the Copenhagen political, economic, and acquis criteria state that membership requires:

(1) that the candidate country has achieved stability of institutions guaranteeing democracy, the rule of law, human rights, and respect for and protection of minorities;
(2) the existence of a functioning market economy, as well as the capacity to cope with competitive pressure and market forces within the Union;
(3) the ability to take on the obligations of membership (the acquis), including adherence to the aims of political, economic, and monetary union.

The political criteria are remarkable, for they allow the EU to judge the quality of democracy, the treatment of ethnic minorities and, in practice, the sagacity of foreign policy in aspiring members—even though existing members have adopted only superficial measures to regulate and harmonize their own behavior in these areas. For many years, the Copenhagen criteria had no legal grounding in the EU treaties. This was ameliorated by the 1997 Amsterdam Treaty, of which Article 6(1) requires members to respect certain principles: the principles of liberty, democracy, respect for human rights and fundamental freedoms, and rule of law, principles which are common to the Members States. Article 7 provides for the exclusion from voting in the Council of a state that falls short of these principles.

The case of a clear and enduring double-standard is in the protection of ethnic minority rights: while EU institutions play no role in how ethnic minorities are treated in the fifteen member states, the EU evaluates with great attention how they are treated in the candidate states. Indeed, the protection of minority rights has been one of the most visibly enforced political requirements of EU membership. Bruno de Witte argues, however, that there is no consensus among EU member states that minority protection should become one of the fundamental values listed in Article 6 in the future, or even that all members should enact modest forms of minority protection (though enlargement may create new pressures in this direction). The Amsterdam treaty addressed the issue only tangentially by calling in Article 13 on the member states to combat discrimination based on racial and ethnic origin. Minority rights protection is, in sum, one of the areas where the asymmetry of power between the EU member states and the candidates is most in evidence, because here, very clearly, the candidates are being required to meet goals that the member states have not set for themselves.[44]

In the words of the Commission, here is how it evaluates whether candidates have met the political criteria: "The Commission not only provides a description of their various institutions (Parliament, Executive, and Judiciary), but examines how the various rights and freedoms are exercised in practice. With regard to human rights, the Commission analyses the way in which the candidate countries respect and implement the provisions of the major human rights conventions, including in particular the European Convention for the Protection of Human Rights and Fundamental Freedoms. As regards respect for minority rights and the protection of minorities, the Commission devotes particular attention to the implementation of the various principles laid down in the Council of Europe Framework Convention for the Protection of National Minorities. Measures undertaken by the countries in order to fight against corruption are also examined."[45] While all of the candidates must satisfy the Copenhagen political criteria in order to begin negotiations for membership, the Commission's scrutiny of these issues continues until accession and so far no candidate has come up with a perfect report card. Each Regular Report and Accession Partnership (described below) lists shortcomings and recommendations for improvement, especially in the area of human rights. Only once the candidates become full members does the pre-accession monitoring of their human rights records come to a halt.[46]

The economic criteria as set out in 1993 were very broad, but the Commission has described them more precisely in later documents. As indicators of whether the candidates have developed a functioning market economy, Agenda 2000 published in 1997 listed a number of indicators.[47] As summarized by the Commission, these indicators

consist of two elements: the existence of a functioning market economy, and the capacity to withstand competitive pressure and market forces within the Union. These two elements are assessed through a number of sub-criteria that have been defined in Agenda 2000. The existence of a functioning market economy requires that prices, as well as trade, are liberalised and that an enforceable legal system, including property rights, is in place. Macroeconomic stability and consensus about economic policy enhance the performance of a market economy. A well-developed financial sector and the absence of any significant barriers to market entry and exit improve the efficiency of the economy. The capacity to withstand competitive pressure and market forces within the Union requires the existence of a market economy and a stable macroeconomic framework. It also requires a sufficient amount of human and physical capital, including infrastructure. It depends on the extent to which government policy and legislation influence competitiveness, on the degree of trade integration a country achieves with the Union and on the proportion of small firms.[48]

There is no rule to the effect that the applicants may simply be too poor to accede.[49] Adjusting for differences in purchasing power, the average GDP per capita of the ten post-communist candidates in 1998 was only about 40 percent of the EU average—though Slovenia's was as high as 68 percent and Bulgaria's as low as 23 percent.[50] As discussed below, EU politicians worried that higher wages and higher welfare benefits would motivate large numbers of Central and East Europeans to move West after accession, while lower wages and lower taxation would convince large numbers of employers to shift production to the East European candidate states.

5.2.2 The Acquis Communautaire (Acquis)

The acquis communautaire is the expression in some 80,000 pages of the high degree of integration among existing member states. EU membership requires that the acceding countries accept in full the current and potential rights and obligations arising from the EU system and its institutional framework (EU acquis). The substance of the acquis cannot be modified by the candidates in any way. The acquis develops continuously and includes: the contents, principles, and political objectives of the primary Treaties; secondary legislation and precedents of the European Court of Justice accepted on their basis; joint actions, common positions, signed conventions, resolutions, and other acts accepted as part of cooperation in the areas of justice and the interior; international agreements entered into by the Communities and those entered into by member states in respect of the Communities' activities.

This means that the new members may not choose to "opt out" of existing EU policies even if current EU members have done so. Some current EU members have, for example, opted out of sharing a common EU border or adopting the common EU currency, the euro. Acceding members may be kept outside the common EU border or the euro-zone because they are deemed unprepared, but in principle the new members cannot *choose* to stay out of these areas of European integration. This also means that the acceding states pledge to accept the acquis in all aspects of the EU's external relations including the EU's negotiations with other candidate states and the EU's emerging foreign and security policies—though in these areas the relevant documents do leave more room for interpretation and reinterpretation later on.[51]

Following on Copenhagen, the Commission was tasked by the Essen European Council in December 1994 to draft a White Paper outlining a comprehensive strategy for preparing the candidate countries to participate in the single market. The goal of the White Paper, published in 1995, was to facilitate the progressive integration of the candidates into the internal market through their phased adoption of the acquis. In the White Paper the Visegrad states finally got a detailed set of instructions for preparing to join the EU—though later candidates would have to be reminded that membership would require much more than simply transposing the rules, norms and standards (the acquis) of the single market into national law. The White Paper accomplished three things: first, it indicated what parts of the internal market acquis were essential in the early stages of preparing for accession. Second, it suggested the sequence for adopting the internal market measures—some of which speak to the fundamentals of any market economy—by listing first-order and second-order measures. All together, the White Paper Annex of laws and regulations listing these measures numbers 438 pages. Third, it took up the question of whether candidates are able to implement the internal market acquis in addition to transposing it into national law.

Implementation of the acquis is a three-step process: adoption of the acquis by a national parliament; implementation of the legislation by the state administration (which may require institutional innovation); and regulatory and legal oversight to ensure compliance, including redress to the legal system. The EU aid program PHARE subsequently set up programs to aid governments in tackling the acquis, aided by the Technical Assistance Information Exchange Office (TAIEX) of the Commission.[52] The question of implementation became the heart of the screening process and the negotiations between the EU and the candidate states regarding all 80,000 pages of the acquis (discussed below).

5.2.3 The Requirements in the Negotiations

The negotiations between the EU and the candidate countries are structured around the acquis, divided into thirty-one chapters (twenty-nine are substantive). In a process called "screening," the Commission scrutinizes to what extent the legislative norms and standards of the EU's acquis have already been adopted by the candidate states. The negotiations then pertain to whether the acquis has been implemented, or how and in what time frame it will be implemented in the future. Whether the national parliaments adopt the acquis is a more or less transparent, technical question; but EU leaders also have insisted that the state administrations actually implement the acquis—an enormous task for each candidate. While states cannot function as EU members without implementing the acquis, verifying implementation involves highly subjective assessments that candidates have feared could be used to stall enlargement.

Meanwhile, certain issues are not part of the negotiations because they are not part of the acquis; these issues only come up as part of the Copenhagen criteria. Fulfilling the Copenhagen political criteria is the key condition for opening negotiations on accession. In theory, however, the EU could close all thirty-one negotiating chapters with an applicant state but postpone accession because, in the judgment of the member states, the quality of democracy, the treatment of ethnic minorities, or the rule of law have deteriorated from the time the applicant originally was found to fulfill the Copenhagen political criteria as a condition for the start of negotiations.

In the end enlargement takes place only when EU leaders make a political decision to conclude the negotiations and the resulting treaties are ratified. The essential point of departure for the EU's negotiating position is that the acquis should, in its entirety, already be adopted and implemented by the candidates at the moment of accession. This, however, is impossible, and in reality the EU accepts the need for numerous transition periods in areas where candidates cannot afford or otherwise cannot manage to meet EU standards in the years to come. The decision about whether a candidate has "done enough"—adopted and implemented enough of the acquis—to qualify for accession is, in the end, a political one.

In addition to the declared requirements of membership, there are also various informal yardsticks by which the Central and East European candidates are measured and which add further ambiguities. There are, of course, no blueprints for how the post-communist applicants should tackle the many aspects of the modern European welfare state, including health, education, the pension system, and the social safety net.[53] But European officials and other specialists observe and sometimes advise on the creation of new systems, and the Commission in its Regular Reports notes whether these are—in its opinion—successful and sustainable. We will return to the impact of the EU's pre-accession process on the reform of the state and the economy in detail in Chapters 7 and 8, surveying also the debate about whether the EU has dictated too much, because so much of the acquis must be adopted without amendment—or indeed too little, because no blueprints exist for reforming many key areas such as the welfare state and the public administration.

5.3 The Toolbox of the Pre-Accession Process

We have explored the characteristics of the pre-accession process and the requirements of EU membership that underpin the process. We now turn to the way that the EU governments and the Commission have structured the process.[54] The different stages that each candidate passes through on the way to membership, described below, afford the EU a range of tools for exercising active leverage. These tools work in two general ways.

First, these tools allow the EU to use the threat of exclusion from the next stage of the process on candidates that are not fulfilling the required reforms. Conversely, it allows the EU to reward states in response to progress in implementing reforms and adopting EU laws. The incremental nature of the pre-accession process works with the meritocracy principle to create a long-term relationship that provides intermediate rewards along the way. Heather Grabbe calls part of this process "gate-keeping" as the EU controls access to each further stage in the pre-accession process.[55] There are seven stages, but only stages three, four, five, and six have been the occasion of routinized and well-enforced conditionality for the six states in this study.

(1) signing trade agreements (Trade and Cooperation Agreements) and receiving PHARE aid;
(2) signing association agreements (Europe Agreements);
(3) beginning screening;
(4) opening negotiations;
(5) opening and closing the thirty-one chapters of the acquis;
(6) signing an accession treaty;
(7) ratification of the accession treaty by the national parliaments and the European parliament.

As we saw in Chapter 4, the Trade and Cooperation Agreements (stage 1) and the Europe Agreements (stage 2) occasioned important debates among EU officials and leaders about the proper uses of conditionality, and contained conditionality clauses, but these were little used for fear of isolating fragile democracies.[56] For the five Balkan states promised the prospect of membership in 1999 (see Table 5.2), however, conditionality has also been used to regulate when states move to stage one and stage two.

Second, the tools described below provide different ways for the Commission to assist each candidate in fulfilling the required reforms, for example, by sharing expertise and information, by setting a list of priorities, and by asking each government to develop a very extensive plan for achieving compliance. These tools all represent the intrusion of the EU into the domestic politics of states that have applied to join it. This intrusion provides a rich alternative source of information and an alternative perspective about how a government is performing that are crucial to our discussion in Chapters 6 and 7 about how the EU's active leverage can have an impact on the polity and the economy of candidate states over time.

Association Agreements

The EU's first potential tool of active leverage was the timing and scope of the association agreements with potential candidates, but this tool was not used.

The association agreements, named the "Europe Agreements," were essentially trade agreements, but they did establish a political relationship as well. As we saw in Chapter 4, the EU delayed signing a Europe Agreement with Romania and also Bulgaria. It also insisted that Europe Agreements signed with Romania and Bulgaria include a clause making the agreement conditional on the respect for human and minority rights. But the EU has never suspended—or even loudly threatened to suspend—a Europe Agreement with a misbehaving associate member, even though the agreements give ample provisions to do so in the case of breaches of democratic standards or human rights. However, the EU has howled very loudly indeed when the commercial provisions of the agreements are violated. In sum, the Europe Agreements pre-date the EU's active leverage and are instead an expression of the commercial interests of EU member states.

Criticism and Démarches in Light of the Copenhagen Criteria

The first tool of the EU's active leverage that was used was the public criticism of aspiring EU members in light of the Copenhagen criteria of June 1993. If an East European government declares to its citizens that the country is on the road to joining the EU, and if EU membership is popular with the citizens (as Table 3.2 indicates), then presumably two things follow from this. First, it gives the EU grounds for comment on the country's progress toward qualifying for membership, especially once the government has submitted a membership application. Second, it indicates that there are political costs for the government if the EU criticizes its performance—unless of course the electorate only hears the government's own version and interpretation of the EU's assessments. After five years of silence, the commentaries and criticisms on the part of EU officials began to flow in late 1994.

The most dramatic and sustained public criticism by the EU was of the third Mečiar government in Slovakia, starting with a démarche in October 1994 and ending only once it lost power in 1998. But in Slovakia, the US ambassador spoke out before the EU, and more sharply. Elsewhere the US government also had an important role in criticizing plainly and loudly the government before the fifteen EU member states could agree to do so.[57] However, the US government had less to offer since an invitation to join NATO was further removed from the immediate political performance of a candidate state, as discussed below. The Council of Europe and the OSCE also mattered, but as I also argue below they chiefly mattered because their good opinion was seen as a prerequisite for EU membership. The criticisms of the EU itself—as well as those of other international actors—were evaluated by domestic actors primarily in light of their impact on the goal of joining the EU.

TABLE 5.3   Toolbox of the pre-accession process

Benchmarks used to exercise conditionality	Official documents available used for evaluation and enforcement
	Agenda 2000 + the Opinions
Beginning screening	Regular reports
Opening negotiations	Accession partnerships
Closing negotiating chapters	National programs for adoption of the acquis
Completing negotiations	Number and timing of closed chapters

Agenda 2000 and the Opinions

The next (and much more effective) tool did not come until some eight years after the collapse of communism in Eastern Europe: in the first comprehens-ive exercise of the EU's active leverage, the European Commission published in July 1997 its "Opinions" on the membership application of each of the ten post-communist candidates as part of its study on enlargement called "Agenda 2000." The Opinions assessed each candidate in light of the Copenhagen criteria and the ability to apply the acquis. William Wallace describes *Agenda 2000* as the culmination of West European ideas and expectations over the past fifty years, hardening into the precise conditions that it spells out. As such, Wallace argues, *Agenda 2000* "provides for some purposes the most precise definition of European values outside the European Convention of Human Rights, extending more widely than that Convention into the details of market rules and public administration."[58]

The Opinions were unique because they not only judged the applicants' readiness for membership in 1997, but also took a medium-term view of whether they would be able to meet the conditions for membership within the period of the negotiations. The Opinions thus gave an overview of the state of political and economic reforms in each candidate in 1997, and speculated how close they might be to being ready for membership after five more years of reform.[59] They also offered an explicit and very well publicized description of each candidate's shortcomings in meeting the Copenhagen criteria and adopt-ing the acquis. On the basis of the Commission's recommendations, as shown in Table 5.4, the Luxembourg European Council in December 1997 decided to start negotiations in 1998 with Poland, Hungary, the Czech Republic, Estonia, and Slovenia (known as the "ins"), and delay the start of negotiations with Romania, Bulgaria, Slovakia, Latvia, and Lithuania (the "pre-ins").[60]

The Regular Reports

The Regular Reports provide a summary of a candidate's progress in meeting the Copenhagen criteria and adopting the acquis during the previous year.

TABLE 5.4   Invitations to open negotiations on EU membership, 2000

Luxembourg European Council December 1997	Helsinki European Council December 1999	On hold
Poland	Latvia	Turkey
Hungary	Lithuania	
Czech Republic	Slovakia	
Slovenia	Bulgaria	
Estonia	Romania	
Cyprus	Malta	

While the negotiations, once underway, revolve around the promises of the candidates to implement the acquis in a certain time frame and in a specific manner, the Regular Reports describe only what has been accomplished; they exclude reforms that are "in the pipeline." The Regular Reports were published for the first time in the autumn of 1998 and have subsequently been published each autumn for every candidate until accession.[61] Widely considered a once yearly "judgment" of the state of reform, the Regular Reports are greeted with considerable media attention in the capitals of the candidate states, and can have considerable political repercussions for the government.[62] The Regular Reports give general descriptions and prescriptions in each policy area. Overall, however, they give an accurate and full picture of where a candidate stands in the pre-accession process measured in two key respects: first, how is it doing in comparison to other candidates; and second, whether it is on track to be included in the upcoming round of enlargement.

In the words of the Commission, "the Regular Reports assess progress in terms of legislation and measures actually adopted or implemented. This approach ensures equal treatment for all candidates and permits an objective assessment of the situation in each country. Progress towards meeting each criterion is assessed against a detailed standard checklist, which allows account to be taken of the same aspects for each country and which ensures the transparency of the exercise. The Reports draw on, and are cross-checked with, numerous sources, starting from information provided by the candidate countries themselves, and many other sources including reports from the European Parliament, evaluations from Member States, or the work of international organizations and non-governmental organizations."[63]

Accession Partnerships and the National Programs for the Adoption of the Acquis

While the Regular Reports look back at progress made during the previous year, the Accession Partnerships look ahead and give the candidate states a clear "work plan" for their future preparations for EU membership. The Accession Partnerships are drafted every year by the Commission and set out in just a few pages the short-term and medium-term priorities for each candidate, according to their individual accomplishments and shortcomings to date. The priorities speak to the acquis, and also to any weaknesses in complying with the Copenhagen criteria. The breakthrough that made EU financial aid a tool of active leverage came in 1999 when the PHARE system was revamped: instead of funding projects proposed by the candidates, PHARE began funding projects that demonstrably furthered one (or more) of the short or medium-term goals set out in the Accession Partnerships.[64]

Each candidate government has been asked to draw up and update regularly a National Program for the Adoption of the Acquis until accession. In this document the government sets out its short and medium-term priorities for the adoption of the acquis in each of twenty-nine substantive chapters, as well as setting out its priorities for improving on the additional political and economic Copenhagen criteria. For each policy area, the government separates the legislative and nonlegislative tasks, and also the short and medium-term tasks, that it plans to undertake to fulfill the goal. It also describes the institutional and the financial resources necessary to attain the goal, and links these needs with financial assistance from the PHARE program. The NPAAs range from 250 to 650 pages, and for most countries they are available on the web in English through the Ministry of Foreign Affairs or the Committee on European Integration.[65] It takes a great deal of political will and administrative effort to compile a NPAA. It is designed to make states set their "own" targets for preparing for membership, and the formality of the document is meant to help it outlive any one national government.

Negotiations and Screening

Screening is the process by which all of a candidate's laws are checked for conformity with the acquis, chapter by chapter. The Luxembourg European Council of December 1997 decided to begin screening with all ten candidates in 1998. Screening therefore coincided with the start of negotiations for the first wave, known as "the ins." For the "pre-ins," screening was a sort of consolation prize that would allow them to move forward in the pre-accession process even though they had been declared unready to begin negotiations. Screening also helped the "pre-ins" get a jump on future negotiations in so far as they benefited from the "pedagogical sessions" with Commission officials.[66] Immediate screening did create the possibility that some of them would be able to catch up to the "ins" once negotiations did begin, enabling them to enter the EU in the first wave. However, some scholars and East European officials questioned whether legislation was scrutinized consistently across different chapters and different countries.[67]

Negotiations between the EU member states and the candidate states are structured around the transposition of the acquis, divided into twenty-nine substantive chapters, thirty-one chapters in all.[68] The EU's negotiating position is that the entire acquis must be adopted and implemented at the moment of accession. The substance of the negotiations is therefore (a) whether the acquis has already been implemented; (b) if not, when and how it will be implemented before accession; and (c) if adoption and implementation are not possible by the time of accession, how long of a transition period will be allowed.[69] As reforms are completed or at least promised, chapters are provisionally closed and the negotiations advance.[70] The candidates compete with one another to close the greatest total number of chapters, and also to close particularly difficult chapters. This competition is helpful in creating momentum to complete difficult reforms that are necessary to close individual chapters. Until the negotiations are completed, chapters are only provisionally closed and the EU can choose to reopen a chapter if a candidate state is not delivering on its commitments.

Calling this process "the negotiations" is widely considered an inaccurate label given that candidates do not negotiate with the EU about the substance of the acquis; they only negotiate about when they will adopt it in full. The only matters open to bargaining are whether, and on what terms, transition periods will be accepted for—or indeed imposed on—new members. New members may seek transition periods in adopting difficult parts of the acquis. Old members, as we will explore in Chapter 8, may seek transition periods as well—for example, in allowing free movement of workers from the new members, or in paying out monies from the EU's agricultural and regional development funds.[71]

To give a technical overview, the accession negotiations between a candidate and the EU take place in the framework of an intergovernmental conference where the parties are the governments of the member states and the government of the candidate. The negotiations take place on two levels. On the level of the Council, the ministers of foreign affairs participate from the member states and from the candidate states. On the level of the COREPER (the Council's permanent representation in Brussels), it is the heads of the delegations of the member states to the EU and the "chief negotiator" of the candidate state that participate. The chief negotiator may be the head of the candidate state's delegation to the EU, or a deputy foreign minister, or the head of a separate committee tasked with conducting the negotiations. The negotiations are conducted mainly in written form. The candidate's negotiating position is "answered" by a common EU position, but first all the member states have to come to an agreement on the substance of this common position. This process repeats itself for every chapter of the acquis separately for each candidate engaged in accession negotiations with the EU. However, there is considerable simultaneity in the timing of the opening and closing of chapters with different candidate states, indicating effective pressure on individual candidate states to not fall behind in the negotiations, but also bureaucratic pressure to keep negotiations moving on similar tracks. It is the complexity, the magnitude, and the length of these negotiations that ultimately demonstrates the significance of a state choosing to join the EU, especially if it was not previously a member of the EEA.

5.4   Joining the Council of Europe and the Atlantic Alliance:
A Comparison

After the collapse of communism, East European states also sought membership in the Council of Europe and (with some delay) in NATO. Did these international organizations have the same kind of influence on domestic outcomes as the EU? We can compare them to the EU using the three factors that I argue have made the EU's leverage so powerful: the benefits of membership, the requirements of membership, and the characteristics of the pre-accession process. I argue in this section that neither the Council of Europe nor NATO exerted influence using the same mechanisms as the EU's active leverage. Simply put, this was because governments, in order to reap the benefits of Council of Europe or NATO membership, did not have to meet substantial entry requirements set by these organizations. Whatever influence these organizations did have was weaker than and different in kind from the active leverage of the EU.

5.4.1   The Council of Europe

Membership in the Council of Europe (COE)[72] was widely regarded as the seal of "democracy" and as a stepping stone to or waiting room for EU membership. East European states sought membership as a credential proving that they had successfully established liberal democracy. This credential was useful for attracting international aid and foreign investment, and it was considered an absolute prerequisite for both EU and NATO membership. The benefits of membership in the Council of Europe were therefore substantial, and so were the requirements: Eastern Europe's new democracies had to demonstrate that they had established liberal democracy including the rule of law and the protection of human rights and fundamental freedoms.

For the period that the applications of Poland, Hungary, the Czech Republic, Slovakia, Bulgaria, and Romania were under consideration in the early 1990s, the Council of Europe consequently did have some leverage on domestic policymaking. It identified deficiencies, and asked candidates to change domestic policies to improve the situation as a condition of entry.

However, it wasted much of its leverage as a result of the characteristics of its enlargement process. There was little enforcement of Council rules, and the enlargement process hardly functioned as a meritocracy. The COE failed to apply its own membership criteria rigorously, embracing what one study has (most aptly) called "democratic underachievers," with serious consequences: "It is beyond dispute that the implicit lowering of admission criteria . . . has allowed in countries with dubious political, legal and human rights practices. This is a state of affairs made that much worse by an unwillingness on the part of certain countries to live up to commitments made at the point of admission."[73] The Council often settled for only a commitment to change domestic policies in the *future*, after membership was granted; but at the moment that a state became a member, virtually all of the COE's leverage evaporated.[74] This led to the admission of illiberal democracies that remained illiberal, and their presence greatly lowered the value of Council membership for other post-communist states. All together, this undermined the COE's claim to be a defender of democracy, the rule of law, and human rights.[75]

Indeed, by the mid-1990s, the COE was admitting new democracies that were openly violating democratic standards and perpetrating serious human rights abuses. Membership in the COE expanded from twenty-three states in 1989 to forty in 1999. The COE has no tools to enforce compliance among its members, except the threat of expulsion; it did follow through on this threat in two cases, expelling Belarus and the rump Yugoslavia. But after Slovakia became a member in 1993 and Romania in 1994 both governments violated COE provisions in serious ways without any sanction. Russia has had perhaps the most egregious record, openly defying the Council of Europe by refusing to implement the conditions attached to its accession in 1996.

The policy of admitting democratic under-achievers was underpinned by the logic of inclusion and by the geopolitical interests of West European states. Making the case for inclusion, COE Secretary-General Daniel Tarschys argued that it was better to accept new members based on their commitment to meeting COE standards, and not on complete compliance.[76] This rationale for inclusion dovetailed with the interests of West European states to have all East European states in the COE for geopolitical reasons, to make them feel included in at least one somewhat exclusive Western international organization since the enlargement of the EU (and NATO) would be long in coming, and much more selective. However, there is little evidence that inclusion has consistently encouraged beneficial change, and much evidence (that we will explore in the next chapter) that illiberal rulers in democratizing states have been able to use COE membership to establish false credentials as democrats and reformers.[77]

The behavior of its members notwithstanding, the Council of Europe has specialized since 1989 in the protection of human rights and ethnic minority rights. Its most visible initiatives have been the 1992 European Charter for

Regional or Minority Languages, the 1995 Framework Convention for the Protection of National Minorities, and confidence-building measures aimed at defusing tensions between majorities and minorities. The COE and the Organization for Security and Cooperation in Europe (OSCE)[78] have pursued joint projects regarding national minority issues in several states including the Slovak Republic and the Baltic states. The COE has also pushed the edge of the envelope by passing Parliamentary Assembly Resolution 120 calling for some form of autonomy for ethnic minorities. Jennifer Preece argues that all together the texts adopted by the Council of Europe and the OSCE from 1990 to 1995 in response to the stresses of democratization in Eastern Europe's ethnically diverse states have established the groundwork for at least a weak regime for the protection of minority rights in Europe.[79]

More important, at least in the short term, the Council of Europe and the OSCE have become powerful standard setters and providers of information for the EU's pre-accession process. Put simply, governments fulfill their obligations to the Council of Europe and the OSCE because the EU has incorporated these obligations (and implicitly the approval of these organizations) into the requirements for EU membership.[80] The centerpiece of the Regular Reports is a general evaluation of how the candidate is meeting those Copenhagen criteria that are above and beyond the norms, rules, and regulations in force among existing EU member states as expressed in the acquis. For the protection of ethnic minority rights, the European Commission has depended chiefly on the evaluations of the OSCE High Commissioner on National Minorities, and also the Council of Europe. Although there has been no formal role for either the High Commissioner or the Council of Europe in the enlargement process, their assessments have in many cases formed the core of the Commission's own assessments. In this way, the benefits of qualifying for EU membership have boosted the influence of both international organizations, granting legitimacy to the standards that they set and creating material sanctions for the violation of those standards.[81] The economic requirements of the Copenhagen criteria also include an overall assessment of whether the candidate has a functioning market economy. On the fitness of the economy, the Commission has listened to the views of the World Bank, the IMF, and the Economic Commission for Europe of the United Nations, boosting their influence in a similar way.

5.4.2   The Atlantic Alliance

NATO emerged as the most effective purveyor of security for East European states after 1989. It therefore had much greater benefits to offer prospective members than the Council of Europe. A state's prospects for NATO membership also became linked to its standing with the EU and to perceptions about the success of its transition to liberal democracy and market capitalism.[82] After all, trade blocks are historically comprised of political–military allies, and many East European elites came to consider NATO membership to be a prerequisite for EU membership.[83] Many East European governments, especially the Visegrad states and the Baltic states, were unsatisfied with the institutions that NATO created as a forum for cooperating with post-communist states, namely in 1991 the North Atlantic Cooperation Council (NACC, later the Euro-Atlantic Partnership Council), and in 1994 the Partnership for Peace.

Despite the tremendous benefits of NATO membership, NATO's leverage on domestic policymaking has been far less powerful than that of the EU for two reasons. First, and most important, states were not invited to join NATO because they had made the most progress in qualifying for membership, for example by restructuring their military. Instead, before the specific requirements were established, NATO governments tapped Poland, Hungary, and the Czech Republic as the post-communist states that should enter NATO in the first round—because of their westerly geographic position, and because of the widespread perception that they were Eastern Europe's liberal democratic frontrunners. The process was a meritocracy only in the loosest form. The Baltic states, whatever the condition of their militaries, were disqualified from the first round of NATO expansion by Russia's displeasure. Five years later, for the second round, the pendulum had swung toward inclusiveness, and all East European states negotiating for membership in the EU were invited to join, reflecting their general success in building democracy—and not their particular success in meeting NATO entry requirements.

Second, the specific requirements of NATO membership pertained to a much smaller part of domestic policy-making, and these limited requirements were not well enforced as a condition of accession. Once the EU decided to enlarge and established the pre-accession process, it provided a stable set of incentives for complying with (some) clearly defined membership criteria. NATO's expansion, in contrast, was driven by the decision whether or not to enlarge. Once the decision was taken to enlarge both in the first and the second round, the qualifications of the candidates seemed peripheral to the outcome.

In the first round, NATO and the United States government asked Poland, Hungary, and the Czech Republic to adopt a new strategic concept, to improve military interoperability, and to accept a "new responsibility" for European security both before and after they were invited to join in May 1997. But NATO never made a credible threat that not completing these tasks could disqualify them from becoming full members. The Czech Republic, for example, delayed adopting a strategic concept until 1998; it fell far below NATO expectations in training military officers in English to improve interoperability; and it attempted to take no responsibility whatsoever for NATO's engagement during the Kosovo crisis.[84] Through all of this, however, the Czech Republic never worried that it would be excluded from the first round of NATO enlargement that depended anyhow on a vote in the US Senate. There, the Czech Republic's widely admired president Václav Havel would matter more than the fact that the Czech government had not bothered to complete NATO's pre-accession tasks.[85]

An important counterexample that may attest to NATO's influence, however, is the transformation of Poland's civil–military relations in the early 1990s in anticipation of NATO's membership requirements. Unlike the Czech Republic or Hungary, Poland had a strong military with a history of independence from civilian authority and of interference in politics. Polish civilian elites knew that NATO would insist on full democratic control of the military, and pushed through the necessary changes.[86] Also, East European politicians believed that the prospect of NATO membership helped, at least on the margins, to strengthen moderate, reform-oriented political parties in domestic politics. Slovak opposition politicians and activists believed that Slovakia's pointed exclusion from NATO on account of the illiberal behavior of the Mečiar governments might have strengthened their position somewhat in the next elections (though not as much as the EU's exclusion since joining NATO was much less popular among Slovak voters than joining the EU). Conversely, Bulgarian politicians believed that the prospect of inclusion in NATO well ahead of membership in the EU helped to shore up public support for modernizing the military and for Westernizing Bulgaria's foreign policy.[87]

Nevertheless, I am arguing that NATO's influence was weaker and also different in kind than the EU's active leverage. In the second round, there has again been little sustained pressure on the candidate states to complete specific reforms before entering NATO. Again, NATO membership has come as a reward for overall progress in building democracy and market capitalism. But even if the same mechanisms for domestic political change do not work in the case of NATO enlargement as in the case of EU enlargement—the incentives of membership are not coupled with extensive and well-enforced entry requirements—what other mechanisms may be at work?

Rachel Epstein argues for a set of mechanisms following a constructivist logic that allow NATO to have an important impact on domestic politics because for some domestic actors NATO's norms and values are very appealing. As a result, domestic actors seeking the social affirmation of NATO comply with NATO norms even in the absence of clear conditionality; and NATO actors succeed in changing domestic policies by targeting certain domestic actors with persuasion. Studying the Polish case, Epstein demonstrates how NATO helped build a civilian consensus in favor of democratic control over the armed forces, and delegitimized arguments for defense self-sufficiency. Epstein concludes that whether NATO has a similar effect on other prospective members ultimately depends on the appeal of NATO's norms and values, manifested in a country's susceptibility to persuasion and to NATO's coalition-building strategies.[88]

Somewhat apart from this debate about how NATO enlargement may impact domestic politics is a more general debate between scholars that argue for and against NATO enlargement as a *desirable* tool for spreading peace and democracy eastward after the end of the Cold War. To give a brief overview, the first phase of this debate occurred from 1994 to 1996, when some American scholars argued that enlarging NATO eastward would indeed bring important geopolitical benefits, stabilizing East Central Europe (ECE) and supporting liberal democracies in the region.[89] Others disagreed passionately, arguing that enlargement would both destroy NATO's effectiveness and strengthen the hand of extremists in Russia.[90] Any benefits that NATO membership might have for stability in ECE would come at too high a price; instead, the EU and other international organizations should step in and reward new democracies with membership.[91]

After Poland, Hungary, and the Czech Republic nevertheless became NATO members in 1999, it became clear that the connection between NATO enlargement and the strength of Russian extremists was extremely tangential, if it existed at all. But was enlargement destroying the effectiveness of the Alliance? How had enlargement impacted the performance of the Alliance during the Kosovo crisis?[92] The debate soon entered its second phase, exploring the impact of NATO's first expansion and asking whether including even more East European states would degrade its capacity.[93] Heedless of the critics, at the Prague Summit in November 2002 NATO members invited seven more states—Slovakia, Romania, Bulgaria, Estonia, Latvia, Lithuania. and Slovenia—to join the alliance in 2004. The debate continues about whether NATO membership is promoting democracy and stability in Eastern Europe—and at what cost (or benefit) to the effectiveness and the relevance of the Alliance.

5.5　Conclusion

The EU's active leverage has depended on three factors: the benefits of membership (passive leverage), the characteristics of the pre-accession process, and the extensive requirements of membership. I explained in this chapter how the EU's active leverage has been strengthened by three characteristics of the pre-accession process: asymmetric interdependence, enforcement, and meritocracy. I also unpacked the membership requirements for East European candidates—the specially designed Copenhagen criteria and also the existing acquis communautaire. The core elements of the EU's active leverage—the benefits of membership and the bulk of the requirements (the acquis reflecting the extent of integration among the member states)—were not designed by EU governments and officials to entice and transform candidate states. Still, the aspects of the EU's active leverage that were deliberately designed—the Copenhagen criteria, the enforcement mechanisms and the meritocratic nature of the pre-accession process—have made the EU's leverage more powerful. Toward the end of the chapter I also explored the various tools and stages built into the pre-accession process that have structured the EU's use of conditionality where both enforcement and meritocracy have been most visible.

Ultimately the pre-accession process is centered on the threat of exclusion: if a candidate does not comply, it can be held back from the next step in the process. The existence of these clearly defined markers where candidates are allowed to (a) begin screening; (b) satisfy the Copenhagen criteria and open negotiations; (c) close particular chapters in the negotiations; and (*d*) complete the negotiations; are the backbone of the EU's active leverage. For the eight East European candidates whose applications for membership were evaluated as part of Agenda 2000 in 1997, these four decisions became indicators for whether they would be able to enter the EU in the first wave. But the process was a dynamic one because the question of whether or not a state would be allowed to move forward to the next stage was decided in a meritocratic way. A candidate could move up thanks to accelerated reform, or slip back as a sanction for unfulfilled promises to implement reform.

For the illiberal governments that were in office until 1996 in Romania, until 1997 in Bulgaria, and until 1998 in Slovakia, comprehensive and accelerated reforms that would satisfy the Copenhagen criteria and qualify the country to join the EU were not on the agenda. These rent-seeking elites remained unmoved by the benefits of EU membership for their societies. Before we explore how the EU's active leverage helped motivate reform in Chapter 7, we turn in Chapter 6 to how the EU's active leverage undermined rent-seeking elites by helping to make the political systems in illiberal pattern states more competitive.

The Impact of Active Leverage I: Making Political Systems More Competitive, 1994–8

The relationship between the EU and credible future members changed the domestic balance of power against rent-seeking elites by helping to make the political systems of illiberal states more competitive. This took place partly because of the shift on the part of the EU from the passive leverage that it exerted in the early 1990s to the active leverage that we explored in the last chapter. How did the EU's active leverage develop traction on domestic politics in states that were prospective members but also illiberal democracies?

We see in the first part of this chapter that the EU's active leverage compelled governments in one liberal democracy, Hungary, to change their foreign policy toward neighboring states. However, it was of little use in moderating the domestic policies of governments in Romania, Bulgaria, and Slovakia because complying with EU rules would undermine the sources of domestic power of the ruling elite. Even in the area of ethnic minority rights in Romania and Slovakia, where the EU and other international actors made their first and arguably their strongest stand, we see only limited compliance despite direct and sustained international pressure.

In the second part of this chapter, we see how the EU did develop at least some traction on domestic politics in illiberal democracies—though not directly on the governments. The EU's active leverage helped create a more competitive political system in two ways. First, it helped change the information environment by undermining the information asymmetries enjoyed by illiberal rulers. Second, it helped change the institutional environment by bolstering the strength and shaping the political agenda of opposition political parties by way of three mechanisms that I call *cooperation*, *adapting*, and *implementation*. Thus in states where no united, organized liberal opposition existed before 1989, the EU's active leverage—in cooperation with other international actors and in synergy with domestic forces—helped to create one.

The disapprobation of the EU may have contributed directly to the electoral defeat of rent-seeking ruling parties in watershed elections in Romania in 1996, in Bulgaria in 1997, and, most likely, in Slovakia in 1998. But it is difficult to prove that concern about their country's EU membership prospects was the chief motivation of swing voters or of new voters that cast their ballots for parties with liberal instead of illiberal political agendas.[1] In other words, the prospect of EU membership may or may not have directly changed how voters responded to political mobilization based on ethnic nationalism and protection from economic reform. However, the EU's active leverage certainly did change how opposition political parties treated both messages in their campaign bids. The greatest and clearest impact of EU leverage was therefore in shaping the political forces that won those elections. By this I mean that EU leverage, in concert with the influence of other international actors, strengthened pro-EU civic groups and shaped how opposition parties portrayed themselves in the election campaign, which parties they chose to cooperate with before and after the elections, and how they governed once in power.

Like previous chapters, this chapter adopts a broadly rationalist explanation for the political choices of elites in East European states in contrast to a constructivist one. I explain the behavior of the ruling elites in illiberal pattern states chiefly by pointing to the rent-seeking opportunities presented in shirking economic reform, and to the political costs for these elites of changing their domestic strategies to satisfy EU requirements. The material incentives of wealth and power that motivate corrupt economic reform and ethnic scapegoating are quite evident. The behavior of opposition political elites and civil society leaders is, however, more complex. There was a long period of time when those opposed to the ruling parties were shunned and even harassed at home, while at the same time being the target of persuasion and socialization by Western actors—not unlike dissidents before 1989 in Poland, Hungary, and Czechoslovakia.[2]

Yet, the material incentives for opposition elites to embrace an EU-oriented political agenda are also evident; getting the state on track for the rewards of EU membership becomes part of a unified, pro-Western ticket that promises opposition elites the rewards of political power over the longer term.[3] As it becomes clear to opposition elites that the pro-EU liberal democratic and market-oriented agenda could be a winner, it becomes the focal point for cooperation among disparate opposition forces. These forces have more to learn about such an agenda than their counterparts in the liberal states who have often spent years either in a democratic opposition movement or in a reforming, technocratic communist party. From my interviews, it is clear that individual opposition actors in Romania, Bulgaria, and Slovakia came to believe deeply in a Western orientation for their countries—just as dissidents in Poland, Hungary, and Czechoslovakia did before 1989. These actors made choices in an effort to obtain the best possible outcome in light of their beliefs as well as their material preferences.[4] In other words, as constructivists would expect, their behavior was motivated not just by material incentives but also by beliefs. However, I found little evidence that their behavior would have been different if they had been motivated purely by the pursuit of political power, using a Western and EU agenda as a tool to win office.[5] Most likely, the material incentives of a Western agenda attracted many elites and put them in a position to be receptive to what constructivists call "social learning" because they needed to adapt to the expectations of international actors. Judith Kelley in *Ethnic Politics in Europe* similarly finds that socialization alone rarely induces policy change, but must be twinned with incentives beyond moral recognition.[6] I return to this debate at the end of the next chapter.

This chapter is divided into three parts. First, I present a short model of how the benefits, the requirements and the tools of the EU's pre-accession process combine to influence domestic politics in illiberal states. Second, once the EU's active leverage has taken shape, I ask: what difference did it make? I show that the EU's active leverage did cause the liberal pattern government in Hungary to rehaul its foreign policy toward neighboring states, but it failed to compel illiberal pattern governments in Romania, Bulgaria, and Slovakia to comply with EU membership requirements. In the third part, I show however that the EU's active leverage did have an impact on the political trajectory of these three illiberal pattern states by helping to create a more competitive political system, bolstering the strength and shaping the agenda of opposition parties. The second and third parts conclude with alternative explanations for, in turn, illiberal intransigence and liberal change.

6.1 Model

Can external actors create incentives for rulers of a democratizing state to implement comprehensive political and economic reform? Let us assume the existence of a powerful international organization of which the emerging democracies are credible future members. The international organization launches a pre-accession process that makes the road to membership conditional on comprehensive reform. There are two main conduits for the influence of this international organization on domestic politics: the rulers and the society.

The rulers all declare that earning membership in this international organization is their state's foremost foreign policy goal because of the tremendous political and economic benefits afforded by membership. We may therefore expect that the international organization would have substantial influence over the domestic policies adopted by all of the rulers. Yet we observe that while the "liberal" rulers (following the model in Chapter 1) adopt domestic policies consistent with qualifying for membership, the "illiberal" rulers do not.

For the liberal rulers, the membership requirements of the international organization reinforce existing domestic strategies of comprehensive reform. Membership provides an impetus and a justification for difficult reform measures that impose short-term costs on society or, even better, that impose discipline on politicians. The priorities of the international organization are mostly compatible with the priorities of the rulers, the groups that support the rulers, and the public. For the illiberal rulers, however, the membership requirements are at loggerheads with the sources of their domestic power. To win elections, the illiberal rulers promise to protect the population from the economic hardship of rapid reform, and from the ethnic enemies of the nation. This allows them to extract economic rents through partial economic reform, and political rents through ethnic scapegoating. Measures to concentrate political power and limit the information available to the citizens allow the illiberal rules to present themselves as reformers working hard to enter the international organization. However, for the illiberal rulers to satisfy the membership requirements—comprehensive economic reform and ethnic tolerance—they would have to abandon their strategies of rent seeking, and thus risk losing their domestic power base. The international organization is not able to pressure or tempt the illiberal rulers into changing their domestic strategies while they are in office.

The society represents an alternative conduit for the influence of an international organization on domestic politics. Here, the international organization can counteract the illiberal rulers' free hand in the democratizing polity. That is, it can make the political system more competitive by pursuing information-oriented and institution-oriented strategies that circumvent the government and interact with other domestic actors.

If qualifying for membership in an international organization offers substantial domestic rewards, the organization may improve the information environment in the democratizing polity. It may disseminate alternative information about what are the best strategies for reform. Most important, it may reveal and criticize the rent-seeking strategies of the illiberal rulers and thereby erode their credentials as reformers in the eyes of the electorate. This is especially effective when the condemnation comes from a powerful international organization with which the illiberal rulers have claimed a deepening relationship as evidence of their commitment to reform. The international organization can drive home its condemnation by excluding the state from the pre-accession process. This reverses some of the conditions that allowed illiberal elites to take control of the polity, and undermines their chances of winning re-election.

The international organization may also improve the institutional environment by strengthening rival groups in society. It may create incentives for the fragmented and weak opposition groups to cooperate with one another, and to adopt political agendas that embrace comprehensive reform. By repeatedly interacting with opposition elites, it may provide information about alternative political and economic strategies, and also help them adapt to its norms and values. These norms and values are especially likely to be attractive for opposition groups if the international organization is popular with the electorate, and can reward opposition groups by moving the state forward in the pre-accession process if they win the next elections. The international organization may also help disparate groups overcome cooperation problems by facilitating communication. More important, an attractive political space in the center of the political spectrum defined by deepening relations with the international organization can serve as a focal point for cooperation among ideologically and ethnically diverse (even feuding) political groups. To sum up, while the domestic sources of power of the rent-seeking ruling elites would have required them to assume great costs in order to adapt to the international organization's domestic requirements, the opposition political parties build a new, different power base centered at least in part on the domestic benefits of qualifying for membership.

6.2 Influencing Governments Directly

Now we turn to the impact of the EU's active leverage directly on the governments of illiberal pattern states. In these states, the West confronted the mistreatment of ethnic minorities, the contravention of democratic standards, and the unsteadiness of progress towards a market economy as well as tense relations between neighboring states.[7] But the EU's active leverage on illiberal pattern states was significantly weaker than on liberal pattern states, as governing elites calculated that meeting explicit and implicit standards of EU membership would require sacrifices that would undermine the domestic sources of their power. For illiberal rules, the call to defend the nation's sovereignty signaled the boundary between Western endorsements—to be solicited—and Western demands on ethnic minority rights and economic reform—to be opposed. Even as the EU's active leverage took shape, illiberal rulers recognized that a "superficially" Western orientation would bring domestic support and legitimacy while placing few real constraints on domestic policy. They were savvy in creating the appearance of a warm relationship with the EU and other international actors to shore up their domestic support and deflect criticism.

Active leverage—the deliberate engagement with the domestic politics of states applying for membership—initially took the form of pressuring illiberal governments to change their ways or else be held back in the pre-accession process. First, beginning in earnest in 1994 and 1995, the EU and other international institutions tried through diplomatic channels to pressure governments to change particular policies, especially to improve the provision of ethnic minority rights. But this pressure was largely unsuccessful. Next, the EU publicly expressed its approval and disapproval of government policies, and linked its judgments to a state's eligibility for EU membership. But even when the threat of exclusion made the costs of not complying with the Copenhagen criteria crystal clear, Western pressure to change particular policies had surprisingly little effect on illiberal governments. As we will see below, however, direct pressure did lead to policy changes in a liberal pattern state, Hungary, after Western actors insisted that the Hungarian government tone down its foreign policy trumpeting the rights of ethnic Hungarians abroad and condemning the governments of neighboring states.[8]

The leaders of the PDSR in Romania, the BSP in Bulgaria and the HZDS in Slovakia all sought to present themselves as pro-Western and moderate, working to bring their countries into the EU while defending the interests of ordinary citizens. They therefore sought Western approbation, or at least the appearance of it, in order to back up their claims at home that they were moving the country toward EU membership. But they resisted actually implementing some of the reforms that would pave the way for membership because to do so also would undermine their domestic power base. Ending the practice of ethnic scapegoating would tarnish their image as the defenders of the nation, and endanger the support of extreme nationalist parties. Ending insider privatization and the various economic advantages stemming from partial reform would threaten the support of powerful economic elites close to the ruling parties who also wield influence on important parts of the media.

In such circumstances, the EU induced "selective compliance," and "formal compliance" on the part of the governments of illiberal pattern states. "Selective compliance" occurred as governments busily transposed large swathes of the EU's internal market acquis into national legislation, but deliberately avoided key components of the Copenhagen criteria concerning the protection of minority rights and the reform of the economy. "Formal compliance" occurred as mounting pressure convinced illiberal pattern governments to promise ambitious reforms as part of formal agreements or treaties on the international stage. They could be convinced to sign the agreements because they wanted the prestige of good relations with the EU—but as we will see below in the case studies they did not implement these agreements fully back home. Formal compliance did have some effect on domestic policy-making at moments when there were clear and immediate pay-offs to cooperation. Even then, however, illiberal ruling elites often changed their domestic policies only in superficial, or short-term ways.

6.2.1   Leveraging Nationalism and Ethnic Tolerance

The disjuncture between foreign promises and domestic implementation was most visible in the sphere of ethnic minority rights in Romania and Slovakia. Western governments became acutely concerned about the possibility of ethnic conflict in other parts of Eastern Europe as the war in Bosnia-Hercegovina became more and more bloody, and as their attempts to stop it coincided with a series of diplomatic and human disasters from 1991 to 1995. Consequently Western governments applied by far the most pressure on illiberal pattern governments to improve ethnic tolerance. Eventually they also extracted the most extensive promises in this area—in the special clauses attached to the Europe Agreements, in the agreements admitting Romania and Slovakia to the Council of Europe, and in the bilateral treaties that both the Mečiar and the Iliescu governments eventually signed with Hungary.

The irony was that Western governments wanted to impose standards of conduct in one of the areas of domestic policy-making—the treatment of ethnic minorities—where they had developed the *least* consensus among themselves about what constituted proper conduct. As discussed in Chapter 5, the EU had no acquis and there were no "European standards" on the protection of ethnic minority rights. Nevertheless, scholars widely agree that Western insistence eventually paid off, making the treatment of ethnic minorities in East Central Europe (ECE) one of the most vivid cases of successful EU conditionality.[9] In Romania and Slovakia, however, we see below that the departure of the illiberal rulers was a precondition for this success—and that even in Hungary the most important changes came immediately after the election of a less nationalist government.

Ethnic Minorities after Communism

Why did ethnic identity become an important factor in the domestic politics of many states emerging from communism? The virtual destruction of civil society twinned with the oppression of ethnic minority groups during communism compounded the saliency of ethnic identity during the transition. At a time when very few civic organizations existed that regrouped citizens *across* ethnic lines, organizations representing ethnic minority groups mobilized quickly to press their claims for cultural and political rights.[10] They viewed democratization as a great opportunity to gain power and protect their identity after long years of oppression. Meanwhile, unreconstructed communists and other opportunists mobilized ethnic majorities against them. The fear on the part of Western governments was that ruling elites in Romania and Slovakia were precipitating a vicious circle of ethnic intolerance by vilifying their minority groups. By 1994, verbal and legislative attacks by illiberal ruling parties and their extremist coalition partners had brought a strong, defensive reaction from the Hungarian government and from organizations representing the ethnic Hungarian minority in both states.[11] These organizations responded to intolerance, intimidation, and also their relative economic weakness by seeking to define and protect the minority's collective rights, to be expressed in various forms of cultural, political or territorial autonomy.[12]

The concept of autonomy is controversial, as it is based on the principle of collective rights that, unlike the principle of individual rights, has not been codified by the United Nations or the OSCE, or accepted by a majority of West European states.[13] From the early 1990s there was a tendency to invoke "European standards" as guidelines for how East European governments should treat their ethnic minorities, even though these did not exist. While Hungarian leaders liked to treat collective rights as a "European standard," many West European governments rejected them as firmly as the Slovak or Romanian government. As the Hungarian government pushed for collective rights for ethnic Hungarians in neighboring states, it portrayed itself as carrying the standard of "progressive" European values.

At first, West European governments kept a distance from the three-way disputes between ethnic Hungarian minorities, the Hungarian government and the Slovak or Romanian government. But the Council of Europe Parliamentary Assembly entered the fray in 1993 by passing Recommendation 1201 that called for autonomy for ethnic minorities in Eastern Europe in general terms, without specifying what kind. The EU then incorporated Recommendation 1201 into its own recommendations for how aspiring EU members in Eastern Europe should protect the rights of their ethnic minorities. By the mid-1990s, the EU was thus asking that East European states adopt more extensive provisions to protect ethnic minority rights than those adopted by most West European states. The only governments heard complaining loudly about Recommendation 1201 were the Romanian and Slovak governments. The Polish, Czech, and Hungarian governments would have had no reason to speak out; as fairly homogenous states, they had no ethnic minorities demanding autonomy.

The support for autonomy by ethnic Hungarian groups, and the opposition to autonomy by nationalist political parties, tended to become more intense over time. Ethnic Hungarian parties in Romania and Slovakia had all aspired to some level of autonomy, but by 1994 they had become radicalized in response to government harassment and were calling specifically for territorial autonomy.[14] The Antall government in Budapest supported their claims. Territorial autonomy, however, was completely unacceptable even to centrist political forces in both Romania and Slovakia. By advocating territorial autonomy, Hungarian parties became impossible allies for moderates and easy targets for nationalists, who seized the opportunity to tar all forms of autonomy with the brush of separatism and irredentism. Nationalist politicians in Romania and Slovakia subsequently equated all calls for autonomy—be it only cultural or educational—with separatism.[15] They "interpreted" the signals sent by the Hungarian minorities—and the Hungarian government in Budapest—in the most threatening possible light in order to lend credence to their claims of defending the nation.[16] To gain political capital, nationalists played up their fear of Hungary, and blurred the distinction between the policy of the Hungarian government and the rhetoric of Hungarian extremists calling for the creation of a "greater Hungary."[17]

The Traction of Western Actors on Hungary, Romania, and Slovakia

EU leverage backed by the careful diplomatic pressure of the OSCE High Commissioner on National Minorities (HCNM) had little traction on the illiberal governments in Romania and Slovakia, or on organizations representing the ethnic Hungarian minorities.[18] But Western leaders did have traction on a third party, the Hungarian government. Laying the groundwork for liberal democracy and a market economy was proceeding apace inside Hungary in conditions of vibrant political competition: the post-communist Socialists (MSZP) and the post-opposition Free Democrats (SZDSZ) were providing a very active and critical opposition to the ruling right-wing Democratic Forum (MDF) since its victory in the 1990 elections. But Hungary's foreign policy was increasingly viewed as nationalistic and destabilizing for the region. As such, it became one of the first targets of the EU's emerging active leverage in 1994 and 1995.[19]

In 1990 József Antall famously declared that he would like to be the prime minister "in spirit" of fifteen million Hungarians—more than the 10.5 million Hungarians in Hungary (and even more than the 13.5 million Hungarians actually living in the region).[20] Improving the conditions of ethnic Hungarians abroad became the priority of the Antall government, trumping even domestic reforms. From the point of view of Western actors, two problems emerged. First, the government implied the possibility of a new European settlement leading to the peaceful revision of borders and allowing Hungary to regain some of the territory that it lost to Romania, Czechoslovakia, and Yugoslavia at the Treaty of Trianon in 1920.[21] Second, the government refused to conclude bilateral agreements known as "Basic Treaties" with Romania and Slovakia recognizing the existing borders unless those treaties also guaranteed collective rights for ethnic minorities. Henceforth, Hungary's relations with neighboring states harboring a Hungarian minority were to be determined by how this minority was treated.[22] MDF Foreign Minister Géza Jeszenszky explained that there could be no question "of making friends over the heads of the Hungarian minorities of three and a half million." Using language criticized in the West, Jeszenszky stated that relations would depend on "when and which of our neighbors recognize the need to abandon the policy of oppressing and applying petty restrictions on Hungarian and non-Hungarian minorities and of trying to create homogeneous nation-states."[23]

In its defense, the Antall government only attempted to leave open the possibility of a peaceful revision of borders sometime in the future, and it pursued exclusively political—never military—channels in its efforts to protect Hungarian minorities. Pál Dunay argues that ambiguity about the borders undermined what was otherwise a responsible and peaceful security policy.[24] The Antall government's chief activity was persistently to bring the issue of the rights of Hungarian minorities to the attention of international fora. It eschewed military strategies even in the face of the threat of very severe harassment of ethnic Hungarians in Vojvodina by the Serbian regime of Slobodan Milošević.

Nevertheless, the tendency of government officials to imply the possibility of border changes and their fixation with ethnic Hungarians abroad earned the Democratic Forum-led government the label "nationalist"—particularly after its vice-chairman István Csurka published an anti-semitic, racist, and revisionist article in August 1992 that received much international attention.[25] Western warnings to Antall and Jeszenszky mounted, leading to the demotion and eventual expulsion of Csurka from the MDF in June 1993.[26]

The Antall government was worked on in several other ways. Western governments made it very clear that they prioritized good relations between Hungary and its neighbors well ahead of the collective rights of ethnic minorities. Many Western actors downplayed Recommendation 1201, and asked the Hungarian government to put regional stability first. The Antall government's vocal criticism of the Romanian and Slovak governments, and its attempts to use international organizations to amplify this criticism, were considered unhelpful, mirroring charges from Bucharest and Bratislava that Budapest was engaged in "excessive dramatization" of the minority rights issue.[27] The West's pressure came most strongly to bear on Hungary when it sought to veto Slovakia's admittance to the Council of Europe in June 1993. The Antall government wanted to use the Council's leverage to force the Slovak government to make further policy changes. But the West Europeans and Americans strongly preferred inclusion in the Council as the way to deal with Slovakia, fearing otherwise that the Mečiar government would turn completely away from the West. The Antall government bowed to Western pressure, and abstained from the vote.[28]

By pressuring Hungary, Western governments also sought to stop statements by the government that gave ammunition to neighboring nationalists, making their message of a "Hungarian threat" more credible and ultimately helping nationalists win elections.[29] Slovak opposition leaders as well as Western and Hungarian observers, for example, believed that Budapest's demands for better treatment of the ethnic Hungarian minority during the summer of 1994 helped the HZDS win the elections in Slovakia that autumn.[30] The Antall government was also asked to put pressure on ethnic Hungarian groups in Slovakia and Romania to abandon their demands for territorial autonomy and "to reconcile themselves with where they live."[31]

In contrast to collective rights for ethnic minorities, Western governments did have unanimous and deeply held views about preserving existing borders and establishing good relations among neighboring states that came through loud and clear in their dealings with Hungary. The "Stability Pact" of French Prime Minister Edouard Balladur, first introduced in 1993, established the requirement of good neighborliness, making absolutely clear that the protection of ethnic minority rights, the marginalization of intolerant discourse in domestic politics, and in particular the resolution of disputes with neighboring states were the sine qua non of any moves toward EU membership, or indeed European respectability. The Stability Pact was born directly of France's frustrations with the EU's inability to bring about a diplomatic end to the Yugoslav wars, and in the context of these wars the Balladur plan was positively received in EU capitals and accepted by EU foreign ministers in December 1993 as the first Joint Action of the EU's Common Foreign and Security Policy (CFSP).[32]

The Balladur Plan was greeted with little interest in Warsaw and Prague. Poland, which had signed treaties of good relations with all seven of its neighbors, declared that it had already accomplished on its own everything that the Pact asked of East Central European states. Poland, like Hungary, had large populations of coethnics in neighboring countries—in Lithuania, Belarus, and Ukraine. But Polish Foreign Minister Krzysztof Skubiszewski had invoked "European standards" quite differently from Hungarian Foreign Minister Jeszensky, in part to subdue any expectations by Polish minority leaders that Warsaw would support extensive collective rights. The Polish government managed to establish good relations with neighboring governments while also renewing ties and extending support to ethnic Polish minority groups.[33] The Czechs, with no coethnics abroad and few minorities at home, were largely indifferent. But the prospect of the March 1995 conference did cause Hungary and Slovakia to sign their long-delayed Basic Treaty, and it pushed the troubled negotiation of a Basic Treaty between Hungary and Romania forward. The debate on which states would be invited to join NATO opened in earnest in 1996, and provided significant additional momentum to the negotiations between Hungary and Romania, including very strong pressure from the American embassies in Budapest and Bucharest.

In Hungary, the election of 1994 had brought a substantially less nationalist government to power. In contrast to Antall's MDF government, the coalition government of the Socialist Party (MSZP) and of the Free Democrats (SZDSZ) led by Prime Minister Gyula Horn declared that Hungarian minorities would no longer be the sine qua non of good relations with Romania and Slovakia. While the basic objectives of Hungarian foreign policy were to remain the same, the methods and style were to change substantially. Socialist Foreign Minister László Kovács promised a foreign policy free of any "sense of mission," history lessons, references to past merits or grievances, and statements that could be misinterpreted.[34] The Horn government demanded provisions for limited collective rights in the Basic Treaties, but it also encouraged the Hungarian minority leaders in Slovakia and Romania to moderate their demands, and overlooked some legislative attacks on ethnic minorities in the Romanian and the Slovak parliament.

Despite provocations by the Slovak and Romanian governments, and despite some protests by Hungarian minority leaders, the Horn government signed Basic Treaties with Slovakia in 1995 and with Romania in 1996 under strong pressure from EU and American officials.[35] Both treaties incorporated Recommendation 1201 on autonomy for minority groups, making it legally binding—but the Mečiar and Iliescu governments broadcast their intention not to implement it. The Slovak parliament stalled ratification until a year later, when it simultaneously passed the Law on the Protection of the Republic that called for the prosecution of individuals who organize "subversive" rallies or spread "false" information that could damage national interests.[36] (In any case, Romania and Slovakia had already made empty promises to abide by Recommendation 1201 as a condition for entering the Council of Europe.) However fervently the Iliescu and the Mečiar governments planned to ignore the provisions for collective rights, it would suit very well the interests of future, less nationalist governments that these bilateral treaties with Hungary—treaties that raised so many difficult questions of history and national sovereignty—had already been signed.

For Hungary, the Antall government's fixation with ethnic Hungarians abroad and its vague statements about peaceful border changes had come into open conflict with its goal of attaining EU and NATO membership. By 1994, some officials and journalists hinted that Hungary was no longer on the list of states likely to join NATO in the first wave.[37] But Western leaders stepped in and put direct pressure on Hungarian governments to sign the Basic Treaties with Slovakia and Romania. Had Hungary not signed the treaties, it would have been excluded from the first group of states to join NATO and begin negotiations with the EU. That Hungary did sign the treaties was celebrated by Western governments who now applauded Hungary as a wellspring of stability in East Central and South Eastern Europe.

History would repeat itself, in a blander form: The next right-wing government of Hungary, led by Prime Minister Viktor Orban (1998–2002) of the Young Democrats (FIDESZ), implemented the "extraterritorial" Hungarian Status Law giving ethnic Hungarians living abroad extensive rights in Hungary. Orban, a consummate populist, amended the law only after sustained and direct pressure from the EU and other Western actors. Raising alarms in the EU, Orban was allegedly courting the far right Hungarian Justice and Life Party as a likely coalition partner after the 2002 elections, but as in the 1994 elections this party did not clear the 5 percent threshold to enter parliament. And like the MDF in 1994, FIDESZ in 2002 was defeated by the Social Democrats (MSZP) in part because Hungarian voters considered that, once again, the right had overplayed its hand at home and immodestly projected Hungarian nationalism into its foreign policy abroad.[38]

6.2.2   *Leveraging Illiberal Rulers in Romania, Bulgaria, and Slovakia*

Western governments and international organizations did succeed in convincing illiberal rulers in Romania and Slovakia to sign the Basic Treaties guaranteeing extensive provisions for the protection of ethnic minority rights with Hungary. However, this was purely "formal compliance" since neither the Iliescu government nor the Mečiar government showed any intention of implementing them. As we look at each of the three illiberal pattern states here in turn, we see that illiberal rulers were savvy in playing it both ways: they acted like liberal Western reformers on the international stage, they presented themselves as such to parts of their domestic audience, but to please their domestic power base they pursued domestic policies that were at loggerheads with liberal democracy, economic reform, and ethnic tolerance. For their part, Western actors were caught between two perceived dangers: isolating the newly democratizing states, or conferring Western legitimacy on their illiberal rulers. As we have already seen, they erred toward legitimacy and inclusion.

Ethnic tolerance was understandably of great importance to the EU and to Western governments; economic corruption, in contrast, was a less urgent concern. The victims were ordinary citizens with more diffuse grievances and also with less information about the causes of their grievances than well-organized ethnic minority groups that were persecuted by ruling elites. Ironically, however, in the early 1990s the West had much more shared knowledge and many more standards to impart in the area of regulating a free market economy. And as we will see in the next chapter, once blatant problems with democratic standards and ethnic minority protection are addressed, the leverage of the EU refocuses on reforming of the economy—and on reforming the state so that it can properly regulate it.

Romania

Romania's Iliescu was a master at presenting himself as a Western reformer to the Romanian electorate, and also making sure that those who argued otherwise were discredited and sidelined in Romanian politics. With a firm hold on power and an absence of ideological affinity for Western liberal democracy, it seems surprising that the Iliescu government would chart for Romania the same foreign policy course as East European governments that were sincerely committed to joining the liberal democratic West. Indeed, ambiguity as to whether Iliescu's National Salvation Front (FSN) preferred a western or an eastern orientation persisted into 1991 as Iliescu looked to Moscow as well as the West for economic and geopolitical support. Romania distinguished itself as the only former Warsaw Pact state that agreed to a clause in its friendship treaty with the Soviet Union precluding membership in NATO (specifically, in any military alliance that could be construed as directed against the other state).[39]

But Iliescu soon recognized that a superficially Western orientation would bring greater domestic legitimacy as well as economic assistance while placing few constraints on his domestic rule. Iliescu pursued a strategy of formal compliance to shore up his image as a democratic leader welcomed in the West. He worked zealously to obtain an association agreement with the EU, membership in the Council of Europe and closer ties with NATO. Agreements with Western institutions lent credibility to the FSN's "reformist" character at home, while qualifying Romania for trade and investment from the West. The Iliescu government sought these rewards of Western acceptance without reference to the violent illiberal political acts it perpetrated at home, taking advantage of the West's deep fear of isolating potentially unstable states after the war broke out in the former Yugoslavia in 1991.[40]

Romania was able to conclude major agreements with the European Union, the Council of Europe and NATO despite few improvements to its democratic standards and its protection of minority rights, though violence directed against ethnic Hungarians and opposition protestors was ended. As discussed in Chapter 4, the EU signed a Trade and Cooperation Agreement in 1991 and later an Association Agreement in 1993 with the Iliescu government. There were substantial delays as EU governments and the EU parliament worried about the undemocratic behavior of the Romanian government, but eventually the EU let Romania conclude both agreements. The delays appear to have had no immediate domestic consequences for Iliescu and his party the FSN, renamed the Democratic National Salvation Front (FDSN) in 1992, and the Party of Social Democracy of Romania (PDSR) in 1993.[41]

The Council of Europe also imposed significant delays on Romania's entry. It commissioned several reports that criticized extensively the rule of law, the security services, the freedom of the press, and the rights of minorities under the Iliescu government. Romania finally became a member in October 1994; the documents by which it was admitted included nine amendments and three sub-amendments calling on Romania to improve substantially in upholding democratic standards and protecting the rights of ethnic minorities. Regardless, Council of Europe membership broadcast that the West accepted the Iliescu-led ruling elite, even as the Iliescu government immediately discounted and even attacked the Council's recommendations.[42] The very week that Romania was admitted, anti-Hungarian attacks by Iliescu, by ruling parties in parliament and by pro-government newspapers, continued apace. The PDSR government "launched a huge mass-media propaganda campaign" against Recommendation 1201 that it had just pledged to uphold.[43] In January 1995, safely admitted to the Council, Iliescu's PDSR entered into a formal coalition agreement with the three extremist parties that had been supporting it informally in parliament since it lost its majority in the 1992 elections.[44]

Iliescu even used Western acceptance as a weapon against the opposition. He sought to blame the delay in Romania's admission to the Council of Europe on the unpatriotic plotting of the opposition and of the Hungarian minority. He asserted that the West had changed its position vis-à-vis Romania and now admitted that "it was wrong to put its faith in Romania's losers and not in those representing the popular option; that is, the election winners."[45] In an unprecedented move, Iliescu sent a new agreement signed with the IMF to parliament for a vote. Paradoxically the reformist parties in opposition abstained or voted against the IMF agreement, while the leftist and nationalist parties pushed it through parliament. The reformers voted against the agreement in an attempt to stem the tide of Western legitimacy being conferred on the Iliescu government.[46]

Another aspect of Iliescu's strategy of seeking Western approbation was the Romanian government's unbridled enthusiasm for NATO's Partnership for Peace program. On January 26, 1994 Romania became the first former Warsaw Pact member state to sign a PFP agreement, which merited several hours of prime time coverage on state-run television. PFP was so attractive because it refrained from differentiating among post-communist states on the basis of whether progress was being made toward liberal democracy.[47]

The Iliescu government did avoid receiving démarches from the EU in 1994, 1995, and 1996—years when the Mečiar government in Slovakia was getting one or two a year. Some observers attribute the change of name of the Democratic National Salvation Front (FDSN) to the Party of Social Democracy of Romania (PDSR) to Iliescu's savvy strategy of deflecting responsibility for his initial three years of violence on the job.[48] It is likely that the EU's budding active leverage moderated the PDSR's extreme scapegoating of ethnic Hungarians, its use of violence against opposition protestors, and its interference in democratic elections. Had such events happened in 1994 or later, they would likely have elicited a flurry of démarches addressed to Bucharest. Instead, the Iliescu government did finally sign the Basic Treaty with Hungary in 1996 (ending its coalition with the extreme right wing parties which withdrew in protest).

What is more, the Iliescu government did not significantly tamper with the 1996 parliamentary or presidential elections, even though it had months of warning that the PDSR was likely to fair quite badly in both of them.[49] Instead, the PDSR launched a vicious campaign centered on anti-Hungarian nationalism, anti-semitism, and charges that the opposition was planning a communist witch-hunt, a ruinous economic reform program, an end to state pension payments, and the restoration of the monarchy.[50] Iliescu himself adopted extreme right-wing rhetoric in his campaign against the opposition candidate Emile Constantinescu between the first round of the presidential election and the runoff. He accused the UDMR of plotting the secession of Transylvania and the "Yugoslavization" of Romania; indeed, his rhetoric was so extreme that Romania's premier extremist Corneliu Vadim Tudor charged him of plagiarism. Iliescu's television spots warned, "Workers, farmers, tenants, Romanians, beware! You will lose your jobs, your land, your homes. The country could break up."[51] Iliescu was caught in his own trap: he realized he would not be able to satisfy both the elite that benefited from corruption and partial reform of the economy, and the ordinary workers whose living standards suffered at the hands of this "directocracy." He tried once again to distract ordinary Romanians with fear for their nation and for their own economic survival. But this time it did not work. While Iliescu again succeeded in capturing most of the rural and peasant vote, it was particularly his loss of votes among manual workers in Romania's more industrialized regions that handed victory to Constantinescu.[52]

Bulgaria

Bulgaria is the most ambivalent case, in part because the Bulgarian Socialist Party (BSP) government itself was more openly ambivalent about the EU in the early 1990s, and in part because it was not as organized in practicing illiberal politics. The BSP won the 1990 election chiefly by promising to protect voters from the harsh consequences of economic reform, and also by presenting itself as the defender of the Bulgarian nation. But in October 1991 the Union of Democratic Forces (UDF) won a narrow plurality in the parliamentary elections, and formed a minority government which depended upon the tacit support of the Movement for Rights and Freedoms (MRF). After Prime Minister Filip Dimitrov's UDF government took office, there were some notable changes of foreign policy: the UDF sought to limit Bulgaria's dependence on Moscow and to render itself a more credible partner for Western states and institutions. The Council of Europe, backed by the EU and the CSCE, had pressured Bulgaria to change Article 11.4 of the Constitution that forbids the creation of ethnic and religious parties. In May 1992, Bulgaria was admitted to the Council of Europe after the Constitutional Court blocked attempts to use this article to exclude the ethnic Turkish MRF from politics.

The UDF-led government fell in just one year and was replaced by an ostensibly non-partisan government of experts headed by Lyuben Berov, and also supported by the MRF. The Berov government was close to the BSP, depending on its support in parliament, and tended to stress Bulgaria's historic and religious ties to Russia. Bulgaria went through the motions of signing a European Agreement with the EU in 1993, but the Berov government was certainly not appealing to Brussels for greater guidance and for accelerating the timetable for EU membership. In contrast, President Zhelyu Zhelev, a former leader of the opposition UDF in the fall of 1989, was a vocal and committed advocate for Bulgaria's Western course. Bulgarian citizens, for their part, were among the most pro-EU in the whole of post-communist Europe. EU aside, by 1994 Bulgarian foreign policy had achieved much that was praiseworthy (though often overlooked by the West): good relations with both Greece and Turkey, early recognition of independent Macedonia, and a successful enforcement of the very costly embargo against Serbia.[53]

The BSP promised voters gradual market reforms leading to a prosperous economy and EU membership. After the BSP won a majority in the 1994 elections, it was just as unresponsive to the EU's emerging active leverage as the HZDS and the PDSR. But the EU and other external actors were paying less attention to the BSP government because it was not involved in a three-way dispute with an ethnic minority and a coethnic government. The BSP did use anti-Turk sentiment in its election campaigns. Yet the Turkish MRF supported several BSP governments and seemed relatively well integrated into the structure of the Bulgarian stae and society.[54] The EU's active leverage was geared in 1995 and 1996 toward solving problems involving ethnic minorities and borders—and not toward curbing the rampant rent-seeking that was impoverishing the Bulgarian people.

As we explored in Chapter 2, the corruption of the partially reformed economy by elites close to the BSP was spectacular. The BSP's economic policies were obviously at complete loggerheads with EU rules—and these policies led to the collapse of the economy in 1996. In the run up to the collapse, the EU did not put significant pressure on the BSP government—in part because of a lack of understanding of what was going on in Bulgaria, since the EU's Opinions were not yet written. Economic collapse accompanied by massive demonstrations—Bulgaria's revolution in the streets, postponed from 1989—brought down the government in late 1996.[55]

Slovakia

Slovakia is the richest and most interesting case of a rent-seeking government forsaking its place in the EU's membership queue, impervious to the very sustained and direct pressure of the EU and other Western actors to change its domestic policies. Slovakia's Movement for a Democratic Slovakia (HZDS) government stayed in office until 1998, outliving the illiberal governments in Romania and Bulgaria. It was thus exposed for the longest time to the EU's active leverage, and the lengths that the EU went to pressure the Slovak government were quite extraordinary. The presumption before 1994 had been that the Slovak Republic would join the EU along with the Czech Republic; its economy and state capacity were generally regarded by EU officials as equal to the task. Most important, economic reforms that took place in the whole of Czechoslovakia from 1990 to 1992 had created a strong foundation for a successful capitalist economy in Slovakia. A place in the first group of post-communist states invited to start negotiations for EU membership was Slovakia's to lose; indeed, to lose that place would take some effort.

As it turned out, Slovakia's second and third Mečiar governments were quite prepared to make this effort. In particular, the third HZDS-led government of Prime Minister Mečiar demonstrated just how little rent-seeking elites would budge under pressure to change domestic policies that were integral to their domestic sources of power. While the third Mečiar government declared in 1994 that joining the EU was its foremost foreign policy task, it practiced "formal compliance," promising but not delivering improvements in areas such as the protection of ethnic minority rights. Thanks to Slovakia's high state capacity, it also practiced "selective compliance," tasking government agencies to adopt large tracts of the acquis, all the while violating basic democratic standards. By the time the EU published its Opinions on the applications of all ten East European candidates in 1997, Slovakia had failed quite spectacularly to meet the Copenhagen political criteria in the areas of democracy and the protection of ethnic minority rights.

In the case of Slovakia, the EU resorted to the "démarche"—a formal diplomatic note criticizing actions taken by the government—as a tool of active leverage.[56] The démarches were unsuccessful in compelling the Mečiar government to end chauvinist and corrupt practices, but it is difficult to know how much the démarches restrained the HZDS and its extremist coalition partners on the margins. Most observers, however, judged the effects of the démarches on Mečiar's behavior to be very small. Still, they were useful to the opposition because they did frighten the government away from a few anti-democratic excesses, such as the expulsion of the democratically elected Democratic Union party from parliament in 1994, and because eventually they did embarrass the government in front of the Slovak public.[57]

The EU's first serious warning came in the form of a démarche on November 23, 1994, condemning in diplomatic language the concentration of political power in the hands of the three ruling parties at the parliament's first post-election meeting on November 3–4 (known as the "night of the long knives"). Slovakia's application for full EU membership was accepted in June 1995, but concern was mounting about the Mečiar government's blatant moves to suppress political competition and evade accountability, including attacks on rival parliamentary parties and the apparent kidnapping of the President's son. The EU's second démarche on October 25, 1995 (followed by a démarche from the US government on October 27) was worded more sharply. It pointed to the continuing concentration of power in the hands of the government, calling for the return of representatives of the opposition to government bodies and expressing concern about the deepening conflict between the prime minister and the president. Referring to Mečiar's attempts to discredit and even dislodge President Michal Kováč, the démarche emphasized the importance of mutual toleration and respect to the different sources of authority in the state.[58]

Following on the second démarche, EU leaders warned that Slovakia risked falling from its place among the leading group in the EU's membership queue, though observers widely agreed that the EU's signals could have been clearer.[59] The European Parliament was more explicit, passing a resolution on November 16, 1995 that criticized specific actions of the Mečiar government, including the efforts by the prime minister to have members of the Democratic Union political party expelled from the Slovak parliament, harassment of politicians and journalists investigating the kidnapping of the President's son, and the failure to grant opposition parties in the Slovak parliament adequate representation. The European Parliament followed up in December 1996 and again in October 1997 with even more critical resolutions in reaction to the intimidation and unconstitutional expulsion of parliamentary deputy František Gaulieder who had defected from the HZDS, and subsequently to the parliament's refusal to reinstate him in violation of the instructions of the Constitutional Court.[60] In May 1997 the HZDS government violated the constitution again by removing a question on the direct election of the president from the ballot in a referendum that was otherwise on NATO membership; the referendum ended in a fiasco.[61] What followed was a chorus of disapprobation from representatives of EU member states, the US government, EU institutions and other international organizations.[62]

What is striking is that Mečiar managed for years to use the démarches as a "confirmation and not a criticism of his own national policies."[63] Mečiar controlled parts of the mainstream media, most importantly the state television, and there he could characterize the démarches as evidence of Slovakia's close relationship with the EU. He would make light of them, downplay their negative tone, and claim that they issued from Slovakia's close relationship with the EU.

He was helped by the fact that many citizens did not find the activities criticized by the EU objectionable—though they might object to Mečiar failing to bring Slovakia into the EU.[64] So Mečiar also claimed that there was no need to worry about the admission of Slovakia "because they need us, for we are a country with an exceptionally good geopolitical situation."[65] Like Iliescu, the Mečiar government also engaged in the "mystification" of its position on EU and NATO membership: government representatives made contradictory statements designed to placate various constituencies, expressing virtually every conceivable position on Slovakia's relationship with the EU. As the prospect of an invitation at the Luxembourg summit to start negotiations faded, government representatives turned to obfuscating the costs of a deteriorating relationship with the EU, suggesting that no countries would be joining the EU in the near term, or indeed that joining would not be all that beneficial for Slovakia.[66]

Also like the PDSR in Romania, the HZDS portrayed the domestic opposition as disloyal, charging that it tarnished Slovakia's image abroad with unfounded criticism of the HZDS government in a naked bid for political power. HZDS agricultural minister Peter Baco, for example, described an article in the *Economist* as part of a "massive disinformation campaign" [by the Slovak opposition] aimed at "the liquidation of Slovakia on international soil."[67] Remarkably, Mečiar managed to persuade his core electoral support—about 25 percent of the population—that the country's failure to be invited to join the EU and NATO was the fault of the opposition, who were accused of "damaging Slovakia's international standing by spreading false and negative information."[68]

By the time the European Commission published the Opinions on each of the candidates for EU membership as part of its Agenda 2000 package in July 1997, elections in Romania and Bulgaria had already replaced rent-seeking political parties with more reform-oriented parties in government. Slovakia was alone among the ten East European candidates to be judged unqualified in the Commission's reports to open negotiations because it was in violation of the Copenhagen *political* criteria. Romania and Bulgaria (as well as Lithuania and Latvia) were also not on the list to open negotiations, but the Commission explained that this was merely because they did not satisfy the Copenhagen *economic* criteria.[69] Even in the period between the publication of the Commission's recommendations in July 1997 and the vote of the European Council at the Luxembourg Summit in December 1997, EU leaders and Commission officials told the Mečiar government that an invitation to begin negotiations could still be possible if the government reversed certain policies, for example, reinstating opposition politicians to parliamentary committees and legalizing the use of ethnic minority languages.[70] This was to no avail: the Mečiar government made no changes.

In the run-up to the December 1997 decision, however, the EU's active leverage was limited by the EU's failure to suspend its Europe Agreement with Slovakia. By the time the Europe Agreement was ratified and came into full effect in 1995, the EU already had very serious doubts about the Mečiar government's democratic credentials. It would have been counterproductive to cut off PHARE aid and other foreign assistance that helped support a mosaic of non-government actors and projects in Slovakia. But Slovak ruling elites relied heavily on revenues from a small circle of economic elites that owned enterprises whose exports were enabled by the Europe Agreement. Suspending access to the EU market would therefore have amounted to a serious economic sanction, but it was never considered—even though the Europe Agreements included provisions stipulating that democracy and ethnic minority rights must be upheld in order for the Agreement to be valid.[71] EU officials explained publicly that the Europe Agreements were viewed as the groundwork for integrating—not isolating—eastern candidates. It was also the case that Western producers would have suffered losses from the suspension of free trade with Slovakia.[72]

The Mečiar government was able to keep up a reformist charade for much of its four-year term. Only in the last year did this become unsustainable as it was condemned as undemocratic by a succession of EU and also American politicians and officials. Still, Mečiar did not change his behavior to stem the flow of Western criticism—instead, he turned against the EU, denouncing what he called a Western plot against Slovakia and embracing Moscow. The EU went furthest in Slovakia in using the tools of active leverage in a deliberate attempt to influence outcomes in domestic politics. Instead of slowly reeling the Mečiar government in and convincing it to comply with EU requirements, however, the EU's active leverage eventually compelled Mečiar to do the opposite: to abandon his pro-Western façade and look for more and more support from Moscow.[73] Forcing Mečiar to go East, however, helped the opposition parties to win the 1998 elections because most Slovak voters clearly preferred to go West.

6.2.3 Alternative Explanations

In Chapter 3 we explored competing explanations for the behavior of East European governments that failed to satisfy the requirements of EU membership. Two come up again here. Did ruling elites in Romania, Bulgaria, and Slovakia have just as much political will to comply with the EU's requirements as neighboring states, only they were hampered by the weakness of the economy, the feebleness of the state administration, or even the backwardness of the political culture in their countries? After all, shortcomings in their economic and administrative performance could be a consequence of the structure of the economy and the state inherited from communism, and not a consequence of the actions of the politicians in power after 1989. In other words, the variation we observe could be attributed to different levels of economic and administrative ability, and not to different political responses to the incentives of EU membership. Second, did the EU treat Romania and Bulgaria unfairly, painting an exaggerated picture of ethnic intolerance and economic corruption, in order to keep them out of the pre-accession process because their relative poverty and backwardness made them undesirable members?

The evidence against both of these competing explanations is very substantial. First, the EU placed great emphasis on democratic standards and the protection of ethnic minority rights when evaluating the candidates. Whatever the weakness of the state administration and the imbroglio of economic reform, EU governments focused on the efforts of governments to support political pluralism and build ethnic tolerance. These were almost wholly under the control of the ruling parties. Had the EU wanted to disadvantage poor states, it could have prioritized economic performance and overall wealth instead.

Second, when the PDSR, BSP, and HZDS governments lost power, the state could very quickly rehabilitate itself in the eyes of the EU. Again, this shows that the fate of the candidate in the eyes of the EU was in the hands of the ruling elites. [74] It was not predetermined by the state's structural weakness, or by the EU's discriminatory treatment. If the agenda of the EU had been to hinder these states in the pre-accession process, it would not have rehabilitated them so quickly after elections brought reform-minded elites to office. After all, problems of state capacity and economic backwardness could not be solved overnight.

The EU was looking first for political changes such as improving pluralism, the rule of law, the transparency of public administration and the protection of ethnic minority rights. The fact that Bulgaria's relationship with the EU and other Western actors improved dramatically during the one-year UDF government of Prime Minister Filip Dimitrov in 1990–1, and so did Slovakia's during the six month coalition government of Prime Minister Jozsef Moravčík in 1994, speaks to the political nature of the EU's judgments of the BSP and HZDS governments. In other words, it was not structural factors such as poverty and administrative incompetence that set the tone. What set the tone were the policies being implemented by ruling elites. This is not to say, however, that the EU did enough to support reformers once they were elected in economically backward candidates where the project of reform was fraught with greater difficulties. Moreover, the point should not be overdrawn: economically more advanced states could much more quickly overcome their years of illiberal rule as measured by their timetable for EU membership, as Slovakia would demonstrate after 1998 (and Croatia after 2000).

A third alternative explanation asks whether the power of international norms would not have sooner or later led to compliance by the illiberal rulers.

Thomas Risse presents a model of "argumentative self-entrapment" whereby oppressive states commit to improving human rights for instrumental reasons, to pacify international criticism—exactly the sort of behavior we see on the part of the Iliescu and Mečiar governments. In Risse's model, however, governments find themselves "increasingly forced to justify their behavior in front of international and domestic audiences until they are engaged in a true dialogue with their critics." Rulers make tactical concessions for instrumental reasons, but these concessions usually mean that they cease to deny the validity of the international norms and instead only reject specific allegations of norm violations. This creates a new "dialogue that results in arguing and processes of persuasion whereby at least some actors listen to argumentation and are prepared to change their views, preferences, or even identities".[75]

Simplifying Risse's argument, we can ask whether the Iliescu government in Romania or the Mečiar government in Slovakia had already fallen into "argumentative entrapment" by signing onto progressive standards of liberal democracy and minority rights in Council of Europe texts as well as in treaties with Hungary and association agreements with the EU. Risse finds no cases where moves along the socialization path were not accompanied by behavioral changes over time. Following Risse's logic, therefore, if Iliescu's PDSR or Mečiar's HZDS had stayed in power after 1996 and 1998 respectively, they would have gradually been socialized away from their brand of illiberal democracy. Mečiar's actions, however, provide the best evidence against socialization, since the violations of democratic standards by the HZDS came in fits and starts, with no trend of improvement despite increasing domestic mobilization and international pressure aimed at forcing the government to reform. If anything, the trend was toward greater (and more desperate) violations of democratic standards, exemplified by the government's obstruction of a referendum in 1997. Individual members of the PDSR and the HZDS, however, did leave the party and change their political agendas. As discussed earlier, it is difficult to prove that they did so because they were persuaded of the intrinsic value of liberal democracy and minority rights, as opposed to being persuaded of their usefulness as part of a promising new political agenda.

6.3   Making Political Systems More Competitive

I argued in Chapter 1 and 2 that what distinguished liberal pattern states from illiberal ones was that they developed a more competitive political system, causing ruling political parties to implement political and economic reforms more completely and more rapidly. I argue in this section that EU leverage helped create what the illiberal pattern states were missing at the moment of transition: a coherent and moderate opposition, and an open and pluralistic political arena. In conditions of regular, free, and fair elections, the EU's active leverage had a hand, over time, in making the political systems of the illiberal states more competitive.

6.3.1   *Leveraging the Institutional and the Information Environment*

Once the EU began to judge the quality of reform in aspiring member states and to link its assessments publicly to a candidate's prospect for EU membership, it influenced domestic politics by helping to change the institutional environment in illiberal democracies. The key was the impact of the EU's active leverage on opposition political parties and other groups in society.[76] These domestic actors served as the interlocutor between the EU and the electorate, and they were the only realistic vehicle for rapid change given the intransigence of the ruling political parties. It was the interplay of domestic opposition actors and the EU's active leverage (and not external pressure alone) that helped bring political change.

The EU helped change the institutional environment in three ways: First, it provided a *focal point for cooperation* among opposition political forces. Second, along with other international actors, it offered information useful to opposition elites that were *adapting* to a political and economic agenda compatible with EU membership. Finally, it offered immediate rewards for political parties that secured the *implementation* of such an agenda once they came to power. All together, these three mechanisms influenced the course of political change in each country by shaping the political parties that took office after the 1996 elections in Romania, the 1997 elections in Bulgaria, and the 1998 elections in Slovakia. Let us look at each of these three mechanisms in turn.

First, securing EU membership became a *focal point for cooperation* among very different opposition political parties and civic groups. In Romania and Slovakia large numbers of small parties of the center left and center right competed (and feuded) with one another, substantially weakening the power of moderate voices in parliament through wasted votes and infighting. Liberal, pro-Western actors in these countries had little or no history of cooperation in an opposition movement against communism to help establish habits of compromise and organizational strength.[77] Meanwhile, the ruling political parties worked hard to undermine and divide the opposition parties by manipulating the electoral laws and labeling critics of government policy as unpatriotic. While their differences on matters of social and economic policy spanned the entire moderate (and sometimes immoderate) political spectrum, electoral defeats in the early 1990s showed that the opposition forces would have to band together in order to unseat the ruling elites. Attacking the ruling elites for forsaking the country's "return to Europe" and promising to move the country decisively toward EU membership formed an important part of an electoral platform that all of the opposition forces could agree on.

Second, Western actors offered information to opposition political elites that were *adapting* to a political and economic agenda compatible with liberal democracy and comprehensive market reform. Parties of the center-right and center-left had been neither strong nor unified in these countries after 1989, nor had they necessarily been "moderate" or "liberal." Over the course of the 1990s, many opposition politicians shifted substantially their position on ethnic minority rights and on economic reform to make their parties fit the increasingly attractive "pro-EU space" on the political spectrum. What motivated individual political elites was in each case a different mixture of political calculation, on the one hand, and a desire to learn about and promote "European" norms and values, on the other. From the PDSR in Romania and the HZDS in Slovakia there was a steady defection of politicians to the opposition parties, suggesting that these individuals considered the long-term prospects of the opposition parties more attractive than the short-term gains of remaining part of the ruling clique.[78]

Western representatives of international institutions, governments and non-governmental organizations were on hand with information for opposition politicians and local civil society leaders on the substance of a liberal democratic agenda, placing particular emphasis on political accountability, on fostering an open pluralistic political arena, and on rights for ethnic minorities within this arena, ideally decoupling questions of ethnicity from those of citizenship. Many different Western organizations and governments were involved in supporting opposition groups with financial assistance, and interacting with opposition elites at meetings, workshops and conferences in national capitals and abroad.[79] Local opposition elites often moved directly from Western-funded NGOs or academic institutions into politics.

In the Slovak case, local NGOs played a special role, compensating for the weakness of opposition parties with extensive surveillance and criticism of the illiberal government, and eventually creating the momentum for cooperation among the opposition parties. Grzegorz Ekiert and Jan Kubik note the "virtuous circle" between Polish domestic organizations and their Western partners, which provided support critical to establishing a strong civil society in Poland in the early 1990s. Yet the most support was channeled to the three liberal states that needed it least—at the expense of "deepening vicious circles" elsewhere.[80] In the mid 1990s, a "virtuous" circle emerged most clearly in Slovakia (and the "Slovak model" for turning civil society against illiberal rulers was then "exported"—by Slovak NGOs"!—to Croatia). By the late 1990s, Western funding for and attention to NGOs in South-eastern Europe, including in Bulgaria and Romania, had increased. Western assistance to

NGOs in post-communist Europe is an important topic that is beyond my scope here. But it is clear that with Western assistance civil society has also become stronger and more vibrant in Romania and especially Bulgaria since the mid-1990s (see Table 7.1).[81]

Third, the character of the EU's pre-accession process required *implementation*: in order to deliver on promises to improve the country's standing in the EU's pre-accession process, opposition politicians would have to follow through with extensive political and economic reforms once in office. To this end, they knew they would have to improve democratic standards, ethnic tolerance, and market reforms in keeping with the Copenhagen criteria. In other words, they knew that their pre-election rhetoric would be judged against their post-election actions in the EU's Regular Reports. This fact lends the adapting and learning process described above much more weight, and pinpoints how the hard-won reward of membership distinguishes the conditionality of the EU from that of other international actors.

The EU's active leverage also helped change the information environment in the country. Most simply, the fact that the EU moved decisively forward with implementing the pre-accession process after the December 1994 Essen summit eventually changed the terms of the debate about who was a Western reformer among Eastern Europe's ruling political parties. While the Commission did not have an information strategy as such, it did make an effort to explain fully and publicly its assessments of the candidates, especially once they had formally applied for membership.[82] The EU's vocal criticism—echoed by a growing number of local civil society groups and opposition parties—gradually revealed that illiberal ruling parties were not, despite their claims, leading their countries into the EU. This criticism undermined the political strategies of ethnic nationalism and economic corruption used by rent-seeking elites, and suggested alternative strategies that were compelling for the voters and usable for opposition elites. It countered two messages: that ethnic nationalism was about protecting the nation, and that slow reform was about protecting the average citizen. The role of the EU in changing the information environment supports Jack Snyder's argument that "the influence of the international community may be essential to help break up information monopolies, especially in states with very weak journalistic traditions and a weak civil society."[83]

The EU was eventually able to circumvent attempts by the government to monopolize information about the EU, interacting with opposition political parties and civic groups. Direct communication with citizens by the EU was limited, but indirect communication through independent media and opposition groups increased steadily after 1995. As the enlargement project became more concrete, EU leaders became more willing to take a decisive stand on issues of domestic politics in the candidate countries, culminating in the more and more specific démarches against the Mečiar government in Slovakia. The EU's good opinion also became a direct factor in the decisions of foreign investors, while credit rating agencies such as Moody's and Standard and Poor adjusted credit ratings in reaction to EU assessments and to the release of the EU's Regular Reports.[84] In this way the EU's statements, Opinions and Regular Reports made the EU the gatekeeper for general Western approbation or disapprobation. Since citizens of Romania, Bulgaria, and Slovakia overwhelmingly favored a westward orientation for their countries and joining the EU, publicity of the criticisms of EU officials helped opposition actors to make a stronger case against the illiberal rulers.

6.3.2 Tracing Change in Romania, Bulgaria, and Slovakia

Let us turn now to a brief sketch of how the mechanisms for influencing the opposition parties and for changing the information environment played themselves out, paying attention also to the significant differences between how (well) they worked in the three cases.

Romania

Given its inauspicious beginnings in 1989, Romania is perhaps the most spectacular case of the EU's active leverage helping to create a more competitive and moderate political system. The PDSR was in power in Romania without interruption for almost seven years. Unlike the power of the illiberal ruling parties in Bulgaria and Slovakia, its power was not checked by other branches of government; instead, it was amplified by Romania's semi-presidential system. As we explored in Chapter 2, Romania had had the weakest opposition to communism before 1989, and the political parties that opposed Iliescu's ruling party from 1990 to 1996 were the least effective in their criticism of the regime. Unlike the Bulgarian or Slovak opposition, they did not control the presidency nor did they have recourse to an independent Constitutional Court. Romania's independent media and civil society groups were also weak and cowed by the considerable power of the Iliescu ruling elite to keep their voices from being heard outside of urban areas.

Romania also stands out because nowhere were the political parties in opposition so fractious and themselves so immoderate. Political competition in Romania was stunted by the disunity and ideological incoherence of the opposition parties in the face of Iliescu's authoritarian policies in the early 1990s. These parties represented widely disparate political views and experienced great difficulty during the on-again, off-again process of uniting under the umbrella Democratic Convention of Romania (CDR) beginning in 1992.

The strongest parties to emerge after 1989 were the so-called historic parties (with their "historic" leadership intact): the National Peasant Christian Democratic Party (PNTCD), the Social Democratic Party (SDP), and the National Liberal Party (PNL). Personal rivalries, personality conflicts and leadership struggles as well as programmatic differences caused opposition disunity, for example accounting for the inability of even the four main "liberal" parties to create one party or even one electoral coalition in the 1990s.[85] How did the mechanisms that I explained in the introduction to this section help improve the institutional environment in Romania?

The initial *focal point for cooperation* among opposition forces was the desire for a clear break with the past combined with a growing antipathy to the Iliescu regime. But embarking in earnest on the political and economic reforms that would qualify Romania for EU membership eventually became the second, more successful focal point for cooperation among the opposition parties in the CDR in the run-up to the 1996 national elections. These parties disagreed on many questions of economic and social reform, but they could agree that meeting EU requirements and joining the EU was the only good road open to Romania. Comprehensive reforms leading to an economic revival and EU membership became the cornerstone of a positive, forward-looking agenda dubbed "The Contract with Romania" that was much more attractive to voters than the anti-communist agenda put forward by the CDR in 1992. Indeed, the Contract with Romania was hugely popular with an almost 70 percent approval rating among the Romanian electorate in 1996.[86] In the 1996 elections, the Iliescu-led ruling elite finally faced a cohesive and organized opposition, and the Romanian polity finally approached the conditions for genuine political competition.

The pro-EU agenda helped bring the CDR together with the Hungarian Democratic Union of Romania (UDMR) and with Petre Roman's Democratic Party (PD) (joined by its coalition partners in the Social Democratic Union (USD)). EU membership was particularly important in providing common ground between the UDMR and some of the more nationalist forces within the CDR, whose attacks on the Hungarian minority in the early 1990s had been rivaled only by those of Romania's extremists like Corneliu Vadim Tudor. Meanwhile, it had become clear to some Romanian politicians within the FSN that adopting a more moderate stance compatible with ethnic tolerance, economic reform and moving towards EU membership could have high political pay offs. Consequently some political elites that had been among Iliescu's most illiberal henchmen changed tack. The most visible political switch was that of Petre Roman: in 1990 he was in the vanguard of FSN politicians using chauvinism and ethnic scapegoating to win the June elections; in 1994 he was one of the very few Romanian politicians who did not condemn Council of Europe Recommendation 1201. Iliescu had called the miners to

Bucharest for a second time in September 1991 in order to remove Roman from his post of prime minister. Roman subsequently led the reformers within the FSN to found a new party, called the Democratic Party-National Salvation Front (DP-FSN). The DP-FSN later merged with several small social democratic parties to form the Social Democratic Union (USD) that ran as part of the opposition (but outside of the CDR) in the 1996 elections.

Nowhere in East Central Europe, meanwhile, did liberal democracy inform so weakly the agenda of the opposition parties in the early 1990s as in Romania, creating such a need for *adapting* to the fundamentals of political pluralism and tolerance. On matters of the nation, the Iliescu ruling elite was able to set the tone, and instead of marginalizing intolerant discourse, it mobilized anti-Hungarian nationalism and set in motion a process of ethnic outbidding. Ethnic intolerance permeated the discourse of almost all of Romania's political parties. As one politician put it, a party could not win on anti-Hungarian rhetoric in the 1992 elections because it was so ubiquitous, but such rhetoric was a prerequisite for becoming a powerful player in the political arena.[87] Opposition parties took nationalist stands, such as endorsing an ethnic definition of the Romanian state, deploring the purportedly sinister intentions of the Hungarian minority, and defending Romania from Western criticism. With reference to the denunciation of the Hungarian minority, the daily *Romania libera* critized the opposition for "permanently giving in to the government's intimidation for fear of being labeled unpatriotic."[88]

On matters of liberal democracy, it was the oppression of the Ceauşescu regime that marked the Romanian opposition, having helped create within its ranks many profoundly illiberal elements in addition to genuine liberal democrats. An important current of intellectuals and some members of the PNL were monarchists, seeking the restitution of a constitutional monarchy under the rule of King Michael. The most popular student leader of the University Square pro-democracy protest went on to found the Movement for Romania, which embraced a crypto-fascist ideology reminiscent of the interwar Iron Guard. Meanwhile, the League of Students that had organized the University Square protest became dominated by Christian ideology and concentrated its efforts on blocking attempts to decriminalize homosexuality, a condition of Romania's admission to the Council of Europe. Learning from Western actors about the substance of a politically attractive pro-Western agenda certainly could not create a homogenous liberal opposition out of this cacophony of forces, but it did move the rhetoric and also the agenda of key opposition political parties toward liberal democracy and ethnic tolerance.

After the defeat in 1992, opposition forces started *adapting* their agenda to promoting a more open political arena and more comprehensive economic reform to set themselves apart from the PDSR and its allies in parliament. Initially opposition actors had a hazy understanding of the concrete reforms and practices that such a program would entail. Politicians in the opposition, like those in Iliescu's ruling clique, were "getting away with" using pro-European rhetoric backed by little substance. From 1990 to 1996, however, representatives of Western organizations, governments, and non-governmental organizations engaged more and more deliberately opposition elites, helping them learn about the substance of a pro-Western agenda, and also training local civil society leaders to take up the project as well.[89] This occurred on a more limited scale than in Slovakia, both because Slovakia had many more Western-oriented civil society actors, and also because illiberal rule in Slovakia lasted a full two years longer.

Should they take power, the CDR-led opposition parties declared that they were resolved to move ahead with political and economic reforms that would qualify Romania for EU membership. They pinned their hopes very strongly and publicly on Romania's early membership in NATO, and on the EU's energetic support for their reform efforts. They expected to gain momentum for the *implementation* of reforms by moving closer to the EU and NATO, but these organizations expected the opposite: inclusion should be a *reward* for successful implementation. As we will see in the next chapter, our third mechanism did not work very well in Romania. Problems in implementing reforms became apparent quite soon after the CDR took power—both because of ongoing disunity in the opposition-turned-coalition, and because of the practices inimical to liberal democracy and a transparent market economy that had become institutionalized and routinized in Romanian public life.

Meanwhile, the EU and other international actors had probably the least success in changing the *information environment* in Romania. It was dominated by the ruling elite because of its ongoing control—from 1990 until the elections of 1996—of Romania's state television. While in the cities the monopoly of the state television had been broken by private television channels, and these new channels were indispensable to the opposition's campaign, in the countryside and the small towns there was usually no alternative to the heavily pro-Iliescu state television that was the only source of information for a majority of the inhabitants.[90] Nevertheless, among especially the urban and working class electorate, political learning did take place as voters abandoned the PDSR in favor of other parties because it had failed to live up to its promises.[91] The EU delegation also became an important alternative source of information in Romania on the EU—even though this was not what the Commission generally did in other candidate states. By 1996 the delegation in Romania was one of the largest anywhere with around twenty-five officials. Given the poor quality of the media, much of the coverage of the EU was "self-generated" by the Commission delegation.[92]

The 1996 Romanian elections, won by the CDR, were a great landmark in Romanian history: this was the first time that a head of state had been changed by the electorate (previous heads of state had either died in office or been forced to abdicate).[93] The CDR received 30 percent in both the Chamber of Deputies and the Senate, and formed a coalition government with the USD and the UDMR. For its part, the PDSR received about 22 percent of the vote; it won 6 percent less than in the 1992 elections while the CDR won about 10 percent more. Overall, the PDSR and its former extremist coalition partners were the clear losers in the parliamentary elections. The CDR's leader Emil Constantinescu won the presidential election with 54.4 percent of the vote while Iliescu received 45.6 percent.

Bulgaria

As the economy deteriorated under BSP rule, opposition mounted: economic crisis in Bulgaria had some of the same effects as EU leverage on mobilizing opposition and triggering debate on the proper course of Bulgaria's domestic and international course. Bulgaria's oppositional UDF was more harmonious than its Romanian and Slovak counterparts, but took many years to mature as a cohesive, forward-looking party that could capture the imagination of Bulgaria's voters. It was economic crisis that captured their imagination in 1997, and the UDF was in position to present itself as the modern, techno-cratic and uncorrupt alternative to the BSP. The realization that Bulgaria was falling far behind because of the mismanagement its own political class loos-ened the grip of BSP propaganda on the information environment. It was brought home by comparisons with the other countries that had applied for EU membership in 1995 and 1996: the Bulgarian newspapers were full of such comparisons, and in the context of such high approval ratings for EU membership, seemed to carry weight.[94]

For Bulgaria's opposition political forces, economic crisis was the principal *focal point for cooperation*. But as demonstrations against the BSP government became stronger over the course of 1996, the idea that the BSP was leading the country away from EU membership became commonplace in political debates: the UDF promised to reverse this trend. Meanwhile, the EU's Commission and other international actors stepped up their presence in Bulgaria (and Romania) as it occurred to them that these states were in greater need of Western assis-tance. The NGO community in Sofia blossomed—though many local NGOs were very small, centering on one or two personalities. Still, by 1997 Bulgaria had an array of EU-funded NGOs analyzing what had gone so dramatically wrong in the Bulgarian economy—and what must be done to put Bulgaria back on course for EU membership. During 1995 and 1996, external actors as well as NGOs aided UDF elites in *adapting* to a strong pro-EU agenda.

The UDF itself put joining the EU at the centerpiece of its domestic reform program, promising to fix the economy and wage war against the corruption and clientalism that had overrun the Bulgarian economy.[95] The reform would be difficult, but the UDF held out the promise that reform would be rewarded by integration; joining the EU mattered to Bulgarian citizens who desired in their great majority to become part of the Western club of democracies.[96] The UDF promised to move Bulgaria forward in the pre-accession process, setting the stage for the *implementation* of EU-oriented reform. As we will see in the next chapter, the economic crisis spawned another kind of discipline: that of an IMF currency board. Still, joining the EU, someday, was central to the program of the UDF-led coalition, the United Democratic Forces (UtDF), and on the minds of Bulgarian voters as they went to the polls in 1997.

Slovakia

Slovakia stands out because illiberal rulers governed so late in the 1990s, and as a result the EU attempted to use its active leverage very directly and deliberately to change their policies and to dislodge them from power. We explore below how the opposition to Mečiar and the HZDS party finally managed to organize itself and cooperate effectively in its bid to win a parliamentary majority in the 1998 elections. This cooperation turned out to be the beginning of Slovakia's dramatic turnaround that culminated in the implementation of sweeping reforms and in full EU membership by the end of 2004. Why has Slovakia ended up as the most successful of the illiberal pattern states? Besides inheriting a stronger economy and a better state administration, Slovakia had the strongest "weak" opposition thanks in particular to the vitality of civic groups, known in Slovakia as "the third sector." The EU's active leverage worked in synergy with these groups and with Slovakia's opposition parties to break the democratic monopoly of the Mečiar government.

Returning Slovakia to "Europe" served as a *focal point for cooperation* among opposition political parties and civic groups, helping to transform the institutional environment in the country. As late as the beginning of 1998, it looked like the inability of the opposition parties to cooperate with one another might hand the HZDS another victory in the September elections. The new Party of Civic Understanding (SOP) emerged, calling for communication and reconciliation between the opposition and the HZDS government. Could the SOP be tempted to break ranks with the opposition and form a coalition government with the HZDS after the elections? SOP leaders ruled this out because of the EU's uncompromising stance toward the HZDS: a SOP-HZDS government would be shunned by the EU and other Western actors. By the early spring of 1998, the SOP had become a loyal member of the anti-HZDS opposition.

Also early in 1998, the Third Sector intervened decisively in the ongoing deliberations and disagreements among Slovakia's various opposition parties.

The Third Sector is an umbrella organization for civic groups in Slovakia. It coordinated the "SOS Campaign" that was launched by civic groups in 1996 to protest the government's attempts to suppress the activities of independent foundations. This campaign created strong feelings of solidarity among disparate civic groups. "Inspiring many citizens to step out in defense of their interests," Pavol Demeš and Martin Bútora argue, "the campaign contributed to the creation of a tradition of civic resistance, exactly the sort of tradition in which Slovakia had displayed a certain deficit" when compared with Poland, Hungary and the Czech lands.[97]

The Gremium of the Third Sector organized in the spring of 1998 what was called the "Democratic Round Table," bringing together representatives of trade unions, the third sector, towns and municipalities, youth groups, and the four major opposition parties—the Slovak Democratic Coalition (SDK), the Party of the Hungarian Coalition (SMK), the Party of Civic Understanding (SOP), and the Party of the Democratic Left (SDL'). The SDK was itself a coalition of five different parties that came together in 1996 and 1997 because the HZDS-led coalition in parliament passed an electoral law that required each party in an electoral coalition to attain 5 percent of the vote. Indeed, we see that important impulses for cooperation among opposition forces came from an unexpected quarter—from laws pushed through by the HZDS, one designed to undermine civic groups and the other to diminish the influence of opposition parties in parliament.

At the Democratic Round Table, the four political parties agreed on close cooperation with each other and with other democratic forces.[98] While the Third Sector provided the forum and the HZDS provided the impulse, securing EU membership for Slovakia provided a substantive focal point for this cooperation. The four parties came from very different backgrounds and had quite different political agendas; they were particularly far apart on their preferred strategies of economic reform. They adjusted their platforms to fit better the pan-European party groupings that they had or hoped to join.[99] And they could all agree on the imperative of defeating Mečiar, reasserting democratic standards, reversing Slovakia's deteriorating relationship with the EU, and qualifying as quickly as possible to start negotiations for EU membership.

Some scholars suggested that Slovakia's opposition parties could take the use of EU membership as a focal point for cooperation to a new level: they should seek out the support of economic elites that had benefited from corrupt privatization, but now found it in their interest to normalize their ill-begotten gains through the rule of the law and the commercial opportunities of EU membership.[100] Access to the EU market could only be guaranteed by putting Slovakia on track for EU membership. As far as I could find out, opposition parties did not promise such economic elites any special protection, and they continued to support the ruling parties. Since this economic nomenklatura had benefited from partial reform as well as insider privatization, it feared—quite correctly—that a change of government would not only bring comprehensive reform but also an attempt to reverse at least some earlier privatizations.

For Slovakia's emerging "democratic" parties, the process of *adapting* their political agendas to EU rules was helped by interacting with Western actors, often in forums that were also sponsored by Slovak NGOs. Before Slovakia's four main opposition parties—the SDK, the SMK, the SOP, and the SDL'— came together at the Democratic Round Table in 1998, many of their members had already changed their political strategies substantially since they entered the democratic political arena in 1989 or the early 1990s. At that time some of the opposition political parties, or at least important currents within them, disagreed with elements of the political and economic reform agenda desired by the EU. Others had had little knowledge when communism fell in 1989 of the various European standards on human rights, or the ongoing debate on ethnic minority rights. A combination of transformation and calculation, however, put all of these political parties more or less on the same page.[101]

Adapting their political agendas to EU rules was particularly important for members of the HZDS that defected to the opposition over time. Indeed, many of the most prominent politicians in the SDK and the SOP had at one time been members of the HZDS, and some had served in top posts in a Mečiar government. For them, adapting was aided not just by conferences and workshops organized in hotels in Bratislava or Brussels by Western foundations and Slovak NGOs. It was also driven by their informal and formal contacts with Western officials and diplomats while in office. Indeed, Mečiar the prime minister managed to lose one foreign minister after another: the impossibility of selling Mečiar to the West combined with the weight of Western disapprobation was apparently too much for any foreign minister to bear. More seriously, the politicians that were in the HZDS, particularly in its early years, did not realize the extent of Mečiar's antidemocratic tendencies, nor did they fully understand the imperative of following Western standards in upholding ethnic minority rights and an open, pluralistic political arena. As these things became clearer, many politicians abandoned the HZDS and adapted their political agenda to suit a political future with the opposition parties.[102]

Slovakia's civic groups regrouped in the Third Sector did more than just push the opposition parties toward cooperation, or partner Western actors in creating forums for learning about a Western agenda. They also orchestrated a very ambitious and successful civic pro-democracy campaign leading up to the 1998 elections that contributed to higher voter registration, higher voter turnout (especially among young people) and more pronounced support for the democratic political forces in the 1998 elections.[103] Sharon Fisher argues that indeed civil society actors deserve the *most* credit in changing the national discourse and turning the tide against the HZDS even as it radicalized its own discourse, attempting to frighten voters about internal and external threats to the Slovak nation.[104]

Under the leadership of the Gremium of the Third Sector and its president Pavol Demeš, Slovakia's civic groups launched the "Civic Campaign OK '98" in March 1998. Building on the gradual awakening of Slovak citizens from "civic unconsciousness" and on widespread dismay with the obstruction of the May 1997 referendum on NATO membership, the Civic Campaign OK '98 led to unprecedented levels of civic mobilization that included unions, the independent media, and sections of the Catholic church.[105] Dozens of NGOs organized educational projects, cultural actions, rock concerts, publications, films, discussion forums with candidates, and meetings with citizens. The largest and most visible of the OK '98 events was the "Road to Slovakia," a fifteen-day march during which approximately 300 civic activists passed through more than 850 towns and villages and covered more than 3,000 kilometers. Meanwhile, back in Bratislava the Institute for Public Affairs (IVO) as well as dozens of other institutes, NGOs and analysts published a rich array of studies chronicling and analyzing the (dismal) performance of the Mečiar government over the past four years, especially its increasingly damaging economic policies.[106]

The NGOs and institutes that formed the core of the Third Sector had very close contacts with international actors and drew a great deal of support from them. The message of Slovak NGOs was amplified by the West's open emphasis on the need for democratization, while their pre-election activities were supported by Western financial assistance.[107] Demonstrating both the vitality of Slovakia's NGOs and the high stakes placed by Western actors on the outcome of the 1998 elections, an informal association called the "Donors' Forum" was created to streamline the application procedures for Slovak NGOs and to facilitate cofinancing, often between private grant-giving foundations and the democratization initiatives of Western governments.[108] While Slovak NGOs could never have accomplished as much as they did without Western support, no amount of Western support could have supplanted or engineered Slovakia's local civic leadership and mobilization.[109]

So it turned out that Slovakia's opposition parties were well positioned to win the 1998 elections. But how committed were they to *implementing* the agenda agreed at the Democratic Round Table? In the election campaign the opposition parties were very explicit about their goal to reverse Slovakia's outcast status immediately after taking power. And once in power they would have greater incentives to move quickly in carrying out the necessary reforms than oppositions in Bulgaria or Romania for two reasons. First, many of Mečiar's most visible transgressions had been political, and these would be easier to reverse than corruption (and backwardness) of the economy.

Second, Commission officials and EU leaders made it very clear that if rapid implementation did occur, Slovakia had a real chance to catch up and join the EU in the first wave.

The EU's active leverage also played an important role in changing the information environment in Slovakia to the benefit of the opposition forces. As the démarches sent to Slovakia became increasingly specific, it became more difficult for the Mečiar government to recast them as general approbation or to reject them as blanket condemnation of Slovakia.[110] The increased institutional capacity of the Commission to follow domestic politics in applicant states enabled it to provide detailed criticisms of the Mečiar government's policies, which meant that they packed more of a domestic political punch. EU démarches in 1995, 1996, and 1997 served as a signal to the electorates and to economic elites that government policies were risking Slovakia's place in the EU membership queue. Referring to the Mečiar government, for example, Jan Marinus Wiersma, rapporteur on Slovakia for the European Parliament, commented "If we took as permanent the current state, we could part ways right now."[111] By April 1998, although three quarters of citizens wished for Slovakia's entry to the European Union, only one third believed that Slovakia was heading in that direction.[112]

The opposition political parties as well as NGOs involved in the Civic Campaign OK '98 capitalized on the EU's more and more visible condemnation of the Mečiar government. One SOP ad that Sharon Fisher argues was characteristic of the opposition's campaign presented opinion polls showing the strength of popular support for EU and NATO membership and noted that

Entry into [the EU and NATO] was a part of the program declaration of the current government. And the reality? . . . None of the prominent world politicians have visited Slovakia in the last several years. Instead of advanced Europe we are moving closer to the unfathomable East. The will of the citizens is key for the SOP. That is why fulfilling the conditions of EU and NATO entry are among our main priorities. . . . The future of the citizens of Slovakia is in a stable and prosperous Europe.[113]

The largest opposition party, the SDK, noted in its party program that Slovakia's exclusion from the first round of candidates for EU and NATO membership was a clear case of "self-disqualification caused by internal factors."[114]

A substantial part of the public "accepted" criticism from abroad that demanded Slovakia's democratization as a precondition for its integration into the EU and NATO, and rejected the Mečiar government's explanation that Slovakia's exclusion was caused by Western unfairness or opposition disloyalty. A survey conducted in October 1997 found that 55 percent of citizens blamed Slovakia's failure to move toward integration on "the ruling coalition, which was reluctant to conduct democratic politics"; 33 percent blamed President

Kováč and the Slovak opposition; 33 percent believed that the EU and NATO were unjustly biased against Slovakia; and 39 percent faulted the Western media and part of the Slovak media (respondents could choose more than one actor).[115]

Opinion polls showed that before 1998 an important segment of those who voted for the HZDS strongly supported membership in the EU, and that concern over Slovakia's deteriorating relations with the EU was rising. One report argued that voters had an incomplete understanding of the criteria of EU membership, that ruling elites were able to shape this understanding through parts of the mainstream media, especially of state-run television STV—but that dissatisfaction with the anti-EU positions of STV was substantial.[116]

Among Mečiar's core voters, trust in the EU and support for Slovakia's accession to the EU had both been quite high in 1992. By autumn 1998 HZDS voters either changed their opinion about the EU, or they stopped voting for the HZDS. Mečiar's propaganda was effective in inspiring his core voters to turn away from the EU (and not away from the HZDS), but swing voters as well as new voters opted overwhelmingly for the opposition parties.[117] According to one poll, support among HZDS voters for joining the EU dropped from 76 percent in April 1998 to 36 percent in January 1999.[118] By 2000, only 16 percent of HZDS voters were certain that they supported EU membership, indicating that the disjuncture between supporting the HZDS and supporting EU membership had narrowed and the HZDS was correctly left with voters opposed to the EU.[119]

The 1998 Slovak parliamentary elections were won by the four opposition parties, the SDK, the SOP, the SDL' and the SMK, which together captured over 58 percent of the vote. The HZDS still gained the most votes of any single political party at 27 percent, but its former coalition partners did far worse: the extreme right wing SNS won 9.1 percent of the vote while the extreme left wing ZRS failed to cross the 5 percent threshold and enter parliament. Individually the SDK won 26.3 percent; the SOP won 8 percent, the SDL' won 14.7 percent and the SMK won 9.1 percent of the vote. All together 58 percent of the vote translated into a constitutional majority in parliament for the opposition parties of 93 out of 150 seats. Once in power, these four parties became ten parties because the SDK and the SMK were "electoral" parties that contained eight "regular" parties between them.[120]

6.3.3 *Alternative Explanations*

The EU's active leverage is only one of many factors contributing to the defeat of illiberal elites in free and fair elections in Romania in 1996, in Bulgaria in 1997, and in Slovakia in 1998. The two most compelling factors are the perils of monopoly,[121] and the toll of economic deterioration or crisis.

The perils of monopoly are analogous to the problem encountered by the communist regimes: as the only actor with any political power before 1989, the communist party could reasonably be blamed for everything that went wrong. This made blaming problems on ethnic minorities and Western enemies all the more tempting for communist leaders. After 1989, a partial monopoly on political power allowed ruling elites to extract rents without much interference from opposing political forces. In Romania, the PDSR's control of the presidency and of parliament, and its moves to exclude the political opposition from decision making, concentrated power in the hands of the Iliescu-led elite. In Bulgaria, the BSP won in 1994 a majority in parliament and also ruled alone. In Slovakia, the HZDS moved dramatically to concentrate all political power in its own hands, attempting to sideline the opposition parties and to undermine rival democratic institutions at every turn. But for a political party to enjoy a real (or perceived) monopoly on power has its costs. Voters may blame it for everything that goes wrong in the country. For this reason, ethnic scapegoating often goes hand in hand with suppressing political competition in illiberal democracies (as well as in authoritarian regimes). Given all of the problems associated with the transition from communism, the perils of monopoly may get the rulers voted out of power unless they have a credible scapegoat, irrespective of the active leverage of the EU.

Economic crisis or the sustained economic hardship brought on by partial economic reform is the second competing explanation for the change in government (or, more accurately, the most important element of the first one). But the economic downturn was exacerbated if not caused by the same inefficiencies of corrupt economic reform and the same disregard for international constraints that retarded accession to the EU. In other words, the severity and the duration of the economic downturn is a result of rent-seeking behavior by ruling elites, which is an outcome of the kind of elites that are in power, and not an independent factor impacting political change.

All together it is quite likely that rent-seeking elites would have been defeated in Romania in 1996, in Bulgaria in 1997, and in Slovakia in 1998 even in the absence of any EU leverage. The perils of monopoly and the long economic malaise may well have been enough to compel the electorate to demand that new political parties take power. This is almost certainly true in the case of Bulgaria, where the population widely (and accurately) blamed the very painful collapse of the economy in 1996 on the BSP government. However, in Romania in 1996 and in Slovakia in 1998 there was no economic crisis (though there was plenty of economic mismanagement and Slovakia's economy was arguably on the verge of crisis), and the total vote for the PDSR and the HZDS was not dramatically lower than at previous elections.

The key development in Romania and Slovakia was the cohesion of the opposition parties and their cooperation with civic groups. This cohesion and cooperation was grounded in the shared political agenda of restarting the transition to liberal democracy and attaining EU membership. EU-based cohesion was also critical in some cases in convincing opposition parties not to defect from the pro-EU bloc after the elections to form a coalition with the former ruling parties. Even if we conclude that the ruling rent-seeking elites would have faired badly in the next elections without it, I argue that EU leverage was decisive in determining what kinds of political parties were on offer to be elected, and what kinds of policies these parties implemented once in power. EU leverage profoundly shaped the campaign platforms and also the policy agendas of the political parties that won the elections.

Did EU approval matter at all for the electoral chances of the opposition forces in Romania, Bulgaria and Slovakia? If politicians did not believe that it did, we would not expect to see the opposition parties using rehabilitation in the eyes of the EU as a prominent campaign slogan. Instead they prepared the electorate to expect the new government to get the country elevated to the next "stage" in the accession process (the opening of negotiations). This would require implementing tough economic reforms that, in the short run, were likely to worsen the economic situation for the bulk of the electorate. It would also require the government to commit valuable political capital to promoting ethnic tolerance and granting ethnic minorities greater rights immediately after taking office. Absent any rewards in public support, it is not obvious why opposition parties would want to commit to such a politically difficult agenda.

6.4 Conclusion

This chapter has focused on when and how the EU and other Western actors influenced the character of domestic politics in the illiberal states. The EU's active leverage was initially brought to bear on the problem of regional instability caused by ethnic intolerance and the question of ethnic minority rights. Here, EU leverage did have a significant impact. Hungary was compelled to change its policy of pressuring and attempting to isolate the Romanian and Slovak government in order to promote the rights of ethnic Hungarians living in Romania and Slovakia. On the demand of the EU, the Hungarian, Romanian, and Slovak governments signed Basic Treaties promising good neighborly cooperation and the protection of ethnic minority rights. Although the signature of these treaties was merely a gesture of "formal compliance" on the part of the illiberal rulers in Romania and Slovakia, it paved the way for downgrading the role of ethnic nationalism in domestic politics, and it lightened considerably the load of future reformers who would have had to face considerable abuse by nationalist forces had they had to sign the treaties themselves.

Beyond "formal" and also "selective" compliance, however, the EU's active leverage was of little use in changing the domestic strategies of ethnic nationalism and economic clientalism pursued by illiberal rulers in Romania, Bulgaria, and Slovakia, because these rent-seeking strategies catered to the rulers' domestic power base. The limits of the EU's active leverage were demonstrated most visibly by the Mečiar government's stark refusal to change its ways in exchange for an invitation to begin negotiations on EU membership at the Luxembourg summit in December 1997. Still, the EU's active leverage did scare illiberal rulers away from certain democratic excesses, such as the (further) use of violence against protesters or the expulsion of democratically elected parties from parliament—excesses so blatant that they could have disqualified the countries from keeping their association agreement with the EU. Whereas the illiberal rulers in Romania and Slovakia had a history of tampering with elections, the EU's active leverage in concert with pressure from other Western actors also ensured that parliamentary elections in all three states after 1995 were free and fair.

The EU's active leverage had the greatest impact on the configuration, the strength and the agenda of the opposition forces competing against illiberal political parties—and not, as we have seen, on the policies of illiberal rulers. What distinguished the liberal pattern states from the illiberal ones in 1989 was the presence of a liberal democratic opposition to communism strong enough to take power and to prevent the democratic monopoly of rent-seeking elites. The EU's active leverage helped create such an opposition in the illiberal pattern states after 1994 by changing the institutional and the information environment to improve the competitiveness of the political system.

The EU along with other international actors helped improve the institutional environment by bolstering the strength and shaping the political agenda of rival groups in society. The goal of getting the country on track to join the EU became a *focal point for cooperation* among ideologically diverse opposition parties and civil society groups. Such groups sought out external contacts with Western actors that promoted learning about and *adapting* to the substance of democratic liberalism, capitalism and minority rights protection. The Western agenda was all the more attractive (and potent) because the EU promised visible rewards to new governments for the *implementation* of reforms. These rewards included immediate financial assistance and foreign investment as part of moving forward in the EU's pre-accession process. Ultimately the character of the elites who won power in post-communist states that were credible future members of the EU no longer depended on domestic factors alone.

The EU helped improved the information environment by working with other international actors to provide an alternative metric for the conduct of the ruling parties and by enriching the debate on alternative strategies for reform. Undermining the information asymmetries enjoyed by the illiberal rulers in turn helped undermine the political strategies of ethnic nationalism and economic corruption in states that had functioned as a democratic monopoly. The EU helped wear away the pro-Western façade of rent-seeking elites by criticizing their performance in government. In so doing it empowered opposition political parties and even substituted for them and for indigenous interest groups that lacked the means to attack the government effectively.

All together, the EU had much greater traction on domestic policy-making in Romania, Bulgaria, and Slovakia after illiberal ruling parties lost elections in 1996, 1997, and 1998, respectively. The opposition parties that took office had used the EU as a focal point for cooperation and had spent time adapting to the EU's agenda for prospective members; once in office, they were tied to implementing this agenda by the expectations of the voters that progress would be made toward membership. Meanwhile, the EU's active leverage became more deliberate and intense over time, paying closer attention to democratic standards and the protection of ethnic minority rights as the actual enlargement of the EU became less abstract (although it still of course allowed many shades of gray). This culminated in the 1998 and 2002 ultimatum to Slovak voters that the EU would not do business with a government that included Mečiar or his HZDS party.

The Impact of Active Leverage II: Reforming the State and the Economy, 1997–2004

Does the blossoming of political competition and the victory of opposition forces that ends the democratic monopoly of illiberal rulers lead to a convergence toward moderate politics across the candidate states? I argue in this chapter that once a state becomes deeply enmeshed in the European Union's (EU's) pre-accession process, the high costs of pulling out of this process motivate even previously illiberal ruling parties to adopt a political strategy that embraces qualifying for EU membership. Stronger political competition in combination with the incentives of EU membership sooner or later drives most political parties in the candidate states toward a consensus on the basic tenor of domestic reform and foreign policy. In conditions of free and fair elections, at a time when so many challenges are being faced by the citizens and the state, political parties learn that they can adapt their agenda to (among other things) the EU pre-accession process—and get back in the political game. On many fronts, keeping ruling elites within the parameters set by the EU's pre-accession process signifies an outstanding success: respect for basic democratic standards, more robust political competition, better protection of ethnic minority rights, and ongoing reform of the economy. It does not, however, by itself guarantee a high quality of democratic policy-making or governance.

This chapter answers two questions about the EU's active leverage. First, what are the mechanisms that translate active leverage into reforms of the state and the economy in all of the candidate states? Once rent-seeking rulers are out of the way, "post-illiberal" as well as liberal pattern states are subject to the challenging but more mundane process of adopting the EU's acquis in step with ongoing reforms of the state and the economy. I argue that the EU's active leverage compels all governments to tackle certain politically difficult and inconvenient reforms, such as creating an independent civil service and accelerating bank privatization, and to stick to them over time.

Three mechanisms translate the EU's active leverage into reforms of the state and the economy. All of them stem from the long-term, incremental nature of the EU's leverage. First, straightforward *conditionality* is at play: moving forward in the EU's pre-accession process is tied to adopting laws and implementing reform. Second, the process itself serves as a *credible commitment* mechanism to ongoing reform because reversing direction becomes prohibitively costly for any future government. As candidates move forward in the process, governments are thus locked into a predictable course of economic policymaking that serves as an important signal to internal and external economic actors. Third, moving towards EU membership changes the character and the strength of different *groups in society*. All together, this is not just plain conditionality but "transformative" conditionality: the state, the economy, and society are transformed as a result of taking part in a process that lasts for many years.

The second question about the EU's active leverage that I attempt to answer in this chapter is an echo of the question originally asked in Chapter 1: what explains the variation that we observe in the political trajectories of the candidate states, particularly among the three "post"-illiberal ones, after years of EU leverage? For Slovakia, Bulgaria, and Romania, how do we explain the variation in the performance of "the reformers"[1] and in the performance of the governments that succeed them? As we learned in Chapter 6, the EU's active leverage cannot work alone but only in synergy with the efforts of domestic political elites. The mechanisms I labeled *cooperation, adapting,* and *implementation* helped create a unified opposition around the goal of moving the country away from illiberal policies and toward EU membership. We can now compare the performance of these opposition forces and conclude that, although these mechanisms helped bring them together to defeat illiberal rulers in all three states, they were not equally up to the task of implementing their EU agenda or, more simply, of governing their country. We will reflect on what the experience of Romania since 1996, Bulgaria since 1997, and Slovakia since 1998 tells us about the ability of these states (and their chosen governments) to overcome the previous years of illiberal rule in the context of the EU's pre-accession process.

It is important here to distinguish between two different phases in the relationship between the EU and the candidate states. The first phase covers the conditionality of enlargement and spans the entire period when the candidates work to comply with the requirements described in Chapter 5, including the "negotiations" about whether they have implemented the acquis. The second phase overlaps with the first, but covers only what I call the "endgame" of the negotiations. Here, the negotiations pertain to two issues: transition periods that are negotiated for technical and financial as well as political reasons (to placate political constituencies in the candidate or the member states); and decisions about how much money new member states will receive from the EU budget. In this endgame, the EU has acted in quite a brutal fashion, imposing its short term political interests on the candidates as asymmetric interdependence allows it to do. This chapter explores only the conditionality phase, but we will return to the endgame of the negotiations in Chapter 8.

This chapter is divided into four parts. In the first part I present a brief model of how the conditionality and credible commitment mechanisms of the EU's pre-accession process promote the convergence of mainstream political parties on a liberal democratic agenda supportive of EU membership. The second part explores the impact of the EU's active leverage on the reform of the state and the economy in the candidate states, and looks at how this played out in Poland, Hungary, and the Czech Republic. The third part analyzes the convergence of domestic politics in the post-illiberal states after reformers take power, but also explains the significant variation in the performance of the three states in qualifying for EU membership. Finally, the fourth part explores alternative explanations for the compliance with EU rules that we observe across all of the candidate states. It asks whether compliance can be explained as a consequence of globalization or the larger processes of Europeanization, making the deliberate conditionality of the EU's active leverage unhelpful or at best unimportant. It also asks whether constructivist as opposed to rationalist mechanisms better explain the behavior of rule-adopting elites in this chapter and the previous one.

7.1   Model

In a competitive political system, the imperative of qualifying for membership in the international organization pushes political parties toward a consensus on the nature and scope of comprehensive political and economic reform. This convergence means that the reform strategies of successive rulers vary only moderately. Why? As accession approaches, the process of qualifying for membership in the international organization becomes more exacting and constrains even further the room to maneuver of any ruler. But the benefits of joining the international organization also increase—or, more precisely, the costs of being excluded become greater and more transparent, making exit from the pre-accession process more costly. This increases substantially the credibility of the state's commitment to reform, attracting foreign investment and locking in new rules governing the economy.

In a noncompetitive political system, what happens when new rulers finally come to power? The new rulers embrace comprehensive reform and embed the country in the pre-accession process of the international organization. As a consequence, other political forces now face compelling incentives to reinvent themselves. On the one hand, the interest groups in society that benefit from eventual membership in the international organization are advantaged over those that do not. This creates incentives for aspiring rulers to reinvent themselves to represent these increasingly powerful interests. On the other hand, the comprehensive reforms implemented by the new rulers are linked to the benefits of moving toward membership in the international organization. Such reforms would be very costly to reverse.

However, since the new rulers are forced to tackle the economic restructuring put off or perverted by the former illiberal rulers, substantial economic difficulties or unfulfilled expectations of the population are likely to create an opportunity for other parties to win the next elections. Old rulers, whatever their prior dependence on economic and political rent seeking, may now discover how easy it is to transform themselves into viable challengers in a more competitive political system. Even if they win, the process of qualifying for membership helps ensure that once a strategy of comprehensive reform has been adopted by one government, it is not abandoned by the next one, whatever the ruling parties' pre-election rhetoric or previous behavior in office. Over time, domestic policies oscillate within an increasingly narrow range because of domestic political competition, on the one hand, and the pre-accession process, on the other. Ultimately, for the country's relationship with the international organization, it no longer matters who wins in national elections.

But the danger is that that the transformation of the polity under the more liberal rulers, and the transformation of the returning (formerly) illiberal rulers, will both be too superficial. There may be enduring scars: political discourse has been ethnicized, habits of corruption have become embedded, and economic backwardness has made the population impatient and liable to vote for extremists. Explaining variation among the success of post-illiberal states returns us to the quality of political competition: for the liberal states, what mattered was the quality of political competition at the very beginning of the transition; for illiberal states, what turns out to matter deeply is the quality of political competition that emerges during the years of democratic but illiberal rule after 1989.

7.2   Reform of the State and the Economy

The EU's active leverage inspires or accelerates reforms of the state and reforms of the economy that strengthen liberal democracy and increase aggregate economic welfare in the candidate states. As Jeffrey Kopstein and David Reilly have also argued, "What the EU has done, especially since the mid-1990s, is to provide the crucial external push that has altered domestic interests in favor of accomplishing some of the key tasks of postcommunism."[2] As already sketched in the introduction to this chapter, I have identified three mechanisms that are at work. First, the *conditionality* of the pre-accession process stipulates that governments adopt certain laws, and embark on certain reforms of the state and the economy. Second, progress in the pre-accession process functions as a *credible commitment* device to ongoing reform, making any reversal very costly. Third, the impact on the polity, the society, and especially the economy of moving towards EU membership changes the nature and the strength of different *groups in society*, generally empowering those that will benefit from EU membership.

More generally, the EU accession process demands that governments adopt long-term strategies for reform of the state and the economy that are to continue well after the end of their own term in office. In this way the EU's active leverage forces politicians to implement long-term policies, improving both the efficiency and the accountability of successive governments. The breadth of the EU's demands across policy areas but also their duration—many taking the form of medium and long-term projects—allow EU conditionality to transform polities and economies in an important way. Overall, the impact of the EU's active leverage has been greater on the illiberal pattern states: there, many reforms that had been initiated in the early 1990s in the liberal pattern states were put off and only came in response to the EU's active leverage after 1997. Table 7.1 provides the Freedom House Democratization scores assigned to all six states for 1997 and 2003, illustrating how much further the illiberal states do travel after 1997 than the liberal ones. The Czech Republic, which instead loses the most ground, is a hybrid case, as discussed below.

TABLE 7.1　Democratization in six ECE states, 1997 and 2003

	Year	Poland	Hungary	Czech	Slovakia	Bulgaria	Romania
Electoral process	1997	1.50	1.25	1.25	3.75	3.25	3.25
	2003	1.50	1.25	2.00	1.50	2.00	2.75
Civil society	1997	1.25	1.25	1.50	3.25	4.00	3.75
	2003	1.25	1.25	1.50	1.50	3.25	2.75
Independent	1977	1.50	1.50	1.25	4.25	3.75	4.25
media	2003	1.75	2.25	2.25	2.00	3.50	3.75
Governance	1997	1.75	1.75	2.00	3.75	4.25	4.25
	2003	2.00	2.50	2.25	2.25	3.75	3.75
Composite	1997	1.50	1.50	1.50	3.80	3.90	3.95
democratization	2003	1.63	1.81	2.00	1.81	3.13	3.25

Note: The scale runs from the highest level of democratization (=1) to the lowest (=7).

Source: Freedom House (2003).

The argument here, as in Chapter 6, depends on a counterfactual: what would domestic policy-making look like in the candidate states absent the demands of EU accession? How do we know that the quality would be worse? We can examine the foot dragging of governments before the EU's active leverage started working in areas such as public administration reform or privatization. We can also listen to the domestic debate on reform in these areas once they are singled out by the European Commission for criticism; the debate in parliament and the testimonies of politicians and policy-makers all indicate that the EU's disapprobation—linked to the country's standing in the pre-accession process—helped mobilize reform. Having posed the counterfactual, we may conclude that reforms in some areas would have been slower, less transparent, and more clientalistic absent the EU accession process.

The outcomes, however, are far from uniform: by arguing that the EU's active leverage did cause reform in all candidates, I am not arguing that it was equally effective in all of them, and certainly not across all policy sectors. Holding the content and character of EU pressure constant across countries, there are myriad domestic factors that mediate the EU's active leverage. Explaining variation in the impact of EU leverage across specific policy areas among the candidates—and among different policy sectors in individual candidates—is a very important subject of current research on EU enlargement, but a systematic survey is beyond the scope of this study.[3] Here I can only sketch the mechanisms that I have identified that promoted compliance with EU rules in the reform of the state and the economy.

Reform of the State: Conditionality and Empowering Domestic Groups

The EU's active leverage has helped inspire reform of the judiciary, the civil service, and other arms of the state administration where political inertia might otherwise block reform. Some reforms of the state turned out to be inconvenient for all political parties elected to office: within the short time horizon of a sitting government, they would bring few political rewards; or indeed they would actually make the government give up existing perks of holding office. In these areas, straightforward conditionality was crucial in forcing governments to adopt and implement change. These reforms became a priority as spelled out in the Accession Partnerships, and their neglect was criticized in the Regular Reports. The EU thus identified and attributed poor performance in the conception and execution of reforms to the state, making the environment for abusing or neglecting such reforms less permissive. It also created a metric for good performance—especially the closing of individual negotiating chapters—that, for all of its faults, was relatively simple and transparent. Ultimately the Commission could refuse to close relevant negotiating chapters until reforms were completed or at least initiated. However, as the negotiations progressed, the Commission tended to close particular negotiating chapters at the same time with many different candidates. This suggests that the conditionality mechanism had been watered down in the service of bureaucratic efficiency—though competition among the negotiating states in closing chapters reportedly played in some cases an important part in keeping parallel negotiations going at a similar pace.[4]

Modernizing the judiciary was one area of critical but politically unrewarding reform where many governments were only galvanized into action by the full use of the EU's conditionality. The EU's demand for a modernized judiciary with judges trained in European law forced governments to embark on this expensive and long-term project. The EU did provide financial assistance and also various training programs and forums for helping local policy-makers, academics, and judges learn about European legal standards and EU law. Creating a professional civil service was another area where governments (except in Hungary and Poland) dragged their feet, not only because such a reform would bring few domestic political rewards but also because it would dilute the power of the ruling parties.[5] They would often prefer to fill the state bureaucracy with their own people rather than crafting and supervising its de-politicization. Finally, and most controversially, reorganizing or even creating a regional level of government in the candidate states has been triggered by the EU acquis and the requirements for fitting most profitably into the existing system of disbursing monies from the EU's regional funds.[6]

Besides simple conditionality, another mechanism is at play in translating the EU's active leverage into changes in the polity: the empowerment of domestic groups calling for reform of the state. While East European publics continued to expect the provision of many services from the state after the end of communism, they also expected greater efficiency, transparency, and accountability on the part of the public administration. Instead, however, governments throughout Eastern Europe developed the habit of not paying much heed to civic groups calling for reforms of the state, because these groups were very weak and because the mechanisms for inputting the views of non-governmental organizations and interest groups into the policy process were virtually absent.[7]

The EU's active leverage empowered domestic groups in two key ways. First, pressure from Brussels acted as a temporary surrogate for pressure from private groups by promoting reforms that were in the interest of the public and the state, but rarely in the interest of bureaucracies or governing elites. These reforms however attracted the interest of certain civic groups. The EU actively encouraged politically oriented "pro-reform" groups through financial and other assistance to take up the cause of being democracy's "watchdog" in the candidate states. Meanwhile, as market access improved for the candidates, the EU created opportunities for producers and entrepreneurs to depend on the

EU market and future membership. As Table 4.2 illustrates, exports to the EU from our six ECE states increased over 400 percent between 1991 and 2002. This trade helped create economically-oriented interest groups that pushed for EU-compatible reforms of the state administration and the economy. Overall, the EU empowered domestic actors who benefited from EU membership in a variety of ways while constraining the power of anti-Western actors in society, the state administration and the parliament.[8] The flip side of this coin, of course, has been anti-EU mobilization on the part of groups that are (or perceive themselves to be) nationally or economically disadvantaged by joining the EU, as discussed in Chapter 8.

Second, the external transparency demanded by the EU's pre-accession process helped foster greater domestic transparency that facilitated the work of pro-reform groups. With so much information on government policies being provided to the EU, it became much more difficult to restrict similar information at home.[9] This had a particular impact on reforms of state structures where governments were inclined to share the least information with outside actors. More broadly, the EU's demands for a modernized judiciary trained in European law and an independent, professional civil service inspired important public debates about (the elusive) "European standards" in these areas. Meanwhile, the perspective of EU membership and the possibility of working in Brussels attracted at least some qualified individuals, including some of my former students, to the state administration instead of the more lucrative private sector.

Reform of the Economy: Conditionality and Credible Commitment

Straightforward conditionality was also critical at many junctures in compelling governments in candidate states to implement difficult economic reforms in order to move forward in the pre-accession process. Here, the argument is parallel to the one above about reforming the state: there are certain economic reforms demanded by the EU that few governments will want to implement because of the risk of rising unemployment, higher prices, or lower state benefits scuttling the chances of future re-election. The majority of such reforms, including the withdrawal of the state from many areas of the economy and creating transparent state institutions to regulate the market, are generally accepted as necessary and desirable components of building market capitalism.[10] (The CAP obviously is quite an exception; many scholars and officials, both in the east and the west, consider it a disastrous, welfare-decreasing market distortion.) However, some of these politically unrewarding economic reforms are, as argued in Chapter 2, usually only implemented when a government's back is to the wall after the onset of an economic crisis. Some are the "hard" institution-building reforms necessary to advance liberal market economies—in contrast to the "easy" market liberalization measures taken immediately after the collapse of communism.[11] At the same time, the EU has strongly promoted the development of social dialog among government, business and labor actors, strengthening "significantly" tripartite institutions in the candidate states.[12] Finally, it has given governments a powerful rationale in explaining difficult reforms to skeptical publics (although "the EU made us do it" is subject to much abuse on the part of governments inside as well as outside the EU).

There are also certain economic reforms that ruling elites will avoid implementing to preserve economic rents for themselves or for economic elites close to the ruling parties. By insisting on reforms such as bank privatization, bankruptcy laws, the restructuring of state aids, and transparent procedures for enterprise privatization, EU requirements reduce (though they certainly do not eliminate) opportunities for economic rent-seeking. The short case study below of the Czech Republic helps illustrate the impact of the conditionality mechanism on corruption. Other reforms demanded by the EU include improving standards and transparency in the provision of basic services such as telecommunications and transportation, ending monopolies in energy and telecommunications markets, decreasing the transaction costs for businesses, and opening up closed markets.

Equally important to the conditionality mechanism in motivating economic reform is the fact that the EU's pre-accession process serves as a commitment device. For domestic and foreign economic actors, especially investors, progress in the EU's pre-accession process serves as a credible commitment to ongoing and predictable economic reforms (and also to certain ongoing political reforms, especially pertaining to state regulation of the economy). Most simply, as Peter Hall and Rosemary Taylor argue, "institutions affect action by structuring expectations about what others will do;" for economic actors, the pre-accession process creates expectations that comprehensive economic reforms will proceed apace.[13] Economic actors had every reason after 1989 to question how far post-communist states would go in implementing liberalizing reforms. Indeed, most stopped at some kind of partial economic reform that privileged insiders and fostered corruption. How could post-communist governments signal that they were serious about comprehensive reform?[14] As Jon Pevehouse argues, governments can make commitments to regional organizations such as the EU in order to signal their commitment to ongoing reform by tying the hands of the country's current and future ruling elites through the rules of the organization.[15]

Once a candidate was well on the way to joining the EU, the costs of losing ground or reversing course became prohibitive—for any government. At the same time, the fact that qualifying for EU membership is such a mammoth project of domestic politics compelled all mainstream political parties to reach a consensus about the underlying thrust of political and economic reform.[16] The exigencies of the EU's pre-accession process thus assured economic actors that the commitment to liberal economic reforms would be protected from two threats: from economic downturns and from government turnover. Continuing economic reform becomes clearly the most likely ongoing strategy for current and future governments.

The credibility of the commitment to ongoing economic reform in the context of the EU's pre-accession process thus serves as a very important signal for domestic and international economic actors, promising them a stable business environment and access to the entire EU market.[17] Lisa Martin argues that the forms of international cooperation that offer states the highest benefits require them to make credible commitments to one another. She finds that for democracies the concerns of economic actors about the credibility of commitments are decreased by the participation of legislatures in international cooperation. In the case of EU candidates, progress in the pre-accession process signals a seriousness of commitment not only to the EU itself as it weighs a candidate's suitability for membership, but also to a range of economic actors as they weigh a country's suitability for investment.[18]

Progress in the pre-accession process builds credibility in the eyes of economic actors using a similar mechanism as legislative participation; namely it makes extrication from and violation of international agreements very difficult. Figure 7.1 depicts the growth in cumulative foreign direct investment in our six East Central Europe (ECE) states from 1990 to 2000. It illustrates the much greater success of Poland, Hungary, and the Czech Republic in attracting FDI, particularly from 1990 to 1994. But it also illustrates that after 1995 Slovakia, Bulgaria, and Romania were able to attract much more FDI than

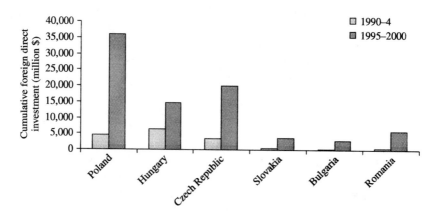

FIGURE 7.1   Growth in cumulative foreign direct investment, 1990–2000.
Source: Calculations based on World Bank (2002*b*).

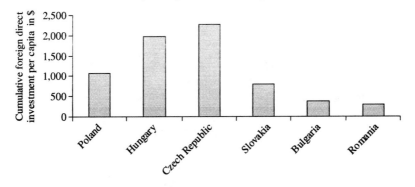

FIGURE 7.2   Foreign direct investment per capita, cumulative 1990–2000.
Source: Calculations based on World Bank (2002*b*).

before 1995, increasing their credibility—and presumably also their interest in sustaining that credibility—with foreign investors. Figure 7.2 shows more clearly that, on an FDI per capita basis, by 2000 the "post" illiberal pattern states had made progress catching up to the liberal pattern ones.

All together, the reforms of the economy that are implemented as part of the effort to qualify for EU membership, and the credible commitment to ongoing reform that comes from moving toward membership in the EU's pre-accession process, bring significant economic benefits. These include a better business environment, better state regulation of the market, higher levels of domestic and foreign investment, and greater opportunities for trade. They overlap of course with the economic benefits of being an EU member, explored in Chapter 3: but the two mechanisms I have emphasized here—conditionality and credible commitment—highlight the benefits for candidates of the process of joining the EU, as opposed to the benefits they enjoy once they are members. And the drive to EU membership, by forcing economic restructuring, improves performance in the world economy over the long run. (This, however, is a controversial argument, and we will listen to the critics in Chapter 8.) Most important, the mechanisms of conditionality and credible commitment help explain why, as we will see later in this chapter, future governments in the candidate states, despite their strikingly different political profiles, do not halt or reverse reform.

Poland, Hungary, and the Czech Republic

Once the EU published its Opinions on the preparation of the ten candidates for membership in July 1997, the tables turned on Poland, Hungary and the

Czech Republic. After years on the high ground, asking the EU what they should do to prepare for enlargement, suddenly they were presented with an elaborate list of their shortcomings. Wade Jacoby in his book *Ordering from the Menu* demonstrates how the modes of emulation varied across candidates, across policy domains and also over time. He identifies four modes called copies, templates, thresholds and patches. Describing the progression of the EU's leverage over time, he observes that "elites began the post-communist period attempting to use a rough template of an existing West European institutional model, only to be confronted . . . in the mid-1990s with a much more specific threshold in the same policy area and then confronted, within a few more years, with the demand that very specific patches be employed if membership negotiations were to proceed."[19]

In 1998 and 1999, the fear of exclusion from the first wave prompted a surge in meeting thresholds and applying patches in Poland and especially in the Czech Republic. Poland, Hungary and the Czech Republic had been invited to begin negotiations along with Slovenia and Estonia at the December 1997 Luxembourg European Council. But it was widely discussed whether Poland and the Czech Republic risked being left behind because, compared to Hungary, Estonia and Slovenia, they were behind on their preparations for membership—though it was also widely agreed that Poland's geopolitical and economic importance would guarantee it a place in the first group. By 2000, it was fairly evident that all five states would enter together, yet competition among the candidates in closing negotiating chapters against the backdrop of the (more and more remote) threat of exclusion kept domestic reforms moving, though at a more selective pace. Despite the generally uniform nature of the EU's pre-accession process, there was a tremendous amount of variation in its impact on the domestic politics of the candidate states that, as explained above, I cannot capture here. Even for two relatively similar candidates such as Hungary and Poland variation in domestic structural and political conditions yielded very different results.

Hungary prompted the least criticism from the EU because of its relatively excellent preparations for membership. The Hungarian Socialist Party (MSZP) government (1994–8) excelled at meeting EU requirements because of the technocratic and bureaucratic abilities of its formerly communist party elite, and because it was very keen to prove its Western, liberal credentials. Excelling in the EU's pre-accession process certainly helped the MSZP establish these credentials; indeed, the right-wing parties accused it of trading servitude to Moscow for servitude to Brussels. Hungary's success underlines yet again the importance of a reformed communist party that transforms or "regenerates"[20] into a strong, moderate and competent left wing party. Part reality and part marketing, the quality of the Hungarian civil service inspired much more confidence than its counterparts in other candidate states that the acquis would actually be implemented.[21]

The MSZP's vigor came against the backdrop of Hungary's comparatively Western-oriented economy. In 1989, it was by far the most open to Western trade and investment, and it attracted the most new foreign investment of any of the EU candidates in the early 1990s (see Figure 7.1). For Hungary, the credible commitment mechanism was consequently less important.[22] The conditionality mechanism, however, did prompt important reforms, particularly those specified in the Accession Partnerships. The right-wing FIDESZ government of Prime Minister Viktor Orban that took power in 1998 tended to require a bit more pressure to comply with EU requests for both reforms of the state administration and liberalizing reforms in the economy.[23]

The record of Poland's post-communist Democratic Left Alliance (SDL) government (1993–7) was not as stellar as that of Hungary's post-communists. Still, the presence of a reformed communist party created a relatively high level of consensus on the thrust of domestic reform, while the credible commitment mechanism of preparing for EU membership helped establish the free market credentials of Poland's post-communist governments. The SDL broke the cycle of Poland's short-lived governments, providing stable government and drawing on the technocratic strengths of the party to prepare Poland for the launch of negotiations with the EU. By 1997, however, it was clear that the post-communist Polish government had slacked in some of its preparations—and the right-wing coalition of coalitions that succeeded it lacked the expertise and discipline to step up the pace.[24] The 1998 Regular Report was particularly critical.[25] Straightforward conditionality was brought to bear on Poland in order to hasten economic reforms in certain key sectors of the economy including energy, steel, banking, and finance. Meanwhile, Polish elites had to balance their future position as one of the largest members of the EU with their current, weak position as an applicant for membership.[26] Still, for Poland's governments the fear of exclusion was always offset by confidence that for geopolitical and economic reasons—centered on the interests of its neighbor Germany—a first enlargement of the EU would not take place without it.[27]

Hungary and Poland, as discussed in Chapter 2, had already experienced eight years of policy-making under conditions of strong political competition before the onset of the full force of the EU's active leverage in 1997. As Antoaneta Dimitrova argues, the EU therefore had the greatest influence in shaping reforms pertaining to the "administrative capacity requirement": the EU demanded that candidates be able to implement the acquis and administer the internal market after accession, even though standards for judging this administrative capacity remained elusive.[28] Other reforms, such as setting up regional government, modernizing the judiciary or creating a professional civil service were underway before 1997. They were the product of indigenous reform efforts mixed in with anticipatory adaptation to EU rules, then "patched" as demanded by the EU during the negotiations.[29] Few would argue that the EU's active leverage has not had a profound and transforming effect on the state and the economy in both Hungary and Poland. And there is abiding concern about the periodic resurgence of nationalism in Hungary's domestic and foreign policy. Yet, absent the EU's active leverage few would argue that these countries would not have constructed liberal democracy and a functioning market economy.

The Czech Republic

The Czech Republic stands out: it shows how the EU's active leverage worked in a state that had a strong liberal start to democratization, but that had suffered from restricted political competition from 1992 to 2002.[30] Even though the Czech Republic has counted as a liberal pattern state in this study, the EU fought against the lack of transparency and the overt corruption in the Czech political system, pushing through reforms as fundamental as creating an independent civil service and bolstering the rule of law.[31] On some measures, the Czech Republic was closer to Slovakia, Bulgaria and Romania than Poland and Hungary when the EU published its Opinions in 1997.

As Anna Grzymała-Busse demonstrates in comparing Poland, Hungary, the Czech Republic and Slovakia, the level of political competition was pivotal in helping to limit how much political parties could manipulate the state for their own benefit. In the more competitive political systems, opposition political parties could make their criticisms heard and check the power of ruling parties.[32] In Gzymała-Busse's study, the Czech Republic resembles Slovakia in that neither state developed an effective opposition in the early 1990s: "Where one party dominated political competition, lax (or nonexistent) regulations allowed the informal extraction of resources from state firms, the procurement of favorable privatization deals, and the accumulation of positions in public administration." Power was more dispersed immediately after 1989 in both Poland and Hungary and, as Table 1.3 indicates, complete turnover of political parties in power took place regularly; this yielded much higher levels of accountability and transparency than in the Czech Republic and Slovakia which instead experienced very high levels of corruption.[33]

The Czech Republic is thus a hybrid case, falling in some ways between the liberal and the illiberal pattern of political change.[34] On the one hand, it had a strong opposition to communism and the first governments put in place certain strong foundations of liberal democracy. On the other hand, the two successive governments of Prime Minister Václav Klaus (1992–6, 1996–7) of the Civic Democratic Party (ODS) made blatant efforts to suppress political party competition, restrict information and obstruct the regeneration of a politically active civil society.[35] Arguably every government attempts some of these things, but the activities of the ODS were in a different league than those of its Polish and Hungarian counterparts. The attempt to control the political arena became even more blatant (though less successful) after the 1998 elections when the right-wing ODS offered its left-wing ideological arch rival, the Social Democratic Party (ČSSD), support for its government in the framework of an "opposition agreement" in exchange for continued political influence and for amnesty from certain prosecutions.

The June 1992 elections set the stage for a decade of Czech politics where the behavior of political parties in power was very poorly controlled by political parties in opposition.[36] Václav Klaus's victorious Civic Democratic Party (ODS) formed a coalition with the Civic Democratic Alliance (ODA) and the Christian Democratic bloc (KDU-ČSL). This coalition controlled 105 out of 200 seats, and held together until the elections of 1996 with high levels of popular support. During this period, Klaus's political power was not threatened by dissent within his own party or by the disintegration of his coalition.

Klaus's power was also not checked by an experienced media, while the weak parties of the fragmented left were very ineffective watchdogs. The ODS-led government thus enjoyed remarkable political freedom. It augmented this freedom by neglecting to establish an independent civil service and by undermining poles of opinion outside of the government, such as universities, non-governmental organizations and interest groups. It generally scorned dialog with civic groups, and delayed establishing a legal framework for non-governmental organizations until 1995. No effort was made to foster public discussion and few public information campaigns were attempted. No freedom of information law was passed. Václav Havel was elected to the Czech presidency, but the powers of the president were restricted and Havel was overshadowed by Klaus.[37] Also telling was Klaus's eagerness to be rid of the Central European University in Prague, which harbored Czech opposition intellectuals and formed part of George Soros's project to create civil society in post-communist Europe. Meanwhile certain members of the ODS-led government engaged in political corruption and financial crime with impunity. All together, these practices stunted the Czech polity by impeding the creation of a new class of Czech elites, and by setting the example that ruling political parties may govern as they please.

Klaus's drive to concentrate power in the hands of the government did not end with his ouster in the autumn of 1997. The elections of June 1998 produced a minority Social Democratic government led by Prime Minister Miloš Zeman. The government was formed after the ČSSD signed an "opposition agreement" with its greatest ideological rival, Klaus's ODS. The ODS had done surprisingly well in the elections by forecasting doom if the left took power, yet it preferred to *give* power to the ČSSD in order to undermine the centrist parties and pave the way for a two-party system. With the "opposition agreement" in force, the ODS did not scrutinize the ways that the ČSSD exercised the powers of government, yet it retained influence over key government decisions, it received many posts in the state administration, and it ensured that few political or economic elites close to the ODS would be investigated and prosecuted for crimes committed during the years of ODS rule.

The ability of the ODS to concentrate power was caused in part by the presence of an unreformed communist party, as discussed in Chapter 2. This has put the Czech Republic at a disadvantage in several ways. The Czech Republic's chronic shortage of able politicians and civil servants stems partly from the repression of the post-1968 communist regime. The Polish and Hungarian communist states bequeathed to their democratic successors more qualified civil servants and talented pro-European politicians than did the Czech communist state. Moreover, the existence of an unreformed communist party over the last decade has made the ČSSD less reformist and more populist. The ČSSD has competed with the Communists for votes on the far left, for example by being ambivalent on NATO membership and on economic reform. Finally, from the point of view of coalition building in parliament, the fragmentation of the left into one useable party, the ČSSD, and one unusable party, the Communists, has made the alternation of power between left and right much less straightforward. This has played into the hands of the ODS: a united, experienced left would have served as a much better watchdog during the seven years of ODS rule, and such a left would not need to enter into an opposition agreement to govern. A united left would have also made the fragmentation of the center-right less tenable.[38]

From 1992 to 1997 the pro-EU comportment of the Czech government, necessary to keep the Czech Republic well within the "first wave" of EU candidates, did not interfere with day-to-day policy-making. The general expectations of the EU in many areas coincided with the political and economic agenda of the coalition government dominated by the ODS and led by Klaus—at least on paper.[39] The Czech Republic was the darling of the West, a self-perpetuating status thanks to the shared impressions of Western policy-makers and the (mostly) favorable, cross-referenced reports of international organizations. Spates of EU protectionism strengthened Klaus's confident message of Czech economic superiority and helped limit the impact of other, more positive Western models of state interference in the economy. By claiming to be "West" of the West Europeans, Klaus ensured that his administration, much of the media and a good deal of public opinion retained a provincial confidence in Czech superiority, rather than opening the country to external influences. EU membership came to be understood as a reward for an economic job that was already well-done.[40]

The turning point came in 1997 when the Czech economy began to slide into crisis, and the European Commission published its Opinion detailing the shortcomings of Czech political and economic reforms. The Klaus government fell in the autumn of 1997 in the midst of financial scandals and the desertion of factions within the ODS protesting the concentration of power and the corrupt practices of the ODS government. In 1998, it became clear that the Czech Republic, far from being superior to other candidates, was not in good standing in the EU's accession process.[41] This explains in part why the Czech Republic lost ground after 1996 in terms of the democratization scores it was assigned by Freedom House (see Table 7.1): these scores capture the assessments of various experts who, like everyone else, realized the extent of the deficiencies in governance and economic reform under ODS rule. This set the stage for both "kinds" of EU leverage to play themselves out in the Czech Republic—influence on the institutional and the information environment, and also directly on the government.

As in the illiberal pattern states discussed in Chapter 6, the EU's active leverage influenced the institutional and information environment. The publication of the EU's Opinion and subsequent Regular Reports provided a very important external evaluation of the quality of Czech reforms, working hand in hand with the struggling economy to destroy the illusion of the superiority of Czech economic reforms and reveal the deficiencies of the Czech privatization process. The EU's active leverage also helped organize and strengthen the opposition to the ruling parties. The parties of the center-left and the center-right performed poorly as watchdogs because of their crippling fragmentation during the 1990s. They were too weak to break up the opposition agreement or to call the ODS and the ČSSD to task for their political and financial misdeeds. However, after the opposition agreement was signed in 1998, EU membership became a *focal point for cooperation* among the Czech Republic's fragmented centrist parties and among various civic groups and initiatives. The civic movement "Impuls 99" was formed as a broad based alliance among civic and political forces seeking to break up the concentration of power signified by the opposition agreement, and to bring the Czech Republic into compliance with the requirements for EU membership.

The second kind of leverage was directly on the government—and here the EU made significant progress working with the ČSSD government after 1998, even during the period of the opposition agreement. Like in Poland and Hungary, the mechanisms of conditionality, credible commitment, and influence on domestic groups compelled the ČSSD government to pursue many of the reforms that the overconfident and Euroskeptic Klaus governments had failed to implement. The Commission put intense pressure on the government, for example, to move quickly on privatizing state-owned banks, writing sensible bankruptcy laws and reforming the truly backward and back-logged judiciary.[42] The most spectacular case of a candidate state reforming its public administration under direct threat of sanctions from the Commission was the creation of an independent civil service in the Czech Republic. The legislation was finally adopted and implemented at the eleventh hour after the Czech Republic's two main parties had spent years dividing the spoils of public administration jobs and influence between them. By 2000, the negotiating team led by Deputy Foreign Minister Pavel Telička, civic groups and opposition parties, and the ČSSD government itself had created momentum for implementing the difficult reforms. The government was egged on by competition with Hungary and Poland, but also granted a reprieve by the slowdown of reform in Poland.

7.3   Convergence in Bulgaria, Slovakia, and Romania

Once "reformers" come to power, how much does the tenor of domestic politics and the output of policy making in post-illiberal states converge with the liberal states? Can our post-illiberal states overcome the inauspicious early years of their transition from communism—the suppressed political competition, economic corruption, and ethnic nationalism of the early 1990s? I argue that the EU's pre-accession process has had an important effect in narrowing the political and economic menu of successive governments, whatever their previous political stripe, causing a convergence around domestic policy goals that are consistent with a polity and an economy that will qualify for EU membership. The narrowing of this menu is reflected in the Freedom House scores assigned to Slovakia, Bulgaria, and Romania, as illustrated in Figure 7.3 for 2001 (and in Table 7.1 for 2003). This kind of convergence does not guarantee a high quality of democracy or of public life. Still, keeping rulers to the parameters of policies consistent with qualifying for EU membership means improvements across the board: respect for basic democratic standards, more robust political competition, protection of ethnic minority rights, and ongoing, supervised reform of the economy.

7.3.1   *The Performance of the Reformers*

Even as we observe the impact of EU leverage on policy-making across the board, we observe substantial variation in the performance of the reformers after they take office from their illiberal predecessors. How do we explain this variation? The performance of the reformers depends in part on structural conditions, such as the prosperity of the economy and the capacity of the state administration when they take office. On these measures, it was clear that once Mečiar was out of the way Slovakia's reformers would have a far easier task than reformers in Bulgaria or Romania.

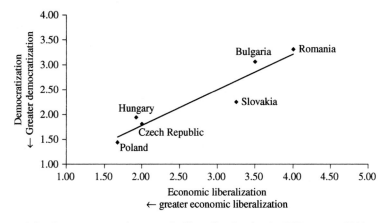

FIGURE 7.3   Democracy and economic liberalization in six ECE states, 2001.
Note: The scale runs from the highest level (=1) to the lowest level (=7).
Source: Freedom House (2001).

Yet, the performance of the reformers also depends on the quality of the domestic institutions that developed after 1989 *in opposition* to the rule of illiberal elites. This follows closely my original argument about the political trajectory of liberal pattern states: the strong opposition to communism brought purposeful liberal democrats to power in 1989, and they were able to lay the foundations of a pluralistic political arena, a capitalist economy and a tolerant society. What the illiberal pattern states were missing in 1989 was a strong democratic opposition. But in Bulgaria and Slovakia the seeds of such an opposition were more visible. Bulgarian and especially Slovak opposition forces hounded and constrained the ruling parties, and even played a role in government in the early 1990s. In both countries (as well as in the Czech Republic) the president stood in opposition to the ruling majority in parliament. While the powers of the office were limited (especially in Slovakia), the president did provide an important counterbalance to the illiberal ruling elite.[43] Overall, though the opposition forces in Slovakia and Bulgaria were weak and immature, they did not leave the excesses of the HZDS and the BSP unanswered. This prevented the institutionalization of clientelism and corruption in Bulgaria and Slovakia on the same level as in Romania, where a much weaker and more ill-defined opposition, further disadvantaged by Romania's semi-presidential system, hardly managed to put any checks on the power of the illiberal elite.

Once elected, the governments of reformers had a very full plate. Under the watchful eye of the EU, they were expected to create a more open political arena, and improve the rule of law. They were also expected to implement difficult economic reforms that were put off by the previous government; indeed, partial reform helped create a warped and corrupt market economy that was in some ways more difficult to reform than the still-socialist economy of 1989. Meanwhile, the population looked to them for substantial improvements in living standards that would be difficult if not impossible to deliver.

For its part, the broader international community expected dramatic improvements in relations between the government and ethnic minorities. In a political environment where ethnic scapegoating had poisoned domestic discourse for years and the nationalist parties remained vocal, this would also require considerable political capital and effort. However, the significant changes in policies toward ethnic minorities that took place in all three states attest to the power of the EU's leverage: politicians made highly contentious concessions regarding ethnic minority issues in order to move forward in the pre-accession process.[44] Finally, NATO and the United States demanded support for NATO's air strikes against the regime of Slobodan Miloševíc during the Kosovo crisis in 1999. All three governments provided some level of support to improve their bid for future NATO membership, and thus had to counter the vigorous condemnation of nationalist political parties and the disapproval of the public for cooperation with NATO against Belgrade.

We turn now to a sketch of the tenure of each of the governments of reformers, evaluating their capacity to govern, to promote ethnic tolerance, to implement political and economic reform, to curb corruption, and to improve the living standards of their citizens. Do they succeed? How is this success motivated by EU leverage, and reflected in progress in the EU's pre-accession process? It is important to recognize both the agency of these new ruling elites, and the intractability of some of the problems that they inherit.

The Dzurinda Government in Slovakia (1998–2002)

The coalition government led by Prime Minister Mikuláš Dzurinda that took office in 1998 in Slovakia was able to fulfill its ambition immediately to end Slovakia's international isolation, and rapidly transform Slovakia's relationship with the EU. The Dzurinda government comprised ten political parties ranging from the post-communist left to the center-right, and included the ethnic Hungarian party. The story of the Dzurinda government is one of constant and spirited debate among the parties in the coalition government—each issue was a "roller coaster ride" that usually ended in some sort of a compromise thanks to the expert leadership of Dzurinda. Passing legislation was not easy; the left wing parties in particular provoked conflict and stalled economic reform, but important reforms were initiated, nevertheless. It helped that several coalition members had experience governing together briefly in 1994.

Under the very close scrutiny of the EU and other Western actors, a sea change occurred in relations between the Slovak majority and the ethnic Hungarian minority after the Dzurinda government took office. By appointing an ethnic Hungarian as deputy prime minister for human rights and minorities, the Dzurinda government impressed ethnic Hungarians as well as Western actors with its positive desire to solve problems; ethnic Hungarian leaders described this political move as equally important to the government's subsequent legislative steps to protect ethnic minority rights in Slovakia.[45] Meanwhile, the composition of the government also demonstrated to ethnic Slovaks that the long-vilified ethnic Hungarian party could take a seat at the table of government with no adverse consequences for Slovakia's territorial integrity, or indeed for the well-being of ethnic Slovaks.

The fundamentals of the Slovak economy had always been promising. The Mečiar government corrupted the privatization process spectacularly, and drove the country into substantial debt in its eleventh hour, but many comprehensive reforms had already been implemented before the division of Czechoslovakia (see Table 2.1). Indeed, Slovakia's 1997 Opinion described it as already having a functioning market economy (unlike Bulgaria and Romania). Still, the government team led by Deputy Prime Minister for the Economy Ivan Mikloš tackled economic reform with great energy, and engineered a belated but impressive turnaround of the Slovak economy. After several years of declining real wages and rising unemployment as a result of austerity measures, both trends were reversed and GDP grew by nearly 4 percent in the first half of 2002. Other successes included macroeconomic stabilization, restructuring the banking sector, legislation to improve the business environment, improving state regulation of the financial sector, and privatizing state-owned companies. In 2001, Slovakia was declared in the Commission's Regular Report to have a functioning market economy and, given ongoing reforms, to be able to withstand competitive pressures within the EU's internal market.[46]

The dramatic transformation of Slovakia after 1998 is captured in the overall change in its Freedom House democratization and economic liberalization scores, illustrated in Table 7.1. For example, the independent media score changed from 4.25 in 1997 to 2.00 in 2001; the electoral process score changed from 3.75 in 1997 to 1.5 in 2003 (the lower the rating, the better).[47]

Meanwhile, the World Bank and the Slovak government registered an overall decrease in corruption in Slovakia between 1998 and 2001.[48] Most important, the secret services were reigned in, and fear was removed from Slovak politics. The Dzurinda government was, however, implicated in several corruption scandals that threatened its popularity, though not on the same scale as the Kostov government in Bulgaria. In several instances economic actors attempted to use their clientalistic ties with one of the ruling parties to influence the outcome of privatization decisions or the award of state contracts. Most of these scandals ended in the resignation of implicated politicians and civil servants (which was already an improvement on the Czech Republic where similar scandals rarely forced anyone to resign), but not in their prosecution. Meanwhile, in some areas such as health care, pensions, and combating high unemployment, observers charged that reforms had hardly even been attempted. Still, by the end of the Dzurinda government's term in 2002, Slovakia had become a "standard" democratic country with a well-functioning economy, a dynamic and open political arena, and at least a vibrant debate on how to improve education, health care, and social policy in the future.[49]

Slovakia's crowning achievement was catching up to Poland, Hungary, and the Czech Republic in fulfilling the requirements of EU membership so that it could join the EU with the other Visegrad states.[50] Foreign Minister Eduard Kukan and his team treated the publication each autumn of the European Commission's Regular Report as one of the most important benchmarks of the Dzurinda government's political, economic, legislative and institutional performance.[51] The government also revived Visegrad cooperation as a way to help Slovakia rejoin its three liberal neighbors.[52] Formal negotiations between Slovakia and the EU began in February 2000, and the Slovak negotiating team led by Ján Fígel lost no time in opening and closing chapters. Eventually Slovakia had done more than catch up: in 2002 it had closed more chapters than Poland, Hungary or the Czech Republic. On the eve of the elections in the autumn of 2002, there was every expectation that Slovakia would be invited to join the EU in the first wave—pending the outcome of the vote.

The Kostov Government in Bulgaria (1997–2001)

The UDF-led government of Ivan Kostov that took office in 1997 enjoyed tremendous legitimacy among the population after popular protests brought down the BSP government that had plunged Bulgaria into economic crisis in 1996. It also enjoyed relative internal harmony, because it had managed to unite many center-left, center-right, and right-wing opposition forces in one political party in a process that began in 1989. The UDF's coalition with two small parties, known as the United Democratic Forces (UtDF), functioned relatively smoothly, and its majority allowed it to pass legislation in parliament. Also, ethnic intolerance faded from the domestic discourse in Bulgaria, though the brutality and violence of the forced assimilation campaign against Bulgaria's Turks in the 1980s remained swept under the rug. The UDF took a positive stance toward Bulgaria's ethnic Turkish minority, and attempted at times even to attract Turkish voters to the party. The UDF did have some experience in government: its original leader Zhelu Zhelev served as president from 1990, and the party had held power for one year from 1990 to 1991. All told, the UDF-led government had much less trouble with infighting and ideological disagreements than coalitions attempting to govern at about the same time in Romania, in Slovakia and also in Poland.

For Bulgaria, the EU's leverage was focused most strongly in the area of economic reform, and intertwined with the conditional assistance program of the IMF. The UDF government turned the Bulgarian economy around from negative growth and hyperinflation in 1996 to an impressive 9 percent inflation and 5 percent growth in 1998. Bulgaria's currency board for the lev and strict austerity program were supervised by the IMF which, well pleased with Bulgaria's success, granted a three-year loan in September 1998 worth $860 million. Meanwhile, under strong pressure and in close communication with the European Commission, the government embarked on an ambitious program to restructure the banks and privatize state-owned enterprises. Compared to Slovakia, Bulgaria's economic reforms were lagging far behind when the reformers took office, while low state capacity and the consequences of the previous governments' policies posed a greater stumbling block.[53] The government ran into trouble, and many second-stage comprehensive reforms were severely delayed. Industrial production and productivity decreased, while foreign buyers for many state-owned enterprises could not be found.

Criticizing the UDF government for slow reform, many observers charged that the austerity measures and other reforms of 1997 were not particularly impressive: the UDF only did what it had to do in view of the profound economic crisis that elevated it to power. While this may be true, it puts the UDF in good company: taking office during an economic crisis (precipitated by the outgoing government) also prompted and dictated the reforms of Poland's Solidarity government in 1989, Hungary's Socialist government in 1995, and the Czech Republic's Social Democratic government in 1998.

The UDF did make important progress in shoring up the rule of law and reigning in activities of Bulgaria's economic nomenklatura that, as we saw in Chapter 2, operated virtually outside of the law under the BSP. Tarnishing the UDF's image more profoundly than stalled reform, however, was a series of corruption scandals directly implicating UDF politicians that made it appear that the UDF was little better than the BSP. Undermining its popularity even more, income levels remained very low, and much of the population experienced little or no benefit from ongoing economic reform. The UDF's comfortable position in parliament meant that widespread poverty and other issues could be sidelined from the domestic debate.[54] Meanwhile, the BSP was completely discredited by the economic fiasco of 1996 yet barely attempting internal reform. In this condition, it could not serve as an effective watchdog or a constructive opposition for the UDF government.

Still, the UDF moved the country visibly forward in qualifying for EU membership, and worked virtual miracles in rehabilitating Bulgaria's image in West European capitals. The relationship between Bulgaria and the EU became much more intense as addressing the deficiencies described in the Commission's Regular Reports and Accession Partnerships became the priority of the government. EU leaders became much more involved in Bulgaria's preparations, and EU officials supported cautiously but enthusiastically the Kostov government.[55] Foreign Minister Nadezhda Mihailova and her team wielded sufficient power in the government to compel other ministries to move on reforms in order to comply with EU rules. That Bulgaria was not invited to begin negotiations for EU membership by the Luxembourg European Council in December 1997 with the five "ins" did not come as a great disappointment; Bulgarian elites and citizens were realistic about when Bulgaria could be prepared for accession. After the 1998 and 1999 Regular Reports detailed Bulgaria's progress under the Kostov government, Bulgaria was invited to begin negotiations by the Helsinki European Council in December 1999 along with the four other "pre-ins."

Most damaging for the dedication of Bulgaria to the EU's pre-accession process was the fact that Bulgaria remained on the EU's negative visa list until April 2001. (Of the ten post-communist candidates, only Romania was also on this list, remaining until January 2002.) Requiring Bulgarian citizens to put themselves through a lengthy, arbitrary and often demeaning process to obtain a Schengen visa to travel to the EU, this created a great deal of ill will among the population and also among the Bulgarian elites that were supposed to be leading the country toward EU membership.[56] When Bulgaria was finally removed from the list, it was a day of striking national celebration that was profoundly meaningful for the many Bulgarians who considered the freedom to travel as the anchor of their return to Europe.[57]

The Constantinescu Government in Romania (1996–2000)

The coalition government led by the Democratic Convention of Romania (CDR) that took office in late 1996 heralded a new beginning for Romania. Bringing together the CDR, the Social Democratic Union (USD) and the Hungarian Democratic Union of Romania (UDMR), it included liberals, peasants, Christian democrats, social democrats, and Hungarians. The invitation to the Hungarians to share power in the government was a "revolution within a revolution," without precedent in the whole of Romania's independent history. It was the charming, sincere, and deeply committed geographer turned politician President Emil Constantinescu who was expected to lead the reformers in transforming Romania. He spoke out eloquently against extreme nationalism, and argued emphatically for accelerated economic reform, for restructuring the security services, and for a zealous battle against corruption in every corner of Romania's public life. The government led by Prime

Minister Victor Ciorbea of the CDR promised in its "Contract with Romania" to tackle all of Romania's most serious problems in its first 200 days.[58] The government's other opening gambit was a mighty diplomatic and domestic campaign for Romania to be invited to join NATO in May 1997 with Poland, Hungary, and the Czech Republic.

Sadly, coalition infighting undermined or blocked virtually all reform. The lion's share of political activity in Bucharest involved bargaining among the three coalition parties—as well as among different parties within the CDR and the USD. Each of the actors in the coalition supported variants of reform that would have benefited its own supporters, vetoing to the extent possible its partners' initiatives. Petre Roman's USD in particular revealed that it had no interest in authentic reform. The reform process soon devolved into a chaos of particularism, stalemate, and factional bartering that Michael Shafir attributes to the absence of compromise as a tradition in Romanian politics.[59] Many Romanians had thought that it would be "enough" to just get the opposition parties into power. They had presented themselves as competent and modern— claiming, for example, to have 15,000 experts on hand. The independent media and civic groups helped them defeat Iliescu without subjecting them to any scrutiny. As it turned out, the opposition leaders were unprepared, incompetent—and incredibly fractious.[60] They could not form a team, and spent much of their time fighting one another.

In comparison to Bulgaria, the situation of the Romanian reformers was less auspicious on four measures—the unity of the opposition, the legitimacy of the opposition, the prospects for economic reform, and the role of ethnic nationalism. Legitimacy was never bestowed on the CDR and its allies by widespread protests against the previous government. The protests and strikes throughout Bulgaria in January 1997 provided legitimacy to the UDF government, while the economic collapse completely discredited the BSP's later attacks on accelerating economic reform. In contrast, the fragmented and ideologically divergent Romanian opposition parties never had the opportunity to turn the support of hundreds of thousands of Romanians cheering them in the streets into a clear program of reform. Iliescu's PDSR and its extremist coalition partners kept Romanian protestors off the streets—and the economy afloat, failing to discredit themselves as overtly as the BSP in their last year in office.

Economic reform could be postponed by the Constantinescu government because in 1996 the Romanian economy was not on the verge of collapse. The desperation of Bulgaria's economic situation in early 1997 left the new government with little to debate: the austerity program and currency board were essential, and they imposed discipline. In Romania, Ciorbea's government made encouraging progress in the first half of 1997, but subsequent infighting until the 2000 elections left reform almost at a standstill while the opposition's promises in the "Contract with Romania" were quickly forgotten. Some observers suggested that an economic collapse—in the summer months when the poor would suffer less—would have been desirable to break Romania's political deadlock.[61]

Ethnic nationalism declined as a force in domestic politics but not as much as in Bulgaria and Slovakia. The victory of the opposition forces on the heels of Iliescu's signature of the Basic Treaty with Hungary did diminish the importance of the issue. However, as a member of the governing coalition, the Hungarian Democratic Union of Romania (UDMR) pursued passionately its quest for political and minority rights and this attracted hostile reactions not just from the opposition, but also from factions within the coalition, deepening the gridlock.[62] Meanwhile, the extremist parties, sometimes supported by the PDSR, filled the parliament and press with accusations that the president and government were committing treason by cooperating with the Hungarians.

What is particularly striking about the Constantinescu government is how much it pinned its hopes on the idea that early NATO membership and closer relations with the EU would provide momentum for subsequent attempts at domestic reform. External affirmation was to precede, indeed to *cause*, internal reforms. Soon after taking office, the government put in motion a grand public relations campaign at home and abroad in support of Romania's inclusion in the first wave of NATO expansion.[63] In a bizarre and desperate twist, it continued this campaign in the Romanian media (especially through television commercials calling on Romanian citizens to support Romania joining NATO right away) long after the foreign ministry had been told explicitly that Romania would not be invited to join with Poland, Hungary and the Czech Republic at NATO's Washington summit in May 1997. When NATO's rejection was finally acknowledged, the dejection of the government and its citizens was blamed for stalled domestic reform.[64]

Despite Romania's dismal track record on reforming the state and the economy, the Commission in its 1999 Regular Report recommended that Romania be invited to begin accession negotiations with the four other pre-ins in recognition of the fact that the Constantinescu government was moving Romania in the right direction. The Helsinki European Council followed through on the invitation, motivated in part by concern about the repercussions for Romanian domestic politics if Romania was the only "pre-in" held back. Some scholars and Romanian officials commented that the EU's invitation at the Helsinki summit deflected pressure from the elite and allowed them to delay or avoid certain economic reforms.[65] The Commission's Regular Reports on Romania each autumn painted a dreary picture; the Constantinescu government accepted the Commission's extensive criticisms with more grace than denial, but at the same time some Romanian politicians remained all too comfortable with the image of Romania as the victim of Western neglect and not the victim of its own legacies, institutions, and elites.

Constantinescu's deep commitment to a pro-Western foreign policy for Romania was indomitable, withstanding the disappointment of not being invited to join NATO in 1997 as well as considerable opposition from nationalist voices at home. During 1999, for example, the Constantinescu government strongly supported NATO's military intervention in Kosovo, standing firm against overwhelming opposition among Romanian citizens and vicious attacks by the opposition parties in parliament. The Constantinescu government described its support for NATO in Kosovo as a way to prove Romania's credentials for future membership.[66] As new elections in 2000 approached, it was impossible to deny that the Constantinescu government had transformed Romania by establishing a fairer and more open arena for political competition, by bolstering the rule of law, by promoting ethnic tolerance, and by anchoring Romania very firmly to a Western foreign policy.

Conclusions about the Performance of the Reformers

From the sketches above, we see that the performance of the reformers in Slovakia, Bulgaria, and Romania varied significantly. This variation was caused in part by the quality of the domestic institutions that developed after 1989 *in opposition* to the rule of illiberal elites. Like oppositions to communism in Poland, Hungary, and Czechoslovakia, activity in opposition to the democratic monopoly of illiberal rulers in Slovakia, Bulgaria and Romania helped build consensus and cooperation among disparate forces that would later take power in these countries. EU membership was an important focal point for cooperation, and complying with EU rules helped construct a common agenda for reform—but success in carrying out this agenda once the reformers took power could not be guaranteed from Brussels.

In Romania, we see that the monopoly on power of the illiberal rulers after 1989 combined with other factors to hinder the development of a unified and purposeful opposition. Instead, the first seven years after communism brought what Aurelian Crăiuțu calls the process of "perverse institutionalization," of clientalism, corruption, and low standards in public life; these are now proving very difficult to dislodge.[67] The consequence for Romania was that the reformers that had managed to unite to win power could not compromise sufficiently in order to govern adequately or to implement much of their agenda. To simplify to a fault, Romania's reformers needed to battle against perverse institutionalization, but this process had also molded and co-opted them. This reveals some of the limits of the agent-based mechanisms of cooperation, adapting, and implementation that we explored in Chapter 6, and that we will dwell on further in the next section. Instead, it highlights the continued salience of historical institutionalist theory that privileges the role of existing institutions in explaining the outcome of policy-making.

7.3.2 The Performance of Successive Governments

New governments are elected in Romania in 2000, in Bulgaria in 2001, and in Slovakia in 2002. What happens? Our "reformers" are completely trounced in Romania and Bulgaria, and they are resoundingly re-elected in Slovakia. The three governments that take power differ from one another quite dramatically. In Romania, Iliescu and the PDSR are returned to power by the failures of the CDR government. In Bulgaria, a new party led by the former King sweeps to power promising economic salvation and technocratic efficiency. In Slovakia, the center-right parties from the previous coalition government make important gains and form a more streamlined coalition government with even greater consensus on political and economic reform.

What are the consequences of these very different electoral outcomes? Do our "post" illiberal states part ways here? No: different as they may be, these governments continue to implement political and economic reforms in order to qualify for EU membership.[68] They all continue on the road to EU membership, demonstrating the profound impact of the EU's active leverage on their domestic politics. For all of the reasons that we explored in the first two sections of this chapter, not one of them reneges on promised reforms, or questions the imperative of complying with EU rules. The tenure of reformers in government has transformed the polity and the economy, empowering groups with stakes in European integration and opening up the flows of funding and foreign investment that accompany the approval of the West. Turning back on the road to EU membership would impose prohibitively high costs on (almost) any new government.

The victory and tenure of reformers was also part of a process that improved and intensified the quality of domestic political competition, heightening accountability and reducing the opportunities for rent seeking. The abrogation of democratic standards, the downgrading of ethnic minority rights, or calling a halt to economic reforms are nowhere on the agenda of the ruling parties—not even on the unspoken agenda of the returning PDSR in Romania. Here we see most clearly the power of the EU's pre-accession process to bring about convergence among the mainstream political parties in a candidate state. While Romania's previous illiberal rulers may have been re-elected, they have not returned to (most of) their old ways. Thus the EU's active leverage has helped encourage formerly illiberal political forces to change their political agendas. Yet there is still a great deal of variation among the three states on the pace of reform, with few surprises: Slovakia has catapulted itself forward, Bulgaria is working hard but struggling in many areas, and Romania trails far behind—a rank order that does not come as a surprise given our analysis in Chapters 2 and 6.

Does it matter anymore who wins? For the quality of preparations for EU membership in the liberal pattern states in the 1990s, it mattered little which constellation of mainstream parties won in national elections. Have the illiberal states converged with the liberal ones so that now, from the perspective of working to qualify for EU membership, the mainstream political parties are also interchangeable? I argue below that yes, this is the case—with two important caveats for future governments in Romania: first, it may not matter anymore which mainstream parties win in a positive way (all are moderate and pro-EU) but also in a less positive way (all are impotent). Second, mainstream parties may not always win. Let us turn now to a brief analysis of the three successor governments, focusing on the momentum for reform, the overall quality of democracy, and the development of viable left- and right-wing parties.

The Second Dzurinda Government in Slovakia (2002–6)

In 2002 the Slovak voters soundly re-elected Slovakia's reformers, giving four center-right parties a majority in parliament. The priority of many Slovak voters was Slovakia's accession to the EU and NATO: a foreign policy issue, albeit a very special one, mattered significantly in this election. The EU made the trade-off faced by the Slovak voter abundantly clear: re-elect Mečiar, and Slovakia will not be invited to become an EU member at the Copenhagen European Council summit in December 2002. Mečiar was not elected, and Slovakia was invited to join the EU with seven other post-communist countries in May 2004 thanks to the work of the first Dzurinda government. Slovakia thus succeeded along with two other "pre-ins," Latvia and Lithuania, in catching up with the "ins." This "big bang" enlargement was caused by the unexpected zeal with which these three "pre-ins" closed the distance between their reforms and those of the "ins." It was also caused by the greater institutional, bureaucratic, and economic ease of admitting together all of the Baltic States, and also the two former parts of Czechoslovakia.

Slovak voters took the imperative of EU-oriented reform a step further than expected in the 2002 elections: they voted out the two left-wing parties in the previous coalition government, the Party of the Democratic Left and SOP. These parties had provoked conflicts among coalition members, attempted to dictate policy, and stalled economic reform. Instead, the Slovak voters strengthened the hand of the ambitious reformers in the previous government.[69] The four new governing parties became the Slovak Democratic and Christian Union (SDKU), the Party of the Hungarian Coalition (SMK), Christian Democratic Movement (KDH), and the Alliance of the New Citizen

(ANO), all of them representing the center-right. Mikuláš Dzurinda was reappointed Prime Minister, Eduard Kukan remained Foreign Minister, and Ivan Mikloš became Finance Minister.[70]

The government immediately laid out an ambitious agenda for reforming the country's tax, pension, healthcare, and social welfare systems, anticipating the ability to push through reforms considerably faster than the previous Dzurinda government. It implemented, for example, sweeping changes in the public finance system that have earned Slovakia acclaim for the lowest tax rates in Central Europe, creating a "paradise" for foreign investors and pressure on neighboring states to follow suit.[71] Ironically, ten years after Václav Klaus's supposedly ultra-liberal Czech Republic parted ways with Vladimir Mečiar's Slovakia, it is Slovakia that has implemented the kinds of fiscal policies that Klaus embraced rhetorically but barely implemented in reality.

It was a surprise that the popularity of the populist Smer party dropped sharply before the elections; it had been expected to come in second after Mečiar's HZDS. Sharon Fisher argues that the drop can be explained partly by the insistence of Smer's leader, Robert Fico, on standing up to the EU at a time when voters, especially young ones, wanted to take no chances on EU membership. One Smer campaign poster featured four people with their pants pulled down, together with the slogan: "To the European Union! But not with naked bottoms!" The SDKU, in contrast, put up billboards with slogans such as "There's just a small step left to NATO and the EU. With us you'll make it." According to Fisher, the SDKU put considerable emphasis on foreign policy, which was probably the most important impetus behind the (unexpected) decision of Slovak voters to hand the SDKU a victory over Smer in the elections.[72]

The 2002 elections demonstrated the convergence of all political parties toward support for EU membership because, as one politician quipped, to do otherwise would be "political self-disqualification." The programs of all of Slovakia's political parties announced their support for Slovakia joining the EU.[73] The HZDS, for its part, appeared increasingly frantic to gain the international respectability that it had squandered in the 1990s, and to assure the electorate that it would not throw away Slovakia's international achievements since 1998 if it returned to power. The party program of the HZDS declared "its irreversible decision to support Slovakia's integration into the EU with all of its might."[74] The HZDS technically won the elections with 19.5 percent of the vote, but no other party would cooperate with it, chiefly because of the character of Mečiar. Had the HZDS been able to form a government after the 2002 elections, we can speculate that not even Mečiar would have tried to turn Slovakia back on the road to EU membership. But the EU would have probably never given him a chance, keeping its promise to exclude a Slovakia led by Mečiar. In 2004, Slovak voters elected a mostly reformed ex-HZDS stalwart as president, reflecting two ongoing trends—the transformation of illiberal politicians to fit the new parameters of Slovak politics, and the inability of the "opposition" parties to settle on a single candidate.

The outstanding feature of Slovakia's emerging democratic polity is the ongoing engagement of civic groups in the content and quality of Slovakia's public life. Neither the influence of the individual civic groups in politics nor the umbrella Third Sector association itself faded away after Mečiar was defeated in the 1998 elections. Nor did all of the civil society leaders rush to join the new government. Instead, many of Slovakia's intellectuals and civil society leaders have sought to advise but also to criticize the coalition government from the outside.[75] The Institute of Public Affairs has continued to publish its annual analysis of the state of Slovakia (called the "Súhrnná správa" or "Global Report") that its editors describe as itself "an agent of change." It has helped to foster "an informal coalition of independent think tanks, non-government organizations, academic institutions and research institutes" that write a critical analysis of Slovakia's domestic politics, foreign policy, economy and society every year. These analyses since 1998 have often formed the basis for the Slovak government's strategies for moving forward with reform.[76] Overall the strength of Slovakia's "third sector" has improved the quality of political competition and debate quite dramatically at a time when the HZDS has hardly been functioning as a constructive opposition.

The Simeon Government in Bulgaria (2001–5)

In June 2001 Bulgarian voters handed power to a party led by an unusual outsider, Simeon-Saxe-Coburg, a former king who fled Bulgaria in 1946. Capitalizing on popular disappointment with corruption and poverty, the National Movement Simeon II (NMSS) captured 42 percent of the vote and a near majority in parliament. Simeon, a second cousin to Britain's Queen Elizabeth, was elected prime minister and much of the party's popularity resided in his personal appeal. The NMSS formed a coalition with the MRF; it made history by appointing the first ethnic Turks to hold cabinet posts since Bulgaria's independence in 1878. The NMSS also included an unprecedented number of women on electoral lists, increasing the percentage of women in parliament from 7.5 to 25.4.[77] Simeon's cabinet included insiders of Bulgaria's political scene, including BSP members, as well as "expert" outsiders. Although generally right-centre in orientation, the party won over many voters with promises to bring significant economic improvement "within 800 days."[78] Immediate change did not come, of course, and Bulgarian voters expressed their discontent later that year by electing Socialist Georgi Parvanov to the presidency.

The consensus on NATO as well as EU membership was cemented by the NMSS. One of Bulgaria's earliest and most passionate advocates of NATO membership, Foreign Minister Solomon Passy, presided over Bulgaria's invitation to join NATO in 2002 and its accession in March 2004. Negotiations with the EU moved steadily forward, with Bulgaria closing chapters more rapidly than Romania. The Commission's 2002 Regular Report declared Bulgaria to have a "functioning market economy."[79] Negotiations were concluded in June 2004, but monitoring of key areas of reform continues, including the state administration, the regulation of the economy, and the fight against corruption. In the event of unsatisfactory reform, the EU may re-open the negotiations.

Bulgarian citizens remain convinced that corruption is endemic, but Transparency International's Corruption Perceptions Index shows improvements for each of the four years from 1998 to 2002.[80] In 2002, the government's Action Plan on corruption created a commission charged with bringing to the courts evidence to try corruption cases. NGOs are also becoming more involved in publicizing and prosecuting corruption cases.[81] Poverty and unemployment remain Bulgaria's most pressing problems. From 2000 to 2004, unemployment has remained close to 20 percent, while roughly one quarter of the population lives below the poverty line.[82] The NMSS government has made progress in reforms neglected by the UDF, particularly reducing the state's overbearing role in the economy. Economic growth has been impressive, above 4 percent each year, and forecast at 4.2 percent in 2004.[83] Overall, the NMSS has kept economic reform and EU accession on track. But Simeon's promises of economic salvation in 2001 stand in stark contrast to the ongoing poverty of average Bulgarians. Once again, reform has not improved living standards and this has led to a sharp drop in the popularity of the NMSS. More worrying, it has contributed to disenhancement with political parties as agents for positive change.[84]

Still, it is to the credit of Simeon that he was there in 2001 to take power; the parties that might otherwise have filled the vacuum would almost certainly have done worse. The NMSS will probably not survive the next parliamentary elections scheduled for mid-2005. The Socialists are the favorites. They finally show signs of reform, embracing EU accession and softening their rhetoric on market reform. The BSP's return to power should hasten its transformation into a modern social democratic party. And if it wins, the once ambivalent BSP will likely preside over Bulgaria's entry into the EU: in December 2004 the commission will make a recommendation to the European Council as to Bulgaria's fitness to join as planned in 2007.

The Third Iliescu Government in Romania (2000–4)

The 2000 elections in Romania returned Ion Iliescu to the presidency, and gave his party, the PDSR a comfortable majority in parliament. The CDR was routed, failing to gain any representation in parliament; and Petre Roman's

USD also did poorly. Deeply disenchanted, Romanian voters were determined to vote against the CDR government; surveys showed, however, that they were not voting for the PDSR or against democracy. The ineffectiveness, gridlock, and corruption scandals of the CDR-led government caused the success of Iliescu, as did the enduring disunity of the center-right parties that could not, for example, even agree on a single presidential candidate in the 2000 elections. Among the center-right forces whose parliamentary representation had been 35.6 percent after the 1996 elections, only the liberals entered parliament in 2000 with 8.7 percent, having left the CDR and founded the National Liberal Party.[85]

The drama of the elections turned out to be the strong second-place finish in the first round of the presidential elections of the extreme right wing politician Corneliu Vadim Tudor. In the run-off election between Tudor and Iliescu, all of the moderate forces in Romania had to rally their supporters to vote for Iliescu in order to defeat Tudor. While Tudor espouses xenophobic, extremist political views, it turned out that his sympathizers and even his voters generally embraced democracy, tolerance and Romania's integration into Western organizations. For them, Tudor stood for using draconian measures to curb corruption and sweep out the entrenched, corrupt, and ineffective political class that had ruled Romania for the past decade.[86]

Installed again in power, Iliescu and the PDSR have behaved quite differently than during their previous seven years of rule.[87] Enmeshed in the EU's pre-accession process, they have had to continue with the reforms of the state and the economy stipulated by Romania's Accession Partnership. The government, formed by Prime Minister Adrian Năstase from the PDSR's reformist wing, has been praised by the World Bank, the European Bank for Reconstruction and Development (EBRD) as well as the European Commission for tackling stalled economic reforms. The government has made important progress in privatizing state-owned banks, shutting down inefficient enterprises and attracting foreign investment. After 2000, the economy returned to positive growth after the long recession from 1997 to 1999 in part thanks to these policies.

More striking, the PDSR has abandoned most uses of ethnic nationalism for political profit; it avoided nationalist appeals in its 2000 campaign, and has even cooperated with the UDMR on legislation to improve the position of ethnic minorities in local administration. Overall, Vladimir Tismaneanu has argued that Iliescu has truly learned to behave like a democrat. After four years of taking his role as the loyal opposition very seriously, he has made a legitimate return to power.[88] The Iliescu government does, however, control too much of the information that is available to many Romanian citizens. The state television is widely described as biased in support of the government, while many of Romania's private media outlets have reason to tread carefully when it comes to criticizing the PDSR because they are owned by people close to the PDSR, they owe debts to banks controlled by such people, or indeed they owe debts to the state. Also, in what can be interpreted as a move to manipulate the information environment, the PDSR renamed itself yet again, becoming in June 2001 the Social Democratic Party (PSD). (We, however, will keep calling it the PDSR until the end of this book.)

There is no question that Iliescu and his team are better able to govern than their CDR predecessors, living up belatedly (and only partially) to their self-styled image as efficient post-communist technocrats. And there are many indications that at least the reform faction within the PDSR would like to implement ambitious reforms. Yet so far they have failed in many areas, and Romania is beset with problems. This third Iliescu government seems to have been caught in its own trap—in the "perverse" institutionalization[89] of clientalism and corruption that it helped create. The fact that comprehensive political and economic reforms were not done quickly gave time for a new class of powerful politicians and businessmen to crystallize out of the former communist nomenklatura. For this new class, it is not beneficial to change the way that Romania is governed; they benefit from the lack of competent politicians and bureaucrats, the lack of transparency, the weakness of civil society, and the shallowness of competition among political parties.[90]

Such a class also developed in other post-communist states: why has it proved more difficult to dislodge in Romania? As argued above, the quality of domestic political competition was much lower in Romania during the years of illiberal rule. The Romanian bureaucracy is perceived as captured by networks going back to the managers of state enterprises and the second and third rank nomenklatura surrounding Iliescu when he gained power (the "directocracy"). Now there seem to be relatively few people pushing to displace this new class—because most political elites are "in" it; because many disenchanted elites have simply left Romania; and because other elites (especially young people) have avoided public life. Consequently, as Alina Mungiu-Pippidi, Sorin Ioniță, and Aurelian Muntean argue, "What is missing is good governance: coherent sets of policies developed by local decision-makers through a legitimate and transparent process engaging the stakeholders involved in their implementation."[91] The government and the state administration lack the capacity to design, adopt, and implement public policies, while civil society groups are too weak to train enough new political elites and exert enough pressure on the old ruling class.

So how do we evaluate Romania's political trajectory? The incentives of complying with EU membership requirements have led Romania's former illiberal rulers to move closer to the political profile of Poland or Hungary's post-communist parties. As a result, the outcome of the 2000 general elections has had little impact on Romania's development goals and strategies. This indicates convergence: like in Poland or Hungary, the policy on joining the

EU and implementing reform is no longer in suspense in the run up to elections (unless the popularity of the extremists surges). As Annette Freyberg-Inan points out, the parties and politicians have converged in presenting the goals and norms of international organizations as fundamental to the national interest.[92] EU integration has become a resource for almost all political elites seeking ways to maintain and consolidate political power—and the search for approbation from Western leaders has been intense.

Yet there are drawbacks to this outward devotion to the EU and other international organizations. Unlike the first and second Iliescu governments, the third Iliescu government does not blatantly violate the requirements of EU membership at home. But many Romanian political parties use a tactical embrace of NATO and EU membership as a substitute for a real political program, and as a way to encourage acquiescence on the part of the Romanian people. By working with the Iliescu government and giving Romania a target date of 2007 for membership, the EU confers legitimacy on the Iliescu government. There are clear and disturbing signs that Romania's EU efforts really are what commentators have feared: minimal reforms done only to please the international community, with no basis in the real and internalized agendas of Romanian political parties and interest groups. It may not matter anymore who gets elected: none of the main political parties are likely to disqualify Romania from the EU accession process. However, who gets elected may not "matter" in another way: no Romanian political parties are able to improve the quality of democracy and governance in Romania.[93]

What should the EU do with Romania? It seems that Romania's political elites have adroitly positioned themselves to secure EU membership for Romania in 2007 without meeting the EU's requirements at least as well as other post-communist candidates. Why would the EU violate its own rules and let Romania in? The same arguments for inclusion and against exclusion are at play as in the beginning of the 1990s. If Romania is excluded, the popularity of the extremists could surge and the country could turn its back entirely on Western liberal democracy. In turn, it could destabilize the region and undermine the EU's project to democratize the Balkans. Also, it is evidently difficult to impose conditionality when the conjuncture of Romania's tyrannical communist past, institutionalized clientelism, low quality political class, and widespread poverty make reform seem so intractable. Perhaps active leverage, for all of its might, can only do so much in this case.

But should the EU give up on using its active leverage to ensure better compliance with EU rules by Romania just because it has not worked as quickly as elsewhere? After all, it is amazing that eight countries made so much progress in order to join the EU in 2004, and that Bulgaria is struggling forward. While the political costs of holding Romanian back may seem very high, they may be much lower for the Romanian polity than squandering the opportunity to push for reform as a condition of EU membership. Once it is gone, it may take many decades to accomplish the same reforms that could have been (mostly) accomplished before accession. Weighing these (and no doubt other) arguments, the European Council will make a decision in December 2004 about whether or not Romania is on track to join in 2007.[94]

Conclusions about Convergence: Could the EU have done more?

We may conclude that institutional and financial assistance from the EU, even EU membership itself, cannot bring salvation (or even good governance) if domestic elites do not rise to the challenge of transforming the polity and the economy. As an aside, we can look at the performance of both sets of governments in Bulgaria and Romania from a different angle and ask: did the EU and other Western actors provide enough help? The question is not whether the EU could have "saved" the UDF and the CDR and got them re-elected. Even if somehow it could (which seems extremely unlikely given the nature of their problems), further alternation of power has been beneficial in both countries: it has brought a new configuration of center-right elites into public life in Bulgaria, and it has moderated the PDSR in Romania. However, could different policies on the part of the EU have helped reform?

All I can do here is make three suggestions. First, the financial assistance provided for Bulgaria and Romania was only adjusted upward to take into account their greater economic backwardness and lower state capacity as part of the 1999 Stability Pact for the Balkans (which we will discuss in the next chapter)—and still the amounts remained modest. More assistance as well as better (complete) access to EU markets should have been provided, sooner. Second, the visa requirements for Bulgarian and Romanian citizens worked at cross-purposes with the EU's active leverage. Resentment of the inability to travel freely decreased the willingness of public figures to portray themselves as pro-European, undermined the popularity of those who did, and fed a sense of futility about ever being allowed into the European club.

Third, the attention and resources for training opposition political elites and promoting civil society groups were insufficient.[95] We can see that the higher quality of political competition during the period of illiberal rule is linked to the greater effectiveness of the first government of reformers, giving Bulgaria a significant edge over Romania even though they shared similarly weak economies in 1989. No amount of funding or cajoling, of course, could undo the legacy of Ceauşescu or the character of the Romanian elites that took power in 1989. However, Western actors may have been able to do more to energize, strengthen and shape Romania's opposition forces and civic groups in the early 1990s.

7.4   Alternative Explanations

We turn now briefly to two alternative explanations, the first questioning the usefulness of the EU's active leverage, and the second questioning the usefulness of a rationalist approach to explaining why and how elites respond to the EU's active leverage. Beginning with the usefulness of the EU's active leverage, was it really a key factor in the convergence of governments in ECE around an agenda of comprehensive reforms of the state and the economy within the parameters of "acceptable" democratic standards and protections for ethnic minority rights?

Absent the EU, one could argue that these countries would sooner or later complete pro-Western reforms. They would do so because of the inescapable pressure of the world economy: globalization, not EU leverage, provides the impetus for reform. Even if candidates were uncertain that they could join, they would be forced to adopt most of the EU's norms and rules because of their dependence on the EU's market and on foreign investors. One could also argue that the rewards of EU membership (passive leverage) are so substantial that eventually all plausible candidates would fulfill the membership requirements. On this account, the EU's deliberate policies (active leverage) are irrelevant. At most, they serve to speed the process up on the margins.

While either of these competing explanations may bear out if you have a long enough time horizon, they cannot explain the variation that we see over the first fifteen years after the collapse of communism. If the main impetus for reform was globalization, we would expect that at least some post-Soviet states that are not credible future members of the EU but that nevertheless could profit from the EU market would exhibit similar patterns of reform. Instead, we see a striking divergence between Poland and Ukraine, or Bulgaria and Georgia. If the main impetus was the EU's passive leverage alone, then it is more puzzling why some credible future EU members did not immediately seek to qualify for the benefits of EU membership. I argue that the EU's active leverage made it impossible for governing elites to pretend to be preparing for EU membership, while at the same time using ethnic nationalism to win elections and corrupt reform to generate economic rents. Without well-developed tools of active leverage, such elites could simply claim discrimination ("the West despises us") and govern with impunity, as in fact they do today in nearby states that are not subject to the EU's active leverage such as Ukraine and Belarus.

Rationalist versus Constructivist Mechanisms for Explaining Compliance

What are the causal mechanisms by which the EU impacts on the course of domestic politics? In other words, how and why do actors in domestic politics respond to the benefits and the requirements of EU membership? I have answered this question in two steps over the course of the last two chapters.

First, I have explored how and why domestic actors outside of government in illiberal pattern states were influenced by the national predicament (and the political opportunity) of being ruled by political parties that were severely undermining their state's prospects for EU membership. I made essentially a rationalist argument: for office-seeking opposition politicians, a pro-Western and pro-EU platform was promising for defeating their opponents, especially given the EU's active leverage that criticized the government; provided a focal point for cooperation with other parties; and promised rewards for compliance. But just what opposition politicians presented as a pro-EU platform was informed and refined by adapting to the rules imposed by the EU for prospective members. By the time these parties were elected to office, they had created a domestic power base that expected, even demanded, progress toward EU membership.

Second, I have explored how and why domestic actors in government in liberal pattern and "post" illiberal pattern states shaped the output of the domestic policymaking process to comply with the requirements of EU membership. Again, I have made essentially a rationalist argument: in light of their promises of attaining full membership in the EU, politicians sought the rewards of building liberal democracy and market capitalism to please their domestic power base including a substantial portion of the electorate. Consequently, governments adjusted domestic policymaking enough to qualify for membership.[96] The structure of the EU's pre-accession process shaped their behavior along the way—they were neither too confident (thanks to asymmetric interdependence), nor were they too disingenuous (thanks to enforcement), nor did they despair that the system was arbitrary (thanks to meritocracy). The interests of office-seeking politicians interacted with the EU's active leverage to produce the reforms of the state and the economy that we have discussed in this chapter.

There are, however, other ways of understanding elite behavior that complement or rival a rationalist approach. What other mechanisms or processes lead domestic actors to comply with EU requirements—but not just requirements, also norms and expectations? Whereas a rationalist approach treats elite compliance as the product of a cost-benefit calculation that is centered on strategies to attain political and economic goods, a constructivist approach takes into account other motivations for compliance. Instead of following the rationalist "logic of consequence," the behavior of actors is motivated by the "logic of appropriateness." Actors do what is deemed appropriate in a given situation and given their social role.[97] International organizations can seek to convince states that their own norms represent "appropriate" behavior: "If their claims and arguments are convincing, domestic actors engage in (complex) learning, that is, they accept the norms as legitimate and comply with them out of moral commitment or a sense of obligation."[98]

Rachel Epstein argues that material incentives cannot fully account for the tremendous influence of international actors on domestic politics in post-communist states. Instead, materialist mechanisms work in tandem with social mechanisms that transform domestic policy choices, not exclusively through coercion, but through the appeal to Western norms and values. Epstein argues that after 1989, domestic elites in post-communist states were the targets of persuasion by Western actors and international organizations that under some conditions were successful in transmitting their norms and values in this way. Also, domestic elites in some situations adopted Western norms and values because they sought affirmation from Western actors and international organizations.[99]

From the interviews that I conducted, the power of persuasion and socialization seemed most clearly at work in shaping the attitudes and political beliefs of opposition parties in Romania, Bulgaria and Slovakia after 1989. Several important political actors of the opposition told me that they had changed their position after they became persuaded that concentrating political power and scapegoating ethnic minorities was "not European" and therefore wrong. This came out most clearly in Slovakia, where many leading members of Mečiar's ruling HZDS left the party in 1993 and 1994 in protest of his abuse of power. However, in Slovakia these same politicians also left the HZDS with an eye on winning the next elections. In other words, they thought that conforming to European standards and qualifying for EU membership was a political platform that could be a winner. They were giving up short-term power in an illiberal government, but for potentially greater power in (what they promised would be) a liberal government.

7.5 Conclusion

I argued in this chapter that in all of the candidates for EU membership, the EU's active leverage promoted reforms of the state and the economy. The most important mechanisms for compelling reform were conditionality, credible commitment, and influence on domestic groups. Governments had to reform in order to move forward in the EU's pre-accession process. Moving forward in this process in turn served as a credible commitment mechanism for many economic actors that treated it as a guarantee of ongoing reform. Moving forward also strengthened groups that benefited from integration in the EU. All together these mechanisms helped create a consensus among all mainstream political parties to continue EU-oriented reforms as falling behind or dropping out of the process became more and more costly.

I also explored how well our "post-illiberal" states implemented reform, and the variation among their compliance with EU rules. I compared the performance of the governments of "reformers" that took power in 1996 in Romania, in 1997 in Bulgaria, and in 1998 in Slovakia, as well as the performance of their immediate successors. The EU's active leverage set in motion positive changes in illiberal pattern states, sanctifying democratic standards, improving the quality of domestic political competition, sidelining ethnic intolerance and creating momentum for economic reform. It also helped set the parameters for competition among political parties. Continuing to move forward in the EU's pre-accession process provided strong incentives for all mainstream political parties to change their political and economic agendas (if not their hearts and minds) in order to prevent their country from falling behind. Even when previous illiberal rulers were re-elected in Romania because of the failure of the "reformers" to govern effectively, they did not return to (most) of their old ways, complying instead with EU rules.

But just as in Chapter 6 we concluded that the key to the EU's leverage was its synergy with domestic opposition groups, in this chapter we can see that an important factor determining the impact of EU leverage on reform is the effectiveness of governments. Reforming the state and the economy cannot be done without committed politicians and skilled officials, and without pressure and assistance from domestic groups. How do we explain the variation in the effectiveness of governments in the three "post-illiberal" states? Structural conditions are certainly important, such as the strength of the economy and the capacity of the state. Yet the performance of the reformers also depends on their own decisions, and more broadly on the quality of the domestic institutions that developed after 1989 *in opposition* to the rule of illiberal elites.

Our model allows for significant change over time, yet the outcomes that we observe underscore that the initial environment continues to matter profoundly. What the illiberal pattern states were missing in 1989 was a strong democratic opposition. But in Bulgaria and Slovakia the seeds of such an opposition were much more in evidence than in Romania. As a consequence, Bulgarian and especially Slovak opposition forces could govern more effectively once in power: their experience in opposition led to better cooperation and a stronger consensus on a common agenda; and their prior success in constraining the illiberal rulers left them with less intractable domestic policy legacies to tackle in office.

The performance of post-illiberal governments in Romania has been the most disappointing. Romania represents the greatest success—and also the greatest failure—of the EU's active leverage. The parameters of domestic politics in Romania have been visibly constrained and moderated by the quest for EU membership, yet successive governments seem incapable of implementing more than superficial reform. In December 2004, the European Council will face the difficult question of whether to commit to a 2007 accession date for Romania.

The Endgame of the Negotiations and the Future of an Enlarged European Union

Ten new members, eight of them post-communist states, joined the European Union (EU) on May 1, 2004. In this chapter I look at the dynamics of an enlarged EU and provide insights into how both the EU itself and the EU's new member states are likely to act in the future. First, I explore competing views on the repercussions of the EU's active leverage for the future quality of democratic institutions and for the prosperity of the economy in the new members. Did it promote robust democratic institutions and a vigorous economy, as I argued in the last chapter, or did it in fact undermine them?

Next, I explain the "endgame" of the negotiations, and consider how the new members are likely to comport themselves in the EU. The unfavorable terms of accession for the new members that emerged from the "endgame" of the negotiations may make them dig in and bargain hard for improvement. But will their intransigence combined with their diversity bring European integration to a standstill? Or will the new members instead be sidelined from partaking in and influencing European integration by being forced to accept a second-class status? I argue that both of these concerns are overblown, and that in many ways the EU will function as it did before enlargement.

Third, I look at why the EU decided to enlarge to these eight post-communist states, and explore how much further it is likely to go. The EU's active leverage has turned out to be the most powerful tool of its foreign policy: On how many more aspiring members will the EU choose to use it? Will the benefits of using the EU's active leverage prove irresistible, even if EU elites and publics are far from reconciled to the consequences of using this tool? As a reference for this chapter, Table 8.1 summarizes the state of play of the EU's membership in 2004. It also indicates both the economic diversity (measured in GDP per capita) among the EU's old members, the economic disparity between old and new members, and also the relative economic weakness of states still left in the queue.

TABLE 8.1   The enlargement of the European Union, 2004

Old EU members 2002 GDP per capita in \$		New EU members 2002 GDP per capita in \$		Estimated years to reach EU-15 average GDP per capita		States with active applications and corresponding 2002 GDP per capita in \$	
Luxembourg	49,100	Cyprus	18,600	Cyprus	21	Croatia	10,100
Ireland	32,600	Slovenia	18,500	Slovenia	31	Bulgaria	7,100
Denmark	29,200	Malta	17,600	Malta	29	Romania	6,500
Netherlands	29,000	Czech Rep	15,100	Czech Rep	39	Turkey	6,400
Austria	28,900	Hungary	13,900	Hungary	34		
U.K.	28,000	Slovakia	12,300	Slovakia	38		
Belgium	27,700	Estonia	12,200	Estonia	31	*SAA Agreement*	
Sweden	27,300	Poland	10,800	Poland	59	*Macedonia*	
France	27,200	Lithuania	10,300	Lithuania	53	*Albania*	
Finland	26,500	Latvia	9,200	Latvia	58		
Germany	25,600					*In SAP Process*	
Italy	25,900					*Serbia-Montenegro*	
Spain	22,400					*Bosnia-Hercegovina*	
Greece	18,400						
Portugal	18,400						
EU-15 average:	27,750	New members average:	13,850			Active applicants average:	7,525

Sources: For old members, OECD (2003). For new members, World Bank (2002*b*). Estimates of number of years for new members to reach EU-15 average are from "A May Day Milestone," *The Economist*, April 30, 2004.

8.1   Debating the Impact of EU Leverage on Domestic Politics

Does political competition help end the democratic monopoly of illiberal rulers only to be replaced by another form of monopoly—the EU monopoly—that takes control of domestic policy-making in all of the candidate states? Or, is the impact of the EU's conditionality on domestic policy-making greatly exaggerated, since many of the demands made by the EU are too diffuse, too vague and too chaotic to be implemented and enforced? After 1989, many observers decried the inactivity of the EU in helping Eastern Europe in the first five or more years after the revolutions of 1989.[1] Since 1998, we will see below that some observers argue instead that the EU's activity in Eastern Europe has been immodest and harmful. Still others take another view and regret that EU leverage did not compel the candidates to implement additional or deeper reforms in a variety of areas.

What has been the real impact of the EU's active leverage? This is a very complex and multifaceted question that will require many more years of study and likely yield many different answers across countries and across issue areas. But already scholars are debating the impact of the EU's conditionality on the development of the polity, the economy and the society in the new member states; they agree that the impact has been substantial in all three areas—but they look at the costs, the benefits and the scope of the task from different angles. After a quick summary of my argument, it is to these debates that I turn below.

Given the existence of an enlarging EU, I argued in Chapter 3 that the benefits of joining outweigh the costs, especially the political and economic costs of being left behind while neighboring states move forward. Indeed, looking through the lens of international relations theory, I argued that East European states would not wish away the existence of the EU in post-Cold War Europe, even if they could not join it. The asymmetry of power between the East European states and the EU, however recalcitrant, has been a more comfortable, diffuse power moderating the special interests of rich and powerful EU member states with a variety of historical claims in the region. Looking through the lens of comparative politics theory, I also sketched the long-term benefits of subjecting a democratizing state to the conditionality of the EU's pre-accession process. Satisfying the requirements of EU membership, I argued, is not just a penance that must be paid for the eventual benefits of being a full member of the EU. Some parts of the EU's pre-accession process are beneficial in their own right, because they cause or at least accelerate changes to the state and the economy that help build a stronger, more prosperous democratic state. I emphasized that the asymmetry of power—caused by the asymmetry of interdependence—has had the positive effect of making the EU's conditionality more credible.

Dictating Rules from Above Undermines Democracy

But how do these benefits measure up to the costs of turning over so much of the domestic political process to compliance with EU requirements? For East European states after communism, this question takes on greater significance since qualifying to join the EU coincides not just with consolidating democracy but also with creating a market economy and reviving and reinventing civic life. Scholars have emphasized that EU candidates pay a high price for submitting to this kind of "reform from above" where so many rules and policies are "imported" from the EU without being crafted and debated by local politicians. Jacques Rupnik put the tension most eloquently, wondering whether the EU's pre-accession process was "a blessed plot" forcing candidates to do efficiently reforms that they had to do anyway; or indeed an elite-driven project that is "emptying" the democratic process of its content. and contributing to premature "democratic fatigue" in Eastern Europe.[2] This tension stems roughly from three concerns—for the domestic policy-making process, for political competition, and for the authority of parliaments in the candidate states. Let us look at each in turn.

The EU compels new applicants to transpose and implement standards of internal democracy, state administration and detailed regulatory protection that the EU-15 had a hand in writing, and a half-century to accommodate. David Cameron notes that "it is not an exaggeration to say that on accession, the new members will be re-created as states, committed to processes of policy-making and policy outcomes that in many instances bear little or no relation to their domestic policy-making processes and prior policy decisions but reflect, instead, the politics, policy-making processes, and policy choices of the EU and its earlier member states."[3] In other words, the domestic policy-making process is degraded by the fact that instead of generating its own solutions to domestic problems, it spends much of its time and resources adopting and implementing the work of an external political organization. Indeed, as Stephen Holmes writes, this may have a disastrous impact on "the prestige of the domestic lawmaking function"; the instruments that the Commission uses to enforce compliance with foreign rules may further erode this prestige.[4]

Regarding policies that affect the nation, Lynne Tesser poses the problem most starkly, pointing to "the illiberal character" of the EU's effort to export liberalism. The best we can hope for, she argues, is that the expected economic returns in the form of higher wages and diminished unemployment will be enough eventually to promote liberal values. In the end, conceptions of the nation may change while the illiberal birth of EU liberalism will eventually be forgotten. In the meantime, however, we must worry about the potential for a backlash where certain sensitive, "national" policies are at stake such as the purchase of land by foreigners or the protection of ethnic minorities. On these issues, the EU can be portrayed as a threat to the nation and thereby strengthen the hand of nationalist parties.[5]

The second concern is for the quality of political competition: the exigencies of the EU's pre-accession process could mean that political parties no longer oppose one another on the basis of rival domestic policies. Anna Grzymała-Busse and Abby Innes argue that EU accession decreases political competition because joining the EU demands very substantial consensus among political parties on policy issues.[6] As a result, at national elections parties compete only on competence. This "de-substantiation" of political competition gives an opening to populist politicians such as Václav Klaus in the Czech Republic and the Samoobrana party in Poland that charge that the country is being turned over to the EU. Moreover, when new institutions are created as a result of this kind of unreasoned policy consensus and not of legitimate and heated domestic debate, the end products—institutions and policy initiatives—are hollow and ineffective because the EU does not provide a comprehensive model in many areas (we return to this point below).

The third, most specific concern is that the exigencies of the pre-accession process are empowering the executive at the expense of the parliament and of other "bottom-up" democratic processes. Margit Bessenyey Williams argues that the EU is weakening East European democracies by privileging the executive over the parliament in the rush to make rapid progress in transposing the acquis into national law. Since the acquis is non-negotiable and so voluminous, all of the candidate states have developed a fast-track procedure for getting EU legislation through parliament that allows for virtually no debate among parliamentarians.[7] (It is worth noting, however, that most if not all EU member states have similar fast-track procedures for adopting the EU acquis.) Heather Grabbe concurs that through the marginalization of legislatures the EU is in danger of "exporting aspects of its own democratic deficit." She also points to the privileging of the core accession team in the executive by the EU's pre-accession process. Grabbe argues that this further concentrates power and resources in a small part of the executive, at the expense of other parts of the government.[8] In these and other areas, Grabbe believes that the pre-accession process is at odds with the EU's broader goal of democratic development because it favors bureaucratic efficiency over democratic legitimacy.

Darina Málová and Tim Haughton also argue that EU pressure on institutional designs that promote efficiency may undermine effective governance in the long run, and that reform driven from outside may "decrease the legitimacy of the state and its institutions." However, in contrast to Williams and Grabbe, they argue that the executive in CEE states is relatively weak in comparison to existing EU members states (all but Romania have a parliamentary system); they counsel strengthening the executive to ensure that CEE states can secure better "representation and articulation of their national interests within the EU decision making framework," and increase their bargaining power.[9]

The arguments that the EU's pre-accession process is imposing foreign rules, suppressing political competition, and undermining parliaments all give genuine cause for concern about the future quality of democracy in the East European states. It also gives us pause in reflecting about how East European states will behave as full members of the EU. The gravity of these perversions and permutations will only become evident after several more years of political development in the EU's new member states. However, there are two realities of post-communist politics that I believe mitigate the dangers.

First, the problem of major institutional rules being "imposed" from the outside and undermining parliament is most likely to occur in the illiberal states that were latecomers to dynamic political competition and indigenous reform. In liberal states, the work of adopting the acquis and conforming to the institutional expectations of the EU only began some eight years after the onset of democratic politics. EU requirements that were satisfied by the liberal states before 1997, as I argued in Chapter 4, generally concerned the internal market acquis and reinforced the existing agendas of the political parties in power. Eight years of democratic politics gave Poland, Hungary, and the Czech Republic time to establish their own domestic policy-making processes, and grapple with alternative reform strategies through lively competition among political parties and heated parliamentary debate. It is important not to devalue the tremendous amount of work accomplished by national governments (at least in the liberal pattern states) after 1989, as we saw in Chapter 2, with little or no input from external actors.

Second, there are many fundamental areas of domestic decision-making that continue to be wholly at the discretion of the government in the candidate states, with little or no guidance from the EU. In many cases, as Wade Jacoby illuminates in his book *Ordering From the Menu*, candidate states pick and choose among templates taken from the existing practices of Western states and from the varied and sometimes conflicting advice of different international actors.[10] This is the case in areas such as social policy, heathcare, and education. So while external influence plays a role, the decision how to govern remains squarely in the hands of the national government in many areas (and indeed, as we see below, this lack of guidance is in turn also a source of consternation for scholars). We also observe a great deal of institutional diversity among the candidate states entering the EU in 2004, indicating that governments have had substantial freedom in redesigning the state after communism.

Vague Expectations Undermine EU Leverage

While the EU's active leverage can be criticized for imposing vast quantities of precise, non-negotiable rules on the candidate states from above, it can also be faulted for the obverse, that is, for not providing precise and detailed guidelines or requirements in important policy areas and on important questions of institutional reform. In many areas of institutional design, the EU lacks institutional templates because it has not been involved in such reforms of the state in existing EU members. Thus, while new members are required to implement the EU acquis, they get little guidance in designing institutions that will make implementation possible.[11] In many policy areas, the EU sets only vague standards, gives inconsistent advice, or lacks transparent benchmarks for evaluating the progress of candidate states in setting up such institutions.[12] These and other factors limit the EU's ability to export "a single model of governance" to the candidate states. Indeed, in major policy areas such as minority protection, social policy, and macroeconomic policy, the EU "has not used its routes of influence persistently to enforce a particular policy agenda"—usually because there exist none or few EU-level policies for it to enforce.[13]

The EU's vague or absent guidelines and requirements in some areas cause consternation among observers and scholars from a variety of perspectives. Here are just a few examples: Gwendolyn Sasse criticizes the EU for only forcing governments to change substantially their policies toward ethnic minorities when a crisis occurs that threatens to cause ethnic conflict or mass migration westward. In other words, the EU makes sure to "put out fires," but lacks both the substantive guidelines and the monitoring tools to supervise more mundane policy change. Indeed, some EU members may worry that "reverse conditionality" could occur as enforcement puts unwanted pressure on them to change their own policies.[14] George Ross advocates a strong EU social policy and regrets that the acquis does not contain rules to prevent the struggling new members from using their relative depravation and backwardness in social policy as a form of comparative advantage. Such rules would forestall the danger of "social dumping" in the future, which has perhaps been made more likely by the limited financial resources that the candidates will receive from the EU budget.[15]

Turning to the role of the EU in promoting economic reform, Bartlomiej Kaminski supports a free market economy with the least state interference possible and credits the EU pre-accession process with opening CEE states to trade and FDI. However, he believes that the Commission "stopped too soon" in pressuring candidates to decrease the size of the state, remove the state from the economy, and improve the regulation of the economy by the state.[16] David Cameron concurs that the new members still fall well short of the standards of advanced industrial economies in many key areas such as corporate governance, competition policy, and the development of regulated securities markets; these shortcomings undermine their ability to attract foreign investment and compete in the EU market.[17]

Moving beyond absent or unenforced requirements, John Glenn questions whether the domestic policies adopted and implemented as part of the negotiations on adopting the acquis represent deep and lasting changes. While he agrees that detailed monitoring and enforcement, even after accession, has ensured that applicant countries could not deceive the EU with superficial changes that led to the premature closing of chapters of the acquis before accession, it is too early to tell how lasting these changes will be after accession. How well will these new institutions function, especially once the EU's active leverage is all but gone?[18] This may be a partial answer to the concerns about the top-down nature of the EU's active leverage that we discussed above: after accession, polities may find ways to replace rules and institutions that were imposed from above and only superficially implemented with more suitable "home-grown" alternatives.

There is also the question of fit: an independent civil service created under EU pressure without adequate domestic consensus may, for example, not be appropriately designed.[19] But it may still allow for greater expression of competing interests than a civil service that would still very likely be highly politicized absent EU pressure, precisely in those new members who postponed reform until they were forced to carry it out under pressure from the EU. In other words, if the policies and institutions adopted "in a hurry" to meet EU requirements turn out to be inadequate, and they very well might, we should still consider the possibility that they provide a better starting point for further reforms than the previous state of affairs. Overall, in light of the discussion in the previous section and in this section, we may wonder at the difficulty, or perhaps the impossibility, of finding the right balance between keeping EU leverage from degrading domestic policymaking, and using EU leverage to promote institutional and policy reform in candidate states.

EU Acquis Undermines Economic Prosperity and Social Policy

Taking another tack, there are also reasons to believe that some aspects of joining the EU are disadvantageous for the economies of the new members. As the negotiations were drawing to a close, some East European politicians overplayed rhetorically the costs of adjustment in an attempt to improve their bargaining leverage. However, beyond any strategic dressing down of the EU, there are valid concerns that the content and the sequencing of economic reforms required of the candidates has disadvantaged local producers and misdirected national budgets. Let us look briefly at arguments that the EU has undermined economic prosperity and social policy in the new members.

Looking back to the beginning of the formal relationship between the EU and East European states, we explored in detail in Chapter 4 how the Europe Agreements imposed a trade regime on East European states that temporarily blocked their most competitive exports, while forcing them to open their markets to EU imports. The Europe Agreements imposed long transition periods for the phase-out of trade barriers in precisely those sectors where the East Europeans had something to export but the EU had powerful interests groups to protect: steel, textiles, chemicals and agriculture (areas where advanced industrial democracies have customarily protected their producers, not just within the EU but within the GATT and the WTO as well). This petty protectionism could have severely hobbled economic recovery, undermining the consolidation of democracy. As I argued in Chapters 3 and 4, it was the EU's protectionism that hardened the resolve of the Visegrad governments to accept nothing short of full EU membership.

Next, meeting the Copenhagen criteria and adopting the acquis has required the removal of the state from many areas of the economy in a sequence that has imposed large adjustment costs on vulnerable countries by insisting that they decrease sharply state subsidies to weak sectors, and privatize relatively quickly large enterprises, banks, and state utilities. Some local enterprises that were able to withstand competition from Western producers depended on state subsidies and loans from state banks to stay afloat. While removing most state aids and restructuring the rest is an integral part of completing the transition to market capitalism, the sequencing and rapidity of the reforms demanded to adopt the acquis may have undermined these domestic producers more than necessary. Moreover, it is expensive for eastern producers to comply with EU product quality, environmental and other standards, further undercutting their ability to compete with western producers. For these and other reasons, David Ellison and Mustally Hussain argue that East European candidates may have experienced a higher level of economic growth had they stayed out of the EU, in particular given the meager financial assistance that they are receiving upon accession.[20]

Finally, the EU required the prospective members to divert state resources to building institutions that make it possible for them to implement the acquis. Since the great majority of the acquis concerns creating an even playing field in the EU's internal market, most of these institutions have therefore been concerned with the state's ability to appropriately regulate the economy. In the condition of transition from communism, however, should this be the dominant concern of the national government? Stephen Holmes argues that government should instead be directing its (meager) national resources to improving education and healthcare, and enhancing social policy to compensate for the economic hardship and dislocation of the population brought on by the transition to capitalism.[21]

Again, it is difficult to identify the right balance—this time between praising and criticizing the EU's role in transforming the economy after communism. Again, the answers to many relevant questions are in the future. Nevertheless, fifteen years on, the evidence is indisputable that it was the EU frontrunners that reformed the most rapidly that also registered the highest rates of economic growth and suffered the lowest increase in income inequality as compared to their eastern and southeastern neighbors that opted for more gradual reforms after 1989.[22] As I demonstrated in Chapters 6 and 7, the absence of EU leverage would have allowed greater economic rent seeking by domestic elites, impoverishing the state and the society. It would have also created a less attractive economic environment for those foreign and domestic actors looking for a commitment to ongoing economic reform, a

Western business environment, and access to the EU market. Overhauling the legal and administrative framework to adopt the acquis, meanwhile, has increased transparency and perhaps also set the stage for positive changes in political habits in the future.

Setting aside the counterfactual about what reforms would have remained undone absent the EU's active leverage, we can be hopeful about the future even if we believe that aspects of the EU's acquis have undermined the economic transition and misdirected state resources. By stimulating foreign direct investment, entrepreneurship, and technology transfers, entering the EU is expected to raise output and growth rates.[23] Over the long run, this should increase the size of the national budget, and therefore the resources available to national governments for healthcare, education, and social policy. Meanwhile, the EU's Stabilization and Cohesion Funds (discussed below) will have some role in offsetting economic inequalities within and among the new members. If East European governments choose to compete for foreign investors by lowering significantly corporate taxes, as Slovakia has done in 2004, then this will have an impact (unknown for now) on government revenue over the medium and long-term. As in many other areas, the EU's new democracies each have important choices to make about how to compete in the EU economy, and we can expect to see a great deal of variation in how they go about it.

8.2   New Members Inside the EU

After years of reform, the impact of the EU's active leverage on the democratic and the economic fitness of the new members has become blurred with the outcome of the "endgame" of the negotiations on their accession. More troubling for the applicants than the membership requirements or the character of the pre-accession process were the specific terms of accession that the candidates were forced to accept in this endgame. While the reasons that the existing EU member states pushed through these terms make perfect sense (briefly, they could), they may regret this choice in the future. In this section I will, first, explain substantively and theoretically the outcome of the endgame of the negotiations. Second, I will speculate about the condition and the behavior of the new members inside the enlarged EU, and about how the EU may function after enlargement.

8.2.1   The Endgame of the Negotiations

The EU's active leverage can be analyzed separately from what I call the endgame of the negotiations. This is the last phase of the negotiations and it consists of bargaining over the terms of accession. The subject is no longer whether or not a candidate has satisfied EU requirements, but what kind of deal they will *initially* get as full EU members. This deal has two components, transition periods and transfers from the EU budget.

Transition periods refer to the time period that old or new members have after enlargement takes place before they must implement certain aspects of the acquis. In many non-contentious areas, new members were able to negotiate a transition period, because to have implemented the acquis by the moment of accession was impossible for reasons of money or of state capacity. In other areas, new members sought transition periods to protect domestic producers and assuage domestic publics. Most visibly, many new EU members were able to secure a transition period of five years before EU citizens can purchase secondary residences, and up to seven years (twelve for Poland) before EU citizens can purchase agricultural land and forests. But transition periods also worked against the new members: old members demanded them in order to protect *their* domestic producers and assuage *their* domestic publics. Most controversially, the old members insisted on the option of a transition period of up to seven years before citizens of the new members would be able to exercise their right to work anywhere in the EU.[24]

Transfers from the EU budget include all monies paid out to the new members, including most importantly transfers from the EU's Common Agricultural Policy (CAP) and from its Structural and Cohesion Funds (regional funds). Commission officials and West European politicians privately agree that the new members are receiving "peanuts."[25] The Berlin European Council in December 1999 placed a ceiling on the EU budget for the 2004–6 period that required that while the EU would grow in size, the EU budget could not. Negotiations about how to apportion monies from the CAP and the Structural and Cohesion Funds thus naturally came at the expense of the new members, whose poor farmers and poor regions had to accept a phase in of transfer payments. Meanwhile, existing recipients of EU transfers, namely farmers in the old member states and regions in Spain, Portugal, Italy, and Greece, kept most of their prior transfers. New member farmers will initially only be eligible for 25 percent of CAP payments, to be increased by 5 percent per year until 2013.[26] New member regions will be limited to no more than 4 percent of national GDP in aid from the Structural and Cohesion Funds.

While these transfers being received by the new members are not negligible (and for some of the smaller ones they are in fact sizeable), they are visibly less than those granted to previous poor states upon joining the EU, and of course visibly less than many old members receive in the 2004–6 period.[27] Some EU leaders now publicly regret that the EU adopted what Jean-Luc Dehaene called "the book keeping approach" as opposed to "the visionary approach" to enlarging the EU.[28]

What happened, in short, is that existing EU members forced the candidates to give up some portion of the near-term benefits of EU membership. The miserliness of the EU can readily be explained by the patterns of asymmetrical interdependence that have marked the EU's relationship with the candidates since 1989. As Andrew Moravcsik and I argued, "the applicants are forced into concessions precisely because the basic benefit offered to them—membership—is of such great value." This benefit so outweighs the costs—particularly those of exclusion—that applicants make extensive concessions. But these concessions contribute to a subjective sense of loss among the applicant states at the close of negotiations even though, overall, they benefit more from the enlargement bargain than existing EU member states.[29]

Yet why did EU governments deploy their superior bargaining power to extract concessions from the applicants? The concessions allow EU governments to satisfy the short-term concerns of their domestic constituents, ranging from narrow special interests to the broad voting publics.[30] The geopolitical and economic benefits of enlargement are diffuse, long-term and, for voters, politically unremarkable. The costs, however, are concentrated, immediate, and politically sensitive. As Table 8.2 indicates, enlargement was quite unpopular with EU citizens in 2002 at the time when EU governments were completing the negotiations with the new members (though France was the only country where more people opposed enlargement than favored it). EU citizens associate enlargement with rising illegal immigration, international crime, and unemployment. While there is little evidence that enlargement will contribute measurably to any of these problems, and may in fact ameliorate them, EU governments nonetheless wanted to satisfy restive publics. In the short-term, the asymmetry of power between the EU and the candidates in the accession process made such accommodation relatively easy: new members will wait for up to seven years before benefiting from the free movement of labor; they receive initially little from the EU's static budgetary pie; and (as discussed below) they are being kept out of the Schengen area.

EU governments were fully aware that the political challenges of an eastern enlargement would be eased for them by their ability to control the terms of accession of the new members. The French government knew, for example, that it would be able to impose a long delay on full payouts for eastern farmers from the CAP and thus mollify the opposition of the French farmers; the German government knew that a long transition on the free movement of eastern workers would stave off fears of rising unemployment on the part of German voters. This underlines in yet a different way that "rhetorical entrapment" (discussed below in Section 3 on why the EU is enlarging) was not necessary to compel EU governments to agree to enlargement;

TABLE 8.2 Support for EU enlargement in the existing EU members, 2002

Country	Supportry for EU enlargement (percentages of those surveyed)	
	For	Against
Greece	76	17
Denmark	71	19
Ireland	67	15
Sweden	65	23
Italy	64	19
Spain	63	14
Portugal	60	20
Netherlands	58	28
Finland	58	31
Luxembourg	56	34
Belgium	53	33
Austria	51	31
Germany	46	34
United Kingdom	42	32
France	41	49

Note: The question asks: "*Do you support enlargement . . . yes, no, don't know?*"

Source: Eurobarometer (2002*b*: 77).

politicians knew they would be able to cushion any short-term costs that might threaten their own popularity by dictating the terms of the enlargement bargain.

To put this endgame into perspective, it is important to emphasize that however unfavorable these terms of accession may be in the short term, enlargement did go forward: these terms may have been necessary to get enlargement by certain West European states. It is also important to emphasize that the latest applicants have not been singled out for special treatment: while their condition may be more fragile and their needs greater, previous applicants to the EU had to deal with very disappointing terms of their accession for exactly the same reasons of relative bargaining power.[31] It is also worth remembering that when it comes to the next enlargement of the EU, the new members may be just as tough in trying to extract concessions from prospective members. Also, as we see below, the game is far from up: new members may yet extract more resources from the EU, perhaps on the example of Greece which demanded a boost in aid immediately after joining in 1981, threatening otherwise to veto the accession of Portugal and Spain.

8.2.2   *The End of Active Leverage: Bargaining and Europeanization After Accession*

After enlargement the EU's active leverage is progressively replaced with two very different dynamics. First, the new members take on the bargaining position of a full member—and not a supplicant for membership—in negotiations among EU member states. Second, more diffuse Europeanization replaces active leverage as the mechanism for EU-driven domestic policy changes in the new members. Yet, some key aspects of the EU's active leverage have been preserved even after accession; meanwhile, as we have just seen, some key benefits of EU membership have been temporarily withheld. This blurry period may be considered as necessary, even positive, because it allows for more gradual adjustments on all sides; or it may be considered unfair, even nefarious, because it creates a temporary second-class status for the EU's newest members.

New Members: High Bargaining Power or Second-Class Status?

Since the eight post-communist candidates became full EU members in May 2004, their bargaining power has increased tremendously. The new members can use their status as voting members of the Council to shape new EU policies. They can also use it to extract concessions by threatening to veto important decisions that require unanimity, such as the EU budget or further enlargement. New members are most likely to try using their bargaining power to reverse or curtail those aspects of the terms of their accession that discriminate against them as new members. The priority will be to hasten their eligibility for full disbursements from the EU budget, shortening the phase-in periods as much as possible. As it stands, for example, the phase-in period for full payments from the CAP to new member farmers will last almost ten years.

In so doing, they will follow in the footsteps of previous new members that used their bargaining power once inside the EU to ameliorate the unfavorable terms of their accession and to extract resources from the EU budget. One striking example is the success of Greece, Spain, Portugal, and Ireland in upping what they received from the EU's regional policy by threatening to veto initiatives such as the Single European Act and the Maastricht Treaty.[32]

TABLE 8.3 Support for EU membership in the EU candidate countries, 2001–3

Country	Support for EU membership "a good thing" ("neither a good nor a bad thing") percentages of those surveyed		
	2001	2002	2003
Poland	51	52	52
	(27)	(30)	(28)
Hungary	60	67	56
	(23)	(20)	(24)
Czech Republic	46	43	44
	(31)	(28)	(34)
Romania	80	78	81
	(11)	(8)	(10)
Bulgaria	74	68	73
	(14)	(19)	(17)
Slovakia	58	58	58
	(28)	(30)	(31)

Note: The question asks: "*Generally speaking, do you think that [country's] membership in the European Union would be . . . 1) a good thing; 2) neither a good nor a bad thing; or 3) a bad thing.*"

Sources: Eurobarometer (2001: 56); Eurobarometer (2002a: 62) and Eurobarometer (2003: 78).

In 2003 and 2004 Poland already took up arms, joining forces with Spain in threatening to veto the proposed EU Constitution in order to protect the number of votes in the European Council that were allocated to both states in the Treaty of Nice.

Though EU members could assert their greater bargaining power and secure many concessions from the new members (and though these concessions may have been a political necessity), it does not mean that EU leaders ultimately did themselves any favors. For less confrontational bargaining to guide the behavior of the EU's new members, it would have been preferable that governments and publics in the new members did not feel that that they had been treated unfairly. Public opinion has turned lukewarm. Table 8.3 shows that among respondents in our six candidates, opposition to joining the EU is still small, but a substantial percent in the new members (though fewer in Bulgaria and very few in Romania) consider EU membership to be

TABLE 8.4   Results of referenda on joining the EU, 2003

Country	Date	Results (percentages)		
		In favor	Against	Turnout
Slovakia	May 16–17, 2003	92	6	52
Lithuania	May 10–11, 2003	91	9	63
Slovenia	March 23, 2003	90	10	60
Hungary	April 12, 2003	84	16	46
Poland	June 7–8, 2003	77	23	59
Czech Republic	June 13–14, 2003	77	23	55
Latvia	September 20, 2003	67	32	73
Estonia	September 14, 2003	67	33	64
Malta	March 8, 2003	54	46	91
Cyprus		No referendum		

Source: EurActive.com

"neither a good nor a bad thing."[33] Table 8.4 shows that while the referenda on joining the EU passed in every single candidate state acceding in 2004, in some cases low turnout made the "yes" vote seem a bit hollow. In some new members, disillusionment with the EU has taken the form of a national obsession with securing more monies from the EU budget. This obsession, in turn, has deflected attention from other, greater benefits of joining the EU and from debates in new members about the desired purpose and substance of future EU policies.

Yet despite the full voting rights that the new members now enjoy in the European Council, the EU's old members and the Commission have preserved at least three avenues for exercising active leverage even after accession. First, upon acceding to the EU the new members did not automatically become a part of the Schengen area where people may circulate freely without any controls at the national borders. Poland and Germany, for example, are therefore still separated by what is called the "Schengen border," requiring Polish citizens to go through border checks before entering what is more or less "the rest" of the EU (the United Kingdom and Ireland are not members by choice). The "Schengen border" separating the new members from the old members will only be dismantled on a country by country basis, once the existing members of the Schengen area vote unanimously that a new member has sufficiently fortified its external border and developed adequate policies for combating international crime. For now the new members are required to adopt all of the Schengen acquis without enjoying the benefits of free movement.[34]

Second, upon acceding to the EU the new members also did not automatically become a part of the European Monetary Union (EMU). For many new members, adopting the euro as soon as possible has become a national priority (even though many economists counsel the new members against hurrying to join). Before they may adopt the euro, however, the new members must convince the existing members of EMU that they satisfy the so-called "Maastricht criteria" of monetary and economic fitness (even though by 2003 many EMU members including Germany were in violation of these criteria). For new members, the quest to qualify for Schengen and for EMU could open them up to pressure from the old members to back down on other issues.

Third, after accession, the Commission retains some power to enforce the ongoing adoption of the acquis by the new members through special monitoring procedures. For some policy-makers in the new members, convinced of the positive role of the EU's active leverage in bringing reforms of the state and the economy, this continued discipline is reassuring.[35] For others, this continued interference signifies the improper use of the EU's active leverage, imposing rules on new members that it never imposed on old members even after accession.

Against the backdrop of the "endgame" of the negotiations and the entry of the new members into the EU in May, two scenarios have come to worry observers, one more in the west and the other more in the east. The first scenario, of greater concern in the west, is that enlargement could bring to a standstill decision making within the EU by bringing in such a diverse, numerous and discontented group of new members. The new members, however, are unlikely to act as a bloc in any matter other than attempting to improve on the terms of their accession. And while the new members may play tough, in particular heightening conflict over the budget, the old members will have some of leverage over them to help counterbalance their newfound bargaining power. In most other matters, the new members hold a variety of views (changing with government turnover just like in the old members). In this vein, Jan Zielonka and Peter Mair argue that there is little reason to fear the various kinds of diversity that enlargement will bring into the EU. Diversity, on the contrary, teaches adaptation, bargaining and accommodation, and hence fosters cooperation and further integration.[36] There may be gridlock, but of a kind that predates enlargement and that stems from pre-existing tensions about empowering EU institutions, deepening European integration and disbursing the EU budget.

Since the mid-1990s, attempts to reform the EU's institutions have yielded difficult negotiations and various institutional contortions. However, there is no straightforward reckoning of the impact of enlargement on the reform of the EU's institutions, or on the relative power of the old members within these institutions.[37] The 2004 enlargement may strengthen the position of small and medium countries against the large countries—though so far they have not had great success. During the Convention on the Future of Europe, small and medium countries from both old and new members allied to oppose the slimming down of the Commission and other changes to the Community method in favor of the larger member states. They were not, however, successful. Seeking equal treatment, the delegates to the Convention on the Future of Europe from the new member states demanded—and received—a representative in the Presidium that was to draft all working documents. The national parliamentarians from the new member states that took part in the Convention did not, however, end up forming a distinct group in the Convention as a whole.[38]

Indeed, as new members join old members in various issue-based (and apparently size-based) coalitions within the EU, their impact is diffuse, shoring up the bargaining position of a particular old member state in some areas and undermining it in others. Again, because the new members are so different from one another, they import a great diversity of positions into the EU. It is important to emphasize, however, that in most cases these positions are not outside of the spectrum of views that already existed in the EU before enlargement. This is true even for the highly controversial support of several new members, especially Poland, for the US war against Iraq; they were in agreement with the Spanish and the British, not on their own, "importing" a new foreign policy position into the EU.

The second scenario, this one of greater concern in the east, is that the eight post-communist states could be condemned to an enduring second-class status in the EU. Such a status would include making permanent the exclusion of East European states from the Schengen border-free area, and from one of the EU's four fundamental freedoms, the free movement of labor. It would also include making permanent the current disparity between funds received from the CAP and the regional funds on the part of old member and new member farmers and regions.[39]

Fear of a second-class status was strongly reinforced by the fact that in the run-up to enlargement in the autumn of 2003 and the winter of 2004 every single EU member took up the option to restrict the flow of workers from the new members. It had been expected that only Germany and Austria would put in place such restrictions. In the end, only the United Kingdom and Ireland allowed workers to come freely in 2004, but restricted their access to unemployment and other benefits.[40] This was largely a political move for most old members since it is widely accepted that few workers are likely to move westward. And indeed the restrictions may help the new members by stemming the brain drain as their most highly talented workers are also the ones most likely to move. Still, the restrictions have been greatly resented in the new members and seem particularly senseless since the need of Western Europe's aging labor forces for legal immigrant workers (paying into national pension schemes) is evident. This need, on the one hand, and the bargaining power of the new members, on the other, makes it unlikely that these restrictions will become permanent. But disillusionment and the perception of a second-class membership on the part of the publics of the new members in the near term could be dangerous. It could, for example, strengthen the hand of those right-wing political parties whose Euroskeptic attitudes go hand in hand with more troublesome chauvinistic and xenophobic views.[41]

The perception of political elites in the new members is also important, and for them the fear of a second-class status has been fed by proposals on the part of the French and also the German government to use "flexibility" or "enhanced cooperation" to create a hard core of the EU from which the new members would be excluded.[42] Once again, they would be left on the outside. As we discussed in Chapter 3, small and weak states seek to join the EU partly to have the same voice in EU matters and the same protection of EU rules as existing members. East European elites are therefore naturally opposed to any kind of a two-tier Europe, placing a high premium on preserving existing levels of equality among all EU members. While in 2003 the French could be heard planning a new inner club that outsiders might someday supplicate to join, these plans seemed to fade away in 2004; perhaps the French realized that all EU members do have an astounding parity of power within the EU's institutions, and that many (old and new members) would use this power to scuttle any plans for a new institutionalized inner circle.

To sum up, in the year that the EU finally enlarged, two concerns domin-ated: in the west, that gridlock caused by enlargement could bring EU inte-gration to a standstill; and in the east that the unfavorable terms of accession of the EU's new members could lead to a permanent second-class status. While there are valid grounds for concern on both counts, they have been overblown. In the new members, however, the perception of a second-class status may have a regrettable impact on public and elite opinion, foreclosing debate on how to take advantage of EU membership in myriad areas while strengthening the hand of xenophobic politicians. In the old members, we can ask whether the low levels of public support for enlargement that necessitated such unfavorable terms of accession for the new members were not caused by a failure on the part of West European governments to explain sufficiently dur-ing the 1990s the long-term benefits of enlargement to their voters.

The Europeanization of the New Members

Putting these concerns for the future aside, across the board there is no question that the EU's active leverage has all but disappeared—and that for the group of states that entered on May 1, 2004 it was already drastically diminished two or three years before accession, once full membership seemed like a done deal. This brings the new members into a new area of academic research: with active leverage fading away, what mechanisms determine the EU's ongoing influence on domestic policy-making in the new members? Scholars of West European politics and the EU define "Europeanization" as the diffusion of common political rules, norms and practices in Europe. This is dominated by the adoption of supranational EU norms and rules in current EU member-states, referred to sometimes as "EU-ization."[43]

Our East European states, having finally "returned to Europe," are now becoming a part of studies of the Europeanization process.[44] The EU's active leverage could be thought of as a form of "Europeanization"; both explain essentially the same outcome. But I find it is better to keep the two research questions separate since the adoption of common rules among existing EU members is often the work of very different mechanisms than compliance among aspiring EU members.[45] Overall, studying the new members should lead to rich insights into whether and why they react differently from one another and from the old members to the forces of Europeanization and indeed EU-ization within the EU.

Beyond the impact on domestic rules and institutions, membership in the EU raises the question of how the new members adapt to the web of relations they must maintain in order, for example, to administer the EU's internal market. Since accession, officials in the new members are interacting with their counterparts in the old members without the same dynamics of conditionality and asymmetric bargaining. Francesca Bignami argues that a great challenge will be establishing cooperative relations based on trust that are indispensable for a common market in the Europe of twenty-five to function. She maintains that the habits of mind formed during accession might compromise the establishment of mutually beneficial regulatory relations post-accession. National administrators in the old members, doubting the capacity of new members for compliance, may withhold certain benefits unfairly, expecting that regardless of the fairness of their actions, administrators in the new members will continue to cooperate. Those in the new members may expect exploitative treatment because of their experiences during the enlargement process and their suspicion of a second-class status; they may thus retaliate when retaliation is unwarranted. If repeated across the board, the cooperation required to create the larger common market will not emerge.[46] This only underscores the potential for negative repercussions from the way that the EU conducted the endgame of the negotiations discussed above.

8.3   Explaining the Past and Future of EU Enlargement

Having examined the condition of the new members in the enlarged EU, let us take a step back and survey the EU enlargement process as such. What is the purpose of EU enlargement for its existing members? Will the EU continue to enlarge? If so, where will enlargement end? In the first section below, I examine alternative explanations for why the EU decided to enlarge to the eight post-communist candidates (ten candidates in all including Malta and Cyprus) in May 2004—with Bulgaria and presumably Romania close behind. In the second section, I ask whether this process will persist to the rest of the Balkans, to Turkey and possibly beyond.

8.3.1   Why Ten New Members in May 2004?

Regarding the EU, what this book seeks to explain is why, how, and under what conditions the EU's passive and active leverage has had an impact on the course of domestic politics in credible candidate states. To this end, we explored in detail why East European governments made full EU membership their foremost foreign policy goal. A separate but related question is why did the European governments already in the EU choose to embark on such an ambitious and extensive enlargement. The argument I make here and in Chapter 5 is a simple one: from the perspective of their economic and geopolitical interests, EU governments preferred an enlarging EU in the context of an undivided Europe (though whether they would not prefer to go back to the simple, divided Europe is another matter). The relationship between the candidate states and the EU is defined, as Andrew Moravcsik and I argue, by asymmetric interdependence: the new members benefit from the EU's eastern enlargement much more than the old members. And yet, the old members also benefit. Straightforward national interest explains not just why the EU's aspiring members have been willing to go through so much to secure EU membership, but also why the EU's existing members have been willing to let them in.[47]

At least two other sets of explanations have emerged for Western motivations for EU enlargement. The first set was prescriptive: in the early 1990s observers considered that the EU should enlarge to make amends for the injustices of twentieth-century European history that witnessed Western Europe abandoning Eastern Europe first to Hitler, then to Stalin. The arguments in favor of enlargement on moral historical grounds may be weighty—France and the United Kingdom violated their treaty obligations to Czechoslovakia in 1938 at Munich in an attempt to appease Hitler; the Allies abandoned the whole of Eastern Europe to Stalin at the end of the Second World War; the West did not come to the aid of the revolutionaries in Hungary in 1956 or in Czechoslovakia in 1968. However, East European dissidents and their Western supporters were quickly disabused of the idea that these kinds of considerations would play an important role in shaping Western policy after 1989.

The second set of competing explanations is broadly constructivist, challenging the idea that West European governments decided to enlarge the EU because it would suit their material interests.[48] K. M. Fierke and Antje Wiener argue that speech acts during the Cold War constructed a set of norms about a united, democratic Europe.[49] When the end of the Cold War changed the context, these speech acts changed their meaning and "constructed" the promise of eastern enlargement, making an interest-based escape from EU (or NATO) enlargement all but impossible for Western governments. If, however, the EU's identity and norms dictated Eastern enlargement as constructivists posit, why was the offer of membership not on the table in 1989? Indeed, we explored in detail in Chapter 4 the EU's tough treatment of the new democracies in the early 1990s including the refusal to recognize them as credible candidates and to grant them access to the EU market. This was a reflection of the material interests of EU members and not of the identity or norms of the institution: after all, the EU's constitutive norms state that any European country can apply for membership, with the Treaty of Rome calling for a "closer union of the peoples of Europe."[50]

Ulrich Sedelmeier provides a theoretically and empirically rich approach, explaining the incremental and not very generous policies of the EU toward the candidate states as the product of competition between material and constructivist (or ideational) forces. Pointing also to the EU's collective identity, Sedelmeier argues that the discursive creation of a specific role of the EU towards the East European applicants has led to a principled advocacy of their preferences inside the EU institutions. EU identity toward the East European applicants includes the notion of a "special responsibility" that constrains the scope for open opposition on self-interested grounds on the part of EU member states.[51]

Taking a similar approach, Frank Schimmelfennig argues that Eastern enlargement was not a rational, efficient institutional arrangement for the EU (or for NATO).[52] First, he argues, the expected transaction, autonomy, and crowding costs of eastern enlargement were higher than the expected benefits of admitting the East Central European (ECE) states as full members. Second, association with the EU through the existing Europe Agreements was a more efficient institutional form for the EU's relations with the ECE states. Third, whereas individual EU member states, particularly Germany, supported enlargement in order to reduce the risk of instability in states along their eastern borders, these EU member states along with the ECE governments did not possess the bargaining power to impose enlargement on the reluctant majority of member states.

In order to overcome this unfavorable trinity, the ECE governments and their Western supporters turned to rhetorical action. Basing their claims on the collective identity and the constitutive liberal values and norms of the EU, Schimmelfennig argues that they shamed the reticent member states into complying with community rules and honoring past commitments. This explains nicely the time lag between the revolutions of 1989 and the promise of membership: the opponents of eastern enlargement eventually found themselves rhetorically entrapped, but it took time to trap them.[53] While the reasons that constructivists give for why materialist explanations cannot account for enlargement are convincing and thought provoking, the "rationalist" counterarguments are also compelling. Let us look at the two most important ones.

First, the economic and geopolitical benefits of EU enlargement are considerable—and they come with lower financial costs and fewer economic adjustments to the old EU members than some initially expected. The new members add 100 million new consumers in relatively fast-growing economies to the internal market. One study projects that the EU-15 states will gain about ten billion euro from enlargement over the long term, well more than the cost to the EU budget of having the new members.[54] In previous enlargements, existing EU members also chose to share power in the EU institutions with new states because of expectations of overall growth in the EU economy, even though each of the previous enlargements also decreased the per capita wealth of the EU.[55] In this enlargement, the new members will also provide a convenient source of legal and politically acceptable (mostly white and Christian) immigrants for Western Europe's dramatically aging labor forces. Turning to the geopolitical benefits, some declare that the greater economic weight and geographical reach of an enlarged EU will give it greater geopolitical clout on the international stage.[56] Finally, surveying the adjustment costs, the new members represent less than 5 percent of the current EU GDP; they receive limited financial transfers; and their industrial and agricultural trade with the EU was liberalized before accession. Consequently, the economic adjustment costs of the May 2004 enlargement have ultimately been small.

The benefits of enlargement must also be weighed together with the costs of foregoing it. Mattli argues that the EU expands when the net cost of excluding countries is bigger than the cost of accepting them; that is, when negative externalities originating in these outsider countries threaten to disrupt the Union's stability, security, and prosperity. The sources of these externalities may reside in political upheaval, economic mismanagement, or social unrest.[57] EU enlargement responds to such threats. It brings the geopolitical stabilization of the European borderlands, reducing political uncertainty, dampening nationalist conflict, and averting economic desolation.[58] This saves the EU blood and treasure while making illegal immigration more manageable. While Schimmelfennig is right to argue that Germany and other EU members directly bordering Eastern Europe were on the whole stronger supporters of enlargement than EU members further west and south, the EU's economic interdependence, its common external border, its emerging common foreign policy and its plans for a common immigration policy all mean that the more distant EU members could not expect to escape the negative externalities of the EU's failure to enlarge.

Second, at the heart of Schimmelfennig's argument is that the material interests of the EU's member states dictated that the EU *stop short* of giving ECE states full membership, continuing instead to deal with them as associate members under the terms of the Europe Agreements. Schimmelfennig does not, however, make a compelling case that this relationship was a stable equilibrium—or indeed that West European politicians believed that it was. On the contrary, it was precisely the realization by West European policymakers that, whether they liked it or not (and many certainly did not), the economic and geopolitical trajectory of the EU's East European neighbors would be intimately linked with the EU's decisions about whether and how to enlarge that led to the full development of the EU's active leverage after 1995. As we saw in Chapter 4, from the earliest moments that EU policymakers could use conditionality to structure relations with ECE states, they worried intensely about turning ECE governments away from the West and toward Moscow for fear that this would compromise their interests in the region.

The economic and geopolitical cost and benefit analysis made by EU governments was not between enlargement, on the one hand, and a stable, democratic, and economically pliant band of post-communist associates on its borders, on the other. This model existed; it was Mitterrand's European Confederation. But it was rejected not because anti-enlargement states were rhetorically entrapped, but because failing to enlarge the EU in an undivided Europe would mean foregoing the benefits of an enlarged EU, and paying the anticipated costs of economic instability, conflict, and uncertainty on the EU's eastern borders. Absent EU enlargement, for example, it is very likely that some ECE states would have reneged on the Europe Agreements while others would have failed adequately to protect ethnic minority rights. To put it another way, if you argue that the EU's pre-accession process has been pivotal to moderation and reform in East European states (as Schimmelfennig has in other work), then this is in some respects difficult to reconcile with the argument that a non-enlarging EU would have brought greater net material gains to the EU-15.

On a cheerful note, if a majority of EU members did decide that EU enlargement was in their material interest (while also conforming to the identity and liberal values of the EU), this is a much more robust and promising starting point for the success of an enlarged EU than the alternatives: that the new members were admitted because of feelings of historical guilt, or indeed that they were admitted because the majority of EU members were trapped by the EU's norms. And even if the EU's liberal norms only *reinforced* material interests in bringing about the decision to enlarge, they were clearly important in other ways, for example, in shaping the EU's pre-accession process and influencing the content of the EU's membership requirements.

8.3.2   What Next? Eastern Balkans, Western Balkans . . . Turkey?

Will the EU choose to continue to use its leverage on states that would like to join it? The EU's leverage on aspiring member states appears to be the single best tool for promoting stability, democracy, and economic prosperity on the European continent.[59] Yet, EU members face a considerable dilemma about how widely to use it. After considering the general debate on the future of enlargement below, we will examine in greater detail the specific challenge of making the EU's active leverage work in the Balkans.

The Future of the EU's Best Foreign Policy Tool: Enlargement

With the first enlargement all but complete in 2004, the EU is being pulled in two different ways. On the one hand, the economic and geopolitical benefits of pacifying and incorporating the periphery continue to be compelling. Here, the credible future candidates in the Balkans are particularly important. They are not just Bulgaria and Romania (the Eastern Balkans), but also Albania, Macedonia, and the post-conflict states of Croatia, Serbia-Montenegro, and Bosnia-Hercegovina (the Western Balkans). Timothy Garton Ash and others have argued that the *absence* of a coherent EU foreign policy toward the former Yugoslavia proved very costly: the EU could have averted some or all of the horrific violence and impoverishment of the Western Balkans by putting in place an ambitious, intrusive, and attractive EU enlargement project right away in 1990.[60] Ten years later, the EU cautiously stepped up to the plate. At the July 1999 Stability Pact Conference in Sarajevo the EU pledged to use the prospect of EU membership to bring stability and democracy to these five additional states, making them what I call "proto-candidates." The EU's inability to deal with the Kosovo crisis without American aid came at a time when aspirations among key EU members to create an effective Common Foreign and Security Policy were high. EU leaders began to realize that the single best foreign policy tool that they possessed was EU enlargement.[61] The benefits of pacifying the periphery thus became intertwined with the goal of creating an effective EU foreign policy, and this boosted the credibility of the EU's membership promise. If the EU could not commit to and succeed at stabilizing its immediate backyard, how could it be taken seriously as a global player?

On the other hand, the prospect of continuing to enlarge has become more contentious as enlargement has moved from the distant future into the daily political reality of EU governments with the accession of ten new members in 2004. The widening-versus-deepening debate continues: how will the EU's institutions function with so many new members, and will further integration not be hobbled or even brought to a standstill by importing such diversity? By the autumn of 2004, Bulgaria, Romania, and possibly even Croatia were slated to join the EU in 2007 or 2008.

What about the membership prospects of the remaining proto-candidates? The EU has already made explicit commitments to admit them if they fulfill the requirements. But I argue below that whether they do qualify for membership or not will be strongly influenced by how they are treated by the EU. Should the EU decide to shelve the possibility of future membership for some of them, financial and political inattention should do the trick. Yet it is unlikely that the EU would deliberately make the choice to neglect the Western Balkans. The potential costs of renewed instability for the EU are high, as is the potential damage of failing in the region for the credibility of its foreign policy.

What about the membership prospects of the states beyond the new members and the officially recognized candidates and proto-candidates? These are to be ruled out for the foreseeable future.[62] In 2003, the EU Commission launched an initiative called the "Wider Europe" which included rethinking the root of the problem: the character of the EU's passive leverage.[63] Can the EU's neighbors such as Ukraine or Moldova be dissuaded from attempting to join the EU for all of the reasons presented in Chapter 3 if the costs of being excluded from the EU decrease? This requires the EU to treat nonmembers significantly better, in particular by granting better access for goods to its markets, and potentially also for people to its territory.[64] In launching the "Wider Europe" policy, the EU aims to postpone or exclude the prospect of EU membership for neighboring states, but also to develop greater traction on national politics and regional stability. So far, however, as Michael Emerson argues, the various clients of this policy are undeterred from seeking the prospect of EU membership, nor do they seem more susceptible to the EU's "good" influence.[65]

Ruling out the possibility that a state can join the EU in the foreseeable future of course sacrifices the potential benefits of using the EU's active leverage to influence domestic politics. In the case of Ukraine, Kataryna Wolczuk argues that many domestic elites have declared EU membership to be Ukraine's foreign policy priority but, just like the illiberal elites in this study, they hardly try to satisfy the domestic requirements of EU membership because there are no costs to noncompliance. If the EU chose to use active leverage backed by a membership promise on Ukraine, a shift to compliance with EU rules could well follow.[66]

The outstanding dilemma, however, is that in addition to the Balkan states, there is another full-blown official candidate for membership: Turkey. Turkey raises the possibility of much greater adjustment costs and financial costs than any of the post-communist candidates because of its size, its relative poverty, the structure of its economy, and the number of its poor workers that could migrate westward. Turkey also raises uncomfortable religious and civilizational questions: will including such a large Muslim country, however secular, change the basic identity of the EU? Will the divergent condition and interests of Turkey destroy any possibility of deepening further European integration? Indeed, will Turkey joining the EU not in fact require unraveling certain aspects of European integration?

The trouble with Turkey is that the EU is not now deciding whether or not it should be a candidate for membership. Turkey has been treated as a credible candidate for membership since the 1980s: its applications to begin negotiations in 1987 and 1997 were turned down, but it remained within the pre-accession process. Beginning in October 1998, the European Commission has published Regular Reports on Turkey's progress in tandem with reports on the other candidates. At the Helsinki European Council in December 1999, the EU made it official: Turkey's status as a credible future member and the EU's (then) thirteenth official candidate was reaffirmed. At the Copenhagen European Council in December 2002, Turkey was told that formal accession negotiations would begin "without delay" if it was judged to fulfill the Copenhagen political criteria in December 2004.[67]

By all accounts, over the last ten years Turkey's governments have pushed through fundamental reforms of the Turkish state and economy in order to qualify for EU membership while improving their record on human rights. EU leverage has worked in bolstering democratic standards, ethnic minority rights, and economic reform, much as it did in the post-communist states. This is impressive, especially because for Turkey the reward of membership at the end of the process is much less certain than for other candidates.[68] At the close of 2003, however, it appeared that Turkey had not yet satisfied the Copenhagen criteria in a number of areas, leaving open for the European Council in December 2004 the possibility of postponing the decision to begin negotiations yet again.[69] We may wonder how much more progress Turkey would have made if indeed EU membership had been a certain reward for its efforts.

Yet the EU will still have to decide by the close of 2004 whether to keep Turkey in the queue for membership. While the preferences of EU members regarding the accession of candidates are shaped by national interests, the decision whether to admit a candidate that is already in the pre-accession process is also constrained by the rules that have been developed to govern the process, in particular the meritocracy rule.[70] In the case of Turkey, member state preferences *seem* to auger against membership, whereas the rules governing the treatment of candidates *seem* to auger for it (assuming that Turkey continues to make progress fulfilling the requirements). Yet there is a very strong case for EU members using active leverage on Turkey and supporting its eventual membership as a matter of national interest. Indeed, this is precisely why the EU has let itself go so far with Turkey. As Timothy Garton Ash observed, "The logic of spreading democracy and respect for human rights, of addressing the deeper causes of terrorism, of helping Islam to adapt to the modern world and avoiding a bloody 'clash' of civilizations cries out for us to say 'yes' [to Turkey's membership]."[71]

In short, will the EU reaffirm its commitment to Turkey's future membership because of the salutary effects it is likely to have on Turkey's domestic politics, and because of the geopolitical benefits of further integrating it into the West? This would require actually admitting Turkey into the EU once it comes close to meeting the requirements. Or, will the EU turn Turkey away completely after stringing it along for some fifteen years? This could create an anti-Western backlash among Turkey's elites and public, with substantial geopolitical costs for the EU. Moreover, it would violate the meritocratic nature of the pre-accession process, because Turkey would have to be turned away for political reasons, and not for failing to make progress toward membership. Indeed, the dilemma with Turkey raises questions about how to treat other neighbors such as Ukraine: should the EU decide against Turkey, would it have been better for Turkey's domestic politics (and for the credibility of the EU's pre-accession process) if the EU had never strung Turkey along? Or would the positive influence of the EU's leverage on Turkey's domestic politics turn out to outweigh the blow to Turkey's moderate political elites of being denied membership at the end of the process?

Making the EU's Active Leverage Work in the Balkans

Less controversial than accepting Turkey is the project of holding out the prospect of EU membership to several more states in the Western Balkans. Can EU leverage work in Croatia, Serbia-Montenegro, Macedonia, Bosnia-Hercegovina, and Albania? (Can it also work someday in an independent Kosovo or Montenegro?) Most of these states still have a long road to travel before they qualify for EU membership, and the obstacles are considerable. Alongside economic backwardness, feeble state institutions, and weak civil societies, some of these states have to overcome hostile relations between ethnic minorities and majorities, and cycles of political extremism brought on by brutal ethnic cleansing and war.

The prospect of EU membership is widely considered to be the cornerstone of any successful strategy to bring democracy and economic revitalization to the Balkan region.[72] But the Western Balkan states need unprecedented economic and political assistance. For the EU, this means exercising active leverage in a more proactive and less confrontational way than with the previous candidates. As Vladimir Tismaneanu argues, it is important to "deprive the illiberal forces of their political and symbolic ammunition" such as "the West despises us" or "the West discriminates against us" which could easily be encouraged simply by passive attitudes and low levels of assistance from the West.[73]

Since the problems are great and membership for many is so distant, *intermediary rewards* for governments and societies engaged in reform are an imperative. They include complete and unilateral access to the EU market for agricultural goods, very substantial economic aid, and visa-free travel to the EU for Balkan citizens. These rewards—especially access to the EU for goods and people—help preserve the domestic political viability of moderate parties. Yet these are the rewards that have been the most difficult for the EU to deliver on account of the short-term costs that they impose (or are perceived to impose) on the EU member states.[74] Putting the CFSP to the test, the provision of effective intermediate rewards requires that the EU's foreign policy preferences overrule the short-term interests of politicians and producers in calibrating the EU's active leverage.[75]

Political elites in distant and poor states such as Macedonia and Albania may legitimately doubt that the EU will ever let them in, even if they fulfill the requirements. Given their economic backwardness and the weakness of their state administration, it will take years to qualify; given their distance from the EU and small size, their political and economic success may be of less relevance. This uncertainty may dovetail with low levels of consensus on the part of domestic political elites on the desirability of certain reforms. Indeed, some elites may be looking for an excuse not to continue EU-oriented reforms. For this reason, like in the illiberal pattern states in this study in the early 1990s, elections may still cause a sea change in efforts to comply with EU rules.

Intermediate rewards help lock in compliance by creating a set of immediate benefits that can be used as a carrot and stick. For elites that seek reform, intermediary rewards provide assistance and immediate domestic benefits for moving forward. For elites that shirk reform, intermediary rewards can be suspended. This imposes immediate sanctions to falling behind on work to achieve the distant goal of EU membership, and may help move political parties toward a consensus on EU-oriented reforms.

How has the EU fine tuned the way it exercises its leverage to take into account the much greater challenge of promoting stability and reform in the Western Balkan states? These states would respond poorly to the treatment that the Visegrad states received after 1989 in three areas: the delay before committing to enlargement; miserly access to the EU market; and negligible financial assistance. Let us look briefly at these three areas—and see that indeed the EU has treated the Western Balkan states differently in each one, at least since 1999.

The EU developed the Stabilisation and Association Process (SAP) in 1999 that gave the Western Balkan states a clear prospect of membership; their status as credible future members has been reaffirmed many times, including at the Thessaloniki European Council of June 2003. The Commission has described the SAP as a strategy designed to help the region secure political and economic stabilization while also developing a closer association with the EU on the way to eventual membership.[76]

As part of the SAP, the EU has also been more generous with market access and financial assistance since 1999 than it was with East Central European states after 1989.[77] All five countries benefit from exceptional trade measures adopted for the Western Balkans in 2000, and from 5 billion euro in financial assistance allocated for the 2000–6 period. The most important reward for reform on the table so far for these states is signing a Stabilization and Association Agreement (SAA). Unlike the Europe Agreements, the SAAs open EU markets almost entirely to imports from the associate members. They also have tougher political criteria: states must have made visible progress in fulfilling the Copenhagen criteria and also requirements specific to the SAP including full cooperation with the International Criminal Tribunal for the former Yugoslavia (ICTY), the creation of real opportunities for refugees and internally displaced persons to return and a visible commitment to regional cooperation. In 2001, Croatia and Macedonia signed an SAA, while negotiations began with Albania in 2003.[78] Using the SAAs as an incentive and a reward for reform seems to be working, but additional intermediary rewards are needed in the form of greater financial assistance and freedom to travel.

The overall characteristics of the EU's active leverage during the 1997–2004 period have been effective, however, and should be protected as the process unfolds in the Western Balkans. In particular, the EU should protect the meritocratic nature of the pre-accession process while also continuing to enforce the requirements of membership from a position of strength. These characteristics of the pre-accession process give elites in troubled and poor states hope of equal treatment without giving them expectations of an easy pass. Indeed, the high geopolitical stakes for succeeding in the Balkans could change the nature of the EU's active leverage by decreasing the credibility of the EU's conditionality. For example, if the EU was anxious to begin accession negotiations with Croatia in order to prove that the SAP is working in post-conflict states, it might be more lenient on compliance, for example, on Croatia's treatment of refugees and war criminals, to the detriment of the credibility of the process.

How much traction does the EU's active leverage already have in the five Western Balkan states? All I can do here is raise some questions and point to some parallels with this study. Macedonia, Albania, and Bosnia-Hercegovina struggle with low state and economic capacity; indeed, Bosnia-Hercegovina is hardly a state at all. For Macedonia and Albania, backwardness appears to be a greater hurdle to qualifying for membership than political will. Serbia-Montenegro and Croatia share the potential for higher levels of state capacity and economic development, but they vary substantially in terms of how political elites are treating the pre-accession process. Let us look briefly at their status.

The defeat in national elections in 2000 of Franjo Tudjman's party in Croatia and Slobodan Miloševic's party in Serbia brought to power much more reform-minded and Western-oriented governments. Prior to these elections, Western governments had little traction on either state because of the make-up of Tudjman's and Milosevic's domestic power base. The EU and other international actors did attempt to moderate, unite and support the democratic oppositions to both rulers. Indeed, they did so more overtly and dramatically, especially in Serbia, than they did in the illiberal pattern states in this study. Taking office in 2000, the new governments launched important political and economic reforms, and sought a much closer relationship with the EU. But both were constrained by conflicting views within the government on the course of reform, and by the continued power of nationalist parties (and, especially in Serbia, criminal groups) in domestic politics. Both struggled with EU demands for full compliance with the ICTY, satisfying them only in part.

Yet the paths of Croatia and Serbia have diverged dramatically since 2000. Croatia is the clear frontrunner because of the strength of its economy and the consensus on qualifying for EU membership among its political elite. After Croatia applied for membership in February 2003, Commission officials stated that Croatia could begin accession talks as early as 2004 if it improved its record on war crimes and the treatment of refugees. The Commission's Opinion on Croatia's application, published in April 2004, recommended that the EU begin negotiations with Croatia. Providing another very clear case of the EU "amplifying" tremendously the leverage of another international organization, the Opinion noted very prominently that the ICTY Prosecutor had declared that "Croatia is now cooperating fully" with the ICTY—and for negotiations to proceed that this cooperation must continue.[79] The European Council in June 2004 agreed to open accession negotiations with Croatia in early 2005. Most striking as a parallel to this study, elections in Croatia in early 2004 returned to power Tudjman's HDZ party, but this government has chosen to comply more fully than the previous government with the EU's membership requirements, including handing over Croatia's "war heroes" to the ICTY. Enlargement Commissioner Günter Verheugen declared that Croatian membership could send a powerful signal to Serbia and other Western Balkan countries that the EU would reward reform.[80] So far Serbia has been far behind Croatia, most vividly in terms of the political will of ruling parties to satisfy EU requirements which has gone hand in hand with persistent economic backwardness and very high levels of corruption in the economy. If these trends continue, Croatia could be far into the negotiations before Serbia even signs an SAA with the EU.

8.4   Conclusion

This chapter tackled three distinct questions. First, it explored the debates among scholars surrounding the impact of the EU's leverage on the future quality of the policy-making process in the new members. The process of joining the EU, especially the imperative of adopting so many foreign-made rules and the content of some of those rules, may have undermined democratic politics in several ways. Nevertheless, I argued that the benefits of being in the EU combined with the benefits of qualifying for membership have outweighed the costs of being subject to the drawbacks of the EU's pre-accession process. It will take more time and further study, however, before scholars come to a better understanding of what the benefits and drawbacks for these new polities really were, making it possible to analyze their longer-term impact on the quality of democracy.

Next, this chapter explored the condition of the new members once they joined the EU in May 2004. There is no question that what I called "the endgame" of the negotiations left the new members with unfavorable initial terms for their membership. But I argued that these terms are indeed "initial," and that there is little reason to fear that the new members will be condemned to a permanent second-class status in the EU. The EU's active leverage has all but disappeared, and as full members they enjoy very substantial bargaining power that can be deployed to further their interests. However, the perception of such a second-class status may have repercussions for domestic politics in the new members, diverting attention from the opportunities of membership and fostering Euroskepticism and xenophobia. While the new members are unlikely to cause gridlock or stall integration, the terms of their accession are likely to elicit hard bargaining at least until the disparities between old and new members are abolished, and the public mood improves.

Finally, this chapter asked the question: why enlarge? Why did the EU's old members put ten post-communist states on the road to membership? I argued that the EU decided to enlarge because the long-term economic and geopolitical benefits of including the new members are considerable, especially in light of the costs of not enlarging, while the short-term adjustment costs for old members can be (and were) minimized. If straightforward national interests explain the decision to enlarge, what about future enlargements? At what point will the costs of enlarging outweigh the costs of not enlarging? This is a tricky question not only from the perspective of deepening European integration and of rousing sensitivities among publics and interest groups in existing EU member states. It is also a tricky question from the perspective of the geopolitical stability of the European continent and the success of the EU's emerging common foreign policy. After all, turning a neighboring state down as a credible candidate for EU membership means relinquishing the influence of the EU's active leverage on its domestic politics.

Conclusion

The European Union (EU) is the most intricate and ambitious project of regional integration in the world. It had a hand in bringing national and ethnic reconciliation, stable democracy and economic revival to parts of Europe after the end of the Second World War, during the Cold War, and then again after the end of the Cold War. Since 1989, building liberal democracies and market economies in East Central European states has been profoundly influenced by the process of attaining membership in the EU. The tremendous benefits combined with the substantial requirements of membership have set the stage for the EU's leverage on the domestic policy choices of aspiring member states. At no time in history have sovereign states voluntarily agreed to meet such vast domestic requirements and then subjected themselves to such intrusive verification procedures to enter an international organization. In 2004, eight formerly communist states joined the EU, and as many or more were credible candidates or future candidates for membership.

I demonstrate in this book that in observing the outcomes of democratization and economic reform, we see an "EU advantage" favoring liberal democracy and market-oriented reforms in states that are credible future EU members. The puzzle is one of causation: does the EU only accept liberal democracies as members? Or, as I argue, does the *condition* of being a credible future EU member (for reasons of geography and geopolitics) create incentives and influence societies such that eventually elites make policy decisions that put states on the road to liberal democracy? If twenty years from now, Serbia or Macedonia look like today's Hungary or Estonia, the case will be clear. And of course we may discover that some domestic conditions are even more intractable than those in Romania; in some credible future members, EU leverage may not work at all.

In this book, I have made the case for the important independent effect of EU leverage on domestic political change in six credible future EU members— under quite different domestic conditions. By no means does EU leverage erase or even diminish many domestic differences: but it does improve the quality of political competition, while narrowing the parameters of domestic policy-making as states comply with EU rules in order to qualify for membership. As we observed in Chapter 7, we see a significant—though certainly far from complete—convergence among liberal pattern and "post"-illiberal pattern states as the latter get closer to qualifying for EU membership. I identified three mechanisms that encourage compliance—conditionality, credible commitment, and influence on domestic groups.

Before convergence could occur, however, the illiberal pattern states had to break the habit of electing illiberal, rent-seeking rulers. At the beginning of this book, I argued that the most important legacy of communism (and pre-communism) is the character of groups of elites present at the moment of regime change, because these groups determine the initial competitiveness of the political system. The presence of an opposition guarantees a certain level of political competition: there are at least two rival, organized political groups. In liberal pattern states, an opposition to communism strong enough to take power in 1989 brings about the all important exit of communist elites from power; it also lays the foundations of liberal democracy and launches comprehensive economic reform. Ideally, a reforming communist party meanwhile creates an active, moderate opposition while transforming itself to get back into the political game.

In illiberal pattern states, however, the opposition is too weak to take power—and the communist party has fewer incentives or resources to attempt transformation. In conditions of limited political competition, rent-seeking elites win and hold power by further suppressing rival groups, promising slow economic reform, and exploiting ethnic nationalism—all the while extracting significant rents from slow economic reform. By influencing the institutional and the informational environment, I argued in Chapter 6 that EU leverage helped create what the illiberal pattern states were missing at the moment of transition: a coherent and moderate opposition, and an open and pluralistic political arena. Under the right conditions, free and fair elections provide opposition parties and civic groups the opening they need to end illiberal rule. Working in synergy with such forces, the EU's active leverage had a hand, over time, in creating those conditions and making the political systems of the illiberal states more competitive.

For its part, the EU did not develop active leverage by design—and it is becoming (again) reluctant to use it. Indeed, the initial credibility of the EU's conditionality flowed from such ambivalence: the EU's tough treatment of the ECE states in the early 1990s not only hardened their resolve to attain full membership, but revealed that EU governments might be pleased to disqualify underperforming candidates. The right balance was struck: candidates were neither too confident (thanks to asymmetric interdependence), nor were they too disingenuous (thanks to enforcement), nor did they despair that the system was stacked against them (thanks to meritocracy).

The aspects of the EU's active leverage that were deliberately designed, including the way that conditionality has been "delivered" through the pre-accession process, have worked remarkably well. No doubt that each observer or participant would suggest changes: from my perspective, a "better" enlargement would include more assistance to civil society and the reform of state institutions, stricter enforcement of the Copenhagen criteria, and more generous terms of accession. Yet it is important to emphasize that the effectiveness of the EU's active leverage stems from its passive leverage—from the benefits of membership (and the costs of exclusion). Change this equation, and the behavior of aspiring members may change as well: this is after all what EU members are hoping will be the outcome of the EU's new "Wider Europe" policy.

Given the EU's singular difficulties, however, in offering what really matters to states on the outside (that are not Switzerland)—access for goods and access for people—efforts to diffuse the EU's passive leverage are not likely to succeed. Moreover, the EU's episodic ambitions as a geopolitical actor on the world stage and the very real benefits of continued enlargement will make it hard for the EU definitively to part ways with some aspiring members, especially Turkey. All of this suggests that the drama of EU enlargement is likely to continue. Let us hope that it does: the most important challenge for EU leaders today is to sustain, adjust, and improve the EU's active leverage so that it can work even in the much tougher cases in the Western Balkans. For better (and not, so far, for worse), the most powerful and successful tool of EU foreign policy has turned out to be EU enlargement—and this book has helped us understand why, and how, it works.

LIST OF INTERVIEWS

The title or affiliation listed is accurate at (or close to) the time of the interview, unless otherwise noted. For those individuals who I interviewed more than twice or who consistently shared their expertise with me I have not listed a date and have listed some of their most important affiliations.

Gabriel Andreescu, Helsinki Committee, Bucharest, November 1998.
Dagmar Ašerová, EastWest Institute, Prague.
Graham Avery, Former Chief Advisor, Enlargement, Directorate-General (DG) IA—External Relations, European Commission, July 1998.
Albena Azmanova, Institut d'Etudes Politiques, Paris, August 2000.

Alyson Bailes, Political Director, West European Union, Brussels, February 1999.
András Barsony, Committee for Foreign Affairs, Hungarian Parliament, June 1998.
Krzysztof Bernacki, European Community Section, Polish Ministry of Foreign Affairs, August 1992.
Gilles Bertrand, Forward Studies Unit, European Commission, July 1998.
Vladimír Bilčík, Slovak Foreign Policy Association, Bratislava, December 2003.
Ludger Blasig, DGIA, European Commission, November 1998.
Krzysztof Bobiński, Financial Times, editor of Unia-Polska, Warsaw, June 1998.
Irina Bokova, EuroLeft Party, Bulgarian Parliament, November 1998.
Olga Borissova, Delegation of the European Commission in Bulgaria, November 1998.
György Boytha, Department of International Law, Eötvös Lorand University, Budapest, June 1998.
András Bozóki, Central European University, Budapest, June 1998 and April 2001.
Daniel Bútora, Slovak Service, Radio Free Europe/Radio Liberty, Prague, July 1998.

Helen Campbell, Cabinet of Hans van den Broek, European Commission, July 1998.
Sergiu Celac, Foreign Minister of Romania 1990; Ambassador and Counsellor, Romanian Ministry of Foreign Affairs, November 1998.
Ludovit Černák, Democratic Union Party of Slovakia, July 1998.
Jerzy Ciechanski, European Integration Department, Polish Ministry of Labour, October 1998.
Rachel Cooper, Chargé d'Affaires, Embassy of the United Kingdom in Slovakia, July 1998.
András Csite, Hungarian Academy of Sciences, Budapest, June 1998.

Slawomir Dabrowa, Department of European Institutions, Polish Ministry of Foreign Affairs, August 1992.
Catherine Day, Director, DG IA, European Commission, July 1998.

Oldřich Dědek, Czech National Bank, Prague, May 1999.

Pavol Demeš, Executive Director, Slovak Academic Information Agency—Service Center for the Third Sector; Former Advisor to Slovak President Michal Kováč, July 1998, August 2000.

Miklós Dérer, Hungarian Atlantic Council, Budapest, February 1999.

Jiří Dienstbier, Foreign Minister of Czechoslovakia 1990–1992, July 1999.

Joly Dixon, Director, DG II—Economic and Financial Affairs, European Commission, July 1998.

Steffen Elgersma, West European Union, Brussels, July 1998.

Tamás Földi, Public Policy Institute, Budapest, June 1998.

Pavel Fischer, Head, Political Department, Office of the Czech President Václav Havel.

Sharon Fisher, Radio Free Europe/Radio Liberty; PlanEcon.

Ivan Gabal, Gabal Analysis and Consulting, October 2001.

Timothy Garton Ash, St. Antony's College, Oxford.

Michael Gold, Crimson Capital, Prague, July 1999.

Peter Green, Journalist, Prague.

Petr Greger, Delegation of the European Commission to the Czech Republic.

Tomáš Halík, Theologian, Prague, March 2000.

Geoffrey Harris, Joint Committee of the European Parliament and Associated Partners, November 1998.

Jiří Havlík, Department of European Integration, Czech Ministry of Foreign Affairs.

Dionyz Hochel, Delegation of the European Commission to the Slovak Republic, July 1998 and May 1999.

Márius Hričovský, Democratic Union, Slovakia, October 1998.

Antoaneta Hristova, Committee on Foreign and Integration Policy, Bulgarian Parliament, November 1998.

András Inotai, Institute for World Economics, Hungarian Academy of Sciences, February 1999.

Wolfgang Ischinger, Ministry of Foreign Affairs, Republic of Germany, June 1999.

Balasz Jarabík, NOS Foundation, Bratislava, October 1999.

Petr Javorčík, Mission of the Slovak Republic to the EU, July 1998 and November 1998.

Leszek Jesień, College of Europe, Warsaw, and Committee for European Integration, Poland.

Géza Jeszensky, Foreign Minister of Hungary 1990–1994, June 1998.

Rudolf Joó, Deputy State Secretary, Hungarian Ministry of Defense, June 1998.

Rastislav Kačer, Director of Policy Planning, Ministry of Foreign Affairs of Slovakia, July 1998.

Jerzy Kalinowski, Committee for European Integration, Poland, October 1998.

Georgi Karasimeonov, Institute of Political and Legal Studies, Sofia, November 1998.

Radek Khol, Institute for International Relations, Prague, July 1999.

Charles King, Georgetown University, November 1998 and July 2000.

Heinz Kluss, Director of the Defence and Security Committee, North Atlantic Assembly, July 1998.

Vladimír Kmec, Center for Strategic Studies and Slovak Ministry of Defense, Bratislava, July 1998.

Maria Koinova, Open Media Research Institute, Prague; European University Institute, Florence.

Petr Kolář, Ministry of Foreign Affairs, Czech Republic, July 1999.

András Kós, State Secretariat for Integration, Hungarian Ministry of Foreign Affairs, February 1999.

Libuše Koubská, Editor in Chief, The New Presence, Prague.

Karel Kovanda, Czech Ambassador to the Atlantic Alliance, 1999.

Ivan Krastev, Center for Liberal Strategies, Sofia, July 2000.

Rudolf Kučera, Department of Political Science, Charles University, Prague, May 1998.

Jacek Kucharczyk, Institute of Public Affairs, Warsaw, February 1999.

Eduard Kukan, Slovak Foreign Minister 1994; Member of Parliament and Chairman of the Democratic Union 1994–1998; Slovak Foreign Minister 1998–present, July 1998.

Gilda Lazăr, Former Senior Counselor and Spokeswoman, Romanian Ministry of Foreign Affairs, November 1998.

Michael Leigh, Chief Negotiator with the Czech Republic; Deputy Director General of DG External Relations, European Commission.

Helmuth Lohan, DGIA, European Commission, November 1998.

Csaba Lörincz, Strategic Planning Department, Ministry of Foreign Affairs, Hungary, February 1999.

Pavol Lukáč, Slovak Foreign Policy Association, Bratislava, May 1999 and December 2003.

Petr Luňák, Czech Ministry of Foreign Affairs, May 1999.

Riccardo Maggi, DG II, European Commission, November 1998.

Jerzy Makarczyk, Deputy Foreign Minister, Polish Ministry of Foreign Affairs, August 1992.

Darina Málová, Department of Political Science, Comenius University, Bratislava, July 1998.

Vassilis Maragos, Delegation of the European Commission to Bulgaria, November 1998.

Elitza Markova, Economic Policy Institute, Sofia, November 1998.

Dobroslav Matějka, Institute for International Relations, Prague, June 1998.

Grigorij Mesežnikov, Institute for Public Affairs (IVO), Bratislava, July 1998 and October 1998.

Anna Michalski, Forward Studies Unit, European Commission, July 1998.

Adam Michnik, Gazeta Wyborcza, Warsaw, November 1999.

Ognyan Minchev, Institute for Regional and International Studies, Sofia, November 1998.

Pierre Mirel, Director, DG Enlargement, European Commission, November 1998 and August 2003.

Jan Mládek, Deputy Finance Minister, Czech Republic, March 1999.

Leo Mullender, Delegation of the European Commission to Slovakia, October 1998.

Alina Mungiu-Pippidi, Romanian State Television and Romanian Academic Society (SAR).

Jerzy Marek Nowakowski, Center of International Studies, Polish Senate, August 1992.

Martin Palouš, Charter 77; Deputy Foreign Minister, Czech Republic; Czech Ambassador to the United States.

Howard J. S. Pearce, Central European Department, Foreign and Commonwealth Office, October 1998.

Jiří Pehe, Radio Free Europe/Radio Liberty; Head, Political Department, Office of the Czech President Václav Havel; Director of New York University in Prague.

Pedro Pick, Patria Finance, Prague, May 1998 and March 1999.

Liliana Popescu, Director of Policy Planning, Romanian Ministry of Foreign Affairs, November 1998.

László Pótí, Institute for Strategic and Defence Studies, Budapest, June 1998.

Martin Potůček, Department of Sociology, Charles University, Prague, May 1999.

Antoaneta Primatarova, Deputy Foreign Minister, Bulgaria, November 1998.

Valeri Ratchev, Bulgarian Ministry of Defense, May 1999.

Jacques Rupnik, CERI, Fondation des Sciences Politiques, Paris.

Michael Rupp, DGIA, European Commission, July 1998 and November 1998.

Jana Ryslinková, Euro-Czech Forum, Czech Republic, July 1999.

Gerhard Sabathil, DGIA, European Commission, July 1998.

Levente Salat, Open Society Institute, Cluj, March 2000.

Ivo Samson, Slovak Foreign Policy Association, Bratislava, July 1998.

Sönke Schmidt, European Commission, November 1998.

George Schöpflin, School of Slavonic and East European Studies, London, April 2001.

Jiří Šedivý, Director, Institute for International Relations, Prague.

Pavel Seifter, Civic Forum; Head, Political Department, Office of the Czech President Václav Havel; Czech Ambassador to the United Kingdom.

John Shattuck, US Ambassador to the Czech Republic, March 2000.

Ivo Šilhavý, Political Department, Office of the Czech President Václav Havel.

Thomas W. Simons, US Ambassador to Poland 1990–94; Stanford University.

Zygmunt Skórzynski, Forum Démocratique Européen, Warsaw, August 1992.

Steffen Skovmand, Delegation of the European Commission to Romania, November 1998.

Aleksander Smolar, Solidarity leader; Stefan Batory Foundation, Warsaw and CNRS, Paris, August 1999.

Jonathan Stein, East-West Institute; Project Syndicate, Prague.

Marianna Stoica, Committee of European Integration, Romanian Parliament, November 1998.

Tomáš Stražaj, Slovak Foreign Policy Association, Bratislava, May 1999.

Réka Szemerkényi, Senior Advisor, Office of Hungarian Prime Minister Viktor Orban, London, January 1999.

Soňa Szomolányi, Professor, Comenius University, Bratislava, July 1998.

István Szonyi, Director, Hungarian Institute of International Affairs, June 1998.

Tamas Szucs, Mission of the Republic of Hungary to the EU, July 1998.

Gerd Tebbe, DGIA, European Commission, July 1998.

Pavel Telička, Deputy Foreign Minister and Chief Negotiator with the European Union, Czech Republic, October 1998 and October 2000.

Boyko Todorov, Center for the Study of Democracy, Sofia, November 1998.

Zdeněk Tůma, Czech National Bank, November 1999.

Jan Urban, Journalist, Prague, October 1998.

László Valki, Department of International Law, Eötvös University, Budapest, June 1998 and May 1999.

Jaroslav Veis, Advisor to Chairman of the Czech Senate Petr Pithart; Journalist, June 1998 and October 2000.

Alexandr Vondra, Deputy Foreign Minister, Czech Republic; Czech Ambassador to the United States.

Kieran Williams, School of Slavonic and East European Studies, London.

Miroslav Wlachowský, Slovak Foreign Policy Association; Director of Policy Planning, Ministry of Foreign Affairs of Slovakia, July 1998 and May 1999.

Josef Zieleniec, Former Foreign Minister of the Czech Republic 1992–7, Czech Senate.

NOTES

Introduction

1. The Soviet Union, Poland, Hungary, Czechoslovakia, Bulgaria, Romania, East Germany, Albania, and Yugoslavia. For the twenty-seven post-communist states on the European continent (without the "east" of unified Germany), see Figure 1.1.
2. I draw on: Ellen Comisso (1997). See also Chapter 1.
3. Valerie Bunce (1995); in debate with Philippe C. Schmitter and Terry Lynn Karl (1994).
4. Terry Lynn Karl (1995); Fareed Zakaria (1997); John Shattuck and J. Brian Atwood (1997); Larry Diamond (2002); and Steven Levitsky and Lucan A. Way (2002).
5. Steven Levitsky and Lucan Way (2003).
6. Philippe C. Schmitter (2001). See also Laurence Whitehead (2001b); and the other contributions to this volume. See also Geoffrey Pridham, Eric Herring, and George Sanford (eds.) (1997).
7. Geoffrey Pridham (ed.) (1991); and Laurence Whitehead (2001c).
8. Stephen Haggard and Steven B. Webb (1994: 5).
9. Edward D. Mansfield and Jack Snyder (1995).
10. In this endeavor I am joined by colleagues and friends whose excellent recently published books have inspired and complemented my own work: Liliana B. Andonova (2003); Wade Jacoby (2004); Judith Kelley (2004a); and the edited volume Frank Schimmelfennig and Ulrich Sedelmeier (eds.) (2005). Earlier important edited volumes include Karen Henderson (ed.) (1999); Jan Zielonka and Alex Pravda (eds.) (2001); Ronald H. Linden (ed.) (2001a) and Paul Kubicek (ed.) (2004a).
11. For the methods that enable comparisons among a limited number of cases to be valuable, Adam Przeworksi and Henry Teune (1970); Gary King, Robert Keohane, and Sidney Verba (eds.) (1994); Charles Ragin (1987) and Valerie Bunce (1999a: 15–17).
12. On the tension in theory building in the field of post-communism between temporally shallow accounts that risk tautology (reformers implement reform) and temporally distant accounts that make it impossible to identify the chain of causation (the boundaries of the Roman empire determine post-communist change), see Herbert Kitschelt (1999) and (2003a).

Chapter 1

1. Comisso (1997); and Valerie Bunce (1999*b*). See also Grzegorz Ekiert and Stephen E. Hanson (eds.) (2003).
2. The democratization index is based on the average of four scores for electoral process, civil society, independent media, and governance (see Table 7.1 for a break-down for the six ECE states). The economic liberalization index is based on the average of scores for privatization, macroeconomic policy, and microeconomic policy. In its wisdom, Freedom House has created indexes that go from 1 (greatest democratization/economic reform) to 7 (lowest democratization/economic reform).
3. Using a World Bank/EBRD Structural Reform index against Freedom House democratization data, others have averaged the scores received for each year between 1990 and 2000 for a similar result. See Chapter 9 in Thomas Oatley (2004: 379–392) and Ånders Åslund (2002: 362). See also European Bank for Reconstruction and Development (2000).
4. World Bank (2002: 16, 73–74, 107).
5. Joel S. Hellman (1998).
6. Ibid., 219.
7. Ibid., 204. Or as Leszek Balcerowicz observed, slow reforms channel "entrepreneurial energies into rent-seeking and corruption rather than the search for greater efficiency," thus destroying the prospects for economic development and increasing inequality. Leszek Balcerowicz (1994).
8. Adam Przeworski (1991: 133). See also Adam Przeworski (1999).
9. Douglass North (1989: 27).
10. Such groups may also be able to repress and therefore exploit labor, generating growth through low wages. See Adam Przeworski et al. (2002).
11. Hellman (1998: 228–231).
12. Paul Pierson (2000: 488). See also Peter A. Hall and Rosemary C. R. Taylor (1996) and Valerie Bunce (2000).
13. Douglass North (1990: 16).
14. Hellman (1998: 228).
15. Timothy Frye (2002).
16. I am creating this term after Valerie Bunce, who observed that "the key question in democratic governance is whether democracy functions as a political monopoly." Valerie Bunce (2002: 306).
17. Andrew Moravscik (1997: 517).
18. Ibid., 525–526.
19. James D. Fearon and David D. Laitin (2000). See also Robert H. Bates, Rui J. P. de Figueiredo Jr., and Barry R. Weingast (1998).
20. Pierson (2000: 489).
21. I am indebted to Anna Grzymała-Busse for a discussion of these points.
22. I argue in Chapter 6 that it is by strengthening the position and shaping the agendas of opposition parties that external actors, chiefly the European Union,

ultimately have the greatest impact on the course of political change in East Central Europe's illiberal democracies.

23. The exceptions are Romania's 1990 and 1992 elections. Still, all six states satisfy minimal definitions of democracy that focus on competitive elections as the mechanisms for bestowing political power on individuals. For the classic, Joseph Schumpeter (1950).

24. On the importance of the accountability of rulers and of "mechanisms of competition other than elections," I draw on Philippe C. Schmitter and Terry Lynn Karl (1991). For the classic on conditions for democracy (polyarchy), Robert Dahl (1971).

25. For a discussion of what constitutes a "satisfying" independent variable that avoids tautology for the causes of democratization, Samuel P. Huntington (1991: 35–36). For post-communist outcomes, Herbert Kitschelt (2003a).

26. For the argument that pre-communist bourgeois–socialist cleavages caused three kinds of communism to develop in Eastern Europe—bureaucratic–authoritarian communism, national–accommodative communism, and patrimonial communism—and that each kind has in turn decisively shaped post-89 democratic politics, see Herbert Kitschelt et al. (1999). See also Herbert Kitschelt (1995).

27. Grzegorz Ekiert (1996: 305–330); Katherine Verdery (1996a); David Stark and Laszlo Bruszt (1998); Bunce (1999a) and many more.

28. Grzegorz Ekiert (2003: 92).

29. Milada Anna Vachudova and Timothy Snyder (1997: 10–11).

30. Valerie Bunce (1999c: 242). See also Bunce (1999b); and Charles King (2000).

31. M. Steven Fish (1998). For a critique, Jeffrey Kopstein and David Reilly (1999).

32. Herbert Kitschelt (2003b: 6). See also Herbert Kitschelt (2001).

33. Michael McFaul (2002: 214). See also Kitschelt (1999).

34. Mitchell Orenstein (2001). See also Shattuck and Atwood (1997: 168).

35. Anna Grzymała-Busse (2003a). See also Anna Grzymała-Busse (2003b).

36. Jon Elster, Claus Offe, and Ulrich K. Preuss (1998).

37. Gábor Tóka (1997). See also Peter Mair (1996).

38. Tóka (1997).

39. Beverly Crawford and Arend Lijphart (1995) and Larry Diamond and Marc Plattner (eds.) (1996).

40. For the correlations, see Kitschelt (2003a).

41. Ken Jowitt (1992). For a critique, Stephen E. Hanson (1995). For a strong argument that the decisive and uniform suppression of civil society across all post-communist democracies is a crippling legacy of communism, Marc Morjé Howard (2003).

42. In 1989, for example, in the six ECE states between 77% and 92% of the population had secondary school education, and between 95% and 99% were literate (these statistics may be somewhat inflated). See UNESCO (2002). On the gender literacy gap, M. Steven Fish (2003).

43. Philip G. Roeder (1999: 751).

Chapter 2

1. On the centrality of a strong opposition to the course of political change, Vachudova and Snyder (1997).
2. John K. Glenn (2001).
3. On the importance of the rapid electoral replacement of the communist elites in 1990 over twenty-six post-communist cases, Fish (1998).
4. Jakub Zielinski (2002).
5. Shock therapy refers to the economic reform program launched by the Polish government on January 1, 1990 that very rapidly liberalized prices and introduced many elements of a liberal capitalist economy as quickly as possible.
6. See Hanson (1995); Ekiert (1996); Bunce (1999a); Ekiert and Hanson (eds.) (2003).
7. H. Gordon Skilling (1973: 97).
8. Ernest Gellner (1993). See also Skilling (1973: 116).
9. The original Charter 77 document was published on January 1, 1977, having been signed by 243 Czechoslovak citizens in late 1976. The document was then open for signature by anyone who agreed to work for human rights in Czechoslovakia. For the personal recollections of many signatories including their persecution by the communist government, see *Charta 77 očima současníků: po dvaceti letech* (1997) and also *Charta 77 očima současníků: před dvaceti lety* (1997).
10. Václav Havel (1986).
11. On normalization, Kieran Williams (1997a). Also Wlodzimierz Brus, Pierre Kende, and Zdeněk Mlynář (1982).
12. On Solidarity, Timothy Garton Ash (2002); Roman Laba (1991); and Jan Kubik (1994).
13. Ekiert (1996).
14. Tony Judt (1988). See also Thomas W. Simons, Jr. (1993).
15. András Bozóki (ed.) (1999). On "refolutions," Timothy Garton Ash (1990). See also Gale Stokes (1993).
16. On the Polish transition, Adam Michnik (1998).
17. For the amazement of Solidarity's leaders at their success, Garton Ash (1990: 25–46).
18. On Poland's shock therapy, Leszek Balcerowicz (1995); and in a comparative context, Åslund (2002).
19. For the argument that the nature and scale of protest in Poland from 1989 to 1993 was a sign of democratic vitality and successful democratic consolidation, Grzegorz Ekiert and Jan Kubik (1999).
20. András Bozóki (ed.) (2002) and Rudolf Tokés (1996).
21. For a vivid depiction of the various groups and traditions of the Hungarian opposition, Timothy Garton Ash (1989: 148–150).
22. For example, Adam Michnik (1985a); Janos Kis (1989) and Jiří Dienstbier (1990).
23. I am indebted to Adam Michnik, Pavel Seifter, and Alexandr Vondra for conversations on this point.
24. Michnik (1985a: 76–99). See also Adam Michnick (1985b).

25. For the different currents of thought within and about Solidarity in the 1980s, including Andrzej Walicki's 1984 article charging that Solidarity was "a democratic movement but not a liberal movement," David Ost (1990).

26. This had little purchase in Poland because of the economic crisis, but rather more in Hungary and the Czech Republic where the proponents of "the third way" were vocal in 1990 (e.g. Valtr Komárek in Prague) but faded away as consensus emerged that a third way did not exist.

27. North (1990: 16).

28. For the role of former dissidents in crafting and defending liberal democracy, Vladimir Tismaneanu (1998).

29. Václav Havel (1990a).

30. Timothy Snyder (2003).

31. Géza Jeszenszky, Foreign Minister of Hungary 1990–4, interview in Budapest, 1998. Also, Rudolf Jóo, Hungarian Ministry of Defense, interview in Budapest, 1998.

32. In all three states, fundamental problems of ethnic tolerance did remain, evinced by severe discrimination (especially in the Czech Republic) against the Roma that governments only addressed later in the 1990s under direct pressure from the EU and other international actors. On the Roma, Zoltan Barany (2002).

33. On implementing institutional change that will be costly in the short run, Haggard and Webb (1994).

34. Alan Jacobs (2004).

35. Within Solidarity there was consensus on the need for radical economic reform, but little consensus on what such reform would entail. Leszek Balcerowicz was willing to take on the post of finance minister and push through his plan for shock therapy after several others had declined the post. Aleksander Smolar, interview in Paris, 1999.

36. Ekiert and Kubik (1999: esp. Ch. 6).

37. I am indebted to Jonathan Stein for conversations on this point. See also Przeworski (1991: 166).

38. For a similar argument that economic crisis can help democratization by flushing out incumbent authoritarian elites, lessening their power over subsequent governments, Stephen Haggard and Robert R. Kaufman (1995) and Karen Remmer (1996).

39. Adam Przeworski and Fernando Limongi (1997).

40. Ralf Dahrendorf (1990). See also Claus Offe (1991).

41. Bela Greskovits (1998).

42. On the communist successor parties, Anna Grzymała-Busse (2002); Mitchell Orenstein (1998); Anna Grzymała-Busse (1998); John Higley, Jan Pakulski, and Włodzimierz Wesołowski (eds.) (1998) and John T. Ishiyama (1997). See also the outstanding collection, András Bozóki and John T. Ishiyama (eds.) (2002).

43. Stephen E. Hanson (2001: 136).

44. Linda J. Cook and Mitchell A. Orenstein (1999).

45. Vachudova and Snyder (1997: 7).

46. Ibid., 7.

47. Ibid., 13.

48. The bright young Communist Aleksander Kwasniewski suggested the compromise that allowed semi-free elections in People's Poland in June 1989; less than seven

years later, he was president of the Polish Republic. For a characterization of the attitude of Communists to liberalism (which treats late Polish and Hungarian communism as exceptional), see Jerzy Szacki (1995).

49. Grzymała-Busse (2002).

50. For the opposing view of the Czech Republic as a more "competitive" democracy, see Kitschelt, Mansfeldová, Markowski, and Tóka (1999).

51. The normalization following the Prague spring left the Czech party "ideologically hidebound" with elites incapable of regenerating the party. But the rigid central party apparatus overlooked a group of reformist elites in the Slovak communist party. These elites took over and transformed the Slovak wing of the Czechoslovak communist party into a social democratic party after 1989. See Grzymała-Busse (2002: 37, 61–62).

52. I am indebted to Jiří Havlík, Jiří Pehe, Pavel Seifter and Alexandr Vondra for interviews and conversations on this point. See Jiří Pehe (2002).

53. Ivo Šilhavý, interview in Prague, 1999. See Milada Anna Vachudova (2001a).

54. Abby Innes (2001). But see Sharon Wolchik (1994) and Bunce (1999a: 77–101) for the role of nationalism and state institutions in the split.

55. Hilary Appel (2001). See also Kevin Deegan Krause (2000).

56. Orenstein (2001). In *Out of the Red* Orenstein describes Leszek Balcerowicz's strategy of reform in Poland as "neo-liberal," and that of Václav Klaus in the Czech Republic as "social liberal."

57. Bunce (2002: 304).

58. On a weak domestic opposition as facilitating the concentration of power by undemocratic elites, M. Steven Fish (2001).

59. By "unreconstructed communists," I mean communist successor parties that were not forced to exit power, divest themselves of their former privileges, and regenerate as modern social democratic parties—even though they may have abandoned their Marxist–Leninist ideology and presided over the end of the communism in their country.

60. For illiberal democracy as a worldwide pattern, Zakaria (1997) and Levitsky and Way (2002).

61. For an intricate discussion of the contrast between elites that formulate a consensual and liberal agenda for their nations, and those that formulate instead a confrontational and anti-liberal one, Tismaneanu (1998).

62. Pauline Jones Luong (2002). For the importance of the balance of power among different kinds of elites, see also Philip K. Roeder (2001).

63. Jack Snyder (2000: 32, 37).

64. Alina Mungiu (1996: 343). Also, Alina Mungiu-Pippidi, interview in Bonn, 1999; and Gilda Lazăr, interview in Bucharest, 1998.

65. Joseph Rothschild (1974) and Piotr S. Wandycz (1992).

66. For this argument with a sultanistic twist, Juan J. Linz and Alfred Stepan (1996: 344–365). See also Tismaneanu (1998).

67. The Civic Forum in Prague also had problems controlling access to its leadership, since it had not existed as an organization as such before demonstrations began in Prague in November 1989. Václav Havel and other long-time dissidents were committed to inclusion, empowering, for example, Václav Klaus. Klaus certainly

did not return the favor once he became prime minister in 1992. Pavel Seifter, interview in London, 2001 and Soňa Szomolányi, interview in Bratislava, 1998.

68. See the essay "Liberalizmus v slovenskej tradícii," in Světoslav Bombík (1995: 48–60).

69. Martin Bútora, Zora Bútorová and Olga Gyárfášová (1994: 243, 255 fn. 3). Also, Grigorij Mesežnikov, interview in Bratislava, 1998.

70. The official estimates of the number dead in the Romanian revolution range between 1,033 and 1,104, although many believe the numbers in Timişoara and also the overall numbers to be higher. The Romanian government has never produced a credible report on the events and the deaths of December 1989. Stokes (1993: 163); and Dennis Deletant (2001: 210).

71. If the Securitate was fighting against the FSN, then it is curious that it did not attack the FSN headquarters or disrupt its access to the state television. Stokes (1993: 165).

72. Mungiu (1996).

73. On the Romanian revolution and the FSN, Matei Calinescu and Vladimir Tismaneanu (1991) and Martyn Rady (1992: 91–144).

74. Jonathan Eyal (1993: 136). See also the excellent article Katherine Verdery and Gail Kligman (1992).

75. President Iliescu faced increasing competition and criticism from Prime Minister Petre Roman. After Iliescu's coterie summoned miners to march on Bucharest again in September 1991, Roman was forced to resign. This forced a split in the FSN: the Democratic FSN (DFSN) becoming the loyal tool of Iliescu, while the FSN (later the Democratic Party-FSN (PD), then Social Democratic Union (USD) in coalition with several social democratic parties) became the party of Petre Roman. In the 1992 elections Iliescu's DFSN received 28% and Roman's FSN received 10% of the vote. Rasmus Bing and Bogdan Szajkowski (1994: 347–349).

76. Loosely aligned in the "National Formation," the three extremist parties were: the ultranationalist Party of Romanian National Unity (PRNU) of Georghe Funar, the Greater Romania Party (PRM) of Corneliu Vadim Tudor, and the Ceauşescu-nostalgic Socialist Labor Party (PSM) of Ilie Verdet. These parties include politicians who are virulently chauvinistic and antisemitic. Some of their most visible members were among the most hated henchmen of Ceauşescu. See Michael Shafir (1995a).

77. Kjell Engelbrekt (1994).

78. Stokes (1993: 176).

79. Richard Crampton (1993: 22). The BSP won 47%, the UDF 36%, and the MRF 6% of the vote in the June 1990 elections.

80. Rumyana Kolarova (1996).

81. The MRF withdrew its support in complicated and rather mysterious circumstances, allegedly linked to the fact that MRF leaders had served as agents for the secret service before 1989 and therefore opposed the UDF's retribution measures and felt comfortable dealing with the BSP. Others argue that the MRF withdrew its support chiefly because its constituents were suffering disproportionately from an economic downturn brought about by UDF reforms. Elitza Markova, interview in Sofia, 1998.

82. Innes (2001).

83. Sharon Fisher (2001).
84. On how Mečiar came to dominate politics in Bratislava, Martin Bútora and Zora Bútorová (1993). See also Carol Skalnik Leff (1996).
85. Fisher (2001).
86. Soňa Szomolányi and Grigorij Mesežnikov (eds.) (1995).
87. For a brilliant exposition of Mečiarism, Kieran Williams (2000). For detailed analysis, Soňa Szomolányi and John Gould (eds.) (1997a).
88. Soňa Szomolányi (2000). See also Kitschelt (1995: 453).
89. Nearly one quarter of the total vote went to parties which failed to enter the parliament. Sharon Fisher (1995).
90. For similar arguments, Mansfield and Snyder (1995: 31) and Linz and Stepan (1996: 254).
91. Vladimir Tismaneanu and Dorian Tudoran (1993: 43).
92. Mungiu (1996: 363).
93. Eyal (1993: 124). Armed miners had been used to violently dispel an anti-FSN rally as early as January 1990. They were brought back again in September 1991 to force the resignation of Prime Minister Petre Roman who had been asserting his independence from Iliescu.
94. Deletant (2001: 219).
95. Bulgarian Helsinki Committee (1995). See also Commission on Security and Cooperation in Europe (1993).
96. For the many facets, Soňa Szomolányi (ed.) (1997). See also Marián Leško (1997).
97. Martin Bútora and Zora Bútorová, Seminar at the Center for European Studies, Harvard University, April 10, 1995.
98. Sharon Fisher (1996a). The stalwart HZDS daily *Slovenská Republika* launched attacks on Slovakia's independent journalists and intellectuals, as well as on foreigners writing about Slovakia such as Sharon Fisher at Radio Free Europe. See Dušan Slobodník (1996).
99. Martin Šimečka (1998).
100. Kieran Williams (2001).
101. For the behavior of the SIS as a political police in chilling detail, ibid.
102. Hellman (1998: 233). See also Haggard and Kaufman (1995: 374) and Joel S. Hellman and Mark Schankerman (2000).
103. John Gould (2004: 278).
104. Stephen Holmes (1997: 6).
105. A World Bank/EBRD study measuring the extent of "state capture" by corrupt firms rated Bulgaria, Romania and Slovakia as "high," and Poland, Hungary, and the Czech Republic as "medium." See Joel S. Hellman, Geraint Jones, and Daniel Kaufman (2000).
106. Heather Grabbe and Kirsty Hughes (1998: 21). See also United Nations (1997).
107. Bartlomiej Kaminski (2001: 40).
108. For data showing that "aggressive liberalizers" have come out ahead, World Bank (1996: 30).
109. Alina Mungiu and Andrei Pippidi (1994: 351–352).
110. Banac (1992: 6).

111. For information on the challenges of reforming the Romanian economy (with scant mention of vested interests), Daniel Daianu (1998).
112. Deletant (2001: 217).
113. Verdery (1996a: 33, 196–197).
114. Michael L. Wyzan (1998: 109–112) and Venelin I. Ganev (1997: 131–132).
115. Freedom House (1998: 166, 171).
116. Ognyan Minchev, interview in Sofia, 1998.
117. Zhelyu Vladimirov (1997: 19).
118. Venelin Ganev (2001). Ganev argues persuasively that throughout the postcommunist cases we should pay greater attention to the deliberate weakening of the state by economic winners from the transition.
119. Freedom House (1996: 96). See also Ganev (1997: 134–135).
120. Hilary Appel and John Gould (2000).
121. Williams (2000: 7).
122. Gould (2004: 295). See also Gould (2001).
123. I am indebted to Sharon Fisher for this point and for many conversations about Slovakia over the last ten years.
124. Williams (2001).
125. Peter Tóth (1997) and Williams (2001).
126. Ivan Mikloš (1998a).
127. "Zoznam I. Mikloša hovorí, že známi a príbuzní politikov sa podielali na privatizácii," *SME*, June 24, 1998.
128. Williams (2001: 7–8).
129. For a related argument, V. P. Gagnon (1994/95) and J. Snyder (2000: 189–259).
130. Janusz Bugajski (1994).
131. For an incisive overview, Jonathan Stein (2000).
132. See Bates, de Figueiredo, and Weingast (1998: 246).
133. Leszek Kolakowski (1992: 52). See also Mark Mazower (1998: 371–372) and Simons (1993: 175–177).
134. Katherine Verdery (1996b: 88).
135. Rady (1992: 145–159, 198).
136. The UDMR was denounced with increasingly astonishing nationalist venom by the extremist parties in coalition with the PDSR. By January 1996, Gheorghe Funar of the PRNU was accusing Iliescu of treason for refusing to ban the UDMR. See "Romanian Extremist Leader Attacks President Again," *OMRI Daily Digest*, January 29, 1996.
137. Tom Gallagher (2001: 107). See also Tom Gallagher (1995).
138. Boyko Todorov and Ognyan Minchev, interviews in Sofia, 1998. I am also grateful to Maria Koinova for discussions on this point. On the forced assimilation campaign referred to in Bulgaria as the "great excursion," Tatiana Vaksberg (2001).
139. Luan Troxel (1993: 413–416).
140. I am indebted to Antoaneta Dimitrova for explaining this perspective.
141. Crampton (1993: 31).
142. Plamen S. Tzvetkov (1992). See also Troxel (1993: 422, 425).
143. Ivanka Nedeva (1993).

144. Antonina Zhelyazkova (1995).
145. Sharon Fisher (1994).
146. András Kós and András Bozoki, interviews in Budapest, 1999.
147. Sergiu Celac, interview in Bucharest, 1998; Christo Halatchev, interview in Budapest, 1999.
148. Sharon Fisher (2002*b*).
149. Bunce (2002: 313).

Chapter 3

1. I use the label "East European" states to refer to post-communist states on the European continent and, depending on the context, specifically to the six states in this study. These six are also sometimes referred to as the East Central European (ECE) states (though Bulgaria and Romania are more accurately part of South Eastern Europe).
2. On enlargement and the international relations debates about institutions and state cooperation, Milada Anna Vachudova (1997).
3. The terms "international institutions" and "international regimes" are used synonymously in much of the literature. Robert Keohane has defined institutions as "persistent and connected sets of rules, formal and informal, that prescribe behavioral roles, constrain activity, and shape expectations." Quoted in John Gerard Ruggie (1992: 570). For the view that international organizations cannot compel states to obey rules (by the most vigorous neorealist critic of the institutionalists), see John J. Mearsheimer (1994).
4. Robert O. Keohane and Stanley Hoffmann (1993: 388).
5. Robert O. Keohane (1993: 296). See also Ruggie (1992: 570–571).
6. Joseph M. Grieco (1995: 34).
7. For the argument that "demand" for institutions will be in part a function of their effectiveness, see Robert O. Keohane (1989).
8. EFTA regrouped the West European states that had so far chosen not to join the EU. See Keohane and Hoffmann (1993: 386–387).
9. On "unilateral adjustment" to EU trade rules, Kalypso Nicolaidis (1993).
10. Walter Mattli (1999: 88).
11. Keohane and Hoffmann (1993: 387).
12. Robert O. Keohane and Joseph S. Nye (1977).
13. Helen Milner (1992: 487). As Milner notes, this contradicts the logic of Joseph Grieco's neorealist theory that states will always seek to minimize the relative gains of others in order to maximize their own security. At least in the short run, the EU's leverage (security) may be increased by giving relative gains to others.
14. Slawomir Dabrowa, Department of European Institutions, Polish Ministry of Foreign Affairs, interview in Warsaw, 1992.
15. Andrew Hurrell (1995: 343). See also Charles Kupchan (1998).
16. In contrast to institutionalists, neorealists hold that institutions have little independent impact on state behavior. International organizations are nothing

more than projections of the power of their member states. See John J. Mearsheimer (1995: 82) and John J. Mearsheimer (1990).

17. Lloyd Gruber (2000: 165).
18. Richard E. Baldwin, Joseph F. Francois, and Richard Portes (1997: 169). See also European Bank for Reconstruction and Development (1999). For costs and benefits across sectors and groups, Helena Tang (2000).
19. Baldwin, Francois and Portes (1997). See also Hearther Grabbe (2001*a*).
20. Kaminski (2001).
21. Kaminski (2001) and Grabbe (2001*a*: 30–32).
22. Richard Baldwin (1995).
23. Mattli (1999: 59–60).
24. Ibid., 81.
25. Jan Mládek, Czech Deputy Finance Minister, interview in Prague, 1999.
26. James Caporaso (1996). See also James Caporaso (2003).
27. Walter Mattli and Thomas Plümper (2002: 570).
28. For extensive reporting and analysis of public opinion in post-communist countries, see the studies written by Richard Rose and his colleagues using The New Democracies Barometer Surveys, including William Mishler and Richard Rose (1996); and Richard Rose, William Mishler and Christian Haerpfer (1998) and Richard Rose (2002).
29. Haggard and Webb (1994).
30. Mearsheimer (1990) and Hurrell (1995).
31. Stephen Walt allows that under unusual conditions two domestic variables—ideological orientation and the domestic costs of compliance with a patron—may affect alliance decisions. But what determines how governing elites evaluate the costs and benefits of accommodating alternative patrons? Walt (1987: 39, 45). See also Gideon Rose (1998) and Jeffrey W. Legro and Andrew Moravcsik (1999).
32. Jeffrey Kopstein and David Reilly (2000: 17).
33. From richest to poorest, the GDP per capita in 1989 at Purchasing Power Parity Rate (1995 Dollars) was: Czech Republic 9,861, Slovakia 8,222, Hungary 7,862, Bulgaria 5,114, Poland 4,821 and Romania 3,858. PlanEcon (2001). Or, according to older data from the World Bank, from richest to poorest, the GDP per capita in 1989 at Purchasing Power Parity (1989 Dollars) was: Czech Republic 12,373, Hungary 9,767, Slovakia 9,235, Romania 6,611, Bulgaria 5,923 and Poland 5,411. (The data at least for Romania is likely inflated.) World Bank (1991).
34. For qualified agreement on this point, Graham Avery, European Commission; Antoaneta Primatarova, Deputy Foreign Minister of Bulgaria; and Liliana Popescu, Director of Policy Planning, Romanian Ministry of Foreign Affairs; interviews in 1998.

Chapter 4

1. Andrew Moravcsik (1991) and Andrew Moravcsik (1998*a*: Chapter 1).
2. Jiří Dienstbier, Foreign Minister of Czechoslovakia 1990–1992, interview in Bratislava, 1999; Géza Jeszensky, Foreign Minister of Hungary 1990–1994,

interview in Budapest, 1998. See also the interview with Dienstbier in "Lekcja przyswojona," *Gazeta Wyborcza*, March 12, 1992.

3. Andrew Moravcsik and Milada Anna Vachudova (2003*a*).

4. Civic Forum document, "Co chceme—programové zásady Obcanského Fora," Prague, 18:00 on November 26, 1989.

5. Contrasting 1989 with past revolutions, Jan Gross observed that this time "the future, the destination, the end point of this revolution is well known. It actually exists. It can be reached by an overnight train." Jan Gross (1992: 68).

6. The defining essay is Milan Kundera (1984). For a similar argument about Slovakia, Bombík (1995).

7. The Spanish transition was often invoked as a model for Poland. The fact however that Poland had to undergo a change of economic system alongside the democratic transition and economic revivification undertaken by Spain made it difficult to draw lessons. Jacek Saryusz-Wolski, remarks at the conference "New Democracies and the European Community," St. Antony's College, University of Oxford, May 2, 1993.

8. For the short-lived Czechoslovak proposal to create a European Security Commission in the framework of the CSCE that would supplant NATO as well as the Warsaw Pact, Czech and Slovak Federative Republic, Ministry of Foreign Affairs (1990). The Polish government expressed some support for the ESC proposal, but the Hungarian government rejected it, attempting already to secure membership in NATO.

9. Jacques Delors (1989).

10. An influential text warning of democratic breakdown in Eastern Europe because the simultaneous transition to a market economy would tar democracy with the brush of economic suffering was Dahrendorf (1990). See also Offe (1991).

11. Václav Havel (1991). See also Géza Jeszensky (1992*b*).

12. On the "demobilization" of the European idea, George Kolankiewicz (1994).

13. Géza Jeszenszky (1991).

14. Steven Weber (1995: 201).

15. Alexandr Vondra, Czech Deputy Foreign Minister, interview in Prague, 1992 and Krzysztof Bernacki, Head of the European Community Section, Polish Ministry of Foreign Affairs, interview in Warsaw, 1992.

16. "East Europe Impatient for Seat at the Top Table," *Financial Times*, December 9, 1994.

17. Josef Brada (1991).

18. Riccardo Faini and Richard Portes (1995: 16–17).

19. UN Economic Commission for Europe (1995: 121–161).

20. Until 1990, the EU had run a trade deficit with Poland, Czechoslovakia, Hungary, Bulgaria, and Romania. In 1991 the surplus was US$2.2 billion, in 1992 it reached US$4.4 billion, and in 1993 US$8 billion. International Monetary Fund (1991) and (1998). See also "Morsels From a Groaning Table," *Financial Times*, June 17, 1993; and "Former Communist States Feel Stranded by EU Club," *International Herald Tribune*, April 18, 1994.

21. Even with tariffs and other restrictions, exports from these sectors amounted to 25–40% of Visegrad exports to the EU in 1993. Jim Rollo, "Maybe not even jam for east Europe," *Financial Times*, June 18, 1993, 15.

22. "EC Protectionism threatens East Europe Growth," *Financial Times*, April 13, 1992.

23. As the economist Jim Rollo put it, "It's like nuclear deterrence: you don't have to use it for it to work." Quoted in "Rising Trade Tension With EU Impedes Eastern Europe's Progress," *The New York Times*, January 25, 1993.

24. As it happened, Germany and the Netherlands were the first to invoke safeguard clauses against Central European goods. John Flemming, EBRD economist, remarks at Merton College, Oxford, February 22, 1993.

25. Jim Rollo and Alisdair Smith (1993).

26. "EU Policies Main Threat to E Europe Exports," *Financial Times*, October 20, 1994, 3. See also David Allen and Michael Smith (1995: 76–78).

27. Respectively: "Blisko coraz dalej," *Rzeczpospolita*, July 12, 1993; and Alan Winters (1992: 127).

28. "Extending the EU Eastwards," *Financial Times*, December 7, 1994.

29. Bartlomiej Kaminski (1994: 6).

30. Rollo and Smith (1993: 165). Anders Åslund declared "protectionism toward so-called sensitive products" as "the worst Western policy" toward the post-communist states since 1989. Åslund (2002: 440).

31. Faini and Portes (1995: 16–17).

32. "Trade and Foreign Investment in the Community's regions: The Impact of Reform in Central and Eastern Europe," Commission of the European Communities, Regional Development Study No. 7, cited in "Structural Barriers to Eastward Enlargement," *Financial Times*, September 13, 1993, 6.

33. András Köves (1992: 95).

34. Alexis Galinos (1994: 22).

35. Overall the image of the EU was positive in the early 1990s, then declined significantly, and then recovered. Generally around a half of respondents saw the EU's image as positive, a further third as neutral, a small number as negative. See Table 4.1.

36. "Czech Republic and EU Reach Accord on Association Agreement," *AP*, May 3, 1993; "Community Lifts Ban on Polish Meat Deliveries," *Financial Times*, July 16, 1993; "Saryusz-Wolski: choroby sa tylko pretekstem," *Zycie Warszawy*, May 26, 1993.

37. "Hungary in EU Trade conflict," *Financial Times*, April 10, 1993; "Polska wstrzymuje import zwierzat i miesa," *Rzeczpospolita*, April 10–12, 1993; "Polskie mieso na pewno nie jest grozne dla Europy," *Zycie Warszawy*, April 9, 1994; "Budapest bars EU Cattle in Trade War," *Independent*, April 12, 1993; "Hungary raises trade defences," *Financial Times*, April 13, 1993; "Morsels From a Groaning Table," *Financial Times*, June 17, 1993; "EWH znosi restrykcje," *Rzeczpospolita*, July 10–11, 1993; "Community Lifts Ban on Polish Meat deliveries," *Financial Times*, July 16, 1993; "Handel rolny z Wspólnota," *Zycie Gospodarcze*, October 3, 1993.

38. "EC Dumping of Farm Produce Upsets Hungary," *Financial Times*, June 22, 1993; and "EU Offers Hope to Eastern Europe's Farmers," *Financial Times*, March 8, 1994.
39. "Wczesne ostrzeganie," *Gazeta Wyborcza*, July 22, 1993; "Sezonowy problem," *Rzeczpospolita*, July 20, 1993; "Handel rolny z Wspólnota," *Zycie Gospodarcze*, October 3, 1993; "Kolej na czerwone porzeczki," *Rzeczpospolita*, August 26, 1993.
40. One study that was quick off the mark in arguing that mere association would not be tenable for the Visegrad states in the long-term: House of Lords (1992).
41. Stephen Haggard et al. (1993: 185).
42. Following the seminal study by Peter Gourevitch (1978).
43. Kaminski (2001: 19–20 and 30–33).
44. This privatization agenda spelled disaster: participating Czech enterprises received no injection of capital, while the weakness of the rule of law and of corporate governance invited Czech managers to strip the assets of many enterprises in an operation dubbed "tunneling." Milada Anna Vachudova (2001*b*).
45. Kaminski (2001: 40).
46. Haggard and Webb (1994: 29).
47. Michael W. Doyle (1997: 476).
48. For the most illuminating accounts of the development of the EU's policies toward Eastern Europe from 1989 to 1997, Karen E. Smith (1999), and Françoise de la Serre, Christian Lequesne, and Jacques Rupnik (1994).
49. "Trouver de nouvelles formes d'association à la Communauté," *Le Monde Diplomatique*, February 1990.
50. For a much richer study of the positions of the EU member states on enlargement during this period, Frank Schimmelfennig (2003). See also the discussion of Schimmelfennig's book in Chapter 8.
51. To make the French give way, Germany insisted on rapid enlargement to the most advanced East European states as a quid pro quo for EMU. Andrew Moravcsik (1998*b*: 38–39).
52. Officials of the French Embassy in the Czech Republic and Belgium, interviews in Prague and Brussels, 1998. See also Milada Anna Vachudova (2001*c*).
53. "MM. Kohl et Mitterand sont d'accord sur l'idée de confédération européenne," *Le Monde*, January 6, 1990.
54. "M. Mitterrand relance l'idée d'une confédération européenne," *Le Monde*, October 10, 1993.
55. Lionel Barber (1993). See also "Brussels sounds out plans for E. Europe," *Financial Times*, May 10, 1993.
56. The transitional agreements went into force on March 1, 1992. The association agreements went into effect on February 1, 1994. "Polska stowarzyszona z Wspólnotami Europejskimi," *Rzeczpospolita*, February 1, 1994.
57. Alan Mayhew (1998: 11).
58. Tony Judt (1996). See also Adam Michnik (1999).
59. See Mattli (1999: 63).
60. Bronislaw Geremek (1990) and Václav Havel (1990). See also Czech and Slovak Federative Republic, Ministry of Foreign Affairs (1992).

61. "První konkrétní krok," *Lidové Noviny*, October 7, 1991.
62. "Trójkat nierównoboczny," *Gazeta Wyborcza*, October 8, 1991.
63. Milada Anna Vachudova (1993).
64. Milada Anna Vachudova (2001*d*).
65. Polish officials did come out in support of partial EU membership from time to time; usually they backtracked in a matter of days in the face of Hungarian and Czech opposition to any such scheme. For Polish President Lech Wałęsa's proposal for an EC-2, *PAP*, Warsaw, May 6, 1992.
66. William Wallace (1992: 45). Also, Pavel Seifter, interview in Prague, 1997.
67. "Central Europe Knocks on the Community Door," *Financial Times*, October 28, 1992; "EC to step up links to central Europe," *Financial Times*, October 29, 1992; "Czy Wspólnota nas chce?" *Gazeta Wyborcza*, October 29, 1992.
68. European Commission (1992: 5).
69. Jan B. de Weydenthal (1993: 21) and Jonathan Eyal (1992).
70. Antall: Hungarian Radio, Budapest, January 3, 1993: *SWB*, January 5, 1993, A1/1. Suchocka: Polish Radio, Warsaw, January 31, 1993: *SWB*, February 2, 1993, A1/1. Klaus: CTK, Prague, December 15, 1992: *SWB*, December 19, 1992, A1/2; and Oesterreich 1, Vienna, interview, January 8, 1993: *SWB*, January 11, 1993, C2/4.
71. "Copenhagen Conference Speaks of Improving Trade With East," *NCA*, April 14, 1993; "E Europe Urged to Renew ex-Soviet ties," *Financial Times*, April 15, 1993; and "East Europe Calls EC's Bluff Over Free Trade," *Financial Times*, April 16, 1993.
72. "Visegrad Group Appeals for EC Membership," *RFE/RL Daily Report*, June 8, 1993.
73. For a comprehensive account of the genesis of the EU's pre-accession strategy, Mayhew (1998: 161–178).
74. Ibid., 164.
75. See Smith (1999).
76. The Polish Sejm voted unanimously, and the Hungarian parliament almost unanimously, to support these applications. See "New Phase for EU as Hungary Asks to Join," *Independent*, April 2, 1994; and Kolankiewicz (1994: 481).
77. "Poland and Hungary Step Up Pressure," *Financial Times*, March 8, 1994; "Hungary and Poland Bang on EU's Opening Door," *International Herald Tribune*, March 8, 1994; "Czechs Delay EU Application," *Financial Times*, March 9, 1994, "Czechs Want Trade Link to EU Now," *International Herald Tribune*, March 11, 1994; "Thirsty for a potion," *Financial Times*, March 23, 1994. See also Michael Mihalka (1995: 73).
78. "Kohl Makes EU Enlargement Pledge to East Europe," *Financial Times*, March 24, 1994. After Hungary's application, Kohl cautioned that expansion would take longer than generally anticipated. See "PM Backs Kohl Over EU Links to Eastern Europe," *Financial Times*, April 28, 1994.
79. "Commission Paves Way for Wider Europe," *Financial Times*, July 28, 1994.
80. David Buchan and Lionel Barber (1994) and "EU to Draw Up Plan for Admitting Six Eastern Members," *Financial Times*, October 5, 1994.
81. On these disagreements, see Lionel Barber (1994). See also "EU's Outstretched Hand to the East Begins to Waver," *Financial Times*, November 23, 1994; "Kohl

invites eastern states to EU summit," *Financial Times*, December 1, 1994; and "Hopes of wider union turn to fear of no union," *Financial Times*, December 9, 1994.

82. European Commission (1994). See also "Kohl Carries EU Debate on New Members," *Financial Times*, December 12, 1994; and "Europe Recovers its Sense of Direction," *Financial Times*, December 12, 1994.

83. "Hungarians and Czechs Set Their Eyes on 2000," *Financial Times*, December 12, 1994. See also Mihalka (1995: 73); Allen and Smith (1995: 76).

84. Smith (1999: 63).

85. Official of the Romanian Foreign Ministry and official of the Delegation of the European Commission to Romania, interviews in Bucharest, 1998.

86. Mungiu (1996: 350).

87. Smith (1999: 97).

88. The break-up of Czechoslovakia provided another opportunity for the EU and other international actors to take a strong stand on domestic political developments. However, the break-up was widely expected to be peaceful. Dubbed the "velvet divorce," it was discouraged, but only half-heartedly, by EU leaders.

89. Sergiu Celac, Foreign Minister of Romania 1990, interview in Bucharest, 1998.

90. Alina Mungiu-Pippidi, interview in Bonn, 1999; Steffen Skovmand, Delegation of the European Commission to Romania, interview in Bucharest, 1998.

91. European Commission (1992).

Chapter 5

1. David Cameron (2001). See the very useful set of tables analyzing the relationship between early democratization, early economic reform, geographic proximity, and ties to the EU.

2. This chapter draws on interviews with many officials in the European Commission, especially Catherine Day, Michael Leigh and Pierre Mirel, and also Graham Avery, Gilles Bertrand, Helen Campbell, Joly Dixon, Helmut Lohan, Anna Michalski, Michael Rupp, and Gerd Tebbe. These interviews were conducted in Brussels in 1998, 1999, 2000, and 2003.

3. Keohane and Nye (1977). On the theory as applied to the EU, see Moravcsik (1991), and Moravscik (1998a, b).

4. Michael Leigh, talk at Harvard University, April 2000; and Eneko Landaburo, talk at European University Institute, September 2000.

5. The EU certainly did not encourage applications for membership in order to gain traction on domestic politics. See Graham Avery (1994).

6. This changed after the Kosovo crisis in 1999 when the EU turned to promulgating a very inclusive enlargement, promising membership to all of the post-communist states of Southeastern Europe as part of its foreign policy to pacify the region. These states became the protocandidates listed in Table 5.2.

7. "Podla Hansa van den Broeka EÚ nemala dôvod menit' názor na SR," *SME*, July 18, 1997.

8. Wade Jacoby (1999a).

9. Miles Kahler (1992: 114–115).
10. On the effectiveness of IMF conditionality, Graham Bird (2003: 93–112).
11. Milada Anna Vachudova (2001*c*).
12. Gilles Bertrand and Anna Michalski, interviews in Brussels, 1998.
13. Anna Krok-Paszkowska and Jan Zielonka found that elites in the candidate states agreed with the EU's policy of conditionality, but were concerned about how the more subjective criteria would be judged. See Krok-Paszkowska and Zielonka (2000).
14. Pavol Demeš and Grigorij Mesežnikov, interviews in Bratislava, 1998; Elitza Markova, interview in Sofia, 1998.
15. "Hans Van den Broek: Slovensko má svoj osud vo vlastných rukách," *SME*, June 18, 1998.
16. Michael Leigh, interview in Brussels, 1998 and 2000; Pierre Mirel, interview in Brussels, 1998.
17. The Commission recommended in July 1997 that the EU open negotiations with Estonia and Slovenia as well as Poland, Hungary, and the Czech Republic. Commission officials demonstrated than in many areas Estonia and Slovenia were performing as well if not better than the three perceived (or politically convenient) frontrunners—though Scandinavian support for Estonia certainly did help as well. As one official put it, the Commission "takes on the advocacy" of candidates that have no powerful patrons. European Commission officials, interviews in Brussels, 1998, 2001. See also Mayhew (1998: 176).
18. On reforming the EU's institutions and rethinking European integration in preparation for enlargement, Helen Wallace (2000*a*); and Mayhew (1998: 312–331). See also Helen Wallace and William Wallace (eds.) (2000).
19. Wolfgang Ischinger, interview in Vaduz, 1999. On this point I am also indebted to conversations with Timothy Garton Ash and Michael Mertes in 2000.
20. Smith (1999: 118).
21. Moravcsik and Vachudova (2003*a*).
22. José I. Torreblanca (2002).
23. The seminal work of neofunctionalism is Ernst B. Haas (1958). The equivalent of intergovernmentalism is Stanley Hoffmann (1966). For an overview of the theoretical debate, James Caporaso and John Keeler (1995).
24. Philippe C. Schmitter (1969); and Wayne Sandholtz and John Zysman (1989). For an institutionalist approach also called "modified neofunctionalism" that includes supranational entrepreneurship, Wayne Sandholtz and Alec Stone Sweet, (eds.) (1998); and Alec Stone Sweet, Wayne Sandholtz, and Neil Fligstein (eds.) (2001*b*).
25. Moravcsik (1991); Andrew Moravcsik (1993); and Moravcsik (1998*a*). See also Geoffrey Garrett (1992).
26. I treat the Commission here as a unitary actor, though recent research shows the substantial heterogeneity of views and purpose among individuals working in the Commission: Liesbet Hooghe (2001).
27. For a strong argument in support of the Commission's autonomous influence, Liesbet Hooghe and Gary Marks (2001). See also Liesbet Hooghe and Gary Marks (2003).
28. Gilles Bertrand and Anna Michalski, interviews in Brussels, 1998.
29. Pierre Mirel, interview in Brussels, 2003.

30. Alec Stone Sweet, Neil Fligstein and Wayne Sandholtz (2001*a*: 11–12).
31. Pierre Mirel, interview in Brussels, 2003.
32. Sonia Mazey and Jeremy Richardson (2001: 92).
33. Desmond Dinan (1998).
34. This view was shared at least partially by the chief negotiators with the EU for the Czech Republic, Slovakia, Poland, and Hungary. Pavel Telička, interview in Prague, 2000; Petr Javorčík, interview in Brussels, 1999; and Leszek Jesień, interview in Krakow, 2001. See also Smith (1999: 106.)
35. Dinan (1998: 39).
36. Robert O. Keohane and Stanley Hoffmann (1991).
37. For a "two-level network manager" theory that allows for limited supranational entrepreneurship by the Commission only when the national aggregation of interests fails for a number of reasons, including capture by producer interests, see Andrew Moravcsik (1999).
38. But for an excellent treatment, Mark Pollack (2003).
39. Michael Rupp, interview in Brussels, 1998; and other European Commission officials.
40. For an incisive treatment of the challenge of "queue-management" and the pressures for ongoing enlargement, Lykke Friis and Anna Murphy (2000).
41. Following the argument in Paul Pierson (1996). See also James Caporaso and Alec Stone Sweet (2001: 224).
42. Karen E. Smith (2003: 119).
43. On the EU's membership requirements: Susan Senior Nello and Karen E. Smith (1998); Heather Grabbe (1999); and Smith (2003).
44. Bruno De Witte (2003: 238–240). See also Bruno De Witte (2002).
45. European Commission (2002*a*: 4).
46. De Witte (2003: 240).
47. European Commission (1997*a*: 42).
48. European Commission (2002*a*: 5).
49. The French did propose GNP per capita minimum requirements for candidates in advance of the 1993 Copenhagen summit, but these were rejected. Smith (1999: 117).
50. European Commission (1999).
51. For the impact of enlargement on the EU's external relations, Marise Cremona (2003).
52. For details and analysis of the White Paper, Mayhew (1998: 208–225).
53. Wade Jacoby (1999*b*).
54. On the enlargement process, Ulrich Sedelmeier and Helen Wallace (2000). See also John Redmond and Glenda G. Rosenthal (eds.) (1998) and Helen Wallace (ed.) (2001).
55. Heather Grabbe (2001*b*).
56. See Smith (1999).
57. I am indebted to conversations with Chris Hill, John Shattuck, and other American diplomats on this point.
58. William Wallace (2002: 81).

59. Grabbe and Hughes (1998: 41–54). See also Jackie Gower (1999).
60. European Commission (1997*b*).
61. The European Commission's Regular Reports can be found at http://europa. eu.int/comm/enlargement/docs/index.htm.
62. Ronald H. Linden (2001*b*: 372).
63. European Commission (2002*a*: 4).
64. Petr Greger, Delegation of the European Commission in the Czech Republic, interview in Prague, 1999; and European Commission officials, interviews in Brussels, 1999.
65. For Hungary's 2001 NPAA as an example: http://www.kum.hu/euanyag/NPAA/-Cover.htm.
66. Leo Mullender, Delegation of the European Commission to Slovakia, interview in Bratislava, 1998.
67. Jan Zielonka and Peter Mair (2002: 5).
68. On the negotiations, see John K. Glenn (2004). The European Commission's site is at: http://europa.eu.int/comm/enlargement/negotiations/index.htm.
69. The implementation the acquis as opposed to just its transposition into national law is the greatest challenge for candidates and for the EU's attempts at enforcement. See Phedon Nicolaides (2001).
70. For the Czech Ministry of Foreign Affairs website on the negotiations in English as an example: http://www.mfa.cz/EU/en/negot/eindex.html.
71. For the complete, final list of transition periods and financial provisions with the states that entered in 2004, European Commission (2003*a*).
72. For the COE's origins, institutional structure, and current programs to support democracy, rule of law and human rights, http://www.coe.int.
73. Stuart Croft *et al.* (1999: 142, 153).
74. For a contrasting view of the Council of Europe's 'soft conditionality,' Jeffrey Checkel (2000).
75. Similarly, the Council's 1994 Framework for the Protection of Minority Rights left monitoring and enforcement wholly to the signatories. Geoff Gilbert (1996).
76. Daniel Tarschys (1995).
77. Croft, *et al.* (1999: 158).
78. For information on the OSCE including current missions to promote democracy and prevent conflict, http://www.osce.org.
79. Jennifer Jackson Preece (1998).
80. Katia Papagianni (2002).
81. Kelley (2004*a*).
82. Before NATO had committed to expansion, membership in the EU was also widely viewed by East Central European states as a second-best solution to their security dilemma. See, for example the interview with Polish Foreign Minister Krzysztof Skubiszewski in "Racja reform i interes panstwa praworzadnego," *Polska Zbrójna*, June 19–21, 1992.
83. Edward Mansfield (1994: 123).
84. Zdeněk Brousil (1997).
85. Martin Kontra and Jaroslav Špurný (1998).

86. Rachel Epstein (2005).
87. Ludovit Černák, Democratic Union Party of Slovakia, interview in Bratislava, 1998; and Valeri Ratchev, Bulgarian Ministry of Defense, interview in Bonn, 1999.
88. Epstein (2005). See also Rachel Epstein (2004a).
89. Richard Holbrooke (1995).
90. For a spirited account of both sides by one of NATO expansion's earliest advocates, Ronald D. Asmus (2002).
91. Michael Mandelbaum (1995). See also Dan Reiter (2001).
92. Milada Anna Vachudova (2000).
93. Robert E. Hunter (1999) and Michael E. Brown (1999).

Chapter 6

1. For the argument that post-communist citizens do use their opinions about EU membership to direct their support toward particular political parties, see Joshua A. Tucker, Alexander C. Pacek, and Adam J. Berinsky (2002).
2. Rachel Epstein develops persuasion and social influence as causal mechanisms translating Western influence into domestic change in East European states in Epstein (2004a).
3. Civil society actors also work hard in many cases to bring about the electoral defeat of illiberal rulers. Even if they stay outside of politics, however, they enjoy much greater access to power and a much-improved environment for their activities after regime change.
4. Epstein (2004a).
5. Many opposition politicians in Romania and Slovakia refused to merge their political parties in the early 1990s despite the fact that their bickering strengthened the illiberal rulers. Casting doubt on their ability to pursue power *or* to act on their Western beliefs, this set the stage for the importance of the EU as a focal point for cooperation later on. On the evidentiary challenge posed by constructivism, see Jeffrey Checkel and Andrew Moravcsik (2001).
6. Kelley (2004a,b).
7. For the first treatment of the power of Western international institutions to stabilize post-communist Europe, Stephen Van Evera (1992). See also Keohane, Nye, and Hoffmann (eds.) (1993).
8. For a rich theoretical discussion of the power of external incentives and a different set of case studies of domestic responses to EU conditionality, see Frank Schimmelfennig, Stefan Engert, and Heiko Knobel (2003). See also Mattli and Plümper (2002).
9. Kelley (2004a,b); Nida M. Gelazis (2000); Katia Papaggianni (2003); and Lynn M. Tesser (2003a).
10. Bugajski (1994). See also Ivan Gabal a kolektiv (eds.) (1999).
11. On nationalism and ethnic minorities after communism, George Schöpflin (2000: 232, 277–297); and Rogers Brubaker (1996). See also Verdery (1996a).

12. Three forms of autonomy have been proposed, although definitions remain fluid: *cultural autonomy:* self-administered schools, universities, churches, and social organizations, funded in part from the state budget; *political autonomy:* self-government in areas where the minority is concentrated; and *territorial autonomy:* more extensive self-government in a *territorially* defined district. See J. F. Brown (1994: 176–178); and Bugajski (1994: 17–23). See also Hurst Hannum (1996).

13. For the contradictions between the rights of individuals in liberal democracies and collective rights for minority groups, Stephen Deets (2002).

14. Karen Henderson (2001: 74–79). See also Martyn Rady (1992).

15. Levente Salat, Open Society Institute, Cluj, interview in Prague, 2000; and Balasz Jarabík, NOS Foundation, interview in New York, 1999.

16. The ethnic Hungarian minority summit held in Budapest in July 1996 revived these charges by calling for "autonomy in line with Western practices," without renouncing territorial autonomy. Zsofia Szilagyi (1996).

17. Slovak nationalists discovered, for example, a Hungarian military threat evinced by "NATO-scale military exercises" along the border in 1992. The Czechoslovak federal defense minister was forced to issue a statement denying the threat. Rudolf Joó, Hungarian Ministry of Defense, interviewed in *Magyar Nemzet*, August 8, 1992, in FBIS-EEU-92-156, August 12, 1992.

18. OSCE HCNM recommendations are at: www.osce.org/hcnm/recommendations.

19. For a brilliant exposition of Hungary's foreign policy and also domestic politics from 1988 to 1998, see László Valki (2001).

20. Valki (2001: 296).

21. While avoiding a direct renunciation of peaceful border changes, Jeszenszky stated that "the peace treaties [signed in Paris in 1947] and the Helsinki Final Act provide a perfectly adequate framework." See Géza Jeszenszky (1992*a*).

22. József Antall (1991).

23. "Where I see the responsibility of the Hungarians," Jeszensky wrote "is in the fact that they made no attempts between 1859 and 1867, and still more when they had attained a position of power after 1867, to forge a multilingual, multicultural Hungaria and, simultaneously, to arrive at a sincere, generous reconciliation with the other Danubian peoples." Géza Jeszenszky (1993: 5, 11).

24. Pál Dunay (1993: 129).

25. Csurka's new party, the Hungarian Party of Justice and Life, won only 1.5% of the vote in the 1994 elections, but 5% in the 1998 elections, enough to enter parliament. See Valki (2001: 303–304).

26. Géza Jeszenszky, Foreign Minister of Hungary 1990–4, interview in Budapest, 1998.

27. The Slovak foreign ministry condemned Hungary's "inordinate, excessive dramatization of some unimportant moves on the part of the Slovak government (such as the removal of Hungarian-language road signs)," and also Hungary's attempts "to threaten our territorial integrity" and "to encourage the irredentist tendencies of the political leaders of ethnic Hungarian political parties in Slovakia." See Slovak Republic, Ministry of Foreign Affairs (1994).

28. Géza Jeszenszky, Foreign Minister of Hungary 1990–4, interview in Budapest, 1998; and Rudolf Joó, Deputy State Secretary, Hungarian Ministry of Defense, interview in Budapest, 1998.

29. Howard J. S. Pearce, British Foreign and Commonwealth Office, interview in Sussex, 1998.

30. László Póti, Institute for Strategic and Defence Studies, interview in Budapest, 1998.

31. Levente Salat, Open Society Fund, Cluj, interview in Bucharest, 1998.

32. "Interest Grows in Stability Pact Plan," *Financial Times*, June 22, 1993; "EC May Keep Out 'Problem' Countries," *Independent*, June 22, 1993; "Action Agreed Over Frontiers," *Financial Times*, December 11–12, 1993; "Paris Talks Aim to Defuse Old Central European Rivalries," *Financial Times*, May 26, 1994; "L'échec des négotiations entre la Hongrie at la Roumanie sur les minorités affaiblit le pacte de stabilité en Europe de M. Balladur," *Le Monde*, March 18, 1995; "52 pays réunis à Paris pour promouvoir la stabilité en Europe de l'Est," *Le Monde*, March 19–20, 1995; "Les nations défiées par les minorités," *Le Monde*, March 21, 1995.

33. On the consistency and success of Poland's foreign policy since 1989, Sarah Meiklejohn Terry (2000). See also T. Snyder (2003: Ch. 12–14).

34. Alfred A. Reisch (1994: 48).

35. For an analysis of the political debates in Hungary, Margit Bessenyey Williams (2001*a*).

36. Eleonóra Sándor (1997) and Sharon Fisher (1996*b*).

37. László Valki, interview in Budapest, 1999. See also Valki (2001: 307, 309).

38. András Bózoki, personal correspondence, 2002.

39. David Phinnemore (2001: 253).

40. Sergiu Celac, Romanian Ministry of Foreign Affairs, interview in Bucharest, 1998.

41. Alina Mungiu-Pippidi, interview in Bonn, 1999.

42. "Council of Europe's Soft Standards for East European members," *RFE/RL Newsline*, July 8, 1997.

43. Gabriel Andreescu (1995: 47).

44. Michael Shafir (1995*a*).

45. Dan Ionescu (1993: 44).

46. Dan Ionescu (1994: 23).

47. Liliana Popescu, Romanian Ministry of Foreign Affairs, interview in Bucharest, 1998.

48. Gabriel Andreescu, Helsinki Committee, interview in Bucharest, 1998.

49. Liliana Popescu (1997).

50. Michael Shafir (1997: 151–152); and Popescu (1997: 175–176).

51. Quoted in Shafir (1997: 153).

52. Shafir (1997: 146, 153–154). "Directocracy" was a term coined by Romanian analysts to describe the system based on corruption and patronage networks where "Ceauşescu-trained managers who run Romania's large state industries and dominate much of the country's economic and political life for their own benefit." On the elections, Daniel Chirot (2000).

53. Kyril Drezov (2001). See also Ganev (1997).

54. For a careful analysis of the Turkish MRF, John T. Ishiyama and Marijke Breuning (1998: 21–50).

55. Kyril Drezov (2000: 196–197).

56. For an incisive treatment of the relationship of the Slovak government with the EU from 1994 to 1998, Karen Henderson (1999*b*).

57. Eduard Kukan, Chairman of the Democratic Union Party, interview in Bratislava, 1998. For an excellent overview, Grigorij Mesežnikov (1998).

58. Miroslav Wlachovský (1997: 46).

59. Grigorij Mesežnikov, Institute for Public Affairs; Dionyz Hochel, Delegation of the European Commission to the Slovak Republic; and Soňa Szomolányi, Comenius University, interviews in Bratislava, 1998.

60. For a chronology, reprinted documents and articles, see "Kauza Gaulieder," *SME*, July 28, 1997.

61. Grigorij Mesežnikov and Martin Bútora (eds.) (1997); and Martin Bútora and František Sebej (eds.) (1998). See also Miroslav Wlachovský and Juraj Marušiak (1998).

62. Generally the US Ambassador and also the British Ambassador to Slovakia made the most forceful private and public statements criticizing the Mečiar government, pushing EU policy forward and leading to more explicit statements by EU officials. Dionyz Hochel, interview in Bratislava, 1998.

63. Leo Mullender, Delegation of the European Commission to the Slovak Republic, interview in Bratislava, 1998.

64. Rastislav Kačer, Director of Policy Planning, Slovak Ministry of Foreign Affairs, interview in Bratislava, 1998.

65. Wlachovský (1997: 47).

66. Vladimír Kmec, Center for Strategic Studies and Slovak Ministry of Defense, interview in Bratislava, 1998.

67. "Slowcoach Slovakia: Has it Got the Democratic Message?" *The Economist*, November 18, 1995. See also *OMRI Daily Digest*, October 18, 1995.

68. Henderson (1999: 234).

69. "Agenda 2000, Commission Opinion on Slovakia's Application for Membership of the European Union," European Commission, DOC/97/20, July 15, 1997. See also the documents, chronology, articles, and editorials in *SME* on July 17, 1997.

70. For example, Leon Brittan quoted in "Európska komisia dá SR odporúčanie, ak si vyriešime svoje politické prolémy," *SME*, September 12, 1997.

71. European Commission officials, interviews in Brussels, 1998 and 1999. One official at the British embassy in Bratislava predicted in July 1998 that the Europe Agreement would be suspended, at least partially, if Mečiar's HZDS won the 1998 elections and re-formed a coalition government with the two extremist parties.

72. We could speculate that the advantages accruing to Western producers thanks to the Europe Agreements made these agreements more difficult to suspend. See Mansfield (1994: 134–137).

73. Pavol Lukáč, Slovak Foreign Policy Association, interview in Bratislava, 1999; and Dionyz Hochel, interview in Bratislava, 1998. See Alexander Duleba (1998).

74. I am indebted to Filip Dimitrov, Prime Minister of Bulgaria 1991–2, for a conversation on this point in Princeton in 1998.
75. Thomas Risse (1999: esp. 531, 539). See also Thomas Risse, Stephen C. Ropp, and Kathryn Sikkink (eds.) (1999); and Thomas Risse (2000).
76. For an important study that also explores the influence of international actors on civic groups and opposition political parties (in contrast to ruling parties), Philippe C. Schmitter and Imco Brouwer (1999).
77. It would be fruitful to analyze this using the literature on the collective action problems faced by "latent groups."
78. Pavol Demeš, leader of the Third Sector, interview in Bratislava, 1998.
79. The organizations included the British Council, the British Know How Fund, the Charles Mott Foundation, the EastWest Institute, the Foundation for a Civil Society, the Konrad Adenauer Foundation, and the National Democratic Institute.
80. Grzegorz Ekiert and Jan Kubik (2000: 48–49).
81. Robert Benjamin, National Democratic Institute, interview in Washington, DC, 2003. For the debate, Sarah E. Mendelson and John K. Glenn (eds.) (2002); and Marina Ottaway and Thomas Carothers (eds.) (2000).
82. Pierre Mirel, interview in Brussels, 2003; Graham Avery, interview in Brussels, 1998.
83. J. Snyder (2000: 355).
84. Joly Dixon, European Commission, interview in Brussels, 1998.
85. Michael Shafir (1995b).
86. Shafir (1997: 143). See also Steven D. Roper (1999: 189).
87. Romanian Parliament member, interview in Bucharest, 1998.
88. Quoted in Ionescu (1993: 42).
89. Romanian parliament members, interviews in Bucharest, 1998. I am also indebted to Aurelian Crăiuțu and Robert Benjamin for conversations on this point.
90. Alina Mungiu-Pippidi, interview in Bonn, 1999. Several studies confirming this are cited in Shafir (1997: fn. 12).
91. Aurelian Crăiuțu (2000: 184).
92. Marianna Stoica, Committee of European Integration, Romanian Parliament, interview in Bucharest, 1998.
93. Roper (1999: 191); and Shafir (1997).
94. Boyko Todorov and Ognyan Minchev, interviews in Sofia, 1998.
95. Ganev (1997: 138).
96. Antoaneta Hristova, Committee for European Integration, interview in Sofia, 1998.
97. Martin Bútora and Pavol Demeš (1999: 156).
98. On Slovakia's Democratic Roundtable, Martin Bútora, Grigorij Mesežnikov, and Zora Bútorová (1999: 18).
99. This was particularly important for the post-communist SDL that adjusted its platform to join the Socialist International. Sharon Fisher, personal correspondence, 2003.
100. Soňa Szomolányi and John Gould (1997b).
101. Ludovit Černák and Márius Hričovský, Democratic Union Party, interviews in Bratislava, 1998.

102. Eduard Kukan, Chairman of the Democratic Union Party, interview in Bratislava, 1998.

103. Surveys showed that the overwhelming majority of voters who voted in 1998 but had not voted in 1994 cast their vote for the opposition parties. Voter turnout was 84.24% of all eligible voters. See Bútora and Demeš (1999: 160).

104. For analysis of the HZDS's rhetoric and the nationalist content of its 1998 election campaign in contrast to the election campaign of the opposition parties, Fisher (2001: Ch. 7).

105. Zora Bútorová (ed.) (1998).

106. Ivan Mikloš (1998*b*).

107. Bútora, Mesežnikov, and Bútorová (1999: 19).

108. These included the EU's Civil Society Development Foundation (PHARE), the Open Society Foundation, the Foundation for a Civil Society, the Charles Stewart Mott Foundation, the German Marshall Fund, the British Know How Fund, the United States Information Service (USIS) and others. See Bútora and Demeš (1999: 163); and the magazine *NonProfit*.

109. Pavol Demeš, interview in Bratislava, 2000.

110. Petr Javorčík, Mission of the Slovak Republic to the EU, interview in Brussels, 1998.

111. "Spravodajca EP je za rozšírenie bez SR," *SME*, September 11, 1997.

112. Zora Bútorová (1999: 201–202).

113. *Slovenký Profit*, August 31, 1998, quoted in Fisher (2001: Ch. 7).

114. Slovak Democratic Coalition (SDK) (1998).

115. Bútorová (1999: 201). See also Zora Bútorová (1998: 213–217).

116. GFK Slovakia (1998).

117. For analysis of the HZDS, Tim Haughton (2001).

118. Zora Bútorová, Olga Gyárfásová, and Marián Velsic (1999: 256).

119. IVO poll of March 2000 cited in Olga Gyárfásová (2001: 202).

120. Martin Bútora and Zora Bútorová (1999).

121. I am indebted to Valerie Bunce for this concept.

Chapter 7

1. I use "the reformers" as short-hand for the more liberal political parties that took power in Romania in 1996, in Bulgaria in 1997, and Slovakia in 1998 from evidently less liberal parties. By using this term, however, I do not suggest that either the reformers themselves or the parties that they were taking power from were all the same, as the case studies in this chapter and the previous one explain in detail.

2. Jeffrey S. Kopstein and David A. Reilly (2000: 28).

3. See Andonova (2003); Jacoby (2004); and Beate Sissinich (2003).

4. Pavel TeLička, Chief Negotiator for the Czech Republic, interview in Prague, 2000; and Leszek Jesień, Polish Committee for European Integration, interview in Krakow, 2001.

5. For details, Antoaneta Dimitrova (2002).
6. Wade Jacoby and Pavel Černoch (2002). See also Glenn (2004).
7. See Susan Rose-Ackerman (2004).
8. See Judith Goldstein (1996).
9. Alexandru Grigorescu (2001).
10. Åslund (2002).
11. Kitschelt (2003*b*: 13–14).
12. Elena A. Iankova (2002).
13. Hall and Taylor (1996: 955).
14. Haggard and Webb (1994: 21).
15. Jon C. Pevehouse (2002).
16. For the related argument that liberal democracies make more durable alliance commitments to one another, Kurt Taylor Gaubatz (1996).
17. For the related argument that voters who are "winners" from the economic transition support EU membership as a guarantee that economic reforms will not be reversed, and therefore cast their vote for pro-EU parties, Tucker, Pacek, and Berinsky (2002).
18. Lisa Martin (2000).
19. Jacoby (2004).
20. Grzymała-Busse (2002).
21. Gerd Tebbe and Michael Rupp, European Commission, interviews in Brussels, 1998.
22. Tamas Szucs, Mission of the Republic of Hungary to the EU, interview in Brussels, 1998. Accession Partnerships for Hungary are at: http://europa.eu.int/-comm/enlargement/hungary/index.htm.
23. András Kós and Csaba Lörincz, Hungarian Ministry of Affairs, interviews in Budapest, 1999.
24. Frances Millard (2002).
25. Leszek Jesień, Polish Committee for European Integration, interviews in Warsaw, 1999. The 1998 and subsequent Regular Reports for Poland can be found at: http://europa.eu.int/comm/enlargement/poland/index.htm.
26. For analysis and documents on Poland's negotiations, Jan Barcz and Arkadiusz Michonski (2002).
27. "Wąsy Dzurindy," *Wprost*, October 22, 1998.
28. Dimitrova (2002).
29. On this point I am indebted to conversations with Jerzy Kalinowski, Polish Committee for European Integration; Anrás Inotai, Hungarian Academy of Sciences, and Wade Jacoby.
30. For all facets of the relationship of the Czech Republic with the EU, Jacques Rupnik and Jan Zielonka (eds.) (2003).
31. This section draws on a longer study: Vachudova (2001*b*).
32. Grzymała-Busse (2003*a*).
33. Ibid., 1133.
34. For insightful analysis of the Czech political scene, see the Prague quarterly *Přítomnost* at http://www.pritomnost.cz.
35. Pehe (2002). See also Michal Klíma (2000).

36. For sharing their insights on Czech politics, I am indebted to Dagmar Ašerová, Pavel Fischer, Peter Green, Jiří Havlík, Pavel Hubáček, Libuše Koubská, Jiří Pehe, Jacques Rupnik, Pavel Seifter, Ivo Šilhavý, Jonathan Stein, Kieran Williams and Jozef Zieleniec.

37. Klaus and Havel disagreed on many issues, most dramatically on the value of civil society for Czech democracy. See Timothy Garton Ash (1995); Kieran Williams (1997*b*) and Martin Potůček (1998).

38. Ratko Kubičko and Petr Příhoda (2001). See also the other articles in the special symposium on Czech political parties in this issue.

39. Michael Leigh (2003).

40. Civic Democratic Party (ODS) (1996).

41. Milada Anna Vachudova (1998) and Jacques Rupnik (1997).

42. Jan Mládek, Deputy Finance Minister, interview in Prague, 1999; and Oldřich Dědek and Zdeněk Tůma, Czech National Bank, interviews in Prague, 1999.

43. Fish (2001: 84–86).

44. Kelley (2004*a*).

45. I am indebted to conversations with Balasz Jarabík on this point.

46. Vladimír Benč an d Anton Marcinčin (2002).

47. Freedom House (2003).

48. Benč and Marcincin (2002: 34); and World Bank (2001).

49. For a ministry by ministry evaluation of how well the Dzurinda government fulfilled its program, Miroslav Kollár and Grigorij Mesežnikov (eds.) (2002).

50. For an excellent analysis, Geoffrey Pridham (2002).

51. Peter Javorčík (2001). For the government's National Program for the Adoption of the Acquis (NPAA), http://www.government.gov.sk/infoservis/dokumenty/acquis/en_nprogram.shtml.

52. Pavol Lukáč (2001). The Visegrad cooperation effort has been popular with both Slovak governments and the public as a way to overcome the international isolation of the Mečiar years, and to regroup Slovakia with its more advanced neighbors. For a report showing that Slovaks support continued cooperation among the four Visegrad states after EU accession the most, with Poles coming in next, then Hungarians, and finally Czechs, see Mateusz Fałkowski, Patrycjja Bukalska, and Grzegorz Gromadzki (2003).

53. Ludger Blasig, European Commission, interview in Brussels, 1998. For an overview of Bulgaria's relations with the EU, see Albena Azmanova (2000).

54. Albena Azmanova, interview in Brussels, 2000. For a critical assessment of the first year of the UDF's Kostov government, Drezov (2000: 210–212).

55. Antoaneta Primatarova, Deputy Minister of Foreign Affairs, Bulgaria, interview in Sofia, 1998; Vassilis Maragos, Delegation of the European Commission to Bulgaria, interview in Sofia, 1998.

56. Elena Jileva (2002*a*).

57. In a public opinion poll conducted in Bulgaria in 2000, the removal of Bulgaria from the EU negative visa list was ranked as the third most important event of the century for the country after, first, the end of the communist regime in 1989 and, second, the communist takeover in 1944. See Jileva (2002*a*: 284).

58. For a description, http://www.info.fx.ro/emil/contract.html.
59. Michael Shafir (2001).
60. Gilda Lazăr, Former Senior Counselor and Spokeswoman for the Ministry of Foreign Affairs, interview in Bucharest, 1998.
61. Romanian parliament member, interview in Krakow, 2001.
62. Shafir (2001).
63. Zoe Petre (1999). See also the other contributions to this volume by insiders of Romania's foreign policy establishment.
64. Sergiu Celac, interview in Bucharest, 1998; Alina Mungiu-Pippidi, interview in Bonn, 1999.
65. Steffen Skovmand, Delegation of the European Commission in Romania, interview in Bucharest, 1998. See also Annette Freyberg-Inan (2002: 152).
66. Vachudova (2000).
67. Crăiuțu (2000: 181).
68. Vladimir Tismaneanu (2002).
69. Pavol Lukáč and Vladimír Bilčík, Slovak Foreign Policy Association, interviews in Bratislava, 2002.
70. For a trenchant analysis, Kevin Deegan Krause (2003).
71. Sharon Fisher (2004).
72. Sharon Fisher (2002a).
73. Vladimír Bilčík (2002).
74. Bilčík (2002: 25).
75. Pavol Demeš, interviews in Bratislava, 1998 and 2001.
76. Miroslav Kollár and Grigorij Mesežnikov (2002: 7). The excellent and voluminous analytical work produced by IVO and other institutes has also made available to researchers a wealth of information that is not available on the same scale in Bulgaria or Romania.
77. Ivan Krastev (2003: 180, 181).
78. Maria Koinova (2001: 139).
79. "Country Briefings: Bulgaria," *The Economist* at: www.economist.com/countries/Bulgaria.
80. Krastev (2003: 192–193). See also "EU: New Membership Road Map for Lagging Candidates Romania, Bulgaria," *RFE/RL*, September 12, 2002
81. Krastev (2003: 188).
82. "Bulgaria, Economic structure," *The Economist Intelligence Unit*, February 9, 2004.
83. "Bulgaria, Economic forecast," *The Economist Intelligence Unit*, April 27, 2004. On the UDF, see Azmanova (2000: 89).
84. Krastev (2003: 177). I am indebted to Aneta Spendzharova for conversations on the Simeon government and also for transcripts of her interviews with economist Tony Verheijen, World Bank, and journalist Georgi Goter, *Sega Daily*, in July 2003.
85. For an excellent analysis of the elections, Grigore Pop-Eleches (2001: 160). See also Alina Mungiu-Pippidi and Sorin Ionita (2001).
86. Pop-Eleches shows, however, that in 2000 the PDSR's voters did hold xenophobic and anti-democratic views that may attract them to Tudor's party in future elections. Pop-Eleches (2001: 164–167).
87. Vladimir Tismaneanu and Gail Kligman (2001).

88. Vladimir Tismaneanu's remarks at the roundtable "Outcome and implications of Romania's Presidential and Parliamentary Elections," Carnegie Endowment for International Peace, December 13, 2000, Washington, DC.
89. Crăiuțu (2000).
90. I am indebted to Charles King for conversations on this point.
91. Alina Mungiu-Pippidi, Sorin Ioniță and Aurelian Muntean (2003).
92. Freyberg-Inan (2002).
93. European Commission officials, interviews in Brussels, 2003.
94. Most likely, the Commission will conclude negotiations with Romania in late 2004 and the European Council will affirm 2007 as the target date for membership. The Commission, however, will continue to monitor key areas of reform with the possibility of re-opening the negotiations should reform falter.
95. Pierre Mirel, interview in Brussels, 2003.
96. For outstanding theoretical development and empirical testing of rationalist and constructivist mechanisms, Kelley (2004a).
97. James March and Johan P. Olsen (1998).
98. Frank Schimmelfennig and Ulrich Sedelmeir (2005).
99. Rachel Epstein (2004a).

Chapter 8

1. Timothy Garton Ash (1998) and (1999).
2. Jacques Rupnik, remarks at the conference "Dilemmas of Europeanization: Politics and Society in Eastern and Central Europe After EU Enlargement," Center for European Studies, Harvard University, December 5–6, 2003.
3. David Cameron (2003: 25).
4. Stephen Holmes (2003: 113).
5. Lynne M. Tesser (2003b); see also Tesser (2003a).
6. Anna Grzymała-Busse and Abby Innes (2003).
7. Margit Bessenyey Williams (2001b).
8. Grabbe (2001b).
9. Darina Málová and Tim Haughton (2002).
10. Jacoby (2004).
11. Phedon Nicolaides (2003).
12. Zielonka and Mair (2002: 5). See also Lykke Friis and Anna Murphy (1999).
13. Grabbe (2001b).
14. Gwendolyn Sasse (2004).
15. George Ross, remarks at the conference "Dilemmas of Europeanization," December 5–6, 2003.
16. Bartlomiej Kaminski, remarks at the conference "Dilemmas of Europeanization," December 5–6, 2003.
17. Cameron (2003: 27–29).
18. Glenn (2004: 24–25).
19. Dimitrova (2002).
20. David L. Ellison and Mustally Hussain (2003).

21. Holmes (2003).
22. Hellman (1998); and World Bank (2002*a*: 16, 73–79, 107).
23. Grabbe (2001*a*); Kaminski (2001); and Baldwin, Francois, and Portes (1997).
24. European Commission (2003*a*: 7, 10).
25. European Commission official and diplomat at the German embassy, interviews in Brussels, 2003.
26. On the political effects of graduated agricultural subsidies, Rachel Epstein (2004*b*).
27. For details, Cameron (2003: 32–34). See also European Commission (2002).
28. Jean-Luc Dehaene, Vice Chairman of the European Convention, remarks at the conference "Dilemmas of Europeanization," December 5–6, 2003.
29. Moravcsik and Vachudova (2003*b*: 49).
30. For details, Vachudova (2001*b*).
31. Moravcsik (1998*a*); and Moravcsik and Vachudova (2003*a*: 4–6).
32. Moravcsik (1998*a*); and Moravcsik and Vachudova (2003*a*: 14–16).
33. See also Cameron (2003: 39).
34. Elena Jileva (2002*b*).
35. Current and former government officials, interviews in Prague and Bratislava respectively, 2002.
36. Zielonka and Mair (2002: 15–16).
37. On enlargement and the functioning of EU institutions, De Witte (2003: 209–227). See also Loukas Tsoukalis (2004).
38. I am indebted to Francesca Bignami for conversations about the Convention. See Peter Norman (2003: 35, 244, 338).
39. Dorothée Bohle and Bela Greskovits, remarks at the conference "The New Face of Europe," Center for European Studies, University of Florida, February 27–28, 2004. See also Holmes (2003).
40. For details, the European Industrial Relations Observatory On-line: http://www.eiro.eufound.eu.int/2004/country/eu.level.html.
41. Paul Taggart and Aleks Szerbiak (2001).
42. On the possible uses, Helen Wallace (2000*b*); and Peter Leslie (2000).
43. For example, Claudio Radaelli (2001); and Tanya Börzel and Thomas Risse (2000).
44. Heather Grabbe (2003). Grabbe treats what I call the EU's active leverage on the candidate states as a part of the Europeanization process.
45. Some striking comparisons, however, may be made between attempts of EU members to qualify for membership in EMU, and attempts of EU candidates to qualify for EU membership.
46. Francesca Bignami (2004).
47. Moravcsik and Vachudova (2003*a*: 10–13).
48. For an excellent contrast of the two approaches, Torreblanca (2002: 9–19).
49. K. M. Fierke and Antje Wiener (1999).
50. Torreblanca (2002: 15).
51. Ulrich Sedelmeier (1999). See also Ulrich Sedelmeier (1998).

52. Frank Schimmelfennig (2003). See also Schimmelfennig (2001).
53. See Schimmelfennig (2001, 2003).
54. Baldwin, Francois, and Portes (1997: 125–176).
55. Torreblanca (2002: 18).
56. Javier Solana, remarks at the Foreign Policy Association, New York, December 1999. Such remarks are commonplace from EU officials, for example recently EU enlargement commissioner Günter Verheugen observed that enlargement had transformed the EU into a continental power, and as such it must become a global player. *Sofia Morning News*, May 14, 2004.
57. Mattli (1999: 95).
58. Fierke and Wiener incorporate security as an interest-driven reason for enlargement into their nuanced anlaysis, but they emphasize that the threat of instability in the East also presented a threat to the *identity* of the EU (and NATO). Fierke and Wiener (1999: 737). For a contrasting view, Helen Sjursen (2002).
59. Garton Ash (1998).
60. Garton Ash (1999: 208–222, 316–331).
61. Milada Anna Vachudova (1999); and Andrew Moravcsik (2003). For the same argument extended to Turkey, Heather Grabbe (2002).
62. For the ramifications, see several of the contributions to Anatol Lieven and Dmitri Trenin (eds.) (2003).
63. European Commission (2003*b*).
64. Anders Åslund predicted in 2002, for example, that if the EU would "open its markets more to sensitive imports from the CIS, notably agricultural produce from Moldova, it could entice enormous changes in the CIS countries at little expense to itself." Time will tell: whether the EU will find the courage, and what changes will follow. Åslund (2002: 455).
65. Michael Emerson (2004).
66. Kataryna Wolczuk (2004).
67. Conclusions of the Copenhagen European Council of December 2002 quoted in: European Commission (2003*c*).
68. Paul Kubicek (2004*b*).
69. European Commission (2003*c*). For the Commision's crucial report on Turkey's progress published in October 2004: http://europa.eu.int/comm/enlargement/turkey.
70. See also Torreblanca (2002: 29).
71. Timothy Garton Ash (2002*b*).
72. World Bank (2000). See also Michael Emerson and Daniel Gros (1999).
73. Tismaneanu (2002: 93).
74. Milada Anna Vachudova (2002).
75. Weber (1999: 212).
76. European Commission (2004*a*).
77. The further opening of the EU market to goods from the Balkans was accompanied by a great deal of pressure from observers and from the US government, and also considerable sensitivity on the part of certain EU politicians and officials to the suggestion that even limited EU protectionism toward the region was counterproductive and, given the EU's relative economic weight, quite stunning.

Günter Burghart, talk at Harvard University, March 2000; and Erhard Busek, remarks in Bratislava, July 2000.

78. European Commission (2004*a*).
79. European Commission (2004*b*).
80. "Croatia Wins Incentive for EU Entry Talks," *Financial Times*, October 9, 2003.

BIBLIOGRAPHY

Allen, David and Michael Smith (1995). "External Policy Developments," *Journal of Common Market Studies* 33(2): 69–86.

Anderson, Richard D., M. Steven Fish, Stephen E. Hanson, and Philip G. Roeder (eds.) (2001). *Postcommunism and the Theory of Democracy*. Princeton: Princeton University Press.

Andonova, Liliana B. (2003). *Transnational Politics of the Environment. The EU and Environmental Policy in Central and Eastern Europe*. Cambridge: MIT Press.

Andreescu, Gabriel (1995). "Political Manipulation at Its Best," *Transition* 1(22): 46–49.

Antall, József (1991). Speech at the United Nations, October 1, New York, published by the Hungarian Ministry of Foreign Affairs as *Current Policy* 34.

Antohi, Sorin and Vladimir Tismaneanu (eds.) (2000). *Between Past and Future: The Revolutions of 1989 and Their Aftermath*. Budapest: Central European Press.

Appel, Hilary (2001). "Corruption and the Collapse of the Czech Transition Miracle," *East European Politics and Societies* 15(3): 528–553.

—— and John Gould (2000). "Identity Politics and Economic Reform: Examining Industry-State Relations in the Czech and Slovak Republics," *Europe Asia Studies* 20(1): 111–131.

Åslund, Ånders (2002). *Building Capitalism: The Transformation of the Former Soviet Bloc*. Cambridge: Cambridge University Press.

Asmus, Ronald D. (2002). *Opening NATO's Door: How the Alliance Remade Itself for a New Era*. New York: Columbia University Press.

Avery, Graham (1994). "The European Union's Enlargement Negotiations," *The Oxford International Review* 5(3): 27–32.

Azmanova, Albena (2000). "Bulgaria," *East European Constitutional Review*, 9, 4: 86–90.

Balcerowicz, Leszek (1994). "Understanding Postcommunist Transitions," *Journal of Democracy* 5(4): 75–89.

—— (1995). *Socialism, Capitalism, Transformation*. Budapest: Central European University Press.

Baldwin, Richard (1995). "A Domino Theory of Regionalism," in Richard Baldwin, Pertti Haaparanta, Jaakko Kiander (eds.), *Expanding Membership of the European Union*. Cambridge: Cambridge University Press, 25–48.

—— Joseph F. Francois, and Richard Portes (1997). "The Costs and Benefits of Eastern Enlargement: The Impact on the EU and Central Europe." *Economic Policy* 12(24): 125–176.

Banac, Ivo (ed.) (1992). *Eastern Europe in Revolution*. Ithaca: Cornell University Press.

—— (1992). "Introduction," in Banac ed., *Eastern Europe in Revolution*, 1–12.

Barany, Zoltan (2002). *The East European Gypsies: Regime Change, Marginality, and Ethnopolitics.* New York: Cambridge University Press.

Barber, Lionel (1993). "The New Hypocrites," *The International Economy,* 7(5): 24–27.

—— (1994). "Variable geometry of measuring up for wider EU," *Financial Times,* September 27.

Barcz, Jan and Arkadiusz Michonski (2002). *Negotiations on Poland's Accession to the European Union.* Warsaw: Ministry of Foreign Affairs.

Bates, Robert H., Rui J. P. de Figueiredo Jr., and Barry R. Weingast (1998). "The Politics of Interpretation: Rationality, Culture, and Transition," *Politics & Society* 26(2): 221–256.

Bell, John D. (ed.) (1998). *Bulgaria in Transition. Politics, Economics, Society, and Culture after Communism.* Boulder and Oxford: Westview.

Benč, Vladimír and Anton Marcinčin (2002). "Príprava Slovenska na integráciu do EÚ," in Anton Marcinčin and Martina Lubyová (eds.), *EÚ-monitoring 2002.* Bratislava: Slovak Foreign Policy Association and the Friedrich Ebert Stiftung, 23–84.

Bignami, Francesca (2004). "The Challenge of Cooperative Regulatory Relations after Enlargement," in George A. Bermann and Katharina Pistor (eds.), *Law and Governance in an Enlarged European Union.* Oxford: Hart Publishing, 97–141.

Bilčík, Vladimír (2002). "Integrácie Slovenskej republiky do Európskej únie," in *Parlamentné vol'by 2002: Zahraničná politika SR vo volebných programoch politických strán.* Bratislava: Slovak Foreign Policy Association, 24–34.

Bing, Rasmus and Bogdan Szajkowski, "Romania," in Szajkowski (ed.) (1994). *Political Parties of Eastern Europe, Russia and the Successor States.* Henlow, UK: Longman, 91–133.

Bird, Graham (2003). *The IMF and the Future, Issues and Options Facing the Fund.* London: Routledge.

Bombík, Světoslav (1995). *Bližšie k Európe.* Bratislava: Slovak Foundation for European Studies.

Börzel, Tanya and Thomas Risse (2000). "When Europe Hits Home: Europeanization and Domestic Change," European University Institute Working Paper, San Domenico di Fiesole, RSC No. 2000/56.

Bozóki, András (ed.) (1999). *Intellectuals and Politics in Central Europe.* Budapest: Central European University Press.

—— (ed.) (2002). *The Roundtable Talks of 1989.* Budapest: CEU Press.

—— and John T. Ishiyama (eds.) (2002). *The Communist Successor Parties of Central and Eastern Europe.* Armonk, NY: M. E. Sharpe.

Brada, Josef (1991). "The Community and Czechoslovakia, Hungary and Poland," *Report on Eastern Europe* 2(49) (December 6): 27–32.

Brousil, Zdeněk (1997). "Příprava na vstup do Aliance," *Vojenské Rozhledy* 6(4): 12–19.

Brown, J.F. (1994). *Hopes and Shadows: Eastern Europe After Communism.* Durham: Duke University Press.

Brown, Michael E. (1999). "Minimalist NATO: A Wise Alliance Knows When to Retrench," *Foreign Affairs* 78(3): 204–208.

Brubaker, Rogers (1996). *Nationalism Reframed: Nationhood and the National Question in the New Europe.* Cambridge: Cambridge University Press.

Brus, Wlodzimierz, Pierre Kende, and Zdeněk Mlynář (1982). *Normalization Processes in Soviet-Dominated Europe,* self-published.

Buchan, David and Lionel Barber (1994). "Road-map sought for EU applicants," *Financial Times,* September 21.

Bugajski, Janusz (1994). *Ethnic Politics in Eastern Europe: A Guide to Nationality Policies, Organizations, and Parties.* Armonk, New York: M. E. Sharpe.

Bunce, Valerie (1995). "Should Transitologists be Grounded?," *Slavic Review* 54(1): 111–127.

—— (1999a). *Subversive Institutions, The Design and the Destruction of Socialism and the State.* Cambridge: Cambridge University Press.

—— (1999b). "The Political Economy of Postsocialism," *Slavic Review* 58(4): 756–793.

—— (1999c). "Lessons of the First Postsocialist Decade," *East European Politics and Societies* 13(2): 236–243.

—— (2000). "Comparative Democratization: Big Bounded Generalizations," *Comparative Political Studies* 33(6/7): 703–734.

—— (2002). "The Return of the Left and Democratic Consolidation in Poland and Hungary," in Bozóki and Ishiyama (eds.), *The Communist Successor Parties of Central and Eastern Europe.* Armonk, NY: M. E. Sharpe, 303–322.

—— (2003). "Rethinking Recent Democratization, Lessons from the Postcommunist Experience," *World Politics* 55(2): 167–192.

Bútora, Martin and Zora Bútorová (1993). "Slovakia After the Split," *Journal of Democracy* 4(2): 71–83.

—— and Zora Bútorová (1999). "Slovakia's Democratic Awakening," *Journal of Democracy* 10(1): 80–95.

—— and Pavol Demeš (1999). "Civil Society Organizations in the 1998 Elections," in Bútora, Mesežnikov, Bútorová, and Fisher (eds.), *The 1998 Parliamentary Elections and Democratic Rebirth in Slovakia.* Bratislava: Institute for Public Affairs, 155–177.

—— and Michal Ivantyšyn (eds.) (1998). *Slovenkso 1997. Súhrná správa o stave spoločnosti a Trendoch na rok 1998.* Bratislava: Institute for Public Affairs.

—— and František Sebej (eds.) (1998). *Slovensko v šedej zone? Rozširovanie NATO, zlyhania a perspektívy Slovenska.* Bratislava: Institute for Public Affairs.

——, Zora Bútorová and Olga Gyárfášová (1994). "Form Velvet Revolution to Velvet Divorce? Reflections on Slovakia's Independence," in János Mátyás Kovács (ed.), *Transition to Capitalism?* London: Transaction Publishers, 229–257.

—— Grigorij Mesežnikov, Zora Bútorová, and Sharon Fisher (eds.) (1999). *The 1998 Parliamentary Elections and Democratic Rebirth in Slovakia.* Bratislava: Institute for Public Affairs.

—— Grigorij Mesežnikov, and Zora Bútorová (1999). "Introduction: Overcoming Illiberalism—Slovakia's 1998 Elections," in Bútora, Mesežnikov, Bútorová, and Fisher (eds.), *The 1998 Parliamentary Elections and Democratic Rebirth in Slovakia.* Bratislava: Institute for Public Affairs, 9–23.

Bútorová, Zora (1998*a*). "Verejná mienka," in Bútora and Ivantyšyn (eds.), *Slovenkso 1997. Súhrná správa o stave spoločnosti*. Bratislava: Institute for Public Affairs, 197–232.

—— (ed.) (1998*b*). *Democracy and Discontent in Slovakia: A Public Opinion Profile of a Country in Transition*. Bratislava: Institute for Public Affairs.

—— (1999). "Development of Public Opinion: from Discontent to the Support of Political Change," in Bútora, Mesežnikov, Bútorová and Fisher (eds.), *The 1998 Parliamentary Elections and Democratic Rebirth in Slovakia*. Bratislava: Institute for Public Affairs, 195–219.

—— Olga Gyárfásová and Marián Velsic (1999). "Verejná mienka," in Mesežnikov and Ivantyšyn (eds.), *Slovensko 1998–1999, Súhrnná správa o stave spoločnosti*. Bratislava: Institute for Public Affairs, 233–272.

Calinescu, Matei and Vladimir Tismaneanu (1991). "The 1989 Revolution and Romania's Future," *Problems of Communism* 38(1): 42–59.

Cameron, David (2001). "The Return to Europe: The Impact of the EU on Post-Communist Reform," delivered at the Annual Meeting of the American Political Science Association, San Francisco, August.

—— (2003). "The Challenges of Accession," *East European Politics and Societies* 17(1): 24–41.

Caporaso, James (1996). "The European Union and Forms of State: Westphalian, Regulatory or Post-Modern?," *Journal of Common Market Studies* 34(1): 29–51.

—— (2003). "Democracy, Accountability, and Rights in International Governance," in Miles Kahler and David A. Lake (eds.), *Governance in a Global Economy: Political Authority in Transition*. Princeton: Princeton University Press, 393–417.

—— and John T. S. Keeler (1995). "The European Community and Regional Integration Theory," in Carolyn Rhodes and Sonia Mazey (eds.), *The State of the European Union: Building a European Polity?* Boulder: Lynne Riener, 29–62.

—— and Alec Stone Sweet (2001). "Conclusion: Institutional Logics of European Integration," in Stone Sweet, Sandholtz, and Fligstein (eds.), *The Institutionalization of Europe*. Oxford: Oxford University Press, 221–236.

Center for the Study of Democracy (1998). *Bulgaria and the European Union: Towards an Institutional Infrastructure*. Sofia: Center for the Study of Democracy.

Charter 77 (1997). *Charta 77 očima současníků: před dvaceti lety*. Prague: Ústav soudobé dějiny.

Checkel, Jeffrey (2000). "Compliance and Conditionality," ARENA Working Paper 00/18, University of Oslo.

—— and Andrew Moravcsik (2001). "A Constructivist Research Program in EU Studies?" *European Union Politics* 2(2): 219–249.

Chirot, Daniel (2000). "How Much Does the Past Count? Interpreting the Romanian Transition's Political Successes And Economic failures," in Werner Baer and Joseph L. Love (eds.), *Liberalization and its Consequences*. Cheltenham, UK: Edward Elgar, 103–122.

Civic Democratic Party (ODS) (1996). "Svoboda a Prosperita," ODS Party Program, April.

Civic Forum (1989). "Co chceme—programové zásady Občanského Fora," Prague, 18:00 on 26 November 1989.

Comisso, Ellen (1997). "Is the Glass Half Full or Half Empty? Reflections on Five Years of Competitive Politics in Eastern Europe," *Communist and Post-Communist Studies* 30(1): 1–21.

Commission on Security and Cooperation in Europe (1993). "Human Rights and Democratization in Bulgaria," CSCE, Washington, D. C., September. http://www.csce.gov/pdf.cfm?file=1993HRinBulgaria%2Epdf&pdf_id=186.

Cook, Linda J. and Mitchell A. Orenstein (1999). "The Return of the Left and Its Impact on the Welfare State in Russia, Poland, and Hungary," in Cook, Orenstein, and Marilyn Rueschemeyer (eds.), *Left Parties and Social Policy in Postcommunist Europe*. Boulder: Westview Press, 47–108.

Crăiuțu, Aurelian (2000). "Light at the end of the tunnel, Romania 1989–1998," in Pridham and Gallagher (eds.), *Experimenting with Democracy, Regime Change in the Balkans*, 169–194.

Crampton, Richard (1993). "Bulgaria," in Whitefield (ed.), *The New Institutional Architecture of Eastern Europe*. London: Macmillan 14–34.

Crawford, Beverly and Arend Lijphart (1995). "Explaining Political and Economic Change in Post-communist Eastern Europe, Old Legacies, New Institutions, Hegemonic Norms and International Pressures," *Comparative Political Studies* 28(2): 171–199.

Cremona, Marise (ed.) (2003). *The Enlargement of the European Union*. Oxford: Oxford University Press.

—— (2003). "The Impact of Enlargement: External Policy and External Relations," in Cremona (ed.), *The Enlargement of the European Union*. Oxford: Oxford University Press, 161–208.

Croft, Stuart, John Redmond, G. Wyn Rees and Mark Webber (1999). *The Enlargement of Europe*. Manchester: Manchester University Press, 142–163.

Czech and Slovak Federative Republic, Ministry of Foreign Affairs (1990). "Memorandum on the European Security Commission," submitted to the CSCE, April 6.

—— (1992). "Declaration of the highest representatives of the Triangle countries adopted at their Prague meeting on 6 May 1992."

Dahl, Robert (1971). *Polyarchy: Participation and Opposition*. New Haven: Yale University Press.

Dahrendorf, Ralf (1990). *Reflections on the Revolution in Europe*. New York: Times Books.

Daianu, Daniel (1998). *Transformation of Economy as a Real Process*. Aldershot, Hampshire: Ashgate.

De La Serre, François, Christian Lequesne, and Jacques Rupnik (1994). *L'Union européenne; ouverture á l'Est?* Paris: Presses Universitaires de France.

De Melo, Martha, Cevdet Denizer, and Alan Gelb (1996). "From Plan to Market— Patterns of Transition," World Bank, Policy Research Working Paper No. 1564. http://econ.worldbank.org/files/448_wps1564.pdf.

De Weydenthal, Jan (1993). "EC Keeps Central Europeans at Arms Length," *RFE/RL Research Report*, January 29.

De Witte, Bruno (2002). "Politics Versus Law in the EU's Approach to Ethnic Minorities," in Zielonka (ed.), *Europe Unbound: Enlarging and reshaping the boundaries of the European Union*. London: Routledge, 137–160.

De Witte, Bruno (2003). "The Impact of Enlargement on the Constitution of the European Union," in Cremona (ed.), *The Enlargement of the European Union.* Oxford: Oxford University Press, 209–252.

Deegan Krause, Kevin (2000). "Accountability and Party Competition in Slovakia and the Czech Republic," Ph.D. Dissertation, University of Notre Dame.

—— (2003). "Slovakia's Second Transition," *Journal of Democracy* 14(2): 65–79.

Deets, Stephen (2002). "Reconsidering East European Minority Policy: Liberal Theory and European Norms," *East European Politics and Societies* 16(1): 30–53.

Deletant, Dennis (2001). "The Successors to the Securitate: Old Habits Die Hard," in Williams and Deletant (eds.), *Security Intelligence Services in New Democracies, The Czech Republic, Slovakia and Romania.* Houndsmills, Basingstoke: Palgrave, 211–262.

Delors, Jacques (1989). Speech at the College of Europe, Bruges, November, published in *Bulletin of the European Communities* 9(22).

Diamond, Larry (2002). "Thinking About Hybrid Regimes," *Journal of Democracy* 13(2): 21–35.

—— and Marc Plattner (eds.) (1996). *The Global Resurgence of Democracy.* Baltimore: Johns Hopkins University Press.

Dienstbier, Jiří (1990). *Snění o Evropě.* Prague: Lidové Noviny.

Dimitrova, Antoaneta (2002). "Enlargement, Institution-Building and the EU's Administrative Capacity Requirement," *West European Politics* 25(4): 171–190.

Dinan, Desmond (1998). "The Commission and Enlargement," in Redmond and Rosenthal (eds.), *The Expanding European Union: Past, Present, Future.* Boulder: Lynne Rienner, 17–40.

Doyle, Michael W. (1997). *Ways of War and Peace: Realism, Liberalism and Socialism.* New York: Norton.

Drezner, Daniel W. (ed.) (2003) *Locating the Proper Authorities: The Interaction of Domestic and International Institutions.* Ann Arbor: University of Michigan Press.

Drezov, Kyril (2000) "Bulgaria: Transition Comes Full Circle, 1989–1997," in Pridham and Gallagher (eds.), *Experimenting with Democracy, Regime Change in the Balkans.* London: Routledge, 195–218.

—— (2001). "Bulgaria and Macedonia: Voluntary Dependence on External Actors," in Zielonka and Pravda (eds.), *Democratic Consolidation in Eastern Europe: International and Transnational Factors.* Oxford: Oxford University Press, 413–436.

Duleba, Alexander (1998). "Slovensko a Rusko," in Bútora and Ivantyšyn (eds.), *Slovenkso 1997. Súhrná správa o stave spoločnosti.* Bratislava: Institute for Public Affairs, 287–299.

Dunay, Pál (1993). "Hungary: defining the boundaries of security" in Regina Cowen Karp (ed.), *Central and Eastern Europe: The Challenge of Transition.* Oxford: Oxford University Press, 122–154.

Ekiert, Grzegorz (1996). *The State Against Society.* Princeton, NJ: Princeton University Press.

—— (2003). "Patterns of Postcommunist Transformation in Central and Eastern Europe," in Ekiert and Hanson (eds.), *Capitalism and Democracy in Central and Eastern Europe,* 89–119.

—— and Stephen E. Hanson (eds.) (2003). *Capitalism and Democracy in Central and Eastern Europe: Assessing the Legacy of Communist Rule*. Cambridge: Cambridge University Press.

—— and Jan Kubik (1999). *Rebellious Civil Society, Popular Protest and Democratic Consolidation in Poland, 1989–1993*. Ann Arbor: University of Michigan Press.

—— and—— (2000). "Civil Society From Abroad: the Role of Foreign Assistance in the Democratization of Poland," Weatherhead Center for International Affairs, Harvard University, Working Paper No. 00–01.

Ellison, David L. and Mustally Hussain (2003). "In the Face of Uncertainty: EU Membership and the Quest for Convergence," paper presented at the Annual Meeting of the Midwest Political Science Association, April 3–6.

Elster, Jon, Claus Offe, and Ulrich K. Preuss (1998). *Institutional Design in Post-Communist Societies: Rebuilding the Ship at Sea*. Cambridge: Cambridge University Press.

Emerson, Michael (2004). "Deepening the Wider Europe," Commentaries, Centre for European Policy Studies, April 6. http://www.ceps.be/Article.php?article_id=296&.

—— and Daniel Gros (1999). *The CEPS Plan for The Balkans*. Brussels: Centre for European Policy Studies.

Engelbrekt, Kjell (1994). "Intolerance in Bulgaria," *RFE/RL Research Report* 3(16): 75–79.

Epstein, Rachel (2005). "NATO Enlargement and the Spread of Democracy: Evidence and Expectations," *Security Studies* 14(1), forthcomming.

—— (2004*a*). "International Institutions, Domestic Resonance, and the Politics of Denationalization," unpublished manuscript.

—— (2004*b*). "International Institutions and the (De)Politicization of Economic Policy in Postcommunist Europe," unpublished manuscript.

Eurobarometer (1993). *Central and Eastern Eurobarometer*, No. 3. http://gesis.org/en/data%5Fservice/eurobarometer/ceeb/topics.htm.

—— (1996). *Central and Eastern Eurobarometer*, No. 6.

—— (1997). *Central and Eastern Eurobarometer*, No. 7.

—— (1998). *Central and Eastern Eurobarometer*, No. 8.

—— (2001). *Candidate Countries Eurobarometer*, No. 2001.2. http://www.gesis.org/en/data_service/eurobarometer/cceb/indexframe_profiles.htm, http://europa.eu.int/comm/public_opinion/cceb_en.htm.

—— (2002*a*). *Candidate Countries Eurobarometer*, No. 2002.2.

—— (2002*b*). *Standard Eurobarometer*, No. 58.1.
http://europa.eu.int/comm/public_opinion/archives/eb/eb58/eb58_en.htm.

—— (2003). *Candidate Countries Eurobarometer*, No. 2003.4.

European Bank for Reconstruction and Development (1999). *Transition Report: Ten Years of Transition*. London: EBRD.

European Commission (1992). "Towards a Closer Association with the Countries of Central and Eastern Europe," SEC (92) 2301 final, December 2.

—— (1994). "Narrowing the Gap: Presidential Conclusions of the European Council, 9–10 December 1994 in Essen," Press Release, DOC 94/4, December 11.

European Commission (1997*a*). "Agenda 2000: For a stronger and wider Union," COM (97) 2000 final, July 15. http://europa.eu.int/comm/enlargement/intro/ag2000_opinions. htm#Opinions.

—— (1997*b*). "Agenda 2000: Summary and Conclusions of the Opinions of Commission Concerning the Applications for Membership to the European Union presented by the candidate countries," DOC/97/8, July 15.

European Commission (1997*c*). "Agenda 2000, Commission Opinion on Slovakia's application for Membership of the European Union," DOC/97/20, July 15. All of the Opinions are at: http://europa.eu.int/comm/enlargement/intro/index_en.htm.

—— (1998–). Regular Reports on the Candidate Countries. http://europa.eu.int/comm/enlargement/report_11_98/.

—— (1999). "Composite Paper—Reports on Progress Towards Accession by Each of the Candidate Countries," October 13. http://europa.eu.int/comm/enlargement/report_10_99/pdf/en/composite_en.pdf.

—— (2002*a*). "Towards the Enlarged Union: Strategy paper and report of the European Commission on the progress towards accession by each of the candidate states," COM (2002) 700 final, October 9. http://www.europarl.eu.int/meetdocs/delegations/latv/ 20021218/04%20EN.pdf.

—— (2002*b*). "Common Financial Framework 2004–2006 for the Accession Negotiations," SEC (2002) 102 final. January 31. http://www.europa.eu.int/comm/enlargement/docs/financialpackage/sec2002-102_en.pdf.

—— (2003*a*). "Report on the results of the negotiations on the accession of Cyprus, Malta, Hungary, Poland, the Slovak Republic, Latvia, Estonia, Lithuania, the Czech Republic and Slovenia to the European Union," prepared by the Commission's departments, at: http://www.europa.eu.int/comm/enlargement/negotiations/pdf/negotiations_report_to_ep.pdf.

—— (2003*b*). "Wider Europe—Neighborhood: A New Framework for Relations with our Eastern and Southern Neighbors," COM (2003) 104 final, March 11. http://europa.eu.int/comm/world/enp/index_en.htm.

—— (2003*c*). "2003 Regular Report on Turkey's progress towards accession," For all of the Commission documents on Turkey's application: http://europa.eu.int/comm/enlargement/turkey.

—— (2004*a*). "The Stabilisation and Association Process for South East Europe, Third Annual Report," COM (2004) 202/2 final, March 30. http://europa.eu.int/comm/external_relations/see/sap/rep3/.

—— (2004*b*). "Opinion on Croatia's Application for Membership of the European Union," COM (2004) 257 final, April 20. http://www.europa.eu.int/comm/external_relations/see/sap/rep3/cr_croat.pdf.

Eyal, Jonathan (1993). "Romania," in Whitefield (ed.), *The New Institutional Architecture of Eastern Europe*. London: Macmillan, 121–142.

—— (1992). "A New Iron Curtain Descends," *The Independent*, September 30.

Faini, Riccardo and Richard Portes (1995). "Opportunities Outweigh Adjustment: The Political Economy of Trade with East Central Europe," in Faini and Portes (eds.), *European Union Trade with Eastern Europe: Adjustment and Opportunities*. London: Center for European Policy Reform, 1–18.

Fałkowski, Mateusz, Patrycjja Bukalska, and Grzegorz Gromadzki (2003). "Yes to Visegrad," The Institute of Public Affairs, Warsaw, Analyses & Opinions Report No. 16.

Fearon, James D. and David D. Laitin (2000). "Violence and the Social Construction of Identity," *International Organization* 54(4): 845–877.

Fierke, K. M. and Antje Wiener (1999). "Constructing institutional interests: EU and NATO enlargement," *Journal of European Public Policy* 6(5): 721–742.

Fish, M. Steven (1998). "The Determinants of Economic Reform in the Post-Communist World," *East European Politics and Societies* 12(1): 31–78.

—— (1999). "Postcommunist Subversion: Social Science and Democratization in East Europe and Eurasia," *Slavic Review* 58(4): 794–823.

—— (2001). "The Dynamics of Democratic Erosion," in Anderson, Fish, Hanson, and Roeder (eds.), *Postcommunism and the Theory of Democracy*. Princeton: Princeton University Press, 54–95.

—— (2003). "How has Democracy Fared in Postcommunist Space?" delivered at the conference "Evaulating Success and Failure in Postcommunist Reform," Claremont-Mckenna College, February.

Fisher, Sharon (1994). "Meeting of Slovakia's Hungarians Causes Stir," *RFE/RL Research Report* 3(4): 42–47.

—— (1995). "Slovakia: Turning Back?" *Transition* 1(1): 60–63.

—— (1996a). "Slovak Prime Minister Listed As One of Ten Worst Enemies of the Press," *OMRI Analytical Brief* 1(97) (May 3).

—— (1996b). "Slovak Parliament Approves Law on the Protection of the Republic and Ratifies Treaty with Hungary," *OMRI Analytical Brief* 1(42) (March 27).

—— (2001). "From Nationalist to Europeanist: The Rise and Fall of National Movements in Slovakia and Croatia," Ph.D. Dissertation, School of Slavonic and East European Studies (SSEES), University College London.

—— (2002a). "Slovak Voters Move Closer to West." *East European Studies Meeting Report* 264, Woodrow Wilson Center.

—— (2002b). "The Troubled Evolution of Slovakia's Ex-Communists," in Bozóki and Ishiyama (eds.), *The Communist Successor Parties of Central and Eastern Europe*. Armonk, NY: M. E. Sharpe, 116–140.

—— (2004). "Slovak and Czech Fiscal Reforms From a Comparative Perspective," unpublished manuscript.

Freedom House (1996) *World Survey of Economic Freedom, 1995–1996*. New Brunswick, NJ: Freedom House and Transaction Publishers.

—— (1998). *Nations in Transit 1998: Civil Society, Democracy and Markets in East Central Europe and the Newly Independent States*. New York: Freedom House. http://www.freedomhouse.org/nit98.

—— (2001). *Nations in Transit 2001: Civil Society, Democracy and Markets in East Central Europe and the Newly Independent States*. New York: Freedom House. http://www.freedomhouse.org/research/nitransit/2001/index.htm.

—— (2003). *Nations in Transit 2003: Democratization in East Central Europe and Eurasia*. Lanham, MD: Freedom House and Rowman & Littlefield. http://www.freedomhouse.org/research/nattransit.htm.

Freyberg-Inan, Annette (2002). "Which Way to Progress? Impact of International Organizations in Romania," in Linden (ed.), *Norms and Nannies*, 129–164.

Friis, Lykke and Anna Murphy (1999). "The European Union and Central and Eastern Europe: Governance and Boundaries," *Journal of Common Market Studies* 37(2): 211–232.

Friis, Lykke and Anna Murphy (2000). "Enlargement: A Complex Juggling Act," in Green Cowles and Smith (eds.), *The State of the European Union, Risks, Reform, Resistance and Revival*. Oxford: Oxford University Press, 186–204.

Frye, Timothy (2002). "The Perils of Polarization: Economic Performance in the Postcommunist World," *World Politics* 54(3): 308–337.

Gabal, Ivan a kolektiv (eds.) (1999). *Etnické menšiny ve střední Evropě*. Prague: Institute for International Relations.

Gagnon, V. P. (1994/95). "Ethnic Nationalism and International Conflict: The Case of Serbia," *International Security* 19(3): 130–166.

Galinos, Alexis (1994). "Central Europe and the EU: Prospects for Closer Integration," *RFE/RL Research Report* 3(29): 19–25.

Gallagher, Tom (1995). *Romania After Ceauşescu: The Politics of Intolerance*. Edinburgh: Edinburgh University Press.

—— (2001). "Nationalism and Romanian Political Culture in the 1990s," in Light and Phinnemore (eds.), *Post-Communist Romania, Coming to Terms with Transition*. Houndsmills, Basingstoke: Palgrave, 104–126.

Ganev, Venelin (1997). "Bulgaria's Symphony of Hope." *Journal of Democracy* 8(4): 125–139.

—— (2001). "The Dorian Gray Effect: Winners as State Breakers in Postcommunism," *Communist and Post-Communist Studies* 34: 1–25.

Garrett, Geoffrey (1992). "International Cooperation and Institutional Choice: The European Community's Internal Market," *International Organization* 46(2): 533–560.

Garton Ash, Timothy (1989). *The Uses of Adversity*. New York: Random House.

—— (1990). *The Magic Lantern: The Revolution of '89 Witnessed in Warsaw, Budapest, Berlin and Prague*. New York: Vintage.

—— (1995). "Prague: Intellectuals and Politicians," *New York Review of Books*, 12 January, 34–41.

—— (1998). "Europe's Endangered Liberal Order," *Foreign Affairs* 77(2): 51–65.

—— (1999). *History of the Present*. London: Allen Lane.

—— (2002a). *The Polish Revolution: Solidarity*, 3rd edn. New Haven: Yale University Press.

—— (2002b), "A Bridge Too Far? In Deciding if Turkey Should Join the EU, the Logic of Unity Clashes With the Logic of Peace," *The Guardian*, November 14.

Gaubatz, Kurt Taylor (1996). "Democratic States and Commitment in International Relations," *International Organization* 50(1): 109–139.

Gelazis, Nida M. (2000). "The Effects of EU Conditionality on Citizenship Policies and Protection of National Minorities in the Baltic States," European University Institute Working Paper, San Domenico di Fiesole, RSC No. 2000/68.

Gellner, Ernest (1993). "Reborn from Below: The Forgotten Beginnings of the Czech National Revival," *Times Literary Supplement*, May 14, 1993, 3–5.

Geremek, Bronislaw (1990). "Pour l'Europe," *Liber*, March 10.

GFK Slovakia (1998). "Public Awareness Campaign," SR 9516 02 02 April–July.

Gilbert, Geoff (1996). "The Council of Europe and Minority Rights," *Human Rights Quarterly* 18(1): 160–189.

Glenn, John K. (2001). *Framing Democracy: Civil Society and Civic Movements in Eastern Europe*. Stanford: Stanford University Press.

—— (2004). "From Nation-States to Member States: Accession Negotiations as an Instrument of Europeanization," *Comparative European Politics* 1(2): 3–28.

Goldstein, Judith (1996). "International law and domestic institutions: reconciling North American 'unfair' trade laws," *International Organization* 50(4): 541–564.

Gould, John (2001). "Beyond Creating Owners: Privatization and Democratization in the Slovak and Czech Republics, 1990–1998," Ph.D. Dissertation, Columbia University.

—— (2004). "Out of the Blue? Democracy and Privatization in Post-Communist Europe," *Comparative European Politics* 1(3): 277–311.

Gourevitch, Peter (1978). "The Second Image Reversed: The International Sources of Domestic Politics." *International Organization* 32(4): 881–912.

Gower, Jackie (1999). "EU Policy to Central and Eastern Europe," in Henderson (ed.), *Back to Europe: Central and Eastern Europe and the European Union*, London: UCL Press, 3–19.

Grabbe, Heather (1999). "A Partnership for Accession? The Implications of EU Conditionality For the Central and East European Applicants," European University Institute Working Paper, San Domenico di Fiesole, RSC No. 99/12.

—— (2001a). *Profiting from EU Enlargement*. London: Centre for European Reform.

—— (2001b). "How Does Europeanisation Affect CEE Governance? Conditionality, Diffusion and Diversity," *Journal of European Public Policy* 8(4): 1013–1031.

—— (2002). "Enlargement puts EU Credibility on the Line, Turkey is the Litmus Test," *The Wall Street Journal*, October 11.

—— (2003). "Europeanisation goes east: power and uncertainty in the EU accession process," in Kevin Featherstone and Claudio Radaelli (eds.), *The Politics of Europeanisation*. Oxford: Oxford University Press, 303–330.

—— and Kirsty Hughes (1998). *Enlarging the EU Eastwards*. London: Royal Institute of International Affairs.

Green Cowles, Maria and Michael Smith (eds.) (2000). *The State of the European Union, Risks, Reform, Resistance and Revival*. Oxford: Oxford University Press.

Greskovits, Bela (1998). *The Political Economy of Protest and Patience*. Budapest: Central European Press.

Grieco, Joseph M. (1995). "The Maastricht Treaty, Economic and Monetary Union and the Neo-Realist Research Programme," *Review of International Studies* 21(1): 21–40.

Grigorescu, Alexandru (2001). "Transferring Transparency: The Impact of European Institutions on East-Central Europe," in Linden (ed.), *Norms and Nannies: The Impact of International Organizations on the Central and Eastern European States*. Lanham, MD: Rowman & Littlefield, 59–87.

Gross, Jan T. (1992). "Poland: From Civil Society to Political Nation," in Banac (ed.), *Eastern Europe in Revolution*. Ithaca: Cornell University Press, 56–71.

Gruber, Lloyd (2000). *Ruling the World, Power Politics and the Rise of Supranational Institutions*. Princeton: Princeton University Press.

Grzymała-Busse, Anna (1998). "Reform Efforts in the Czech and Slovak Communist Parties and Their Successors, 1988–1993," *East European Politics and Societies* 12(3): 442–471.

—— (2002). *Redeeming the Communist Past*. Cambridge: Cambridge University Press.

—— (2003*a*). "Political Competition and the Politicization of the State in East Central Europe," *Comparative Political Studies* 36(10): 1123–1147.

—— (2003*b*). "Party Politics and Informal Institutions in East Central Europe," delivered at the conference "Evaulating Success and Failure in Postcommunist Reform," Claremont-Mckenna College, February.

—— and Abby Innes (2003). "Great Expectations: The EU and Domestic Political Competition in East Central Europe," *East European Politics and Societies* 17(1): 64–73.

Gyárfásová, Ol'ga (2001). "Slovensko a Svet," in Gyárfásová et al. (eds.), *Krajina v Pohybe, Správa o politických názoroch a hodnotách l'udí na Slovensku*. Bratislava: Institute for Public Affairs, 195–224.

Haas, Ernst B. (1958). *The Uniting of Europe: Political, Social and Economic Forces, 1950–1957*. Stanford: Stanford University Press.

Haggard, Stephen and Robert R. Kaufman (eds.) (1992). *The Politics of Economic Adjustment*. Princeton: Princeton University Press.

—— and Robert R. Kaufman (1995). *The Political Economy of Democratic Transitions*. Princeton: Princeton University Press.

—— and Steven B. Webb (1994). "Introduction," in Haggard and Webb (eds.), *Voting for Reform: Democracy, Political Liberalization, and Economic Adjustment*. New York: Oxford University Press, 1–36.

—— Marc A. Levy, Andrew Moravcsik, and Kalypso Nicolaidis (1993). "Integrating the Two Halves of Europe: Theories of Interests, Bargaining, and Institutions," in Keohane, Nye, and Hoffmann (eds.), *After the Cold War: International Institutions and State Strategies in Europe, 1989–91*. Cambridge, MA: Harvard University Press, 173–195.

Hall, Peter A. and Rosemary C. R. Taylor (1996). "Political Science and the Three New Institutionalisms," *Political Studies* 44: 936–957.

Hannum, Hurst (1996). *Autonomy, Sovereignty, and Self-Determination, The Accommodation of Conflicting Rights*. Philadelphia: University of Pennsylvania Press.

Hanson, Stephen E. (1995). "The Leninist Legacy and Institutional Change," *Comparative Political Studies* 28(2): 306–314.

—— (1998). "Analyzing Postcommunist Economic Change: A Review Essay," *East European Politics and Societies* 12(1): 145–170.

—— (2001). "Defining Democratic Consolidation," in Anderson, Fish, Hanson, and Roeder (eds.), *Postcommunism and the Theory of Democracy*. Princeton: Princeton University Press, 122–151.

Haughton, Tim (2001). "HZDS: The Ideology, Organization and Support Base of Slovakia's Most Successful Party," *Europe-Asia Studies* 53(5): 745–769.

Havel, Václav (1986). *Living in Truth*. London: Faber and Faber.

—— (1990*a*). Speech at Prague castle on the occasion of the visit of German President Richard von Weizsacker, March 15. All speeches in English at: http://old.hrad.cz/ president/Havel/speeches/index_uk.html.

—— (1990*b*). Speech at the European Parliament, Strasbourg, May 10.

—— (1991). Speech at NATO Headquarters, Brussels, March 21.

Hellman, Joel S. (1998). "Winners Take All: The Politics of Partial Reform in Postcommunist Transitions," *World Politics* 50(2): 203–234.

—— and Mark Schankerman (2000). "Intervention, Corruption and Capture: The Nexus Between Enterprises and the State," European Bank for Reconstruction and Development, Working Paper No. 58.

—— Geraint Jones and Daniel Kaufman (2000). "Seize the State, Seize the Day," World Bank, Policy Research Paper No. 2444.

Helsinki Committee, Bulgarian (1995). *Annual Report 1995.*

Henderson, Karen (ed.) (1999*a*). *Back to Europe: Central and Eastern Europe and the European Union.* London: UCL Press.

—— (1999*b*). "Slovakia and the Democratic Criteria for EU Accession," in Henderson (ed.), *Back to Europe: Central and Eastern Europe and the European Union.* London: UCL Press, 221–240.

—— (2001). *Slovakia: The Escape From Invisibility.* London: Routledge.

Higley, John, Jan Pakulski, and Włodzimierz Wesołowski (eds.) (1998). *Postcommunist Elites and Democracy in Eastern Europe.* New York: St. Martin's Press.

Hoffmann, Stanley (1966). "Obstinate or Obsolete? The Fate of the Nation-State and the Case of Western Europe," *Daedalus* 95: 862–914.

Holbrooke, Richard (1995). "America, A European Power," *Foreign Affairs* 74(2): 38–51.

Holmes, Stephen (1997). "Crime and Corruption after Communism: Introduction," *East European Constitutional Review* 6, 4: 6–8.

—— (2003). "A European *Doppelstaat?*" *East European Politics and Societies* 17(1): 107–118.

Hooghe, Liesbet (2001). *The European Commission and the Integration of Europe, Images of Governance.* Cambridge: Cambridge University Press.

—— and Gary Marks (2001). *Multi-Level Governance and European Integration.* Lanham, MD: Rowman & Littlefield.

—— and —— (2003). "Unraveling the Central State, but How? Types of Multilevel Governance," *American Political Science Review* 97(2): 233–243.

House of Lords (1992). "Enlargement of the Community," Select Committee on the E.C., June 9.

Howard, Marc Morjé (2003). *The Weakness of Civil Society in Post-Communist Europe.* Cambridge: Cambridge University Press.

Hunter, Robert E. (1999). "Maximizing NATO: a Relevant Alliance Knows How to Reach," *Foreign Affairs* 78(3): 190–203.

Huntington, Samuel P. (1991). *The Third Wave, Democratization in the Late Twentieth Century.* Norman: University of Oklahoma Press.

Hurrell, Andrew (1995). "Explaining the Resurgence of Regionalism in World Politics," *Review of International Studies* 21(4): 331–358.

Iankova, Elena A. (2002). *Eastern European Capitalism in the Making.* Cambridge: Cambridge University Press.

Innes, Abby (2001). *Czechoslovakia: The Short Goodbye.* New Haven: Yale University Press.

International Monetary Fund (1991), (1998), and (2003). *Direction of Trade Statistics Yearbook.*

Ionescu, Dan (1993). "Romania Admitted to the Council of Europe," *RFE/RL Research Report* 2(44): 40–45.

Ionescu, Dan (1994). "Romania's Standby Agreement with the IMF," *RFE/RL Research Report* 3(18): 21–26.

Ishiyama, John T. (1997). "The Sickle or the Rose? Previous Regime Type and the Evolution of Ex-Communist Parties," *Comparative Political Studies* 30: 299–234.

—— and Marijke Bruening (1998). *Ethnopolitics in the New Europe*. Boulder and London: Lynne Rienner.

Ishiyama, John T (ed.) (1999). *Communist Successor Parties in Post-Communist Politics*. Commack, New York: New Science Publishers.

Jackson Preece, Jennifer (1998). *National Minorities and the European Nation-State System*. Oxford: Clarendon Press.

Jacobs, Alan (2004). "Governing for the Long Term: Democratic Politics and Policy Investment," Ph.D. Dissertation, Harvard University.

Jacoby, Wade (1999a). "Priest and the Penitent: The European Union as a Force in the Domestic Politics of Eastern Europe," *East European Constitutional Review* 8(1–2): 62–67.

—— (1999b). "Exemplars, Analogies, and Menus: Eastern Europe in Cross Regional Comparisons," *Governance* 12(4): 455–478.

—— (2004). *The Enlargement of the European Union and NATO: Ordering from the Menu in Central Europe*. Cambridge: Cambridge University Press.

—— and Pavel Černoch (2002). "The Pivotal EU Role in the Creation of Czech Regional Policy," in Linden (ed.), *Norms and Nannies: The Impact of International Organizations on the Central and Eastern European States*. Lanham, MD: Rowman & Littlefield, 317–339.

Javorčík, Peter (2001). "Slovensko a Európska únia," in *Ročenka zahraničnej politiky Slovenskej republiky 2000*. Bratislava: Slovak Institute for International Studies.

Jeszenszky, Géza (1991). Speech at the Hungarian Parliament, Budapest, October 15, published by the Hungarian Ministry of Foreign Affairs as *Current Policy* 38.

—— (1992a). Interview in Magyar Nemzet, February 6, *Current Policy* 2.

—— (1992b). "Eastern Europe: The West Could Lead Us Forward," *International Herald Tribune*, October 22.

—— (1993). "Hungary's Foreign Policy Dilemmas," *The Hungarian Quarterly* 34(130): 3–13.

Jileva, Elena (2002a). "Insiders and Outsiders in Central and Eastern Europe: The Case of Bulgaria," in Kees Groenendijk, Elspeth Guild and Paul Minderhound eds., *In search of Europe's borders*. The Hague: Kluwer Law International, 273–288.

—— (2002b). "Visa and Free Movement of Labour: The Uneven Imposition of the EU acquis on the Accession States," *Journal of Ethnic and Migration Studies* 28(4): 683–700.

Jowitt, Ken (1992). *New World Disorder: The Leninist Extinction*. Berkeley: University of California Press.

Judt, Tony (1988). "The Dilemmas of Dissidence: The Politics of Opposition in East-Central Europe," *East European Politics and Society* 2(2): 185–240.

—— (1996). "Europe: The Grand Illusion," *New York Review of Books* 43(12) (11 July).

Kahler, Miles (1992). "External Influence, Conditionality, and the Politics of Adjustment," in Haggard and Kaufman (eds.), *The Politics of Economic Adjustment*, 89–136.

Kaminski, Bartlomiej (1994). "What Kind of Deal Have Central European Associates Got from the European Community?" World Bank, Working Paper.

—— (2001). "How Accession to the European Union has Affected External Trade and Foreign Direct Investment in Central European Economies." World Bank, Policy Research Paper No. 2578.

Karl, Terry Lynn (1995). "The Hybrid Regimes of Central America," *Journal of Democracy* 6(3): 72–87.

Kelley, Judith (2004a). *Ethnic Politics in Europe: The Power of Norms and Incentives*. Princeton: Princeton University Press.

—— (2004b). "International Actors on the Domestic Scene: Membership Conditionality and Socialization by International Institutions," *International Organization* 58(3): 425–457.

Kenny, Padraic (2002). *A Carnival of Revolution: Central Europe 1989*. Princeton: Princeton University Press.

Keohane, Robert O. (1989). "The Demand for International Regimes," in Keohane ed., *International Institutions and State Power*. Boulder: Westview Press, 101–131.

—— (1993). "Institutional Theory and the Realist Challenge after the Cold War," in David A. Baldwin (ed.), *Neorealism and Neoliberalism*. New York: Columbia University Press, 269–300.

—— (2002). *"Power and Governance in a Partially Globalized World,"* New York: Routledge.

—— and Stanley Hoffmann (1991). "Institutional Change in Europe in the 1980s," in Keohane and Hoffmann (eds.), *The New European Community: Decisionmaking and Institutional Change*. Boulder: Westview, 1–39.

—— and —— (1993). "Conclusions: Structure, Strategy, and Institutional Roles" in Keohane, Nye, and Hoffmann (eds.), *After the Cold War: International Institutions and State Strategies in Europe, 1989–91*. Cambridge, MA: Harvard University Press, 381–404.

—— and Helen Milner (eds.) (1996). *The Internationalization of Domestic Politics*. Cambridge: Cambridge University Press.

—— and Joseph S. Nye (1977). *Power and Interdependence*. Boston: Little Brown.

—— Joseph S. Nye, and Stanley Hoffmann (eds.) (1993). *After the Cold War: International Institutions and States Strategies in Europe, 1989–91*. Cambridge, MA: Harvard University Press.

King, Charles (2000). "Post-Postcommunist: Transition, Comparison, and the End of 'Eastern Europe,' " *World Politics* 53(1): 143–172.

King, Gary, Robert O. Keohane, and Sidney Verba (eds.) (1994). *Designing Social Inquiry: Scientific Inference in Qualitative Research*. Princeton: Princeton University Press.

Kis, Janos (1989). *Politics in Hungary: For a Democratic Alternative*. Boulder: Social Science Monographs, distributed by Columbia University Press.

Kitschelt, Herbert (1995). "Formation of Party Cleavages in Post-Communist Democracies: Theoretical Propositions," *Party Politics* 1(4): 447–472.

—— (1999). "Accounting for Outcomes of Post-Communist Regime Change. Causal Depth and Shallowness in Rival Explanations," delivered at the Annual Meeting of the American Political Science Association, Atlanta, September.

—— (2001). "Post-Communist Economic Reform. Causal Mechanisms and Concomitant Properties," delivered at the Annual Meeting of the American Political Science Association, San Francisco, August.

Kitschelt, Herbert (2003*a*). "Accounting for Postcommunist Regime Diversity, What Counts as a Good Cause?," in Ekiert and Hanson (eds.), *Capitalism and Democracy in Central and Eastern Europe: Assessing the Legacy of Communist Rule.* Cambridge: Cambridge University Press, 49–88.

—— (2003*b*). "What Helps To Advance Market Liberal Economics in Post-Communist Countries?," unpublished manuscript.

—— Zdenka Mansfeldova, Radoslaw Markowski, and Gábor Tóka (1999). *Post-Communist Party Systems: Competition, Representation, and Inter-Party Cooperation.* Cambridge: Cambridge University Press.

Klíma, Michal (2000). *Kvalita Demokracie v České Republice a volební inženýrství.* Prague: Radix.

Koinova, Maria (2001). "Saxcoburggotsky and His Catch-All Atitude: Cooperation or Cooptation?" *Southeast European Politics* 2(2): 135–140.

Kolakowski, Leszek (1992). "Amidst Moving Ruins," *Daedalus* 121(2): 43–56.

Kolankiewicz, George (1994). "Consensus and Competition in the Eastern Enlargement of the European Union," *International Affairs* 70, 3: 477–483.

Kolarova, Rumyana (1996). "Bulgaria: Could We Regain What We Have Already Lost?," *Social Research* 63, 2: 543–559.

Kollár, Miroslav and Grigorij Mesežnikov (2002*a*). "Introduction," in Kollár and Mesežnikov (eds.), *Slovenkso 2002, Súrnná správa o stave spoločnosti.* Bratislava: Institute of Public Affairs, 7–15.

—— and —— (eds.) (2002*b*). *Predsavzatia a Skutočnost', Hodnotenie Plnenia Programového vyhlásenia vlády Milukáša Dzurindu.* Bratislava: Institute for Public Affairs.

Kontra, Martin and Jaroslav Špurný (1998). "Třetí pokus se jmenuje NATO: Ospalost' hlavní překážkou na cestě k diplomatickému úspechu století," *Respekt,* 9(9) (March 9), 9–11.

Kopstein, Jeffrey and David Reilly (1999). "Explaining the Why and When: A Comment on Fish's Determinants of Economic Reforms in the Post-Communist World," *East European Politics and Societies* 13(3): 613–626.

—— and —— (2000). "Geographic Diffusion and the Transformation of Postcommunist Europe," *World Politics* 53(1): 1–37.

Kornai, János and Susan Rose-Ackerman (eds.) (2004). *Building a Trustworthy State in Post-Socialist Transition.* New York: Palgrave MacMillan.

Köves, András (1992). *Central and East European Economies in Transition.* San Francisco: Westview Press.

Krastev, Ivan (2003). "Bulgaria" in Adrian Karatnycky, Alexander Motyl and Amanda Schnetzer (eds.), *Nations in Transit 2003: Democratization in East Central Europe and Eurasia,* Lanham, MD: Freedom House and Routledge, 176–193.

Krok-Paszkowska, Anna and Jan Zielonka (2000). "The EU's Next Big Enlargement: Empirical Data on the Candidates' Perceptions," European University Institute Working Paper, San Domenico di Fiesole, RSC No. 2000/54.

Kubicek, Paul (ed.) (2004*a*). *The European Union and Democratization*. London: Routledge.

—— (2004*b*). "Competing Views of Turkey's Place in Europe," paper presented at the conference "The New Face of Europe," Center for European Studies, University of Florida, February 27–28.

Kubičko, Ratko and Petr Příhoda (2001). "Kam to dopracovaly naše strany," *Přitomnost*, Spring, 7–10. http://www.pritomnost.cz./index.php?clanek=1862.

Kubik, Jan (1994). *The Power of Symbols Against the Symbols of Power*. University Park: University of Pennsylvania Press.

Kundera, Milan (1984). "A Kidnapped West, or Culture Bows Out," *Granta* 11: 95–118.

Kupchan, Charles (1998). "After Pax Americana: Benign Power, Regional Integration, and the Sources of a Stable Multipolarity." *International Security* 23(2): 40–79.

Kurtz, Marcus J. and Andrew S. Barnes (2002). "The Political Foundations of Post-Communist Regimes: Marketization, Agrarian Legacies, or International Influences," *Comparative Political Studies* 35(5): 524–553.

Laba, Roman (1991). *The Roots of Solidarity*. Princeton: Princeton University Press.

Legro, Jeffrey W. and Andrew Moravcsik (1999). "Is Anybody Still A Realist?," *International Security* 24(2): 5–55.

Leigh, Michael (2000). "Public Attitudes to EU Enlargement," in Bruno Cautrès and Dominique Reynié (eds.), *L'Opinion Européenne*. Paris: Presses de la Fondation Nationales des Sciences Politiques, 85–93.

—— (2003). "The Czech Republic as an EU candidate: strengths and weaknesses," in Rupnik and Zielonka (eds.), *The Road to the European Union: The Czech and Slovak Republics*. Manchester: Manchester University Press, 87–97.

Leško, Marián (1997). *Mečiar a mečiarizmus, Politik bez skrupúl, politika bez zábran*. Bratislava: VMV.

Leslie, Peter (2000). "Abuses of Asymmetry: Privilege and Exclusion," in Karlheinz Neunnreither and Antje Wiener (eds.), *European Integration After Amsterdam: Institutional Dynamics and Prospects for Democracy*. Oxford: Oxford University Press, 192–217.

Levitsky, Steven and Lucan A. Way (2002). "The Rise of Competitive Authoritarianism," *Journal of Democracy* 13 (2): 51–65.

—— and —— (2003). "Ties that Bind? International Linkage and Competitive Authoritarian Regime Change in the Post-Cold War Era," delivered at the Annual Meeting of the American Political Science Association, August, Philadelphia.

Lieven, Anatol and Dmitri Trenin (eds.) (2003). *Ambivalent Neighbors, The EU, NATO and the Price of Membership*. Washington DC: Carnegie Endowment for International Peace.

Light, Duncan and David Phinnemore (eds.) (2001). *Post-Communist Romania, Coming to Terms with Transition*. Houndsmills, Basingstoke: Palgrave.

Linden, Ronald H. (ed.) (2001*a*). *Norms and Nannies: The Impact of International Organizations on the Central and Eastern European States*. Lanham, MD: Rowman & Littlefield.

—— (2001*b*). "Conclusion: International Organizations and East Europe—Bringing Parallel Tracks Together," in Linden (ed.), *Norms and Nannies: The Impact of*

International Organizations on the Central and Eastern European States. Lanham, MD: Rowman & Littlefield, 369–382.

Linz, Juan J. and Alfred Stepan (1996). *Problems of Democratic Transition and Consolidation: Southern Europe, South America, and Post-Communist Europe.* Baltimore: John Hopkins Press.

Lukáč, Pavol (2001). "Visegrad Cooperation: Ideas, Developments and Prospects," *Slovak Foreign Policy Affairs* 2(1): 6–23.

Luong, Pauline Jones (2002). *Institutional Change and Political Continuity in Post-Soviet Central Asia.* Cambridge: Cambridge University Press.

Mair, Peter (1996). "What is Different About Post-Communist Party Systems?" *Studies of Public Policy* 259, University of Strathclyde.

—— and Jan Zielonka (eds.) (2002). *Enlarged European Union: Diversity and Adaptation.* London: Frank Cass.

Málová, Darina and Tim Haughton (2002). "Making Institutions in Central and Eastern Europe, and the impact of Europe," *West European Politics* 25(3): 101–124.

Mandelbaum, Michael (1995). "Preserving the New Peace: the Case Against NATO Expansion," *Foreign Affairs* 74(3): 9–13.

Mansfield, Edward (1994). "Alliances, Preferential Trading Arrangements and Sanctions," *Journal of International Affairs* 48(1): 119–139.

—— and Jack Snyder (1995). "Democratization and the Danger of War," *International Security* 20(1): 5–38.

March, James and Johan P. Olsen (1998). "The Institutional Dynamics of International Political Orders," *International Organization* 52(4): 943–969.

Martin, Lisa (2000). *Democratic Commitments, Legislatures and International Cooperation.* Princeton: Princeton University Press.

Mattli, Walter (1999). *The Logic of Regional Integration, Europe and Beyond.* New York: Cambridge University Press.

—— and Thomas Plümper (2002). "The Demand-Side Politics of EU Enlargement: Democracy and the Application for EU Membership," *Journal of European Public Policy* 9(4): 555–574.

Mayhew, Alan (1998). *Recreating Europe: The European Union's Policy towards Central and Eastern Europe.* Cambridge: Cambridge University Press.

Mazey, Sonia and Jeremy Richardson (2001). "Institutionalizing Promiscuity: Commission-Interest Group Relations in the European Union," in Stone Sweet, Sandholtz, and Fligstein (eds.), *The Institutionalization of Europe.* Oxford: Oxford University Press, 71–93.

Mazower, Mark (1998). *Dark Continent, Europe's Twentieth Century.* London: Vintage Books.

McFaul, Michael (2002). "The Fourth Wave of Democracy *and* Dictatorship: Noncooperative Transitions in the Postcommunist World," *World Politics* 54(2): 212–244.

Mearsheimer, John J. (1990). "Back to the Future: Instability in Europe After the Cold War," *International Security* 15(1): 5–56.

—— (1994). "The False Promise of International Institutions," *International Security* 19(3): 5–49.

—— (1995). "A Realist Reply," *International Security* 20(1): 82–93.

Mendelson, Sarah E. and John K. Glenn (eds.) (2002). *The Power and Limits of NGOs: A Critical Look at Building Democracy in Eastern Europe and Eurasia.* New York: Columbia University Press.

Mesežnikov, Grigorij (1998). "Vnútropolitický vývoj a systém politických strán," in Bútora and Ivantyšyn (eds.), *Slovensko 1997, Súhrnná správa o stave spoločnosti.* Bratislava: Institute for Public Affairs, 19–98.

—— and Martin Bútora (eds.) (1997). *Slovenské referendum '97: Zrod, priebeh, dosledky.* Bratislava: Institute for Public Affairs.

Michnik, Adam (1985a). *Letters from Prison and Other Essays.* Berkeley: University of California Press.

—— (1985b). *Takie Czasy... rzecz o kompromisie.* London: Aneks.

—— (1998). *Letters from Freedom.* Berkeley: University of California Press.

—— (1999). "The Return to History," speech delivered at the Forum 2000 conference, Prague, October 12. All Forum 2000 speeches at: http://www.forum2000.cz/forum2000.html.

Mihalka, Michael (1995). "The Bumpy Road to Western Europe," *Transition* 1(1): 73–79.

Mikloš, Ivan (1998a). "Privatizácia," in Bútora and Ivantyšyn, (eds.), *Slovensko 1997, Súhrnná správa o stave spoločnosti.* Bratislava: Institute for Public Affairs, 405–431.

—— (1998b). "Odpočet," *Domino-fórum* 7 (July 2–9): 7–9.

Millard, Frances (2002). "Polish Domestic Politics and accession to the European Union," in Henderson (ed.), *Back to Europe: Central and Eastern Europe and the European Union.* London: UCL Press 203–219.

Milner, Helen (1992). "International Theories of Cooperation Among Nations: Strengths and Weaknesses," *World Politics* 44(3): 466–496.

Mishler, William and Richard Rose (1996). "Trajectories of Fear and Hope, Support for Democracy in Post-Communist Europe, "*Comparative Political Studies* 28(4): 553–581.

Moravcsik, Andrew (1991). "Negotiating the Single European Act: National Interests and Conventional Statecraft in the European Community," *International Organization* 45(1): 19–56.

—— (1993). "Preferences and Power in the European Community: Liberal Intergovernmentalist Approach," *Journal of Common Market Studies* 31(3): 473–524.

—— (1997). "Taking Preferences Seriously: A Liberal Theory of International Politics." *International Organization* 51(4): 513–553.

—— (1998a). *The Choice for Europe: Social Purpose and State Power from Messina to Maastricht.* Ithaca: Cornell University Press.

—— (1998b). "Europe's Integration at Centruy's End," in Moravcsik (ed.), *Centralization or Fragmentation? Europe Facing the Challenges of Deepening, Diversity, and Democracy.* New York: Council on Foreign Relations, 1–58.

—— (1999). "Supranational Entrepreneurs and International Cooperation," *International Organization* 53 (2): 267–306.

—— (2003). "The Quiet Superpower," *Newsweek*, June 17.

Moravcsik, Andrew and Milada Anna Vachudova (2003*a*). "National Interests, State Power and EU Enlargement," Center for European Studies, Harvard University, Working Paper No. 97.
http://www.ces.fas.harvard.edu/working_papers/CES_papers.html.
—— and —— (2003*b*). "National Interests, State Power and EU Enlargement," *East European Politics and Societies* 17(1): 42–57.
Mungiu, Alina (1996). "Intellectuals as Political Actors in Eastern Europe: The Romanian Case," *East European Politics and Societies* 10(2): 333–364.
—— and Andrei Pippidi (1994). "Letter from Romania," *Government and Opposition* 29(3): 348–361.
Mungiu-Pippidi, Alina and Sorin Ioniţă (2001). "Interpreting an Electoral Setback," *East European Constitutional Review* 10(1): 86–91.
—— and Aurelian Muntean (2003). "The Failure of Public Governance in Romania," Paper presented at the NISPAcee Conference, April 9–12, Bucharest, Romania.
Nedeva, Ivanka (1993). "Democracy Building in Ethnically Diverse Societies: The Cases of Bulgaria and Romania," in Ian M. Cuthbertson and Jane Leibowitz (eds.), *Minorities: The New Europe's Old Issue*. New York: Institute for EastWest Studies, 123–150.
Nicolaides, Phedon (2003). "Preparing for Accession to the European Union: How to Establish Capacity for Effective and Credible Application of EU Rules," in Cremona (ed.), *The Enlargement of the European Union*, Oxford: Oxford University Press, 43–78.
Nicolaidis, Kalypso (1993). "East European Trade in the Aftermath of 1989: Did International Institutions Matter?" in Keohane, Nye, and Hoffmann (eds.), *After the Cold War International Institutions and State Strategies in Europe, 1989–91*. Cambridge, MA: Harvward University Press, 196–245.
Norman, Peter (2003). *The Accidental Constitution*. Brussels: EuroComment.
North, Douglass (1989). *Structure and Change in Economic History*. New York: W. W. Norton & Company.
—— (1990). *Institutions, Institutional Change and Economic Performance*. Cambridge: Cambridge University Press.
Oatley, Thomas (2004). *International Political Economy: Interests and Institutions in the Global Economy*. New York: Pearson Longman.
OECD (2003). GDP per capita, 2002, at current prices in US dollars. http://www.oecd.org/dataoecd/48/5/2371372.pdf.
Offe, Claus (1991). "Capitalism by Democratic Design? Democratic Theory Facing the Triple Transition in East Central Europe," *Social Research*, 58(4): 865–892.
Orenstein, Mitchell (1998). "A Genealogy of Communist Successor Parties in East Central Europe and the Determinants of their Success," *East European Politics and Societies* 12(3): 472–499.
—— (2001). *Out of the Red: Building Capitalism and Democracy in Postcommunist Europe*, Ann Arbor: Michigan University Press.
Ost, David (1990). *Solidarity and the Politics of Anti-Politics*. Philadelphia: Temple University Press.
Ottaway, Marina and Thomas Carothers (eds.) (2000). *Funding Virtue: Civil Society Aid and Democracy Promotion*. New York: Carnegie Endowment for International Peace.

Papagianni, Katia (2002). "The Making of Minority Policies in the Context of an Emerging European Regime on Minority Rights," unpublished manuscript.

—— (2003). "The Role of European Integration and International Norms on Minority Rights in Estonian and Latvian Ethnic Politics in the 1990s," Delivered at the Annual Meeting of the American Political Science Association, Philadelphia, August.

Pehe, Jiří (2002). *Vytunelovaná demokracie*. Prague: Academia.

Petre, Zoe (1999). "The Role of the President in Romania's Approach to NATO Integration," in Kurt W. Treptow and Mihail E. Ionescu (eds.), *Romania and Euro-Atlantic Integration*. Iaşi: The Center for Romanian Studies, 91–102.

Pevehouse, Jon C. (2002). "Democracy from the Outside-In? International Organizations and Democratization," *International Organization* 56(3): 515–549.

Phinnemore, David (2001). "Romania and Euro-Atlantic Integration since 1989: a Decade of Frustration?," in Light and Phinnemore (eds.), *Post-Communist Romania: Comming to Terms with Transition*. Houndsmills, Basingstoke: Palgrave, 245–269.

Pierson, Paul (1996). "The Path to European Integration: A Historical Institutionalist Analysis," *Comparative Political Studies* 29(2): 123–163.

—— (2000). "The Limits of Design: Explaining Institutional Origins and Change," *Governance* 13, (4): 475–499.

PlanEcon (2001). *PlanEcon Review and Outlook for Eastern Europe*.

Pollack, Mark (2003). *The Engines of European Integration: Delegation, Agency, and Agenda Setting in the EU*. Oxford: Oxford University Press.

Pop-Eleches, Grigore (2001). "Romania's Politics of Dejection," *Journal of Democracy* 12(3): 156–169.

Popescu, Liliana (1997). "A Change of Power in Romania: The Results and Significance of the November 1996 Elections," *Government and Opposition*, 32(2): 172–186.

Potůček, Martin (1998). "Havel versus Klaus: Public Policymaking in the Czech Republic," Lecture at the Institute for Human Sciences (IWM), Vienna, January 27.

Pridham, Geoffrey (ed.) (1991). *Encouraging Democracy: The International Context of Regime Transition in Southern Europe*. Leicester: Leicester University Press.

—— (2002). "The European Union's democratic conditionality and domestic politics in Slovakia: the Mečiar and the Dzurinda governments compared," *Europe-Asia Studies* 54(2): 203–227.

—— and Attila Ágh (eds.) (2001) *Prospects for Democratic Consolidation in East-Central Europe*. Manchester: Manchester University Press.

—— and Tom Gallagher (eds.) (2000). *Experimenting with Democracy, Regime Change in the Balkans*. London: Routledge.

—— Eric Herring, and George Sanford (eds.) (1997). *Building Democracy? The International Dimension of Democratization in Eastern Europe*. London: Leicester University Press.

Przeworski, Adam (1991). *Democracy and the Market, Political and economic reforms in Eastern Europe and Latin America*. Cambridge: Cambridge University Press.

—— (1999). *Democracy, Accountability, and Representation*, New York: Cambridge University Press.

Przeworski, Adam and Fernando Limongi (1997). "Modernization: Theories and Facts," *World Politics* 49(2): 155–183.

—— and Henry Teune (1970). *The Logic of Comparative Social Inquiry*. New York: Wiley-Interscience.

—— Michael E. Alvarez, Jose Antonio Cheibub, and Fernando Limongi (2002). *Democracy and Development, Political Institutions and Well-Being in the World, 1950–1990*. Cambridge: Cambridge University Press, 142–179.

Radaelli, Claudio (2001). "Whither Europeanization? Concept Stretching and Substantive Change," *European Integration Online Papers (EIOP)* 4(8) (July).

Rady, Martyn (1992). *Romania in Turmoil*. New York: St Martin's Press, 91–144.

Ragin, Charles (1987). *The Comparative Method: Moving Beyond Qualitative and Quantitative Strategies*. Berkeley: University of California Press.

Redmond, John and Glenda G. Rosenthal (eds.) (1998). *The Expanding European Union: Past, Present, Future*. Boulder: Lynne Rienner.

Reiter, Dan (2001). "Why NATO Enlargement Does Not Spread Democracy," *International Security* 25(4): 41–67.

Reisch, Alfred A. (1994). "The New Hungarian Government's Foreign Policy," *RFE/RL Research Report* 3(33): 46–57.

Remmer, Karen (1996). "The Sustainability of Political Democracy: Lessons from South America," *Comparative Political Studies* 29(6): 611–634.

Risse, Thomas (1999). "International Norms and Domestic Change: Arguing and Communicative Behavior in the Human Rights Area," *Politics & Society* 27(4): 529–559.

—— (2000). "Let's Argue! Communicative Action in World Politics, "*International Organization* 54(1): 1–39.

—— Stephen C. Ropp, and Kathryn Sikkink (eds.) (1999). *The Power of Human Rights: International Norms and Domestic Change*. Cambridge: Cambridge University Press.

Roeder, Philip G. (1999). "The Revolution of 1989: Postcommunism and the Social Sciences," *Slavic Review* 58(4): 743–755.

—— (2001). "The Rejection of Authoritarianism," in Anderson, Fish, Hanson, and Roeder (eds.), *Postcommunism and the Theory of Democracy*, Princeton: Princeton University Press, 11–53.

Rollo Jim (1993). "Maybe Not Even Jam for East Europe," *Financial Times*, June 18.

—— and Alisdair Smith (1993). "EC Trade with Eastern Europe," *Economic Policy* 8 (16): 139–181.

Roper, Steven D. (1999). "Romania," in Julie Smith and Elizabeth Teague (eds.), *Democracy in the New Europe, The Politics of Post-Communism*. London: The Greycoat Press, 173–191.

Rose, Gideon (1998). "Neoclassical Realism and Theories of Foreign Policy," *World Politics* 51(1): 144–172.

Rose, Richard (2002). "A Bottom up Evaluation of Enlargement Countries, "*Studies of Public Policy* 364, University of Strathclyde.

—— William Mishler, and Christian Haerpfer (1998). *Democracy and Its Alternatives: Understanding Postcommunist Societies*. Baltimore: Johns Hopkins University Press.

Rose-Ackerman, Susan (2004). "Public Participation in Consolidating Democracies: Hungary and Poland," in Kornai and Rose-Ackerman (eds.), *Building a Trustworthy State in Post-Socialist Transition*. New York: Palgrave Macmillan, 9–28.

Rothschild, Joseph (1974). *East Central Europe between the Two World Wars*. Seattle: University of Washington Press.

Ruggie, John Gerard (1992). "Multilateralism: The Anatomy of An Institution," *International Organization* 46(3): 561–598.

Rupnik, Jacques (1994). "Europe's New Frontiers: Remapping Europe," *Daedalus* 123(3): 91–115.

—— (1997). "Still Underestimating the European Union," *The New Presence* 11 (November). http://www.pritomnost.cz/index.php?clanek=1059.

—— (2000). "Eastern Europe: The International Context," *Journal of Democracy* 11(2): 115–129.

—— and Jan Zielonka (eds.) (2003). *The Road to the European Union: The Czech and Slovak Republics*. Manchester: Manchester University Press.

Rupp, Michael Alexander (1999). "The Pre-Accession Strategy and Governmental Structures of the Visegrad Countries," in Henderson (ed.), *Back to Europe: Central and Eastern Europe and the European Union*. London: UCL Press, 89–106.

Sandholtz, Wayne and John Zysman (1989). "1992: Recasting the European Bargain," *World Politics* 42(1): 95–128.

—— and Alec Stone Sweet (eds.) (1998). *European Integration and Supranational Governance*. Oxford: Oxford University Press.

Sándor, Eleonóra (1997). "The Slovak-Hungarian Basic Treaty," in Martin Bútora and Péter Hunčík (eds.), *Global Report on Slovakia, Comprehensive Analyses from 1995 and Trends from 1996*. Bratislava: Sándor Márai Foundation, 55–61.

Sasse, Gwendolyn (2004). "Minority Rights and EU Enlargement: Normative Overstretch or Effective Conditionality?," in Gabriel N. Toggenburg (ed.), *Minority Protection and the Enlarged European Union: The Way Forward*. Budapest: OSI, Local Government and Public Service Reform Initiative, 59–83.

Schimmelfennig, Frank (2001). "The Community Trap: Liberal Norms, Rhetorical Action, and the Eastern Enlargement of the European Union," *International Organization* 55(1): 47–80.

Schimmelfennig, Frank (2003). *The EU, NATO and the Integration of Europe*. Cambridge: Cambridge University Press.

—— Stefan Engert, and Heiko Knobel (2003). "Costs, Commitment and Compliance: The Impact of EU Democratic Conditionality on Latvia, Slovakia and Turkey," *Journal of Common Market Studies* 41(3): 495–518.

—— and Ulrich Sedelmeier (eds.) (2005). *The Europeanization of Central and Eastern Europe*. Ithaca: Cornell University Press.

Schmitter, Philippe (1986). "An Introduction to Southern European Transitions," in Guillermo O'Donnell, Philippe Schmitter, and Laurence Whitehead (eds.), *Transitions from Authoritarian Rule: Southern Europe*. Baltimore: Johns Hopkins University Press, 3–10.

Schmitter, Philippe C. (1969). "Three Neofunctional Hypotheses about International Integration," *International Organization* 23: 161–166.

Schmitter, Philippe C. (2001). "The Influence of International Context Upon the Choice of National Institutions and Policies in Neo-Democracies," in Whitehead (ed.), *International Dimensions, of Democratization: Europe and the American, Expanded Edition*. Oxford: Oxford University Press, 26–54.

—— and Imco Brouwer (1999). "Conceptualizing, Researching and Evaluating Democracy Promotion and Protection," European University Institute Working Paper, San Domenico di Fiesole, SPS No. 99/9.

—— and Terry Lynn Karl (1991). "What Democracy Is... and Is Not," *Journal of Democracy* 2 (3): 75–88.

—— and Terry Lynn Karl (1994). "The Conceptual Travels of Transitologists and Consolidologists: How Far to the East Should They Attempt to Go," *Slavic Review* 53(1): 173–185.

Schöpflin, George (2000). *Nations, Identity Power. The New Politics of Europe*. London: Hurst and Company.

Schumpeter, Joseph (1950). *Capitalism, Socialism and Democracy*, 3rd edn. New York: Harper & Brothers.

Sedelmeier, Ulrich (1998). "The European Union's Association Policy Towards the Countries of Central Europe: Collective EU Identity and Policy Paradigms in a Composite Policy," Ph.D. Thesis, University of Sussex.

—— (1999). "Accommodation Beyond Self-Interest: Identity, Policy Paradigms, and the Limits of a Rationalist Approach to EU Policy Towards Central Europe," paper presented at the European Community Studies Association (ECSA) Conference, Pittsburgh, June 3–5.

—— (2003). "EU Enlargement, Identity and the Analysis of European Foreign Policy," European University Institute Working Paper, San Domenico di Fiesole, RSC No. 2003/513.

—— and Helen Wallace (2000). "Eastern Enlargement: Strategy or Second Thoughts?," in Wallace and Wallace (eds.), *Policy Making in the European Union*. Oxford: Oxford University Press, 427–461.

Senior Nello, Susan and Karen E. Smith (1998). *The European Union and Central and Eastern Europe: The Implications of Enlargement in Stages*. Aldershot: Ashgate Publishing.

Shafir, Michael (2001). "The Ciorbea Government and Democratization: A Preliminary Assessment," in Light and Phinnemore (eds.), *Post-Communist Romania, Coming to Terms with Transition*. Houndsmills, Basingstoke: Palgrave, 79–103.

—— (1997). "Romania's Road to Normalcy," *Journal of Democracy* 8(2): 144–158.

—— (1995a). "Ruling Party Formalizes Relationship with Extremists," *Transition* 1(5): 41–46.

—— (1995b). "The Centripetfugal Process of Unifying the Liberals," *Transition* 1(15): 49–53.

Shattuck, John and J. Brian Atwood (1997). "Defending Democracy: Why Democrats Trump Autocrats," *Foreign Affairs* 76(6): 167–170.

Šimečka, Martin (1998). "Média na Slovensku—monopol vlády a monopol opozice," *Nová Přítomnost* 1(January), 26–27.

Simons, Thomas W., Jr. (1993). *Eastern Europe in the Postwar World*, 2nd edn. New York: St. Martin's Press.

Sissenich, Beate (2002). "The Diffusion of EU Social Policy in Poland and Hungary," in Linden (ed.), *Norms and Nannies: The Impact of International Organization on Central and Eastern European States*. Lanham, MD: Rowman & Littlefield, 287–315.

—— (2003). "State-Building by a Non-State: European Union Enlargement and Social Policy Transfer to Poland and Hungary," Ph.D. Dissertation, Cornell University.

—— (2004). "European Union Policies Toward Accession Countries," paper presented at the conference "Public Opinion About the EU," Indiana University, April 2–3.

Sjursen, Helen (2002). "Why expand? The Question of Legitimacy and Justification in the EU's Enlargement Policy, "*Journal of Common Market Studies* 40(3): 491–513.

Skalnik Leff, Carol (1996). "Dysfunctional Democratization? Institutional Conflict in Post-Communist Slovakia," *Problems of Post-Communism* 43(5): 36–50.

Skilling, H. Gordon (1973). "Opposition in Communist East Europe," in Robert A. Dahl (ed.), *Regimes and Oppositions*. New Haven: Yale University Press, 89–119.

Slobodník, Dušan (1996). "Sharon Fisherová (a kto v tieni za ňou?) versus Slovenkso: Informačný smog zahmlieva a deformuje pravdu," *Slovenksá Republika*, November 4.

Slovak Democratic Coalition (SDK) (1998). "Volebný program: Spolu za lepšie Slovensko."

Slovak Republic, Ministry of Foreign Affairs (1994). "Správa o plnění úloh a aktuálnych ceil'och zachraničnej politiky Slovenskej republiky," Document No. 50472/94, January 1994.

Smith, Karen E. (1999). *The Making of EU Foreign Policy: The Case of Eastern Europe*. London: Macmillan.

—— (2003). "The Evolution and Application of EU Membership Conditionality," in Cremona (ed.), *The Enlargement of the European Union*. Oxford: Oxford University Press, 105–139.

Smolar, Aleksander (2001). "History and Memory: The Revolutions of 1989–91," *Journal of Democracy* 12(3): 5–19.

Snyder, Jack (2000). *From Voting to Violence: Democratization and Nationalist Conflict*. New York: W. W. Norton & Company.

Snyder, Timothy (2003). *The Reconstruction of Nations: Poland, Ukraine, Lithuania, Belarus, 1569–1999*. New Haven: Yale University Press.

Stark, David and Laszlo Bruszt (1998). *Postsocialist Pathways: Transforming Politics and Property in East Central Europe*. Cambridge: Cambridge University Press.

Stein, Jonathan (2000). "National Minorities and Political Development in Post-Communist Europe," in Stein (ed.), *The Politics of National Minority Participation in Post-Communist Europe—State-Building, Democracy, and Ethnic Mobilization*. New York: M. E. Sharpe, 1–30.

Stokes, Gale (1993). *The Walls Came Tumbling Down, The Collapse of Communism in Eastern Europe*. New York: Oxford University Press.

Stone Sweet, Alec, Neil Fligstein, and Wayne Sandholtz (2001a). "The Institutionalization of European Space," in Stone Sweet, Sandholtz, and Fligstein (eds.), *The Institutionalization of Europe*. Oxford: Oxford University Press, 1–28.

Stone Sweet, Alec, Wayne Sandholtz, and Neil Fligstein (eds.) (2001*b*). *The Institutionalization of Europe*. Oxford: Oxford University Press.

Szacki, Jerzy (1995). *Liberalism After Communism*. Budapest: Central European University Press.

Szajkowski, Bogdan (ed.) (1994). *Political Parties of Eastern Europe, Russia and the Successor States*. Harlow, UK: Longman.

Szilagyi, Zsofia (1996). "Hungarian Minority Summit Upsets Slovak and Romanian Leaders," *OMRI Daily Digest*, July 9.

Szomolányi, Soňa (1997). *Slovenkso: Problémy konsolidácie demokracie, Spor o pravidllá hry pokračuje*. Bratislava: Nadácia Friedricha Eberta.

—— (ed.) (2000). "November 1989: Otvorenie kl'ukatej cesty k demokracii," in Jan Pesek and Soňa Szomolányi (eds.), *November 1989 na Slovensku*. Bratislava: Nádacia Milana Šimečku, 92–110.

—— and John Gould (eds.) (1997*a*). *Slovakia: Problems of Democratic Consolidation and the Struggle for the Rules of the Game*. New York: Columbia International Affairs Online. http://www.ciaonet.org/book/gould/gould.html.

—— and —— (1997*b*). "Vít'az neberie všetko," *Domino-fórum* 37.

—— and Grigorij Mesežnikov (eds.) (1995). *Slovakia: Parliamentary Elections 1994*. Bratislava: Friedrich Ebert Foundation.

Taggart, Paul and Aleks Szerbiak (2001). "Parties, Positions and Europe: Eurscepticism in the EU Candidate States of Central and Eastern Europe," Sussex European Institute, Working Paper No. 46.

Tang, Helena (2000). *Winners and Losers in EU Integration: Policy Issues for Central and Eastern Europe*. Washington, DC: World Bank.

Tarschys, Daniel (1995). "The Council of Europe: The Challenge of Enlargement," *World Today* 51(4): 62–64.

Terry, Sarah Meiklejohn (2000). "Poland's Foreign Policy Since 1989: The Challenges of Independence," *Communist and Post-Communist Studies* 33: 7–47.

Tesser, Lynn M. (2003*a*). "The Geopolitics of Tolerance: Minority Rights under EU Expansion in East-Central Europe," *East European Politics and Societies* 17(3): 483–532.

—— (2003*b*). "Europeanization and Prospects for Nationalism in East-Central Europe," Ph.D. Dissertation, University of Chicago.

Tismaneau, Vladimir, (1998). *Fantasies of Salvation, Democracy, Nationalism and Myth in Post-Communist Europe*. Princeton: Princeton University Press.

—— (2002). "Discomforts of Victory: Democracy, Liberal Values and Nationalism in Post-Communist Europe," in Mair and Zielonka (eds.), *Enlarged European Union*, 81–100.

—— and Dorian Tudoran (1993). "The Bucharest Syndrome," *Journal of Democracy* 4(1): 41–52.

—— and Gail Kligman (2001). "Romania's First Postcommunist Decade: From Iliescu to Iliescu," *East European Constitutional Review* 10(1): 78–85.

Tóka, Gábor (1997). "Political Parties in East Central Europe," in Larry Diamond, Marc F. Plattner, Yun-han Chu, and Hung-mao Tien (eds.), *Consolidating the Third Wave Democracies*. Baltimore: Johns Hopkins Press, 93–134.

Tokés, Rudolf (1996). *Hungary's Negotiated Revolution*. Cambridge: Cambridge University Press.

Torreblanca, José I. (2002). "Accomodating interests and principles in the European Union: The Case of Eastern Enlargement," in Helen Sjursen (ed.), *Enlargement and the Finality of the EU*. ARENA Report No. 7/2002, 7–33.

Tóth, Peter (1997). "Vláda sposobila nárast organizovaného zločinu," *SME*, December 3.

Troxel, Luan (1993). "Socialist Persistence in the Bulgarian Elections of 1990–1991," *East European Quarterly* 26(4): 413–416.

Tsoukalis, Loukas (2004). *What Kind of Europe?* Oxford: Oxford University Press.

Tucker, Joshua A., Alexander C. Pacek, and Adam J. Berinsky (2002). "Transitional Winners and Losers: Attitudes Toward EU Membership in Post-Communist Countries," *American Journal of Political Science* 46(3): 557–571.

Tzvetkov, Plamen S. (1992). "The Politics of Transition in Bulgaria: Back to the Future?" *Problems of Communism* 41(3): 34–43.

United Nations (1997). *World Investment Report*. New York: United Nations.

United Nations Economic Commission for Europe (1995). *Economic Survey of Europe in 1994–1995*. New York: United Nations.

United Nations Educational Scientific, and Cultural Organization (UNESCO) (2002). *World Education Indicators*. Institute for Statistics Paris: UNESCO. http://earthtrends.wri.org.

USAID (2002). "Monitoring Country Progress in Central and Eastern Europe & Eurasia," No. 8. http://www.usaid.gov/locations/europe_eurasia/country_progress.

Vachudova, Milada Anna (1993). "The Visegrad Four: No Alternative to Cooperation?," *RFE/RL Research Report* 2(34): 38–47.

—— (1997). "The Systemic and Domestic Determinants of the Foreign Policies of East Central European States" D.Phil. Dissertation, Faculty of Politics, University of Oxford.

—— (1998). "Přijetí do EU v první vlně nemáme jisté," *Lidové Noviny*, August 20.

—— (1999). "The EU Needs to Change Its Spots," *International Herald Tribune*, August 8.

—— (2000). "The Atlantic Alliance and the Kosovo Crisis: The Impact of Expansion and the Behavior of New Allies," in Pierre Martin and Mark R. Brawley (eds.), *Alliance Politics, Kosovo, and NATO's War: Allied Force or Forced Allies?* New York: Palgrave, 201–220.

—— (2001*a*). "Ten Years of Czech Party Politics," *The New Presence* 3(2) (Summer): 24–26. http://www.pritomnost.cz/index.php?clanek=1749.

—— (2001*b*). "The Unexpected Force of Institutional Constraints, The Case of the Czech Republic," in Pravda and Zielonka (eds.), *Democratic Consolidation in Eastern Europe*, 325–362.

—— (2001*c*). "The Trump Card of Domestic Politics: Bargaining over EU Enlargement," *East European Constitutional Review* 10(2): 93–97.

—— (2001*d*). "The Division of Central Europe," *The New Presence* 3(3) (Autumn): 12–14. http://www.pritomnost.cz/index.php?clanek=1774.

—— (2002). "Strategies for Democratization and European Integration in the Balkans," in Cremona (ed.), *The Enlargement of the European Union*. Oxford: Oxford University Press, 141–160.

Vachudova, Milada Anna and Timothy Snyder (1997). "Are Transitions Transitory? Two Types of Political Change in Eastern Europe Since 1989," *East European Politics and Societies* 11(1): 1–35.

Vaksberg, Tatiana (2001). "Technology of Evil," documentary on forced assimilation campaign against Bulgarian Turks, 1980–1989.

Valki, László (2001). "Hungary: Understanding Western Messages," in Pravda and Zielonka (eds.), *Democratic Consolidation in Eastern Europe: International and Transnational Factors*. Oxford: Oxford University Press, 281–310.

Van Evera, Stephen (1992). "Managing the Eastern Crisis: Preventing War in the Former Soviet Empire," *Security Studies*. 1(3): 361–381.

Verdery, Katherine (1996a). *What Was Socialism and What Comes Next*. Princeton: Princeton University Press.

—— (1996b). "Nationalism, Postsocialism, and Space in Eastern Europe," *Social Research* 63(1): 77–95.

—— and Gail Kligman (1992). "Romania after Ceauşescu: Post-Communist Communism?" in Banac (ed.), *Eastern Europe in Revolution*. Ithaca: Cornell University Press, 117–147.

Verheigen, Tony with Alexander Kotchegura (eds.) (1999). *Civil Service Systems in Central and Eastern Europe*. Chelterham, UK: Edward Elgar.

Vladimirov, Zhelyu (1997). "The Value Crisis and the Weakness of Democratic Institutions in the Post-Totalitarian Societies in Eastern Europe, The Bulgarian Case," Final Report, NATO Fellowship Programme, 1995–1997.

Wallace, Helen (2000a). "EU Enlargement: A Neglected Subject," in Green Cowles and Smith (eds.), *The State of the European Union, Risks, Reform, Resistance and Revival*. Oxford: Oxford University Press, 149–163.

—— (2000b). "Flexibility: A Tool of Integration or a Restrain on Disintegration?" in Karlheinz Neunnreither and Antje Wiener (eds.), *European Integration After Amsterdam: Institutional Dynamics and Prospects for Democracy*. Oxford: Oxford University Press, 175–191.

Wallace, Helen (ed.) (2001). *Interlocking Dimensions of European Integration*. Houndsmills, Basingstoke: Palgrave.

—— and William Wallace (eds.) (2000). *Policy Making in the European Union*. Oxford: Oxford University Press.

Wallace, William (1992). "From Twelve to Twenty-Four? The Challenges to the EC Posed by the Revolutions in Eastern Europe," in Colin Crouch and David Marquand (eds.), *Towards Greater Europe?* Oxford: Oxford University Press, 34–51.

—— (2002). "Where does Europe End? Dilemmas of Inclusion and Exclusion," in Zielonka (ed.), *Europe Unbound: Enlarging and reshaping the boundaries of the European Union*. London: Routledge, 78–94.

Walt, Stephen (1987). *The Origins of Alliances*. Ithaca: Cornell University Press.

Wandycz, Piotr S. (1992). *The Price of Freedom*. London: Routledge.

Weber, Steven (1995). "European Union Conditionality," in Barry Eichengreen, Jeffrey Frieden, and Jurgen von Hagen (eds.), *Politics and Institutions in an Integrated Europe*. Berlin: Springer, 193–213.

Weiss, Martin (2003). "Czech Republic" in Adrian Karatnycky, Alexander Motyl, and Amanda Schnetzer (eds.), *Nations in Transit 2003: Democratization in East*

Central Europe and Eurasia. Lanham, MD: Freedom House and Routledge, 216–237.

Whitefield, Stephen (ed.) (1993) *The New Institutional Architecture of Eastern Europe.* London: Macmillan, 14–34.

Whitehead, Laurence (ed.) (2001*a*). *The International Dimensions of Democratization: Europe and the Americas, Expanded Edition.* Oxford: Oxford University Press.

—— (2001*b*). "Three International Dimensions of Democratization," in Whitehead (ed.), *International Dimensions of Democratization: Europe and the American, Expanded Edition.* Oxford: Oxford University Press, 3–25.

—— (2001*c*). "Democracy by Convergence: Southern Europe," in Whitehead (ed.), *International Dimensions of Democratization: Europe and the American, Expanded Edition.* Oxford: Oxford University Press, 261–284.

Williams, Kieran (1997*a*). *The Prague Spring and its Aftermath: Czechoslovak Politics, 1968–1970,* Cambridge: Cambridge University Press.

—— (1997*b*). "National Myths in the New Czech Liberalism," in George Schöpflin and Geoffrey Hosking eds., *Myths and Nationhood.* London: Hurst, 79–89.

—— (2000). "What was Mečiarism?" in Williams (ed.), *Slovakia After Communism and Mečiarism.* London: School of Slavonic and East European Studies, University College.

—— (2001). "Slovakia since 1993," in Williams and Deletant (eds.), *Security Intelligence Services in New Democracies, The Czech Republic, Slovakia and Romania.* Houndsmills, Basingstoke: Palgrave, 123–158.

—— and Deletant (eds.) (2001). *Security Intelligence Services in New Democracies, The Czech Republic, Slovakia and Romania.* Houndsmills, Basingstoke: Palgrave.

Williams, Margit Bessenyey (2001*a*). "European Integration and Minority Rights: The Case of Hungary and Its Neighbors," in Linden (ed.), *Norms and Nannies: The Impact of International Organization on the Central and Eastern European States.* Lanham, MD: Rowman & Littlefield, 59–87.

—— (2001*b*). "Exporting the Democratic Deficit," *Problems of Post-Communism,* 48(1): 27–38.

Winters, Alan (1992). "The Europe Agreements: With a Little Help from Our Friends." *The Association Process: Making it Work.* London: Centre for Economic Policy Research (CEPR), Occasional Paper No. 11, 18–28.

Wlachovský, Miroslav (1997). "Foreign Policy," in Martin Bútora and Péter Hunčík (eds.), *Global Report on Slovakia, Comprehensive Analyses from 1995 and Trends from 1996.* Bratislava: Sándor Márai Foundation, 33–53.

—— and Juraj Marušiak (1998). "Hlavné trendy v zahraničnej politike," in Bútora and Ivantyšyn (eds.), *Slovensko 1997, Súhrnná správa o stave spoločnosti,* Bratislava: Institute for Public Affairs, 233–243.

Wolchik, Sharon (1994). "The Politics of Ethnicity in Post-Communist Czechoslovakia," *East European Politics and Societies* 8(1): 153–188.

Wolczuk, Kataryna (2004). "Integration without Eurpeanisation: Ukraine and its Policy towards the European Union," European University Institute Working Paper, San Domenico di Fiesole, RSC No. 2004/15.

World Bank (1991). *Global Development Network Growth Database.* http://www.worldbank.org/research/growth/GDNdata.htm.

World Bank (1996). *From Plan to Market: World Development Report*. Oxford: Oxford University Press.

—— (2000). *The Road to Stability and Prosperity in South Eastern Europe: A Regional Strategy Paper*. Washington, DC: World Bank.

—— (2001). "Corruption in Slovakia. Results of Diagnostic Surveys." Washington, DC: World Bank and USAID.

—— (2002). *Transition: The First Ten Years. Analysis and Lessons for Eastern Europe and the Former Soviet Union*. Washington, DC: World Bank.

—— (2002). *World Development Indicators*. http://devdata.worldbank.org/ dataquery and http://earthtrends.wri.org.

Zakaria, Fareed (1997). "The Rise of Illiberal Democracy," *Foreign Affairs* 76(6): 22–43.

Zhelyazkova, Antonina (1995). "Reaching out to Minorities," *Transition* 1(13): 58–60.

Zielinski, Jakub (2002). "Translating Social Cleavages into Party Systems, The Significance of New Democracies," *World Politics* 54(2): 184–211.

Zielonka, Jan (ed.) (2002). *Europe Unbound. Enlarging and reshaping the boundaries of the European Union*. London: Routledge.

—— and Peter Mair (2002). "Introduction: Diversity and Adaptation in the Enlarged European Union," in Mair and Zielonka (eds.), *Enlarged European Union: Diversity and Adaptation*. London: Frank cass, 1–18.

—— and Alex Pravda (eds.) (2001). *Democratic Consolidation in Eastern Europe: International and Transnational Factors*. Oxford: Oxford University Press.

Press

"52 pays réunis à Paris pour promouvoir la stabilité en Europe de l'Est," *Le Monde*, March 19–20, 1995.

"A May Day Milestone," *The Economist*, April 30, 2004.

"Action Agreed Over Frontiers," *Financial Times*, December 11–12, 1993.

"Blisko coraz dalej," *Rzeczpospolita*, July 12, 1993.

"Brussels Sounds Out Plans for E Europe," *Financial Times*, May 10, 1993.

"Budapest Bars EU Cattle in Trade War," *Independent*, April 12, 1993.

"Bulgaria, Economic Structure and Forecast," *Economist Intelligence Unit*, February 9, 2004 and April 27, 2004 (respectively).

"Central Europe Knocks on the Community Door," *Financial Times*, October 28, 1992.

"Commission Paves Way for Wider Europe," *Financial Times*, July 28, 1994.

"Community Lifts Ban on Polish Meat Deliveries," *Financial Times*, July 16, 1993.

"Copenhagen Conference Speaks of Improving Trade With East," *NCA*, April 14, 1993.

"Council of Europe's soft standards for East European members, *RFE/RL*, July 8, 1997.

"Croatia Wins Incentive for EU Entry Talks," *Financial Times*, October 9, 2003.

"Czech Republic and EU Reach Accord on Association Agreement," *AP*, May 3, 1993.

"Czechs Delay EU Application," *Financial Times*, March 9, 1994.

"Czechs Want Trade Link to EU Now," *International Herald Tribune*, March 11, 1994.

"Czy Wspólnota nas chce?" *Gazeta Wyborcza*, October 29, 1992.

"E Europe Urged to Renew ex-Soviet Ties," *Financial Times*, April 15, 1993.

"East Europe Calls EC's Bluff Over Free Trade," *Financial Times*, April 16, 1993.

"East Europe Impatient for Seat at the Top Table," *Financial Times*, December 9, 1994.

"EC dumping of Farm Produce Upsets Hungary," *Financial Times*, June 22, 1993.

"EC May Keep Out 'Problem' Countries," *Independent*, June 22, 1993.

"EC Protectionism Threatens East Europe Growth," *Financial Times*, April 13, 1992.

"EC to step up links to central Europe," *Financial Times*, October 29, 1992.

"EU: New Membership Road Map for Lagging Candidates Romania, Bulgaria," *RFE/RL*, September 12, 2002.

"EU Offers Hope to Eastern Europe's Farmers," *Financial Times*, March 8, 1994.

"EU Policies Main Threat to E Europe Exports," *Financial Times*, October 20, 1994, 3.

"EU to Draw Up Plan for Admitting Six Eastern Members," *Financial Times*, October 5, 1994.

"EU's Outstretched Hand to the East Begins to Waver," *Financial Times*, November 23, 1994.

"Europe Recovers Its Sense of Direction," *Financial Times*, December 12, 1994.

"Európska komisia dá SR odporúčanie, ak si vyriešime svoje politické prolémy," *SME*, September 12, 1997.

"EWH znosi restrykcje," *Rzeczpospolita*, July 10–11, 1993.

"Extending the EU Eastwards," *Financial Times*, December 7, 1994.

"Former Communist States Feel Stranded by EU Club," *International Herald Tribune*, April 18, 1994.

"Handel rolny z Wspólnota," *Zycie Gospodarcze*, October 3, 1993.

"Hans Van den Broek: Slovensko má svoj osud vo vlastných rukách," *SME*, June 18, 1998.

"Hopes of Wider Union Turn to Fear of No Union," *Financial Times*, December 9, 1994.

"Hungarians and Czechs Set Their Eyes on 2000," *Financial Times*, December 12, 1994.

"Hungary and Poland Bang on EU's Opening Door," *International Herald Tribune*, March 8, 1994.

"Hungary in EU Trade Conflict," *Financial Times*, April 10, 1993.

"Hungary Raises Trade Defences," *Financial Times*, April 13, 1993.

"In the Waiting Room; Bulgaria, Romania and the EU," *The Economist*, November 1, 2003.

"Interest Grows in Stability Pact Plan," *Financial Times*, June 22, 1993.

"Kauza Gaulieder," *SME*, July 28, 1997.

"Kohl Carries EU Debate on New Members," *Financial Times*, December 12, 1994.

"Kohl Invites Eastern States to EU Summit," *Financial Times*, December 1, 1994.

"Kohl Makes EU Enlargement Pledge to East Europe," *Financial Times*, March 24, 1994.

"Kolej na czerwone porzeczki," *Rzeczpospolita*, August 26, 1993.

"L'échec des négotiations affaiblit le pacte de stabilité en Europe de M. Balladur," *Le Monde*, March 18, 1995.

"Lekcja przyswojona," *Gazeta Wyborcza*, March 12, 1992.

"Les nations défiées par les minorités," *Le Monde*, March 21, 1995.

"M. Mitterrand relance l'idée d'une confédération européenne," *Le Monde*, October 10, 1993.

"MM. Kohl et Mitterand sont d'accord sur l'idée de confédération européenne," *Le Monde*, January 6, 1990.

"Morsels From a Groaning Table," *Financial Times*, June 17, 1993.

"New Phase for EU as Hungary Asks to Join," *Independent*, April 2, 1994.

"Ousted King's Party Leads Bulgarian Vote," *Washington Post*, June 18, 2001.

"Paris Talks Aim to Defuse Old Central European Rivalries," *Financial Times*, May 26, 1994.

"PM Backs Kohl Over EU links to Eastern Europe," *Financial Times*, April 28, 1994.

"Podl'a Hansa van den Broeka EÚ nemala dôvod menit' názor na SR," *SME*, July 18, 1997.

"Poland and Hungary Step Up Pressure," *Financial Times*, March 8, 1994.

"Polska stowarzyszona z Wspolnotami Europejskimi," *Rzeczpospolita*, February 1, 1994.

"Polska wstrzymuje import zwierzat i miesa," *Rzeczpospolita*, April 10–12, 1993.

"Polskie mieso na pewno nie jest grozne dla Europy," *Zycie Warszawy*, April 9, 1994.

"První konkrétní krok," *Lidové Noviny*, October 7, 1991.

"Racja reform i interes panstwa praworzadnego," *Polska Zbrójna*, June 19–21, 1992.

"Rising Trade Tension With EU Impedes Eastern Europe's Progress," *The New York Times*, January 25, 1993.

"Road-Map Sought for EU Applicants," *Financial Times*, September 21, 1994.

"Romanian Extremist Leader Attacks President Again," *OMRI Daily Digest*, January 29, 1996.

"Saryusz-Wolski: choroby sa tylko pretekstem," *Zycie Warszawy*, May 26, 1993.

"Sezonowy problem," *Rzeczpospolita*, July 20, 1993.

"Slowcoach Slovakia: Has it got the democratic message?" *The Economist*, November 18, 1995.

"Spravodajca EP je za rozšírenie bez SR," *SME*, September 11, 1997.

"Structural Barriers to Eastward Enlargement," *Financial Times*, September 13, 1993.

"Thirsty For a Potion," *Financial Times*, March 23, 1994.

"Trójkat nierównoboczny," *Gazeta Wyborcza*, October 8, 1991.

"Trouver de nouvelles formes d'association à la Communauté," *Le Monde Diplomatique*, February, 1990.

"Visegrad Group Appeals for EC Membership," *RFE/RL Daily Report*, June 8, 1993.

"Wąsy Dzurindy," *Wprost*, 22 October 1998.

"Wczesne ostrzeganie," *Gazeta Wyborcza*, July 22, 1993.

"Zoznam I. Mikloša hovorí, že známi a príbuzní politikov sa podiel'ali na privatizácii," *SME*, June 24, 1998.

INDEX

Index